MW01123065

JAMAICA

IN THE

CANADIAN

EXPERIENCE

A Multiculturalizing Presence

edited by
Carl E. James & Andrea Davis

Fernwood Publishing
Halifax & Winnipeg

Copyright © 2012 Carl E. James & Andrea Davis

All rights reserved. No part of this book may be reproduced or transmitted in
any form by any means without permission in writing from the publisher,
except by a reviewer, who may quote brief passages in a review.

This project was carried out with the support of the Centre for Research on Latin America and
the Caribbean and the York Centre for Education and Community at York University, Toronto.

The editors gratefully acknowledge the financial support for this publication from the
International Development Research Centre (IDRC).

Editing: Brenda Conroy
Cover design: John van der Woude
Printed and bound in Canada by Hignell Book Printing

Published in Canada by Fernwood Publishing
32 Oceanvista Lane, Black Point, Nova Scotia, B0J 1B0
and 748 Broadway Avenue, Winnipeg, Manitoba, R3G 0X3
www.fernwoodpublishing.ca

Fernwood Publishing Company Limited gratefully acknowledges the financial support
of the Government of Canada through the Canada Book Fund and the Canada Council
for the Arts, the Nova Scotia Department of Communities, Culture and Heritage,
the Manitoba Department of Culture, Heritage and Tourism under the
Manitoba Publishers Marketing Assistance Program and the Province of Manitoba,
through the Book Publishing Tax Credit, for our publishing program.

Library and Archives Canada Cataloguing in Publication

Jamaica in the Canadian experience : a multiculturalizing
presence / Carl E. James & Andrea Davis, editors.

Includes bibliographical references.
ISBN 978-1-55266-535-0

1. Canada--Civilization--Jamaican influences. 2. Jamaicans--
Canada--History. 3. Jamaica--Civilization. 4. Canada--Civilization.
5. Multiculturalism--Canada. I. James, Carl- II. Davis,
Andrea, 1963-

FC106.J27J32 2012   971.004'9697292   C2012-903241-7

CONTENTS

for Kamau Davis-Locke

FOREWORD

Mary Anne Chambers

"So what will happen to Jamaica when young people like you leave?" This was certainly not what I had expected when we took a break for lunch, to enjoy delicious hot and juicy beef patties with soft drinks that I had gone out to buy. We had been working hard. Moving was hard work, physically. Packing all our belongings, including the beautiful mahogany furniture that had been stored in the spare bedroom for months, never used, waiting for this day. With the house sold and more cash than we could legally take out of the island, the alternative was to spend as much as we could on things we wouldn't be able to afford in Canada, at least not for the foreseeable future.

The year was 1976. Our sons were five and two years of age. Moving was hard work, emotionally. "Second class citizens" was what we were told we would be, living in Canada. So claimed those people who said they weren't going anywhere. "Five flights to Miami every day," was the prime minister's message, if we were unhappy.

So why was this old man playing with our heads at this stage of the game? He helped people move their belongings out of the country every day. Business was good for the moving companies in those days. "Put whatever you want in the drawers and lock them" had been his advice. We knew what that meant. We had heard how money was being moved out of the country. Foreign exchange restrictions meant creativity on the part of those who didn't want to leave all of their fortunes behind. How else would they manage to care for themselves and their families abroad?

It was easy to mess with our heads. No one really wanted to leave the rock. We felt we had no choice if we were to secure the kind of future that we wanted for our sons. There was no answer for the old man. We ate quietly and got back to the task at hand: leaving Jamaica. Canada would be good for us. We would be good for Canada. There would be no looking back.

So here we are in 2012. Canada has been good for us. We have been good for Canada. We have never looked back. But I have been going back often, as a visitor. And as the airplane starts the descent for landing, flying low enough for me to see the beautiful Caribbean Sea, followed by the stunning lush green mountains and all the places I wish I could identify, the goose pimples surface every time. And as I step out of the airport terminal building and that warm breeze caresses my face, I take deep breaths like I can't get enough of that air, several deep breaths, in fact. And I feel like I am home.

Jamaica needs me. Jamaica needs all daughters and sons of the rock. Or so I have chosen to believe. That old man is still in my head.

So Jamaicans go back. And we do what we can to show our love. The Honourable Robert Nesta Marley was well ahead of his time, and his words have proven to be timeless. *One Love* plays out in so many different ways.

Educational initiatives are the beneficiaries of much of the love. Dozens of alumni associations exist in Canada that provide primary, secondary and tertiary level institutions with much needed financial support. Scholarships for outstanding students who struggle financially, libraries, science laboratories, computers, building renovations and additional classrooms, transportation and lunch programs are some of the ways these associations are helping schools, colleges and universities throughout Jamaica.

The little children of Jamaica are a big attraction for me. They are beautiful. They are joyful. They are affectionate. They are so easy to love. Too many of them live in poverty, but they have immense potential. Jamaica's villages and towns have given life to highly successful individuals of every skill and profession, whose contributions are being felt in Canada and indeed on every continent. And what all of these success stories share is the opportunity to access the quality of education necessary to lift young women and men out of the poverty of their surroundings. PACE Canada, the project for the advancement of childhood education, was established in 1987 by renowned Jamaican Canadian educator Dr. Mavis Burke, to give three to six year olds a lift along the road to a brighter future. Now, this registered Canadian charitable organization's Adopt-A-School program provides financial assistance to more than 300 Basic Schools and Early Childhood Institutions, approximately 12,000 children each year. Other initiatives include the provision of computers, musical instruments and other learning resources, as well as funding for the training of teachers in the sector.

Alumni associations and organizations like PACE Canada are able to do what they do because Jamaicans and others who have had the opportunity to experience Jamaica find it just about impossible to leave Jamaica behind. Jamaica's national anthem says it best: "Jamaica, Jamaica, Jamaica, land we love."

What lies ahead in the prose and poetry of the essays collected by Carl James and Andrea Davis is a blend of history and current reality that will strike a note of familiarity for Jamaicans who have chosen to call Canada home, even when the contributing author knows of Jamaica not by birth or ancestry but through the good fortune of having been touched by its magic and its magical people. The essays speak thoughtfully of lived experiences, contributions, challenges and achievements. Contradictions are revealed in the demand for skilled workers and professionals that exists alongside the racialization of the same immigrants who are *visible* because of their race. *Visibility* is a key differentiator. My daughter-in-law, who was born in Guyana and came to Canada as an infant, is asked where she is from. My other daughter-in-law, whose parents came to Canada from Holland, is not asked where she is from. Similarly, white Jamaicans who are not betrayed by that beautiful accent generate surprise when it is discovered that they are Jamaican.

Race factors heavily in the accounts of the contributing authors of this anthology. There can be no doubt that unlike the socio-economic or class distinctions that seem to sidestep the "Out of Many, One People" motto of Jamaica, there is no escaping the racialization that exists in Canada, at times even imposed upon us by ourselves. "Don't be disappointed when you don't get too far" was the advice of a white Canadian-born colleague at Scotiabank, shortly after I arrive in Canada. That concern turns out to be unnecessary when, at thirty-eight years of age, I am appointed a vice-president and, later, a senior vice-president. "We need to stick together" is the advice of a Black colleague from the Caribbean, who turns out to be anything but supportive of me.

In the essays there are also reflections on the expectations that are held of Jamaicans in the diaspora. History and lived experiences also come into play here. It should not be surprising that any such expectations are tempered by the level of trust and the memory of the reasons that influenced the choices that were made when we aligned ourselves with another place to call home. Jamaicans in the Canadian diaspora direct their trust selectively.

We know we are better than the negative stereotypes and definitions that speak to the lowest common denominator of the racial profiles. We know that even if only for the sake of our children and their children we must continue to believe that Canada will be good for us. Indeed, Canada has been good for many of us. Jamaicans are proud and remarkably resilient people, who are known to be capable of excelling at whatever we do. Jamaicans have been, and will continue to be, good for Canada.

INTRODUCTION
Changing the Channel
Andrea Davis and Carl E. James

In 2012, as Jamaica celebrates the fiftieth anniversary of its independence from Britain, Jamaicans at home and abroad have a unique opportunity to reflect on the achievements of this small island nation in the relatively short period of its existence. Perhaps most significantly, Jamaica's increasingly powerful influence on global culture cannot go unremarked. The growth of Jamaican diasporas beyond Britain to the United States, Canada and West Africa, beginning shortly after independence, has served to strengthen Jamaica's global reach, so that today Jamaica's cultural, economic and political achievements are felt way beyond its national borders. This anthology commemorates the fiftieth anniversary of Jamaica's independence by acknowledging the immense and widespread contributions of Jamaica and Jamaicans to Canadian society.

As an officially designated multicultural society that has relied, and continues to rely, on immigration as a tool of economic and social development, Canada is defined by its racial, ethnic and cultural diversity. Yet, Canada's multicultural practices have tended to promote conformity to a British Canadian cultural "ideal" (Fleras 2004; Foster 2007; Saloojee 2004). It is this ideal, which represents only one aspect of Canadian cultural reality, that Jamaicans and other minority immigrant groups — as part of Canada's powerful third force (Leman 1999) — have consistently challenged, urging Canadian society to rethink its definitions of nation, multiculturalism and social citizenship. From the "rebellious" Jamaican Maroons, who were re-located to Nova Scotia in 1796, to the Jamaican immigrants who arrived in British Columbia in the late nineteenth century, Jamaicans have long provided a critical multiculturalizing presence in Canada (James in press). In the years following the introduction of immigration reforms in the 1960s, Jamaica's importance in defining Canadian society has become even more significant. The Canadian *Immigration Act* of 1967, which introduced a new points system judging immigrants on education and skill training, allowed small but newly independent nations like Jamaica to take advantage of uniform immigration quotas for the first time. Post-1960s immigrants have boosted the ranks of Canada's skilled labour force, excelling in the areas of education, health, business and culture. Yet, the popular Canadian perception of these immigrants, like Jamaicans, who originate in the Global South and are largely racialized and minoritized, is that they contribute little to the building of society. In Canada, where narratives of historical Black communities are largely silenced, Jamaicans, in particular, have come to stand in for a homogenized and problematic Black Canadian identity, marked by performances of hyper-masculinity and physical aggression (Davis 2006: James, in press).

This anthology provides a counter-narrative to this construction of Jamaica and Jamaicanness by chronicling the diverse and immense contributions of Jamaican Canadians across all sectors of society. By recounting Jamaica's contributions to Canadian development from a trans-Canada perspective — from British Columbia in western Canada to Nova Scotia in the east — the chapters in this book allow us to articulate a new understanding of engaged multicultural citizenship that positions Jamaica as integral, rather than marginal, to Canada's developed economy. In recognition of the wide reach of Jamaica's influence on Canada, this collection brings together the critical reflections of individuals from across Canada representing disciplines such as history, cultural studies, health, education, economics, art, literature and sociology. These reflections are organized into eight thematic sections that set the context and speak to issues of migration, language and cultures, diaspora experiences, education, transnational relations, economic and social relations, and social and geographic mobility.

The interdisciplinarity of this volume is reflected in its multiplicity of genres, from social science writings to life stories, interviews, fiction and poetry. Contributors include medical practitioners, educators, students, community activists, journalists and artists. In addition to exemplifying various professional fields, contributors also represent the ethnic, racial and regional diversity of Jamaicans — which no doubt informs their range of perspectives and the positions from which they write as well as the complexity and richness of Jamaican cultural influences. The anthology explores the interconnections between Jamaica and Canada, paying attention to the countries' shared colonial and commonwealth relations, and seeks to build knowledge and understandings of the two countries.

We recognize our presence on this land and the place of Aboriginal peoples in its historical development. So too, we recognize the contributions of Canada's Black communities that laboured in the service of Canada before and after slavery, and which advocated for the changes in immigration policy that enabled the cultural and political influence of today's Black communities. This celebration of Jamaican Canadians is not meant to undervalue the role of other Caribbean or immigrant groups in Canada's development and the construction of its national identity. Rather, it is meant simply to provide a moment of reflection in the year of Jamaica's fiftieth anniversary for two nations and their people to assess how far we have come collectively. For Jamaicans who live in Canada this collection is also a powerful recognition that their lives bridge at least two borders and that their historical memories are entangled in at least two nations. To this end, we hope this anthology provides all of us as Canadians with renewed commitment to an acceptance of our cultural diversity, multiculturalism and responsible civic engagement.

References

Davis, A. 2006. "Translating Narratives of Masculinity across Borders: A Jamaican Case Study." *Caribbean Quarterly* 52: 2/3 (June–Sept.).

Fleras, A. 2004. "Racializing Culture/Culturalizing Race: Multicultural Racism in a Multicultural Canada." In C.A. Nelson and C.A. Nelson (eds.), *Racism, Eh? Critical Interdisciplinary Anthology of Race and Racism in Canada*. Concord, ON: Captus Press.

Foster, C. 2007. *Blackness and Modernity: The Colour of Humanity and the Quest for Freedom*. Montreal: McGill-Queen's University Press.

James, C.E. in press. "The Jamaicans Are Here and Working": Race and Community Responses. In L.L.M Aguiar, L. Berg and D. Keyes (eds.), *Hinterland of Whiteness: White Fantasies in the Okanagan Valley*. British Columbia. Vancouver: UBC Press.

Leman, M. 1999. *Canadian Multiculturalism*. Ottawa: Government of Canada/Political and Social Affairs Division.

Saloojee, Anver. 2004. "Social Cohesion and the Limits of Multiculturalism in Canada." In C.A. Nelson and C.A. Nelson (eds.), *Racism, Eh? A Critical Interdisciplinary Anthology of Race and Racism in Canada*, 410–28. Concord, ON: Captus Press.

PART ONE – SETTING THE CONTEXT

1. CROSSING BORDERS AND NEGOTIATING BOUNDARIES

Olive Senior

I have been observing "border crossings" all my life, for like many West Indians of my generation, I grew up knowing members of my family and the wider community who had gone "away" and, in some cases, returned. In my Jamaican mountain village, the travellers' tales, the stamps, the letters, the photographic images and the whole *idea* of travel represented true exotica. These early images of travel shaped my consciousness and fuelled my own desire to cross not just geographical but also psychological and cultural boundaries. Travellers of one sort or another have continued to appear imaginatively in all my writings.

The fiftieth anniversary of Jamaica's independence provides a time for reflection on this aspect of our heritage. Migrant travel for Jamaicans and other Caribbean peoples is not new; what has not been much explored though is what it means to be the traveller. In moving from one place to another, we are automatically confronted by boundaries that are set by others. But we often fail to note that we also travel with boundaries, some of which are an intrinsic part of our inheritance and some of which we set ourselves. How do we negotiate these boundaries and redefine our identities? Find our new place in the world? To do so we perhaps need to look deeply into the prism of the journey itself and the way it plays out in the dream that carried us here. I'd like to share informally some of my thoughts on the subject.

Journeys — like well-told stories — shape themselves into beginnings, middles and endings, encompassing the three movements of departure, landfall or "arrival" at a new mode of being, and return (a paradigm which, perhaps not surprisingly, also reflects the archetypal journey of the hero as conceptualized by Joseph Campbell (1968)). The "return" can refer to the actual return to one's own home or the desire to do so, or to finding home where one is; in the ideal world, "away" elides into "home" and home and nation don't have to coincide. I'd like to use these three movements of the journey as a framework for discussing border crossings.

Departure

To emigrate implies an activist approach. You are the actor. You start off optimistic, expansive. You take the steps necessary to make the move. Success in getting your "papers" energizes you. You have a terrific sense of accomplishment. You depart from home.

Arrival

You arrive with high expectations. You are immediately acted upon. You experience a seismic shift in your psyche. You are circumscribed by the questions, plagued by the insecurity of arrival in a place where you do not yet know your place; you do not know the rules of the game or even what the game is. You learn early on that your role is no longer at centre stage — you are no longer the actor or optimist who left home. You move quickly to the wings. You are no longer the would-be traveller but the immigrant. You realise that your new role is to proceed cautiously from the margins, testing the boundaries of the Other.

You might argue that one of the reasons for the journey is to enhance your own opportunities, your own status, your own visibility both where you are now and back "there." Even if you travel alone, you do not journey only for yourself. Part of the process is that you wish to see and be seen, i.e., recognized both here and there, for there is no humanity in apart-ness. How can you "arrive" if there is no one to see you? At the same time, you do not want to be too visible. Where you come from, you know that too high visibility attracts unwanted attention.

In coming to this place, you learn a new iconography that is both visible and internalized. Some immediate symbols of arrival define "personhood": without plastic artefacts — your health card, your SIN card, your bank card, your driver's licence and so on — you do not exist because you cannot be officially seen. There are also essential sightings you must learn from the ground up (in the city of Toronto a notion of the four directions and how to find your way around by ground transportation). You have to learn how to dress for winter (the only thing you need to learn from the inside out). In short, you need to quickly assimilate different values, codes, rules of behaviour, references, images. In some ways this is a world upside down, for your own ways of seeing no longer hold true. Here, nothing can be taken for granted. And yet you do precisely that. Like those who were here before you came, you accept what you see.

The following few examples show ways in which your perceptions might betray you: How do you evaluate wealth and poverty in a country with a "poverty line" which is still higher than the income of most people in your country? Can there be poor people here too? Where do you place the doctors and other professionals used to a life of privilege in their own country who spend many years as janitors or taxi drivers before they can qualify to practise their profession in the new land? How do you judge success here versus there? The nature of "waste"? Charitable giving? Exchange or gift-giving when the concept of "hand wash hand" no longer holds?

Part of the problem is that the whole experience of border crossings exists in an ahistorical framework. The people who come know little of where Canadians are coming from, and Canadians already here know even less about the new arrivals. And yet if we were to examine each other historically, we would be able to affirm that we are not such strangers after all; in the long ago and not so distant past, people like us met and mingled. Newfoundlanders have been feeding cod to West Indians for centuries, and the West Indies bananas to Canadians. Canadian Presbyterian clergy and their wives journeyed to the Caribbean to minister to a people brought half-way across the world from India. Some of the missionaries left descendants in the Caribbean while the descendants of the Indians come to Canada. The Irish and Scots who came and settled Canada were the brothers and sisters of the Irish and Scots who settled Trinidad or Jamaica or Montserrat and shaped elements of our cultures. Jamaican Maroons were shipped off to Nova Scotia shortly after Acadians from Maritime Canada were shipped off to Haiti as well as Louisiana.

Awareness of history would affirm that our connections are not one-way flows but are built up of past exchanges; we have a shared history of imperialism, for instance, in the similarities of the education we all received just a few generations ago. To be able to affirm that we have met before, that our meeting today in Toronto is not new, might help to reduce the barriers between "us" and "them," bring "here" closer to "there," get the conversation going. It might also enable us to see better just who is changed by the experiences of border crossings, and how. What might be revealed are not just the cosmetic changes but the deeper cultural interchanges, such as the veranda and yard of the Caribbean manifest in the patio and terrace of Toronto's summer cafes. We might acknowledge that we can learn from each other, that the new arrival has something to teach, for example, what we have already learnt about the deleterious effects on society from structural adjustment policies. We might learn that many skills and much knowledge are, after all, transferable and do not require "Canadian experience." That in this new global village we are in our respective homelands already beginning to take on features of each other. Canadian suburbanites, for instance, are seen as people who drive in a car with the windows up into a garage with doors that open and close automatically behind them as they disappear into a house with drapes drawn and doors and windows closed: people who at the end of each working day retreat into privacy. How different from our

Caribbean style, we might say. But is this very thing not happening now in island societies? This retreat behind burglar bars and automatic garage doors, into gated communities, to all-inclusive tourist resorts? What does this signify more than a retreat to isolation, a re-creation of the paradigm of the Great House and the hut, the mansion and the shanty outside the gates, and the corresponding social divisions we thought we were breaking down?

Regardless of the depth of our perception, some form of incorporation is nevertheless desirable and desired. For what does "arrival" really mean but the achievement of community with people you can break bread with, where you can have a seat at the table. You might argue that Canada's policy of multiculturalism implies not one but separate tables. And you might also argue that for many of the so-called visible minorities, even people who are born in Canada, there are sometimes no place settings in crucial institutions — the school system, the work place. While immigrants are encouraged to both maintain their identities and adapt to the host country, the host country itself is sometimes ill-prepared to adapt to the immigrant. The process of sensitizing the hosts to the need for fundamental changes in, for example, the school environment to make all students feel welcome, for an ideology that recognizes at the deepest level the changing demographics of the society, does not always go far enough.

I myself set off resisting this new place: feeling too close an embrace would signify disloyalty to the place that had nurtured me — the place I call motherland. Most of all, as a writer I feared a loss of "voice," which of course is based on not just what but how I hear. I think my original confusion resulted from the belief that crossing borders means transference — that in choosing to feel comfortable in one country I was rejecting the other. Now, having spent some time consciously working through this, I feel differently. As an artist, I realise that my work occupies an intercultural space and had done so long before I left home. I have also discovered that I am happy to live in two different countries because each fulfils different needs in me. To be able to move between the two for me represents the ideal and makes me a privileged person.

So for me, "home" is not so much place as "community" — the latter based on human interactions that are intelligible to all the actors. If such a condition is not present, the traveller exists in a state of perpetual unease, a condition that might be called exile. In real life as well as in the literature, this unease is often expressed in sensory terms, a sign that no matter what government legislates, true arrival can only take place in our hearts. Much of the sensory language is multifaceted, our usage reinforcing the idea of striking a balance.

While the notion of seeing/being seen can serve as an affirmation of arrival and personhood, we don't want to be too visible. Embodied in the concept of seeing is the concept of "overlooking." If the look is too cold, we are being ignored or left out; if it is too hot, if there is too strong an eye, then we might fear witchcraft or the evil eye. Just as we hope to be seen in the right way, we also have to learn degrees of the political correctness of looking as well as of touching. We have to learn balance so that we can keep our distance but not be distanced.

But it is perhaps in sound that our desire for balance is most revealed. As I have stated before (Senior 2005), I regard "resonance" as a key word for the reading of one's sense of arrival, of place or placement. My dictionary definition of resonance is "sound produced by a body vibrating in sympathy with a neighbouring source of sound." It seems to me that the condition of resonance is what the traveller seeks to achieve. Thus, one might see the condition of internal exile as signifying a lack of resonance, a state which in literature is often signified with words like emptiness, coldness, silence. Loss and exile, spiritual or otherwise, are equated with loss of sound, the distancing from the other.

Home for me is a place where there is a condition of resonance or sound returned, that is, a place where you speak to a community and it speaks back to you. This does not necessarily involve dialogue; resonance can be achieved without speech. It can be felt in a look, a gesture, a place setting. What immigrants fear most is silence — being alone, being beyond community, being "exiled."

I used to think that the fact of being Caribbean and its implied hybridity meant that we were better prepared for crossing borders than others, that it is something ingrained in our blood, partly because of our maritime location and all that it implies. In the past, "away" came to us, not just through enforced and indentured labour, migrants and settlers but through widespread contact with those other inhabitants of the floating world, sailors and soldiers (something we tend to forget about our past). Our history is one of forced dislocations, of having to forge community from disparate and sometimes unwilling peoples. We already possess a dual language of here and there, of English and Creole. If journeying implies preparation, then we should be well prepared, many of us already having undertaken the search for both individual and national identity; we have explored the ideology of differences. Because of the fragile nature of our societies, we know what it is to live constantly between hope and despair and to survive. We have presumably already learnt accommodation.

Mobility is part of Caribbean identity. From birth we know personally the dislocations brought about by our family structures, which to a great extent are based on the widespread displacement of children and the absence of parents; the requirements of schooling, which usually take us away from home; the movement demanded by work opportunities; and the possibilities for upward social mobility. Moving upwards, socially and economically, often implies moving away — from village, home, family, language — and in the process of reconstructing oneself, acquiring a new persona. We might say we as Caribbean people are born into a kind of duality in which "away" is programmed into our ambitions, hopes, expectations.

Yet little of this seems to help in coming to a society such as Canada, for to come here is to suddenly become a member of a visible minority and all that it entails. Visibility here implies over-exposure; you are too readily seen, but you can fade and vanish in the harsh glare of overlooking.

Return

The notion of resonance refers not just to here but also to there, the place left behind, the place to which you may return. I asked earlier, what is the point of arrival if there is no one to see you, here or there? If you are invisible and silenced in the country to which you have journeyed, then home, the place you left behind, functions at least in your mind as the place with resonance, the place where you are both seen and heard.[1]

We who cross borders worry a great deal about our changing too much in relation to the places we left behind. But I have found that the problem is not so much that *we* are moving away from home but how fast home is moving away from us. It is not just a question of change, for that we are accustomed to, what is significant is the speed and nature of change.

If we look briefly at the history of Caribbean emigration, which began on a large scale in the mid-nineteenth century,[2] we might be able to remark on some of these changes, especially the ways in which the relationship of the migrant to "home" has shifted. In the early years, most of the emigrants were wage labourers drawn to large-scale industrial and agricultural enterprises in Latin America, starting with the building of the Panama Railroad in the 1850s and continuing until the 1930s. The objective for most was simply to earn the "living wage," denied them in the colonial backwaters the British West Indies had by that time become, and most left with the intention of returning home. But largely because of the harsh nature of their experiences abroad, these emigrants as well as those who participated in both world wars, returned as changed men and women. And it was these returning migrants who over succeeding decades played an influential role in the transformation of their home societies, if only by their presence and their changed attitudes. Some had acquired not just cash but skills and know-how and helped to develop their societies economically, socially and culturally. For the most part, they were now educated in the "university of life," which included a new self-confidence, new political ideas and the bitter experience of racism in a more naked form than they had experienced at home. Many were in the forefront of the spread of radical ideas, the formation of trade unions, political parties and nationalist groups, and the widespread labour disturbances throughout the West Indies of 1937–8. They formed a core of support for Marcus Garvey and Pan-Africanism. Condemned by the elite, they were nevertheless heroic figures to the ordinary people, as manifested in popular culture. Returning emigrants and ex-soldiers were a driving force for change up to the 1950s.

The composition of emigrants since the 1950s has changed, and their going has impacted their home society differently. First, there was the large movement of skilled and semi-skilled people to Britain, later of more trained and educated people and larger proportions of women to North America. Many do not return. And those who do return have less and less impact, partly because of the conditions at home. The transformative force in our Caribbean societies is no longer the returning emigrant but the global corporation, which sees these societies exclusively as low-end markets and sources of cheap labour. Transformative change is now mainly in the hands of others — those who control technology and communications and — one might add — the global drug trade. Under these pressures and other, internal ones as well, these small, fragile nation-states have assumed a momentum of their own — not comprising the economic and social transformation hoped for, but rather as runaways with no one in control. In societies now largely ruled by materialism, attitudes to returning migrants seem purely cynical. Regardless of the political rhetoric, it appears that all they are expected to contribute to their island societies is their remittances. The environment and ethos of small island societies are shifting rapidly; in the blink of an eye they have changed. So the question for the traveller is: how do you fit yourself back into a place which is no longer the one you left?

One example of this phenomenon is provided by the Caribbean migrants who went to England starting fifty-odd years ago with the arrival of the first set on the *Empire Windrush*, on June 22, 1948. Many of these people are now retired and returning home for good, the fulfilment of a lifelong dream. While I have no doubt that there are significant numbers of these returnees for whom the move is a satisfactory one, in Jamaica (and other West Indian territories, I am told) their presence is largely visible in the construction all over the countryside, including the remotest areas, of houses characterized by their huge size — eight or ten bedrooms are not uncommon — many to be occupied by one elderly couple. These houses are so grand in conception (if not design or execution) and so ubiquitous, their imagery is startling. I see them as icons of arrival, the reconstruction by people who left fifty years ago with the "great house" image in their heads as the premier symbol of status.[3] The problem is that the attitude to the great house has changed. Instead of being the recipients of deference and respect, these new occupants quite often find themselves preyed upon, even by their own families. Many of these returning residents have spent their whole lives working, sacrificing to educate their families and save enough for the move back home, and many are ill-prepared to deal with the place they have come back to. The fit between home and return appears to be an uneasy one; the boundaries are indefinable.

Another recent phenomenon is that many Jamaicans returning for holidays now come as tourists, staying in guest houses and hotels and not with their families as was formerly the case. This not only reflects more disposable income and perhaps more sophisticated tastes but also an acknowledgement of the changed society, a shift in perception, an awareness, perhaps, of wanting to be "seen" differently, or of not wanting to be seen at all. Too high a visibility attracts danger, the evil-eye hidden behind the dark glasses of the gangster. A new wariness seems to have crept into the returning residents' views of family relationships, including those with the larger family of the nation.

But we must also recognize that emigrants themselves have contributed to what I call the syndrome of "waiting," which for me characterizes much of the Jamaica I know today — the phenomenon of people, many of them children, who spend their time not in productive activity but in waiting for the return of the absent one, waiting to be sent for, waiting for the money and goods to be sent, waiting for the barrel.[4] Waiting too soon contributes to the feeling of abandonment that characterizes society, and I use that word in its various senses, including what is frequently described as indiscipline, a general "breakdown" in society. How much of this abandon springs from the abandonment of children that is a byproduct of emigration? And from the migrants themselves returning, feeling abandoned or marooned on their own islands? In such a situation, with resonance replaced by dissonance, there can be little sense of community.

Despite all the studies on the subject, perhaps too many of these are quantitative and not addressed to the border crossers themselves; people who cross borders often do so in a haze of ignorance, the impulse and desire to leave home, to arrive somewhere, is often so strong that their only source of knowledge is often anecdotal. But should it be any other way? Can adventure be anything more than individual experience?

If I were to be asked what I have learnt from the experience of crossing borders it would be that nothing is permanent or finite. What is the desirable alternative to staying put? In this new floating world of the twenty-first century, is it simply finding new moorings? In order to understand border crossings, do we need to redefine our notions of home? Should it still be firm attachment to roots? Or should we aim to be moored yet flexible, learning and absorbing new experiences in order to make ourselves into better citizens, wherever we happen to locate ourselves?

Notes

1. It is interesting that in modern Jamaican language usage, someone asking if you understand or are in agreement will ask "seen?" implying sight or inner vision.
2. For an overview of this early emigration see Insanally et al. 2006.
3. Jean Besson (2002: 305) presents a different view, making a distinction between two variants of such houses and assigning an important role "for the circulation of transnational lineages" to those houses that are built on family land.
4. In Jamaica, the children left behind are known as "barrel children" as goods sent from abroad are often the only connection with parents. Crawford-Brown (1999) has pointed out the deleterious effects on the children. See also "Barrel Children" entry in *Wikipedia*.

References

Besson, J. 2002. *Martha Brae's Two Histories: European Expansion and Caribbean Culture Building in Jamaica.* Chapel Hill and London: University of North Carolina Press.

Campbell, J. 1968. *The Hero With a Thousand Faces*. Princeton, NJ: Princeton University Press.

Crawford-Brown, C. 1999. *Who Will Save Our Children?* Mona, Jamaica: UWI Canoe Press.

Insanally, A., M. Clifford and S. Sheriff (eds.). 2006. *Regional Footprints: The Travels and Travails of Early Caribbean Migrants.* Mona, Jamaica: Latin American-Caribbean Centre, University of the West Indies.

Senior, O. 2005. "The Poem as Gardening: The Story as su-su. Finding a Literary Voice." *Journal of West Indian Literature* 14, 1 and 2 (November).

2. JAMAICANS AND THE MAKING OF MODERN CANADA

Barrington Walker

Canadians tend to think that the Jamaican presence in Canada is a story of the "recent" arrival of dark skinned strangers to Canada's large urban centres in the late 1960s, dramatically altering the racial landscape of the country.[1] These people, so the story goes, amongst other similarly foreign non-White arrivals, thrust the country into the modern era of "multiculturalism," the latest, most advanced and most enlightened stage of Canada's national history. There is a small element of truth to this story, but this is not the whole truth. This essay will suggest that Jamaica and Canada have had long historic links: imperial, social, economic, and cultural. The relationship between the two countries runs deep; and it has often been a difficult relationship traversing a history of nearly 300 years through the histories of slavery, emancipation, British colonization, and independence. This chapter — indeed this collection of essays — will show that the Jamaicans in Canada (*Jamaican-Canadians come Canadians*), have not been recent arrivals by any means but rather that Jamaica and Jamaicans, on the contrary, have had a significant role in shaping Canada's history and in making modern Canada.

The Triangular Trade: Cod, Rum and Slaves

Jamaica's long history with what is now Canada was forged in the crucible of Atlantic World slavery and the ascendance of the British as the pre-eminent naval power by the mid-eighteenth century with a deep commercial interest in slavery and the slave trade. The earliest bonds between Canada and Jamaica were a product of each region's role in a British imperial world built in large part on the backs of African descended peoples, the slaves who survived the horrors of the middle passage from Africa to the Caribbean. The triangle trade was the economic (and social) system that linked Europe and its colonies to the slave frontiers of West, and over time, Central Africa. Slave-holding and slave-trading European powers shipped their finished goods to the African kingdoms that engaged in slave raiding and trading.

Prized European goods and technologies were traded for slaves, who were bound for the Americas. The raw materials harvested from the colonies were sent to the imperial centres, where they were processed into finished goods for consumption in domestic and export markets.

Canada's earliest ties with Jamaica within the British Empire were forged when Newfoundland became a node in the triangle trade when it began to export its salted cod to the British West Indian slave owners in return for (locally bottled) Jamaican rum (Karlansky 1998: 83). Salted cod is still a staple of the Jamaican diet today, a national dish, while the rum imported from Jamaica and bottled at home, commonly referred to as "screech," is embedded in the cultural fabric of Newfoundland. But while trade in commodities like sugar and bauxite have always been an important part of the relationship between Canada and Jamaica, so too have movements of Jamaica's people, variously labelled as migrants, sojourners and immigrants, shaped Canada in indelible ways.

The Maroons

The Maroons were the first Jamaican migrants to land ashore today's Canada. Although the Maroon's history is relatively unknown in Canada, they hold a central place in the imaginations of most Jamaican people as they exemplify a fiercely independent culture of resistance to slavery in the British Caribbean. Just as important, however, are the ways in which the Maroons shaped Canada and Canadian history. The Maroons were an integral part of what some scholars call an emerging "Afro-Atlantic World," a society born out of Africans' desire for freedom in a world that insisted they be chattel slaves (Pulis 1999). Their origins lie with the Spanish, who allied with them to fight the British. When Jamaica passed to British hands, the Maroons, strengthened by runaway British slaves, fought the British in a series of battles during the years of 1665 to 1795, a period that historians refer to as the Maroon Wars. There is some debate as to whether the Maroons actually suffered at the hands of the British or whether they were tricked into surrendering their arms in 1795. The Jamaican governor, Lord Balcarres, under the advice of the Jamaican legislature, decided to exile those who had not surrendered within a ten-day period, despite assurances that those who surrendered after the deadline would be allowed to stay on the Island (Winks 1997: 79–80; Walker 1984: 8). The colonial government was determined to rid itself of the scourge of the Maroons and shipped them to Nova Scotia, where, it was hoped, they might be permanent settlers in the same vein as the Black Loyalists and the Refugees — Blacks who settled there in the aftermath of the American Revolution and the War of 1812 respectively.

In 1796, the Maroons arrived in Halifax, where they faced immense difficulties, partly wrought by the suddenness of their exile and their difficulty in adjusting to the culture and climate of a cold colony in British North America. The Maroons also suffered discrimination from the colony's White population, which looked upon them with the same distain they reserved for the other Blacks settlers, who many felt had been unceremoniously dumped upon their doorstep by their imperial masters. So like the Blacks who arrived before them, the Maroons suffered the prejudices of the host society. Some Whites believed them to be "arrogant, rude, heathenish and superstitious" (Winks 1997: 83). Others regarded them primarily as a source of cheap labour. Settled on the outskirts of Halifax (again like other Black communities), the Maroons were employed to help build the Halifax Citadel. But as James W. St. G. Walker (1984: 8) notes, the Maroons, "proud, independent and nursing a memory of betrayal … refused to become compliant Nova Scotian settlers." Deeply dissatisfied with their time in Nova Scotia, the Maroons decided in 1800 to leave for Sierra Leone, where they joined many Black Loyalists who had left Nova Scotia eight years earlier.

British Columbia's Black "British"

The Maroons were one of the first and most significant groups to enter the region now known as Canada from Jamaica, but they were far from the last. In the mid-nineteenth century, British Columbia received an influx of Black settlers from the United States — primarily California — and from Jamaica. Blacks fled California to escape the social, political and economic discrimination. Although California had entered the union of the United States of America as a free state in 1850, slavery was still widely practised illegally, and the free Black population suffered myriad indignities of White supremacy. Many of these Blacks decamped for Victoria, where, joined by White settlers from British North America and the United States, they attempted to forge a non-native settler colony on un-ceded First Nations territory (Harris 2003). Though it is not clear what brought Blacks from elsewhere in the British Empire — for instance, Jamaica — once in British Columbia, they became an important part of a burgeoning settler colony. They identified as British subjects and displayed a rather profound loyalty to the British Crown. These two qualities proved useful to a colony under pressure from the White American migrants, who were in favour of the United States annexing Victoria and British Columbia (Killian 1978: 76).

In 1860, in this context of fear of American annexation, these "British" (West Indian and largely Jamaican) Blacks, approached the governor of the colony with a proposal to start a volunteer rifle corps with the aim of pro- tecting Victoria from the threat of an attack from the Americans. Governor Douglas, short of money but in need of a bulwark against the United States' expansionist desires in the Pacific Northwest, gave his permission and began to recruit troops for this special corps. The Victorian Pioneer Rifle Company

(VPRC, or the "African Rifles," as it came to be known) initially consisted of fifty men, none of whom had any prior military experience. They were poorly equipped but nonetheless benefitted from the tutelage of a naval drill sergeant from a vessel in the local harbour (Killian 1978: 77; Winks 1997: 278). By 1861, the VPRC was the only military corps on Vancouver Island; the group was also, rather impressively, initially largely self-financed (Killian 1978: 77).

In 1861, the Pioneers approached the colonial government for money out of a sum of $1200 that had been set aside for "volunteer corps of the colony." The Rifles, the only corps in Victoria at the time, were granted only $250 by the governor. They later applied for the remaining $1000 but were denied it (Killian 1978: 77). In the summer of 1861, other settlers started the Vancouver Island Volunteer Rifle Corps for Whites only. Indeed, when the Pioneers sent a delegation asking to vote in the elections of the new corps' lieutenant-colonel, they were rebuffed amidst loud applause (Winks 1997: 279).

The Pioneers continued until 1864, when they suffered two fatal blows. First, the group was no longer able to support itself financially, and partly because of racial discrimination, its members were asked to surrender their arms. Second, when Governor Douglass's successor, a man who had governed the African colonies of Sierra Leone and The Gambia, arrived, he asked that the Pioneers be disbanded (Winks 1997: 279). Given his past as a colonial governor in Africa, it is not surprising that the new governor blanched at the notion of having armed Black men policing and guarding the colony, be they loyal British subjects or not. The Pioneers were rudely informed that they could not participate in the new governor's reception nor could they bear arms. It is also true, as Robin Winks (1997: 280) points out, that the Pioneers were an ill equipped and perhaps inadequately trained corps to protect the island from the threat of American annexation.

Despite this setback, B.C.'s Black British (Jamaican) community continued to wield influence in the early colony. In 1864, the same year the Pioneers were disbanded, the Jamaican community found itself at the centre of an election controversy when a bi-election was called to fill a seat in the colonial assembly. Only British-born subjects could hold office; naturalized citizens — many of whom were American-born Blacks — could not. American born Blacks did not like a law which seemed to have been passed to keep them from holding office. One of the candidates for office, in a bid to win the support of the Black community, campaigned on a promise to introduce the Alien Bill, which allow naturalized citizens the right to hold office. Many of the colony's Jamaicans, however, picked Empire over "racial" affinities and voted for a candidate who opposed the proposed legislation. As historian Crawford Killian (1978: 131) tells us, the Jamaicans' refusal to support the Alien Bill raised the ire of many of the bill's proponents in the colony, sparking virulent anti-Jamaican sentiment, including "a boycott of Jamaican businesses."

Jamaicans in Canada from the Age of Restriction to Selective Admission

The Blacks of British Columbia entered Canada not through, but during the time of, the Underground Railroad. Though this era was no golden age of Black life in Canada, it was one of the most important and indeed liberal periods for Blacks in Canada for it offered them freedom from slavery and equal rights under the law (though not social equality). The promise of the Underground Railroad was not to last. Anti-Black racism and racism in general were to become much worse after the mid-nineteenth century. During this time Jamaican migration to Canada slowed to a trickle, a consequence of larger intellectual, social and policy developments in Canada that had profound effects on the Black presence. At the turn of the century, anti-Black racism was at its peak (Winks 1997), with Blacks being inundated with racist depictions of Black life in materials used in school curricula (e.g., *The Story of Little Black Sambo*). The 1906 and 1911, immigration legislation ushered in the era of racially preferential immigration policy. From this time until the 1960s, few West Indians were able to emigrate to Canada. Between 1900 and 1909, only 374 were admitted. This number rose to 1,133 between 1910 and 1919, a spike that was largely a result of the decision of Cape Breton's coal miners to bring in West Indian labour amidst wartime labour shortages. From 1920 to 1929 the number of West Indians admitted to Canada stood at a level similar to the first decade of the twentieth century: 315. During the Great Depression, 673 West Indians were admitted, and during the years of 1940 to 1949, the number grew to 2,936 (Walker 1984: 8–9; Mensah 2010).

The historical records give us glimpses of the Jamaican past in Canada, but it is difficult for historians to tease out from the records the relatively small number of Jamaicans (certainly when compared to the 1960s) from the small number of West Indians who were able to get past Canada's formidable immigration colour bar in the early twentieth century. For example, in the early part of the century, we know that "Jamaicans were among those recruited to the coal mines and the shipyards. United Negro Improvement Association (UNIA) chapters existed in several major Canadian cities in the interwar period. These chapters had both Canadian-born and West Indian-born membership. Those chapters in cities that were most heavily influenced by West Indian immigrants were Toronto, Sydney and Montreal" (Marano 2010: 236). Many of the West Indian members hailed from Jamaica; for example, in interwar Toronto, Jamaican Reverend Stewart was the pastor of an Elm Street church where the city's first UNIA meeting was held (Brand 1991: 38–39).[2] Stanley Grizzle (1998: 31), a founding member of the Brotherhood of Sleeping Car Porters and a towering figure in Black Canadian human rights activism, was born to Jamaican parents who immigrated to Canada in 1911 and found a home in the small but robust interwar Black Canadian and West Indian community of Toronto. Grizzle's mother came as a domestic and his father to work on the railroad. As Grizzle writes: "While Canada had blanket restrictions on immigration from British colonies that had large non-White populations, the Crown made exceptions for people who came as porters and domestics" (31). Memoirs of two other prominent Jamaican-born Black Canadians — Harry Gairey and Bromley L. Armstrong, both of whom played a role in breaking down Canada's immigration colour bar after World War II — are also helpful in fleshing out the experiences of Jamaicans in early twentieth century Canada.

Harry Gairey

Human and civil rights leader Harry Gairey was born in Jamaica in 1898 into a family of seven; he had three brothers and three sisters. His father died when Gairey was five years old, and he grew up in Cuba with his mother, his brothers and sisters and a man with whom his mother formed an acquaintance after his father's death. At the age of sixteen, Gairey left Cuba for New York City. After a brief layover, Gairey made his way to Niagara Falls and shortly thereafter on to Toronto. Interestingly, Gairey remembers entering Canada with relative ease:

> They took us off the train, into the Immigration room, but it didn't take very long because the train stayed only about fifteen or twenty minutes. I didn't have a passport; at that time you didn't need one. We didn't take a medical or anything. They just asked how much money you had. I had $362 of my own money, that I worked for. Not stolen, not hustled just my own hard work. "Where are you going?" — they did ask that (Gairey and Hill 1981: 6).

Gairey gives us no direct answer to the question of why he was able to enter the country with relatively little difficulty, but the historical record and context give us some clues. Gairey arrived during the relative boom years of West Indian immigration in the age of restrictions. Once in Canada, Gairey, failing to find factory work, took a job on the railways, which, as noted above, was one of the few occupations where the Canadian government was willing to set aside its distain for prospective Black immigrants. Gairey went on to work as a railway porter, an occupation he stayed with for several years because as he put it, "When I got a job on the road, I never turned anywhere else. Never bothered because I knew I was blocked everywhere I went; it was no use to butt my head against a stone wall; I'd have a railroad job and make the best of it" (7).

Gairey's first job was on the Grand Trunk Railway (GTR), where he worked as a dishwasher, enduring long hours of taxing work and non-unionized status. During his time on the GTR, he met Harry Burnett, who became an important civil rights leader at the forefront of the struggle against "Jim Crow" laws in Dresden, Ontario, in the early 1950s. Gairey worked on the railroad through the 1930s, during which time the Canadian National (CN) railway had amalgamated with GTR. Gairey went on to work at the Canadian Pacific (CP) railway. Gairey was also one of the self-described "instigators" for the unionization of Black railway porters in the 1940s, through the Brotherhood of Sleeping Car Porters.

In 1947, Gairey's son, Harry Gairey Jr., was denied access to the Icelandia, a Toronto skating rink. Gairey, sought the assistance of the sitting alderman in Toronto for Ward Five, Joe Salsberg, a well-known Jewish-Canadian community leader, labour leader and human rights activist. With Salsman's help and outside pressure from protesters who picketed the arena, Toronto City Council passed an ordinance on January 14, 1947, making it illegal to discriminate against anyone seeking access to recreational or amusement facilities that were licensed by the police commission. Gairey's involvement in this important victory portended his human rights activism in later years (Gairey and Hill 1981: 8–27).

Bromley L. Armstrong

Bromley L. Armstrong was born in Kingston, Jamaica, on February 9, 1926, the fourth of seven children. Two years after the end of World War II, Armstrong decided to leave Jamaica. For Jamaicans who wished to emigrate in the postwar era, the United States, Canada and Britain were all considered difficult places to gain entry; each had taken measures to keep Black immigrants (as well as other non-White immigrants) out. Armstrong briefly considered signing up as a sailor in hopes of getting on one of the "Ladyboat" trade routes between the Caribbean and Canada (Armstrong and Taylor 2000: 22).

Armstrong's older brother, Eric, had departed Jamaica in 1943 for service in the Canadian armed forces, which allowed him to apply for landed immigrant status after de-enlistment, a strategy that was effective in the age of restrictive immigration policy. After a number of unsuccessful attempts to bring Bromley and another younger brother to Canada, Eric settled upon applying for student visas for both. Since it was impossible to secure landed permanent status for them, student visas were an often successful strategy for cracking open the door to Canada.[3]

Once he arrived in Toronto, Armstrong had the usual difficulties trying to find work in a city where, like Harry Gairey before him, Black men in search of employment were funnelled toward work on the railways. Unlike

Gairey, however, Armstrong was fortunate that Everald (yet another older brother who had emigrated to Canada prior) had managed to secure a job at Massey Ferguson. Thus, his family connections were instrumental in Armstrong obtaining a job at the factory. He later joined the UNIA and became active in the labour movement.

Selective Admissions

Gairey, Armstrong and Grizzle were instrumental in pushing the cause for human rights in Canada. Much of their efforts focused on breaking down the barriers to Black immigration. Their efforts were channelled through the institutional mechanism of the Negro Citizenship Committee (NCC), founded in 1951 and shortly thereafter renamed the Negro Citizenship Association (NCA) (Armstrong and Taylor 2000: 102). The founding members of the group included Harry Gairey, Barbadian-born Don Moore and his wife, Bromley Armstrong and Stanley Grizzle (Gairey 1981: 32).

The association was born in the home of Don Moore on Dundas Street in Toronto. The NCA's mission was stated in its constitution, to "petition the government to enlarge the section of the *Immigration Act*, in order to permit freer entry of Negroes into the Dominion of Canada" (Armstrong and Taylor 2000: 102). During the early years, much of the NCA's time was spent on gathering data on the problems that plagued Black West Indian immigrants who were denied entry into Canada (103).

What differentiated the NCA from earlier organizations such as the UNIA was its mainstream and middle-class leadership[4] and its willingness to enter into partnership with other groups, such as organized labour, who were also fighting for a more inclusive Canada. As Bromley Armstrong reflects in his memoirs, the NCA made appeals to the Canadian state for the increased entry of Blacks into the country based on arguments centred on "nation building" rather than more "radical" appeals to social justice. The NCA, in short, sought to impress upon the Government of Canada that its failure to admit West Indians in anything more than a trickle was having a negative impact on the country's growth and development (Armstrong and Taylor 2000: 105). The NCA's main point of contention with Canada's immigration policy was order-in-council P.C. 2856, which gave immigration officials the discretionary power to bar immigrants on the basis of climatic unsuitability (105). This was one of the more egregious forms of discrimination that potential Jamaican immigrants to Canada faced.

From 1952 onwards, the NCA continued to fight to break down barriers to West Indian immigration to Canada. That year, the organization was instrumental in helping a young immigrant nurse from Jamaica, Beatrice Massop, enter the country, successfully persuading the government to allow Massop entry under the "exceptional merit" category. Increasing numbers of Caribbean nurses were being admitted to Canada under this category. Buoyed by this gain, the NCA began to ratchet up pressure on Louis Saint Laurent's government. New legislation was passed in 1952, but the reality was that racial preferences still persisted in Canada's immigration laws and the practices through which it selected immigrants. In 1954, Don Moore and the other leaders of the NCA requested a meeting with the prime minister (108), but the prime minister dispatched an underling, Immigration Minister Walter Harris, to attend the meeting on his behalf (108–9).

The meeting, held on April 27, 1954, was widely publicized, and demonstrations in favour of lowering the colour bar against Black immigrants were held in Toronto in a public show of support for the NCA. While Harris was willing to listen to the oral submissions of the NCA leadership, he did not offer the response they were looking for: the repeal of P.C. 2856. Nor was he willing to clarify the intentionally vague and highly discretionary "exceptional merit" clause of the *Immigration Act*. On July 1, Prime Minister Laurent appointed a new immigration minister, Jack Pickersgill. The NCA, which had been waiting for months for an official reply from the government, appealed to Pickersgill to render his verdict. Still the government refused to change its position and continued to insist on its right to admit prospective Black immigrants under the "exceptional merit" provisions of the *Immigration Act* (115).

Meanwhile, diplomatic pressure from the Caribbean on the Canadian government to open up its borders began to grow.[5] By 1955, Jamaica's Peoples National Party leader, Norman Manley, met with the NCA in Toronto and agreed to continue to press the Canadian government to open up its borders to West Indians. At this time, Minister Pickersgill was meeting with the Jamaican minister of trade and industry in Ottawa. The Canadian government was faced with answering poignant questions about why it was reluctant to allow West Indians into the country when the United States had already implemented such a program. Canada was also under considerable pressure from Britain, which had also just moved to lower restrictions on West Indian immigration (Walker 1984: 9). On June 10, 1955, the Canadian government announced that it would "admit a certain number of domestics from the British West Indies on an experimental basis, 75 of these domestics to be selected from Jamaica and 25 from Barbados" (116). Though the challenges faced by West Indian domestic workers in Canada cannot be cavalierly dismissed[6] — the relationship between employers, backed by Canadian state power, and these immigrant women was fundamentally exploitive — the importance of this scheme cannot be overstated. Prior to 1960, the scheme, which inched open Canada's doors to Black Caribbean migration, was one of only a handful of legal routes Blacks had to gain admission to this country (Mensah 2010: 105). West Indian students, who had been admitted into

Canada since the 1920s, comprised one of the only other groups allowed entry in the pre-1962 era (Mensah 2010: 103).

In 1962, the *Immigration Act* was amended to eliminate racial preferences under the Diefenbaker government by Minister of Immigration Ellen Fairclough. (Kelley and Tebilclock 2000: 314–5. In 1967, further amendments introduced the points system, which assessed prospective immigrants on "education and training; personal assessment, by an immigration officer; occupational skills; arranged employment in the area of destination" (Armstrong and Taylor 2000: 167). As a result of these changes in Canadian immigration policy, Jamaican immigration to Canada swelled between 1973 and 1977. But by the end of the 1970s, the numbers of Jamaicans decreased because the emphasis in immigration requirements shifted from education to occupation and work history. More emphasis was also placed on the independent immigrant class at the expense of family class immigrants (Mensah 2010: 105–6). Nonetheless, by 2006, the Canadian census revealed that some 231,110 persons in Canada were of Jamaican origin (107).

After Racial Restrictions: Jamaicans in Canada

As we have seen, Jamaicans were an integral part of pre-Confederation Canada in British Columbia and Nova Scotia. After the emergence of racially preferential immigration policies and practices in Canada in the early twentieth century, Jamaican lived in small enclaves amidst other West Indians and Black Canadians in places such as Toronto, Montreal and Sydney, Nova Scotia. Jamaicans were instrumental in breaking down immigration barriers, but the road to end racial restrictions was a long one. Jamaican-born Harry Gairey and Bromley Armstrong played pivotal roles in the struggle to open up Canada's borders to non-Whites, as did Stanley Grizzle, who was of Jamaican parentage. All fought alongside the energetic and charismatic Barbadian-born Don Moore. Jamaicans in Canada were part of larger West Indian communities and Black Canadian communities as well. They certainly had differences amongst them, but they also had a common cause in combatting the pervasiveness of racism and racial exclusion.

Jamaican Canadians in the more recent past, like their predecessors, have left an indelible mark on the Canadian past. Lincoln Alexander, a first-generation Canadian of a Jamaican-born mother, was Canada's first Black Member of Parliament (1968) and the first Black Lieutenant Governor of Ontario. In fact, Lincoln Alexander was the first Black person in Canada to occupy a vice-regal position in Canada.[7] Olympic gold-medalist Donovan Bailey and entrepreneur Michael Lee-Chin are two other examples of exemplary Jamaican Canadians (Abdel-Shehid 2005: 79–83).[8]

This chapter self-consciously choses to focus on the positive aspects of the Jamaican story in Canada. But it would be naïve to suggest that Jamaican

Canadians have not had to and do not have to overcome struggles. Jamaicans in Canada are a stigmatized group, over-policed, under-employed and hyper-incarcerated. We are branded in the mainstream media as inherently criminal, and we continue to suffer from pervasive patterns of social and economic marginalization (Henry 1994; Mensah 2010). It is also sadly true that even those of us who achieve the status of national icon, such as sprinter Ben Johnson, can quickly find themselves the object of scorn and derision should they falter (Abdel-Shehid 2005: 67–93). Nonetheless, it is hoped that this chapter at least in small part serves as a corrective to the overwhelmingly negative picture that has been painted of Jamaicans and their descendants in Canada. Ours is a story of positive accomplishments in the face of long odds, and it is still being written.

Notes

1. I recognize that Jamaica is a multi-"racial" and perhaps multicultural country that has been "settled" and colonized by people of diverse origins who by design or circumstance displaced its indigenous population. Nonetheless, in this chapter the Jamaicans I refer to are peoples of African descent.
2. It is difficult to pinpoint the exact year from Blackman's narrative.
3. Sheldon Taylor, Bromley's biographer (Armstrong and Taylor 2000), notes rather sardonically that West Indian immigrants were being denied permanent status at a time when the government was beginning to grant it to for German prisoners of war.
4. The term middle class is a difficult concept when applied to Jamaican Canadians and other Black Canadians, who have to tended to live at the economic margins of society. What I mean to denote is not only a sense of their economic standing relative to others in the Black community but the style and substance of their political engagement and tactics.
5. The Barbadian government met with Canadian government officials in order to lobby Canada to help alleviate its population growth by allowing Barbadians temporary access to Canada as agricultural workers and domestics.
6. For a critical, poignant and at times painful look at the travails of West Indian domestic workers in Canada see Silvera (1983).
7. <http://swaymag.ca/people-community/lincoln-alexander-lives-the-canadian-dream>.
8. <http://archives.cbc.ca/sports/olympics/clips/81161/>, <http://portland-holdings.com/Info.aspx?disp=history-founder>.

References

Abdel-Shehid, G. 2005. *Who Da Man? Black Masculinities and Sporting Cultures*. Toronto: CSP.
Armstrong, B.L., and S. Taylor. 2000. *Bromley: Tireless Champion for Just Causes: Memoirs of Bromley L. Armstrong*. Pickering. ON: Vitabu Publishing.
Brand, D. 1991. "Violet Blackman." In D. Brand (ed.), *No Burden To Carry: Narratives of Black Working Women in Ontario, 1920s to 1950s*. Toronto: University of Toronto

Press.

Gairey, H., and D. Hill. 1981. *A Black Man's Toronto, 1914–1980: The Reminiscences of Harry Gairey*. Toronto: Multicultural History Society of Ontario.

Grizzle, S. 1998. *My Name's Not George: The Story of the Brotherhood of Sleeping Car Porters in Canada: Personal Reminiscences of Stanley G. Grizzle*. Toronto: Umbrella Press.

Harris, C. 2003. *Making Native Space: Colonialism, Resistance and Reserves in British Columbia*. Vancouver: UBC Press.

Henry, F. 1994. *The Caribbean Diaspora in Toronto: Learning to Live with Racism*. Toronto: University of Toronto Press.

Karlansky, M. 1998. *Cod: A Biography of the Fish that Changed the World*. New York: Penguin.

Kelley, N., and M. Tebilclock. 2000. *The Making of the Mosaic: A History of Canadian Immigration Policy*. Toronto: University of Toronto Press.

Killian, C. 1978. *Go Do Some Great Thing: The Black Pioneers of British Columbia*. Vancouver: Douglass and McIntyre.

Marano, C. 2010. "Rising Strongly and Rapidly: The Universal Negro Improvement Association, 1919–1940." *Canadian Historical Review* 91(2).

Mensah, J. 2010. *Black Canadians: History, Experience, Social Conditions* (second ed.). Black Point, NS: Fernwood Publishing.

Pulis, J.W. (ed.). 1999. *Moving On: Black Loyalists in the Afro-Atlantic World*. New York: Garland Publishing.

Silvera, Makeda. 1983. *Silenced: Talks with Working Class Caribbean Women about Their Lives and Struggles as Domestic Workers in Canada*. Toronto: Sister Vision Press.

Walker, J.W.S.G. 1984. *The West Indians in Canada* Ottawa: Canadian Historical Association/Multiculturalism Program, Government of Canada.

Winks, R. 1997. *The Blacks in Canada: A History* (second ed.). Kingston: McGill-Queen's Press.

PART TWO – MIGRATION: OPPORTUNITIES AND CHALLENGES

3. "TO ENSURE THAT ONLY SUITABLE PERSONS ARE SENT"

Screening Jamaican Women for the West Indian Domestic Scheme

Michele A. Johnson

Since the late 1960s, scholars have tracked the process, meaning and impact of the recruitment of Caribbean women, many of them Jamaican, to perform domestic service in Canadian households (Henry 1968). Building on those foundations, some analysts have discussed the ways in which the experiences of Caribbean migrant domestic workers revealed an intersection between Canada's historically restrictive immigration policies/legislation and concerns about citizenship, including contested meanings about who could/ could not be allowed into the nation (Harris 1988; Daenzer 1993; Cohen 1994; Satzewich 1993–1994; Carty 1994). Other scholarship has focused on the interruptions and disruptions which have emanated from the insertion of these primarily Black women (and later, their families) into a Canadian society which is perceived of and narrated as White (Calliste 1993/1994, 1991; Macklin 1994; Bakan and Stasiulis 1997, 1995, 1994. The working lives of these women – held in place through their closely monitored labour contracts – have received the attention of some scholars (Arat-Koç 1989; Giles and Arat-Koç 1994), while others focused on the challenges their recruitment meant to gender relationships generally and to automatic claims of intra-gender solidarity specifically (Schecter 1998). Further, the daily work and personal experiences of the women, as they cleaned houses which they did not own and nurtured children who were not theirs (while many had left their *own* children behind in order to pursue these positions), have been the focus of scholars who examined what life was like for those who were recruited, as Silvera (1989) writes, quoting Molly, "to do the dirty work" (see also Anderson 2000).

While the scholarship on domestic service in Canada has been growing steadily, the sector remains relatively under-researched in the Caribbean context (Aymer 1997; Higman 1983; Johnson 2007, 2002, 1996, 1993; Mohammed 1986). In fact, the attention given in the Canadian context to the experiences of Caribbean domestic workers recruited to work in the West Indian Domestic Scheme has not been mirrored from the Caribbean side of the equation (Henry 1968; Douglas 1968; Silvera 1989). Such examinations would illuminate the region's general socio-economic and political contexts which made such a scheme desirable. Although it is beyond the purview of this chapter to examine the many territorial specificities which together coalesced into "the Scheme," it does discuss the policies and processes of recruitment within the Jamaican context which determined who among the many applicants were chosen "to uphold the highest standard of West Indian womanhood" (Anon n.d.) and by extension, to convince historically unaccommodating Canadian officials that Caribbean (in this case Jamaican) residents were worthy of an "opportunity" of admission to the "Great White North."[1]

Agnes Calliste reminds us that, although the West Indian Domestic Scheme, launched in 1955, has been the focus of many of the discussions of the "domesticated" connections between Canada and the Caribbean, there was an earlier scheme which has not received as much attention (Calliste 1993/1994). While Jamaican workers did not participate in that earlier formal labour recruitment scheme, the possibility of performing domestic work in Canadian households was not entirely foreign in the island's domestic service sector in the period prior to 1955. Indeed, from as early as 1920, classified advertisements in Jamaica's longest running newspaper, the *Daily Gleaner*, sought to recruit Jamaican women to work as domestic servants in Canadian households. In March of that year, the Royal Employment Bureau, located on Orange Street in Kingston, advertised for a "general house worker" for a "wealthy Canadian lady" in Ontario, Canada. Potential applicants were advised to apply in writing and that "experience [was] not necessary" since the successful applicant "[would] be taught." Promises were made of "good wages and prospects; passage advanced." However, the advertisement also made it clear that in order to be even considered, applicants "must be respectable" (*Daily Gleaner* 1920a). Later in the year, the same Bureau sought nine "general helps" to work for "several well-to-do Canadians"; and assured that they would also receive "good wages and prospects; passage advanced," the recruits were required to be "honest, respectable, industrious ... healthy, [and] have some experience in general housework." Importantly, in order to be hired, each applicant had to be a "girl or unencumbered young widow" (*Daily Gleaner* 1920b). On another occasion, the Bureau tried to secure positions for twenty-three women to work with "Canadian [families]: Doctor, Merchant or other well-to-do [families]" as "general servants"; good wages and advanced passages were advertised as part of the package and for their part, recruits "[had] to have good guarantee[s]" (*Daily Gleaner* 1920c). Although agencies such as the Royal Employment Bureau, Reliable Employment Bureau, Bell's Employment Agency and Overseas Employment Service[2] were active in the recruitment of domestic workers, some employers sought to recruit workers on their own behalf. One such employer, "Mrs.--, well-to-do Canadian" sought a "nursemaid to assist with 2 children"; potential applicants were informed that the successful applicant "must have previous experience" and "must have good references" (*Daily Gleaner* 1920d).

Whether it was locally based employment agencies or individual Canadian employers, the focus on the honesty, respectability, industriousness and health of potential recruits, which could be vouched for through "good guarantees or references" was in keeping with some of the major issues addressed during recruitment in the Jamaican domestic service sector (see Johnson 1996, 2007). Concerned about the introduction of persons who were not family members into the intimate spatial and relational parameters of the household, employers (or their proxies) tried as best as they could to screen applicants in order to eliminate those workers whose supposed lack of these qualities (often simply referred to as "decency") would prove not only disruptive but potentially threatening. These anxieties would also preoccupy those associated with the recruitment of Jamaican domestic workers for Canadian households in the 1950s.

In January 1954, G.H. Scott of the Jamaican Ministry of Labour wrote to the island's Executive Council about the "Recruitment of Jamaicans for Agricultural and Domestic work in Canada." Placing the memorandum in a wider context, Scott reported that from as early as 1946, the Executive Council had considered sending a delegation to the Dominion "to explore the possibilities of recruiting Jamaicans for agricultural and domestic work in Canada." However, the idea was shelved since "the reply received was that after consideration by all the Canadian Departments concerned, the conclusion was reached that there was no need to draw on Jamaican sources of labour and that the Canadian climate was not likely to prove favourable for such a scheme." Scott argued that the idea for a scheme to recruit Jamaican workers to perform domestic service in Canada should now be reconsidered since "from time to time applications from prospective employers of Jamaican domestic workers in Canada are made to the Labour Department" but that "due to immigration restrictions … it is not possible to take advantage of these offers." Noting that the possibilities for such a scheme could be positively evaluated through the experiences of a group of highly placed Canadian employers, Scott went on to say:

> A number of carefully selected domestic workers have been supplied, on request, for employment under diplomatic sponsorship

by members of the staff of the Canadian Embassy in Washington, and satisfactory reports on their services have been received. The Ministry of Labour is confident that were such workers given the opportunity to work in the Dominion itself, the same satisfaction would result.

And further, said Scott, since Jamaicans in the U.S. had a "creditable record" as agricultural and domestic workers, "as a consequence of which there is an increasing demand for them, the time may be opportune to approach the Canadian authorities again to enquire whether they would now be prepared to consider a scheme for the migration of selected Jamaicans for employment in the Dominion."

G.H. Scott did not indicate who among the Canadian diplomatic services sought Jamaican domestic servants, nor was there any consideration about *why* Canadian authorities working in Washington would turn to Jamaicans to fulfil their domestic labour needs. One would have expected Canadian diplomats to have recruited domestics from among Canadian workers. Still, at issue for our purposes in this chapter is that it was the Jamaican government which envisioned (temporary) emigration through a domestic scheme as a means of addressing the unemployment and under-employment of the island's female workforce. This is of interest especially since the Scheme is often presented as "initiated by the Canadian Government in 1955" (Henry 1968: 83). It seems more accurate to argue, as Audrey Macklin (1994:16) has done, that "pressure from Canadian employers and British Caribbean governments" led to the initial agreements between Canada and Jamaica (as well as Barbados) that became the Scheme.

Based on Scott's submission, by April 1954, J.A. McPherson, Minister of Labour, reported that on January 25, 1954, the Executive Council had accepted that "a further approach should be made to the Canadian Authorities with a view to ascertaining whether they would be prepared to consider a scheme for the migration of selected Jamaicans for employment in the Dominion, particularly in the fields of agriculture and domestic work." The Council agreed to approach the British West Indies trade commissioner in Canada to make "preliminary enquiries into the matter." The response of the trade commissioner, which was submitted to Jamaica's Executive Council by the minister of labour, is worthy of note.

The commissioner reported that the Canadian authorities indicated that "the entry of labour on a temporary basis into Canada interfered with the standing regulations governing the entry of labour on a permanent basis and is a question which in all probability would be resisted in official quarters." And since the Canadian government was already engaged in sponsoring numerous immigrants – particularly from Europe on a permanent basis and was having "some difficulty … placing many of these immigrants in the labour market" (the latest figures indicated that there were about 280,000 unemployed persons in Canada), it was felt that "there is little or no demand for temporary labour from outside for work on farms, etc. as there is in the United States." In essence, the Canadian government at that time indicated that "there [was] no shortage of such labour in Canada," essentially ruling out the possibility of domestics from Jamaica entering Canada to work on a temporary basis – thereby rejecting the Jamaican government's request. Given that there was no need for domestics in Canada, Minister McPherson concluded that "in the circumstances, it is suggested that no further action be taken in the matter for the time being" (McPherson 1954).

That the requests for the recruitment of domestic workers were rebuffed by the Canadian authorities in the face of substantial *European* immigration and on the premise that there was resistance to temporary workers (even though the likelihood of recruitment of Caribbean migrants for permanent positions was extremely low) was entirely in keeping with Canadian immigration policy. From as early as 1910, when a "restricted, exclusive, and selective" Canadian immigration law was passed, the tendency to prevent the potential immigration of persons of African descent was clear (Winks 2000: 307). And should Blacks be mistaken about what was meant, the government of Wilfrid Laurier passed an order-in-council in August 1911 which declared: "For a period of one year … the landing in Canada shall be … prohibited of any immigrants belonging to the Negro race, which race is deemed unsuitable to the climate and requirements of Canada."[3] By 1947, the categorization of Canadian immigration as selective and exclusionary was reiterated by William Lyon Mackenzie King, who stated: "Canada is perfectly within her rights in selecting the persons whom we regard as desirable future citizens. It is not a 'fundamental human right' of any alien to enter Canada. It is a privilege." This answered the concerns, said King, of Canadians who did not wish, as a result of any mass migration, "to make a fundamental alteration in the character of our population."[4] In other words, the Great White North desired and intended to remain "White."

Having apparently rejected the solicitations of the Jamaican government in 1954, the Canadian authorities reversed their intentions one year later, and in 1955 the West Indian Domestic Scheme was launched. According to Frances Henry (1968: 83), under the Scheme, after the Ministry of Labour in each island selected the women: "Final applicants [were] interviewed by a team of Canadian immigration officials who visit[ed] the islands once a year specifically for this purpose." The role of the Jamaican government in seeking to screen and recruit segments of its female force to perform domestic service in Canada played into the classist, racist and gendered legacies of a long colonial heritage, which remained in the island well into the second half of the twentieth century. It was primarily lower-class women, most of whom were the descendants of the enslaved populations in the island, who had themselves performed similar labour for their enslavers, who were the targets of this proposed scheme. Unable to solve the deep, structural problems that accompanied the small, vulnerable economy, still largely driven by agriculture and dominated by the cultures of King Sugar and Queen Banana, if not their economic buoyancy, the Jamaican government in the 1950s envisioned a partial solution through recruitment of some of the island's women into foreign domestic work. The hope was at least two-fold: that the women be taken out of the large and growing pool of unemployed and under-employed persons in the island and that through their earnings in Canada, they would help in the maintenance of family members in Jamaica, for whom there was only the barest of governmental provision – and that only for the most destitute (Moore and Johnson 2000). And since there was a possibility that the domestic workers might, in time, "send for" family members, the expectation was that the pressures on the economy and society would be further alleviated in some small measure. That the women would perform tasks in positions that had long, deeply engrained, racialized and gendered associations in North America and the Caribbean may not have been consciously stated considerations, but they lurked in every room where "the problems" of poor, Black, Jamaican women's lives were being discussed and their "solutions" formulated in spaces into which they were not invited.

For those who desired to acquire one of the positions offered each year, the first phase of screening was crucial. The determination of which applicants would be placed on the "short list" from which Canadian officials would choose involved a rarely examined process of local recruitment which bears some comment. This was where Jamaicans measured their fellow citizens to decide who among them possessed the domestic skills, temperament and other qualities which made them suitable for Canadian households. This was where some Jamaicans decided which *others* would take advantage of the "wonderful opportunity" while at the same time embracing "the responsibility to make good, so that in future years other … [Jamaican] women can look forward to similar opportunities." After all, the recruits were told: "Remember, if you fail you will let down not only yourself but your country. If you make good you will be a credit to your country and contribute toward the continuation of the scheme" (Anon n.d.). The pressure on the Selection Committee to choose well must have been enormous; the burden on the selected women to perform as domestic workers *and* as representatives of Jamaican womanhood must have been incredible.

In June 1957, the office of the Permanent Secretary in the Jamaican Ministry of Labour contacted Mrs. Leila Tomlinson to advise her that "the Canadian Government [was] again accepting a number of West Indian household helps for employment in Canada" and that Jamaica had been allocated "66 of these workers" (Permanent Secretary to the Ministry of Labour, 1957a).[5] Mrs. Tomlinson was informed that applications had arrived to meet the June 1, 1957, deadline.

> It will therefore be necessary for the Ladies' Selection Committee to meet at an early date to commence the eliminations.... The Minister has asked me to express to you again his appreciation of your valued and devoted service in connection with the interviewing of applicants under the scheme last year and to say that he would be most grateful if you could find it possible to assist again in the interviewing and selection of these women this year.

There was a recognition of the "great sacrifice … [of her] valuable time" and a request for Mrs. Tomlinson to participate in the recruitment process, especially "in view of the splendid results achieved in last year's selections."

Mrs. Tomlinson's responded that she would be "happy to serve again … on the panel of ladies for the selection of West Indian Household helps for the Canadian Government."[6] She received a reply in which the Minister of Labour invited her "and all members of the Ladies Committee, who will select this year's quota of girls, to have Tea with him at the Ministry of Labour, 110 East Street, Kingston, at 5 P.M. on Tuesday, 18th June 1957, and to discuss this year's arrangements for the recruitment, as well as any suggestions which you might wish to offer relating to the selection of these workers" (Permanent Secretary to the Ministry of Labour, 1957b). These "ladies," invited to tea with the Minister of Labour, were expected to serve as the gatekeepers for the Scheme and to determine who among the applicants would be sent forward for consideration by the Canadian selection team.

That the Ladies' Selection Committee was dominated by middle- and upper-class women, most of whom were married, was entirely in keeping with the class-gender ideology which had been imported into and taken root in the island and which defined them as "ladies."[7] According to the ideas about idealized gender roles, women who fulfilled the essence of "the cult of true womanhood" performed superlative versions of piety, purity, submissiveness and domesticity.[8] While Mary Louise Roberts (2002: 150–7) contends that "in Europe, the cult was more likely to go under the name of 'real womanhood' or 'the domestic ideal,'" Donna Guy (2000:170) argues that "true women" made their appearance in Latin America (including the Caribbean) in the twentieth century. For her, in the Caribbean region, "the ideologies that guided them were inspired less by religion and literacy than by nationalism and public health campaigns," but the results were similar. The ladies who served on the Selection Committee were believed to be supreme examples of "the domestic ideal" and so were qualified to sit in judgement of *other* women (referred to by the Permanent Secretary as "girls") who had applied to work as domestic servants in Canadian homes. These "girls" had to be carefully screened, since they represented the nation and carried upon their shoulders not only their hopes for personal and familial improvement but the local authorities' desires for extended immigration opportunities in Canada. How would the "ladies" make sure that they selected the right "girls"?

Included in one letter from the Permanent Secretary to Mrs. Tomlinson was a three-page memorandum that set out "certain points which have been prepared in this Ministry for your guidance in selecting these household helps" (1957b). Grouped under twelve sub-headings, the guidelines for the selection of the Jamaican women who would serve in the Scheme covered a range of considerations, including the following:

> Selection is to be confined to single women without children within the age group 21 to 35 years (applicants to furnish birth certificates).... They should have a minimum of 5 years formal education (equivalent locally to the Sixth Standard, Elementary School) with preference to those with higher qualifications. Credit should be given for special courses taken in housecraft, domestic science, etc., and experience [is] to be taken into account, particularly with modern household appliances. (Ministry of Labour 1957: 1)

Having been given the parameters for selection, the Selection Committee was reminded that it was "important that the information given ... be true, otherwise applicants might be regarded as having breached their conditions of admission to Canada" (2). Not only were the "ladies" being asked to invoke the standards of recruitment but they were also to verify that those who presented themselves as likely candidates for recruitment were, in fact, worthy of these "wonderful opportunities."

One additional issue that was raised and which might have been directly connected to the preceding concern was that of dependents. The Ministry was adamant that the Ladies' Selection Committee impress upon the prospective recruits that theirs was a solitary recruitment. Other workers, from other parts of world, might have been sought and admitted to Canada as permanent settlers, preferably accompanied by their families, but neither of these conditions held for Jamaican and other women recruited under the West Indian Domestic Scheme. According to the guidelines, "Selectees should not expect, after arrival in Canada, to send for dependents. In any case arrangements should be made to the satisfaction of the Ministry of Labour for the care and support of dependents." The Jamaican authorities not only upheld the requirement of a single and "unencumbered" status of the women who were carefully selected for the program, but they went one step further to ensure that, should the recruited women *have* dependents, they would be cared for and supported to the satisfaction of the Ministry. How was it that these women, who were supposed to have had no dependents, were to ensure that their dependents were cared for and supported? This is, at best, mysterious. Unless those dependents were other than partners and children (since the requirement clearly said they were to be "single women without children"), the internal contradictions, which would come back to haunt the program, were already apparent.[9]

As the two-member selection panels from the Ladies' Selection Committee met the applicants between Monday, June 24, and Friday, June 28, 1957, they were asked to work "in order to ensure that only suitable persons are sent." The decisions about who those "suitable persons" could be were determined by a number of factors. Not only was the selection proscribed according to gender (no male servants were expected to be recruited), age (relatively young persons) and educational attainment, it was also limited by the financial ability of the applicants. The Ministry's guidelines stated:

> Selection is to be restricted to applicants who are able to pay their passage and other transportation expenses and have sufficient funds to buy suitable clothing, if they are not already so equipped. Successful applicants will be required to make a deposit of £50 with the Ministry of Labour to meet their transportation and incidental expenses. They should clearly understand this. (Ministry of Labour 1957: 1)

Part of these funds was to be used to purchase winter coats and "a minimum of warm clothing to provide against the change in climate they will experience in Canada." For those who might have had the training and/or experience to qualify as skilled domestic workers, an inability to find those significant funds disqualified them and skewed the selection away from the most economically marginal workers – away from the poorest women in the sector.

Up to the mid-twentieth century, there was a general preference among workers in the domestic service sector in Jamaica to seek, wherever they could, clearly defined specialist positions. From cooks, pantrymaids, pastrymaids, nursemaids and laundresses to ladies' maids, chambermaids and butleresses, many Jamaican domestic workers sought to (and often expected to) work as members of a domestic staff (see Higman 1983: 124). Prospective recruits for the Scheme were encouraged to think in another direction. The guidelines advised: "While there are openings in Canada for experienced cooks, housemaids, and other specialized domestic help, the greatest demand is for more general help and selection should be confined to this type of worker. A general domestic worker is expected to perform general household duties, ordinary cooking and to look after children" (2). While the "general maid" who was required to assume a wide range of duties was also present in many middling and less-affluent Jamaican households, the idea that Canadians (who, by virtue of being in a relatively wealthy country were believed to be better off than most Jamaicans) wanted to hire one general servant might have come as a surprise to many Jamaican domestic workers.

Among the most fundamental issues that preoccupy persons who participate in the domestic service sector are those of work hours and time off. To some extent, this was determined by factors such as whether or not workers resided in their employers' homes, the type of domestic work performed (nursemaids and laundresses, for example, tended to work quite differently) and the prevailing legal and customary expectations. In the Jamaican context, well into the 1970s, domestic workers did not benefit from the labour laws which dictated maximum working hours, time off and holidays.[10] Applicants to the Scheme may well have expected that the Canadian labour scene would be an improvement on the extreme variations in local working conditions and would entail the removal of personal employer whim from their labour contracts. However, this was not the case; instead, prospective recruits were to be informed that in the Canadian context:

> Usually working hours are from breakfast time to dinner time with a rest period during the day and half day or day off per week. In some households Sunday is free, in others every second Sunday. It is difficult to be specific with respect to hours of work as usually this is worked out between employer and employee. It is common practice after one year of service to give two weeks holidays with pay. (3)

The expectation that the hours of work would be "worked out between employer and employee" usually placed the domestic worker at a great disadvantage. Since it was the employer who demanded, recruited and could replace workers, the negotiation around hours left little room for workers' preferences to be taken seriously. Where the worker resided in their employer's home, their ability to resist the demands of employers became even less possible, and where, as was the case with the Scheme, they were solitary workers in a foreign context without familial or community support, their vulnerability to pressures for long work hours were tremendous. Insofar as those who created the guidelines within the Ministry of Labour were willing to take this "flexible" stance regarding the working hours of the women whose labour they recruited meant that they endorsed the traditions of domestic service in the Jamaican context. That the Jamaican government would allow for those ill-defined expectations to remain unresolved in the agreement which lay at the heart of the Scheme and made no demands on behalf of the island's "exported" workers, placed those workers in positions of relatively heightened vulnerability.

Similarly, the fact the domestic workers were not covered by Jamaica's minimum wage laws until the 1970s may have made it easier for the Ministry of Labour to accept the undefined nature of remuneration for the workers they recruited for the Scheme. According to its instructions to the Ladies' Selection Committee:

> The salaries paid [to] domestic workers in Canada cover a wide range and are dependent to a very large extent upon ability and experience. Wages range from $55.00 to $100 a month, including board, separate lodging and laundry. Those starting at the lower end of the scale would qualify for increases depending on their proficiency. In this connection those domestics selected should be informed that they must reasonably expect to start in the lower bracket, at least until they become accustomed to Canadian methods. (2)

Since the Ministry of Labour was prepared to leave it to Canadian employers to determine the wages they would pay based on the "ability and experience" of the women who were recruited, it is not a surprise that there was a tendency for the women to be paid poorly. And since the Ministry, and its proxies through the Ladies' Selection Committee, was willing to instruct the women to "reasonably expect to start in the lower bracket," the authorities seemed content to assist in the low categorization of the island's women and to allow for the possibility of their exploitation. What, exactly, constituted "Canadian methods" and how the domestic workers would be able to prove that they had "become accustomed" to them in order to be paid at a higher rate was not clarified. No doubt, like their hours of work and with similar results, recruits were expected to "work out" these issues with their employers.

The question of exactly *who* it was that the Jamaican Ministry of Labour sought to recruit to the Scheme was captured in the "general policy" given to the Ladies' Selection Committee. According to the Ministry of Labour, the selection of domestic workers should reflect "as much as practicable a representative cross-section of the different types of persons who apply, but it is most essential that those selected should comply with the basic standards and requirements in order to ensure that only suitable persons are sent" (1). It is not at all clear what sorts of "different types of persons" might have applied, but the Ministry's anxiety that "only suitable persons" should be selected was not in doubt. What that suitability entailed was made quite clear throughout the guidelines, which stated that in addition to an "ability to read and understand recipes" and knowledge about household appliances, the prospective recruits should be judged according to their "good personal appearance and hygiene ... neatness and tidiness ... [and] good decorum and manners" (1). Further, the Ministry reminded the Selection Committee that "Character, Marital Status, Age and Compulsory Service Period" were issues to which they should pay attention: "Persons selected must be in good physical and mental health, of good character and must agree to remain at domestic employment for at least one year." Recruits were expected to show a "Sense of Responsibility – They must have a sense of responsibility (be able to 'stand on their own feet')." They should be able to display "Health and Efficiency"—"A state of very good health is necessary because of difference in climatic and housing conditions." And if the Selection Committee was in any doubt about the unease that ran through the Ministry, the last sentence in the last "Note" to the Committee re-emphasized those anxieties in block capitals: "PERSONAL HYGIENE SHOULD BE A MOST IMPORTANT CONSIDERATION" (3).

These foci on the prospective recruits' clean, neat and tidy bodies along with their behaviour and manners were in keeping with the concerns voiced by many Jamaican employers of domestic labour (see Johnson 2007, 1996). They were no doubt represented among the policy drafters in the Ministry and the Ladies' Selection Committee, and they would have expected Canadian employers to have had similar apprehensions. Given the necessity for domestic workers to be inserted into the intimate spaces of the households they served and given the personal entanglements which were likely to result from that intimacy, perhaps those concerns were understandable. What is interesting, however, was the preoccupation with the recruited women's bodies and manners, as opposed to the training, skills and experience that the domestic workers were expected to possess.

These former issues were given even more emphasis when the Selection Committee was asked to focus on recruits' "Moral Standard, Social Conditions and Adjustments" since "Moral standards in Canada are different from those in Jamaica and should any recruit, after taking up employment in Canada, become an expectant mother, that may be regarded by employers as grounds for dismissal" (2). The question of children's "illegitimacy" had preoccupied the cultural elite and those who aspired to join that class since the nineteenth century. However, while the framers of the "civilizing mission" made shrill demands that Jamaicans engage in monogamous Christian marriage, the majority of the population saw no contradictions in starting families without official marriages and felt little or no shame in their children born "out of wedlock" (see Moore and Johnson 2005, 2004). There is little doubt that the Jamaican women who offered their services under the Scheme must have thought very carefully about what all of this Canadian "morality" meant for them and their families.

While the acquisition of political independence in 1962 might have meant a fundamental change in Jamaica's methods of governance, there was no desire on the government's part to end the exportation of the island's female labour force through the Scheme. Indeed, the new independent government sought to expand the program and to add other labour schemes to its increasingly dependent relationship with Canada. In October 1962, the minister of labour confirmed that the Cabinet had agreed that he and his permanent secretary should visit Canada "for the purposes of exploring the possibility of securing the recruitment of nursemaids for work in the Dominion, as well as an enlarged quota for household helps" (Newland 1962). Concerned to establish the system by which Jamaica would receive a quota of the positions for household helps, since the West Indies Federation, "now defunct," could no longer serve that function, the minister wanted not only the "establishment of a nurse-maid's scheme" and the "expansion of the household helps scheme" but to examine "the possibilities of recruiting kitchen porters and bus boys for restaurants in the Toronto area." However, despite the existence of the Scheme since 1955 (and assurances that it would continue), as well as what Minister Newland referred to as "a shortage of these categories of workers in Canada," the Canadian authorities

> expressed the view that the objective could be achieved through the normal channels of selection of Jamaican immigrants to Canada by the establishment of a branch of the Canadian Immigration and Naturalisation Service in Jamaica. It is expected that pending the setting up of a permanent Service in Jamaica, the Canadian Government will carry out "ad hoc" consideration of applications from *suitable persons* who would make application for admission to Canada through the High Commissioner for Canada. (emphasis added)

Instead of special schemes, according to Minister Newland, the Canadian position was that "Persons falling into the categories of nurse-maids, household helps, kitchen porters and bus boys would qualify for admission to Canada subject to these persons fulfilling the requirements of the Canadian Immigration and Naturalisation Service." On this occasion, the attempts by the Jamaican government to promote schemes for the exportation of portions of the Jamaican labour force were unsuccessful, and recruitment processes, such as those spearheaded by the Ladies' Selection Committee, were not necessary. However in 1973, according to Minister of Labour and Employment Ernest G. Peart, the Ministry was *still* processing applications for domestic workers "with the aid of a voluntary Ladies Committee … with final selection being made by the Canadian High Commission." The Jamaican government sanctioned and facilitated process of exporting female reproductive labour continued, and local "ladies" continued to choose "women" or "girls" to perform paid domestic labour in the homes of those who, invoking the vision of a classist perspective, would have been perceived as Canadian "ladies."

While a great deal of the scholarly investigation focused on the international and transnational nature of domestic service has examined this phenomenon in the late twentieth century, this chapter urges us to think of an earlier period, when this movement was facilitated by official channels. These Jamaican (and other Caribbean) women were part of what Noeleen Heyzer (1994: xv) refers to as "the export of women's labour as domestic workers [which] has become an increasingly important source of foreign exchange, or regular remittances to supplement household incomes, and of labour absorption in a situation of chronic unemployment." As increasing numbers of women in Western countries, including Canada, entered the formal labour force, they generated an "increasing reliance on the import of migrant women for their domestic labour to resolve problems of labour shortage and social reproduction – household maintenance, the care of the young, the old and the sick" (xv). As Bridget Anderson (2000: 2) argues, this transnational process facilitated circumstances in which "racist stereotypes intersect with issues of citizenship, and result in a racist hierarchy which uses skin colour, religion, and nationality to construct some women as being more suitable for domestic work than others." Further, says Anderson, often these migrant domestic workers are required not only to sell their labour power but also to sell their "personhood" in complicated and often oppressive intra-gender relationships where their female employers demand that they "do the dirty work."

In the case of the Scheme, the fact that the recruitment process began with Jamaican "ladies" who sat in judgement of the "women/girls" who applied in order "to ensure that only suitable persons [were] sent" provides a glimpse of the unexplored links between Jamaica and Canada, which had shared an imperial connection for centuries. And since the Jamaican "ladies" no doubt believed that they shared a class and cultural, if not necessarily a racial, affinity with the Canadian households, supposedly run by "ladies" for whom they performed this voluntary service, the intertwined and complicated intra-gender, international and transnational relationships are fascinating. For those who were deemed *suitable* for consideration by the Canadian authorities, the next hurdle involved convincing the visiting recruiters that they could perform not just domestic work but a host of other functions tied to the ideologies of domesticity and "ideal womanhood." But further, they had to persuade the recruiters (and later their employers) that they were not simply domestic workers but that they understood that the performance of their duties occurred within a context where an intersection of race, class and gender prescribed and proscribed their place and status. Having gone through screening and recruitment, after working in Canada, many would echo the sentiments of "Primrose," who declared to Makeda Silvera (1989: 88):

Canadians have the feeling that we are coming here to rob them, to take their jobs, yet we are the ones who clean up all their mess, pick up after them. We take the jobs that they wouldn't take, and yet they hate us so much.

> Sometimes I sit down and consider, and I say that our government (in Jamaica) are very slack too. I say this when I face all the problems that we live-in domestic workers have.... When I go back to JA (Jamaica), I'm going to RJR and JBC radio station and announce to all the people the true story of Canada and Canadians. I want somehow to get the government of Jamaica to let them know they are slack, cause if they had done better we wouldn't be under this pressure.

For what had been declared to be "great opportunities," the Jamaican domestic workers in Canada had been carefully screened and chosen. As they struggled to survive the conditions of work, they may well have wondered what had been meant when they were deemed to be "suitable persons" for the positions.

Notes

1. According to some scholars, Canada has traditionally linked its identity to the idea of a "Great White North," with images of snow, wilderness, emptiness and innocence. However, in publications like *Rethinking the Great White North*, the very idea of "Whiteness" is challenged by critical race theory and is thus centred and problematized in debates about Canadian history, geography and identity (see Baldwin, Cameron and Kobayashi 2011).
2. Reliable Employment Bureau was located at 91 East Street; Bell's Employment Agency was to be found on Church Street; and Overseas Employment Services was at 30 Beeston Street, all in Kingston.
3. In his book, *Deemed Unsuitable: Blacks from Oklahoma Move to the Canadian Prairies in Search of Equality in the Early 20th Century*, Bruce Shepard (1997), reproduced a document of the Government of Canada, Order-in-Council no. 1324, 12 August 1911, image facing page 1.
4. Winks (2000: 435) points to "Canada, *House of Commons Debates, 1947*, 1 May, 352, 365" as his source.
5. Mrs. Tomlinson also received a similar letter the following year; see Acting Permanent Secretary, Ministry of Labour, Letter to Mrs. L. James Tomlinson, M.B.E., 8 Central Avenue, Mountain View Gardens, Kingston 3, 9 June 1958, C 1035/S12 (III), JA 3/24/1068.
6. Although Mrs. Tomlinson's written affirmative response to the Ministry is dated 14 June 1957, she must have contacted the Ministry informally earlier than that date since the Ministry's further correspondence with her is dated 12 June 1957.
7. The membership of the Ladies' Selection Committee for 1957 was: Mrs. E.R.D. Evans, Mrs. M. Richardson, Mrs. C. Greaves Hill, Mrs. Braham, Mrs. S. Levy, Mrs. Joe DeCordova, Mrs. A.C.V. Graham, Mrs. W.S.K. Gordon, Miss Doris Morant, Mrs. D.T.M. Girvan, Miss Amy Bailey, Mrs. Ewart Forrest, Mrs. H.G.

Duffus, Mrs. D. Fletcher, Mrs. S.T. Ellington and Mrs. L. James-Tomlinson. See Ministry of Labour, "Recruitment of Household Helps for Work in Canada: Roster of Interviews for Week Ending 28/6/57," JA 3/24/1068. For short biographies of some of these women see Vassell (1993). For a discussion of the attempts to "civilise" and "engender" post-slavery Jamaican society, see Moore and Johnson (2004), particularly chapters 4–7.

8. For an influential discussion of the principles that guided the lives and experiences of White, middle-class, nineteenth-century American women, see Welter (1996).

9. In 1975 the Canadian government decided to deport some of the women who had been recruited to work as domestic servants in Canada. According to Silvera, "The charge was that they had submitted fake immigration applications claiming they had no children, but were now attempting to apply for landed status for children they now acknowledged in Jamaica." See Silvera's discussion of the case against the "Seven Jamaican Mothers" and the support they received from individuals as well as the "International Committee Against Racism, Canadians Against the Deportation of Immigrant Women, the Universal African Improvement Association, the Canadian Labour Party, teachers, trade unionists, church leaders and the Sikh community" (Silvera 1989): vii–viii.

10. The *Master and Servants Act* of 1842 was finally overturned by *An Act to Repeal the Masters and Servants Law, 1974.* In its stead the *Employment (Termination and Redundancy Payments) Act* was passed in 1974.

References

Anderson, Bridget. 2000. *Doing the Dirty Work: The Global Politics of Domestic Labour.* London: Zed Books.

Anon., n.d. *Advice to West Indian Women Recruited for Work in Canada as Household Helps.* Bridgetown, Barbados: Government Printing Office.

Arat-Koc, Sedef. 1989. "In the Privacy of Our Own Homes: Foreign Domestic Workers as the Solution to the Crisis in the Domestic Sphere in Canada." *Studies in Political Economy* 28 (Spring).

Aymer, Paula L. 1997. *Uprooted Women: Migrant Domestics in the Caribbean.* Westport, CT; London: Praeger.

Bakan, Abigail B., and Daiva K. Stasiulis. 1994. "Foreign Domestic Worker Policy in Canada and the Social Boundaries of Modern Citizenship." *Science and Society* 58, 1 (Spring).

____. 1995. "Making the Match: Domestic Placement Agencies and the Racialization of Women's Household Work." *Signs: Journal of Women in Culture and Society* 20–21 (Winter).

____ (eds.). 1997. *Not One of the Family: Foreign Domestic Workers in Canada.* Toronto: University of Toronto Press.

Baldwin, Andrew, Laura Cameron and Audrey Kobayashi (eds.). 2011. *Rethinking the Great White North: Race, Nature and the Historical Geographies of Whiteness in Canada.* Vancouver: UBC Press

Calliste, Agnes. 1991. "Canada's Immigration Policy and Domestics from the Caribbean: The Second Domestic Scheme." In Jesse Vorste (ed.), *Race, Class and Gender: Bonds and Barriers* (136–69) Toronto: Garamond Press.

____. 1993/1994. "Race, Gender and Canadian Immigration Policy: Blacks from the

Caribbean, 1900–1932," *Journal of Canadian Studies* 28, 4 (Winter).

Carty, Linda. 1994. "African Canadian Women and the State: 'Labour Only, Please.'" In P. Bristow et al. (eds.), *"We're Rooted Here and They Can't Pull Us Up": Essays in African Canadian Women's History*, Toronto: University of Toronto Press.

Cohen, Rina. 1994. "A Brief History of Racism in Immigration Policies for Recruiting Domestics." *Canadian Woman Studies* 14, 2.

Daenzer, Patricia. 1993. *Regulating Class Privilege: Immigrant Servants in Canada, 1940s–1990s*. Toronto: Canadian Scholars' Press.

Daily Gleaner. 1920a. Classified advertisements, 13 March.

____. 1920b. Classified advertisements, 12 June.

____. 1920c. Classified advertisements, 14 August.

____.1920d. Classified advertisements, 10 July.

Douglas, E.M.K. 1968. "West Indians in Canada: The Household Help Scheme: A Comment." *Social and Economic Studies* 17, 2 (June).

Giles, Wenona, and Sedef Arat-Koç (eds.). 1994. *Maid in the Market: Women's Paid Domestic Labour*. Halifax: Fernwood Publishing.

Guy, Donna J. 2002. "True Womanhood in Latin America." *Journal of Women's History* 14.1Spring.

Harris, Ruth Lynette. 1988. "The Transformation of Canadian Policies and Programs to Recruit Foreign Labor: The Case of Caribbean Female Domestic Workers, 1950's–1980's." PhD. dissertation: Michigan State University, Ann Arbor: UMI.

Henry, Frances. 1968. "The West Indian Domestic Scheme in Canada." *Social and Economic Studies* 17, 1 (March).

Heyzer, Noeleen, Geertje Lycklama à Nijeholt and Nedra Weerakoon (eds.). 1994. *The Trade in Domestic Workers: Causes, Mechanisms and Consequences of International Migration*. Kuala Lumpur: Asian and Pacific Development Centre. London: Zed Books Ltd.

Higman, B.W. 1983. "Domestic Service in Jamaica, since 1750." In B.W. Higman (ed.), *Essays Presented to Douglas Hall: Trade, Government and Society in Caribbean History, 1700–1920*, Kingston: Heineman Educational Books Caribbean.

Johnson, Michele A. 1993. "Intimate Enmity: Control of Women in Domestic Service in Jamaica, 1920–1970." *The Jamaican Historical Review* XVIII.

____. 1996. "Decent and Fair: Aspects of Domestic Service in Jamaica, 1920–1970." *Journal of Caribbean History* 30, 1&2.

____. 2002. "Young Woman from the Country: A Profile of Domestic Service in Jamaica, 1920-1970." In V. Shepherd (ed.), *Working Slavery, Pricing Freedom: The Caribbean and the Atlantic World since the 17th Century*. Kingston: Ian Randle Press.

____. 2007. "'Problematic Bodies': Negotiations and Termination in Domestic Service in Jamaica, 1920–1970." *Left History: An Interdisciplinary Journal of Historical Inquiry & Debate* 12: 2 (Fall/Winter).

Macklin, Audrey. 1994. "On the Inside Looking In: Foreign Domestic Workers in Canada." In W. Giles and S. Arat-Koç (eds.), *Maid in the Market: Women's Paid Domestic Labour*. Halifax: Fernwood Publishing.

McPherson, J.A. 1954. Minister for Labour, "Executive Council Submission: Recruitment of Jamaicans for Agricultural and Domestic Work in Canada." M.L. C. 3203, 21 April, JA 1B/31/342.

Ministry of Labour. 1957. "Selection of Household Helps for Employment in Canada: Points for Guidance of Ladies Committee." JA 3/24/1068.

Mohammed, Patricia. 1986. "Domestic Workers." In P. Ellis (ed.), *Women of the Caribbean*. Kingston: Kingston Publishers.

Moore, Brian L., and Michele A. Johnson. 2000. *"Squalid Kingston" 1890–1920: How the Poor Lived, Moved and Had Their Being*. Kingston: Social History Project.

___. 2004. *Neither Led Nor Driven: Contesting British Cultural Imperial in Jamaica 1865–1920*. Kingston: University of the West Indies Press.

___. 2005. "'Married but not Parsoned': Attitudes to Conjugality in Jamaica, 1865–1920." In G. Heuman and D. Trotman (eds.), *Contesting Freedom: Control and Resistance in the Post-Emancipation Caribbean*. London: Macmillan.

Newland, L.G. 1962. Minister of Labour, Cabinet Submission, M.L. No. C-1138, 354/ML-22, 26 October, JA 1B/31/354.

Peart, Ernest G. 1973. Minister of Labour and Employment, Cabinet Submission. "Canadian Household Help Scheme." M.L. No. C1035, No. 258/ML&E – 21, 25 April, JA1B/31/258.

Permanent Secretary to the Ministry of Labour. 1957a. Letter to Mrs. Leila J. Tomlinson, 8 Central Avenue, Vineyard Town. 11 June. C 1035/S13 (11), JA 3/24/1068.

___. 1957b. Letter to Mrs. Leila J. Tomlinson, 8 Central Avenue, Vineyard Town. 12 June. C 1035/S13 (11), JA 3/24/1068.

Roberts, Mary Louise. 2002. "True Womanhood Revisited." *Journal of Women's History* 14.1.

Satzewich, Vic. 1993/1994. "Racism and Canadian Immigration Policy: The Government's View of Caribbean Migration, 1962–1966." *Canadian Ethnic Studies* 28, 4.

Schecter, Tanya. 1998. *Race, Class, Women and the State: The Case of Domestic Labour in Canada*. Montreal, New York, London: Black Rose Books.

Scott, G.H. 1954. For Minister of Labour, "Executive Council Submission: Recruitment of Jamaicans for Agricultural and Domestic work in Canada." M.L. C 3203, 20 January, JA 1B/31/14.

Silvera, Makeda. 1989. *Silenced: Talks with Working Class Caribbean Women about Their Lives and Struggles as Domestic Workers in Canada*. Toronto: Sister Vision.

Vassell, Linnette (ed.). 1993. *Voices of Women in Jamaica, 1898–1939*. Mona, Kingston: Dept of History, University of the West Indies.

Welter, Barbara. 1996. "The Cult of True Womanhood, 1820–1860." *American Quarterly* 18 Summer.

Winks, Robin W. 2000. *The Blacks in Canada: A History*. Carlton Library Series 192. Montreal and Kingston: McGill-Queen's University Press.

4. ODYSSEY HOME TO A PLACE WITHIN

An Autobiography of One of Jamaica's "Lost Children"

Tamari Kitossa

It is obvious we are products of histories and are shaped by the experiences of our interactions. We are also, obviously, agents in the shaping of our experiences as well as those of others. On both counts, what is obvious has the power to be taken for granted. That is, as contended by Antonio Gramsci, in the dialectic between self and society, we are unavoidably "one in the mass" (1992: 324). But the question is, in what way? This question is really an invitation to undertake a project of self and social discovery in order to arrive at an understanding of one's distinctiveness and place in the world. Moreover, having subjected one's understanding of the world to scrutiny, the next step is to develop a consciousness of one's membership in a group or number of groups. The aim is to develop a critical and coherent understanding of the world from one's own vantage point, to develop oneself as a liberal subject who acts with free-will and reason, and to contribute to a broader humanistic goal of working toward the betterment of society. According to Gramsci (1992: 324), "The starting-point of critical elaboration is a consciousness of what one really is, and is 'knowing thyself' as a product of the historical process to date which has deposited in you an infinity of traces, without leaving an inventory." Conspicuously and without explanation, Edward Said notes in *Orientalism* (1979: 25), that the only available English translation of Gramsci's *Prison Notebooks* excludes the logical conclusion that "therefore it is imperative at the outset to compile such an inventory."

This chapter is my effort to compile a coherent inventory of the world of shadows in which I live: as a Jamaican immigrant *in* but not *of* Canada and as a Jamaican *from* Jamaica but who can "never return home" even though I visit. I seek to make sense of my ambivalence about my *place* in the world as a Canadian and Jamaican. I do so from the vantage point of a Jamaican-born person whose formative attachment to my grandmother was abruptly and violently broken at age eight, when I was forcibly brought to Canada to live with my parents and siblings in 1973. I seek not only to craft an account that explains who I am, who I have come to be, and the nature of my ambivalence toward my identity as Jamaican, but more broadly to suggest that I am part of a larger group experience which has yet to be fully explored by sociologists. I suspect that little scholarly work has been done because Jamaicans themselves have taken for granted the painful losses and injuries some of their children suffered during the heyday of immigration to Canada in the 1970s and 1980s. I do not suggest that good quality scholarly or fictional work on the Caribbean immigrant experience is unavailable (Bobb-Smith 2003; Flynn 2011; Foster 1995; Prince 2001). On the contrary, my point is that more work lies ahead of us.

It is impossible to know exactly how many immigrant Jamaican children came to Canada between the ages of five and twelve and in so doing were dispossessed of their primary caregiver attachments. These individuals cannot be easily identified because immigration statistics are aggregate in nature and don't distinguish between children born in Jamaica and those born in Canada. Thus, they can only suggest the size and composition of this population. Nonetheless, the 2001 census indicates that foreign-born Jamaicans comprise 53 percent of all Jamaicans in Canada. Fifty-eight percent of this group, however, immigrated between 1970 and 1990 (Statistics Canada 2007). Using the 1991 census, George Eaton showed that in the early phase of immigration in the 1960s, there were relatively few Jamaican immigrants, 2,662, the majority of them males. But, with the changes in Canada's immigration policy, the second half of the 1960s saw a significant increase in numbers, 13,439, and a significant shift in demographics. In the second half of the 1960s, about one third of this latter group were immigrant dependents and "as late as 1969 young children and teenagers were 26 percent of the dependents" (Eaton 1999: 835). This demographic change became more marked in the 1970s by the number of dependent children. Women and children accounted for between 50 and 58 percent each year of Jamaican immigrants over this period. But even as Jamaican immigration dropped by half (34,124) in the 1980s, Eaton reminds us that "the bulge of under-nineteens persisted, averaging 43 percent from 1980–1989" (835–6). Based on Canada's labour recruitment policies, this skewed gender and age immigration pattern would have a profound impact on the structure of Jamaican families and influence a broad range of social problems (see the Appendix at the end of this chapter). This chapter presents a reflection on my experience of self-interrogation and conversations with other Jamaicans who, like me, had our formative development, and as such our identity as Jamaicans, irreparably altered by our immigrant experiences. While this study could have benefitted from research in which I interviewed the appropriate number of participants about their experiences, I use my experiences and what C. Wright Mills calls the "sociological imagination" to grasp and connect the broad outlines of the history and psychology of individuals and the groups to which I belong.

Taking Gramsci and Mills seriously, I seek to articulate how and in what ways my experiences and related issues are shared by many other Jamaican-born children who were between the ages of five and twelve when they entered Canada in the late 1960s to the late 1980s. This particular group of children, especially those raised and nurtured by women other than their mothers, underwent a psychically violent detachment process from their primary caregivers and significant others. As a consequence, their formative development was severely disrupted and they were compelled to take on roles and identities for which there was little preparation by anyone in their family. More study is required of this population for without doubt they suffered a highly traumatic experience, as a result of which they developed personality traits and characteristics akin to other children who suffered trauma. I believe that few adults from this group have in fact mourned their loss of familial relations and the disruption of their childhoods. Fewer still have come to terms with how their spontaneous survival modes have shaped the persons they have become and, for some, their role as parents. The parents of my generation, some of whom have repatriated to Jamaica, likely recognized and, dealt with the traumas of all their children as best they could. But, as research indicates, distracted and stressed parents often do not attend to the needs of their children as well as when conditions are otherwise (Maccody 1980: 403). Confronted with a racist immigration policy and White supremacy in Canada (Bobb-Smith 2003: 167), Jamaican parents were likely under serious economic and psychological pressure to conform to Canadian society. Nonetheless, there is little by way of public conversation or research about the massive impact this small group of children had on the structure of Jamaican families and their ability to adapt to and cope with the broad range of social issues presented to them in Canada.

If this group of Jamaican Canadians experienced the quality of loss I suggest and if this has had a significant impact on family and community life in Canada, what were and are the implications for Jamaica? I believe that Jamaica too experienced a psychic loss that must also be repaired. Communities in Jamaica, especially in the 1970s, likely grieved over their "lost children," grandchildren, brothers and sisters and nieces and nephews who went to "foreign," tearing apart, but fortunately not destroying, the caring fabric of their communities. In losing its children in their formative years, Jamaica lost the chance to confer on this group strong and firm identities as Jamaicans. In my estimation, Jamaica has yet to come to terms with the impact of having lost a generation of its young. The fiftieth anniversary of Jamaican independence is an opportune time to reflect on how Jamaica and its lost children can begin to meaningfully repair the damaging costs of immigration.

Jamaica: A Place Within, a Place of Loss

It was in 1973, when I was eight years old, that my family immigrated to Canada. Including my first return trip in 1988, I have since visited my birth country six times. Certain memories stay with me. Since that first visit, a quiet voice from the land whispers for me to come "home" every few years. That voice often presents itself with sights and smells that are as real as if I were in Jamaica: the sweet-tasting smell of burning brush and timber carried in the cool evening air high in the hills of St. Ann. I visualize the grey-white smoke against a verdant backdrop that rises over peak after peak as the car taking me to my hill-top district bounces, bobs and weaves along roads which were probably Arawak trails later cut into roads by my African ancestors. The soft hellos to and from dignified, humble farmers making their way from their fields — walking in their water boots and cutlasses under their arms — remain as an inspirational symbol of struggle. But, I have earlier memories too — from the time when I lived in Jamaica as a child.

One early memory is at five years old being held aloft on my father's shoulders at a Jamaica Independence Day celebration. I remember only stadium lights turning the night into day, a sea of people and plumes of white smoke from outdoor cooking. I remember also visiting my parents and siblings in Kingston. As though it were yesterday, I recall the smell of diesel spewing from the buses as they came to and from the bus terminal on Hope Road. I remember too, the smell of carbolic soap, which my mother would use to bathe me and my siblings, the Christmas harvests and community merry-making in St. Anns, jankunu parades in Kingston and the smell of my grandfather's hard dough bread wafting over the district.

No memories, however, stand out with as much distinctiveness as the unqualified love of my grandmother and the awful day I was taken from her. The story goes that my mother had me when she was seventeen. Finding it difficult to deal with a premature baby with special needs, my paternal grandmother made my mother an offer I don't think she was free to reject: "Give the child to me and go back to school." Thus, from the age of six months until I was eight, I was, for all intents and purpose, my grandmother's child. She would, by arrangement, send me to Kingston in the summer to stay with my parents and by 1971, my three siblings. My grandmother, however, was my world, and it was hard for me to be away from her during those summers. Where my grandmother was, so too was I, clinging to her frock tail and sucking my thumb. That world of love, nurture and total security ended when I was eight years old. I am told that it was a pitiful sight when it dawned on me that I was being taken away from my grandmother to live in a place called Canada. Apparently, I was hysterical and clung so tightly to her legs that it took two grown men to pry me from her. That was not the end of the matter. I understand that I dodged multiple strong-armed men to hide under my grandmother's bed. They had to pull me out by my legs, clawing, scratching and screaming. When all the fight and tears were out, my last gesture was to give my grandmother the only memento I valued — my toothbrush. Interestingly, of all of my childhood life in Jamaica, this is the only memory that remains blocked from my consciousness. I have no images of the experience save for those created by the memories of others who were there. What I do have is a deep foreboding sense that on that day something was taken from me and I have never been able to retrieve it — that sense of wholeness. So, what becomes of a child, or indeed a group of children, who were, in the classic psychological sense of *attachment* (Maccoby, 1980: 53), removed from relationships in which they were cared for, nurtured and feel secure? This question is not intended to romanticize the life of Jamaican childhood between 1970 and the late 1980s since without doubt, there were many difficulties and in some instances, outright sexual and physical abuse in the waiting period before reunification with parents who immigrated earlier. Yet, the fact remains that there are many like me who suffered dispossession of ties to primary caregivers.

In any case, this was not an auspicious start to my adventure in Canada — a stranger in a strange land. Given the destruction of my relationship with my grandmother and a lifetime of repressed anger at her, when I was thirty, I asked my mother why she and my father took me from my grandmother. It was a difficult question for my mother, who understandably for years struggled with the decision to allow my grandmother to be my surrogate mother. To this day, that decision casts a shadow on our relationship that we try to transcend. The answer: "Your grandmother didn't want your siblings to have opportunities you would miss out on if you stayed with her." If my mother felt guilt, what must my grandmother have felt?

While I have visited Jamaica numerous times since 1988 and I feel myself being called by the land every few years, my removal from grandmother is part of a broader feeling of alienation that is not repaired by any subsequent visit. There is a quality to the alienation that is unshakeable; maybe it befits the statement that "one can never go home again!" It is amusing, though, that on my first few visits to Jamaica total strangers in Ocho Rios would shout out, "Yo English!" I'd smile, more out of bemusement than anything else. It is as if I have "foreign" stamped on me. Yet, to be so easily marked as "foreign," on one hand suggests there is an authenticity I lack. On the other, I am confronted with my ambivalence toward my Jamaican identity. My identity as Jamaican is not something I reject. In Canada, where blackness is always presumed to mean immigrant, with my dreadlocks and crown (tam), it is assumed, if not transparent, that I am Jamaican. But, when I am in Jamaica, it is difficult to feel at home though the sights, sounds, smells and the beauty of the people themselves, more often than not, are welcoming.

Jamaica's "Lost Children," or Children Lost to Jamaica?

Those Jamaicans who struck out after independence to seek their fortunes abroad are celebrated in the nation's lore as having had pluck, courage and a good dose of luck on their side. They were not blamed for leaving; they were encouraged. Lacking industry and technology sufficient to compete on the global stage, Jamaica sent abroad a vibrant, young, intelligent and skilled labour force which the country could not make use of. This worked to the benefit of Canada, the United States and the United Kingdom. Counted among the "exports" are those who are now famous and wealthy, infamous and, of course, regular folks who worked hard, saved and raised families in the best way they could. Some in this latter group have even become modestly wealthy from their foresight and industriousness. There are of course also those who will be judged as spectacular failures, to be scoffed at for not making better of themselves and, of course, their homeland. Despite those deemed as failures at the mission, we count as a benefit the gains from Jamaica's exporting, not long after independence, of many of its young gifted adults and their young families. The results are often measured in terms of remittances (Simmons, Plaza and Piché 2005) and more recently, in the return of expatriate seniors and young entrepreneurs. Ledgers, however, have a minus column also.

This chapter is an opportunity to reflect on that minus side and the hidden cost, yet in my estimation to be fully appreciated. It is about the psychic cost to Jamaica in general but particularly to the children whose emotional development and sense of self were severely disrupted when their full socialization into Jamaica's deep web of caring was destroyed. I often wonder what must it have been like for the elders to hear and feel the increasing silence of children's voices as yet another of their grandchildren was sent off to "foreign." Sure, new children were born. Nevertheless, I imagine that for the elders this experience was akin to the destitution in Africa in the aftermath of enslavement raids, which emptied towns and villages of their children and many of the child-bearing parents. It seems we have not thought seriously enough of emigration as a massive imposition of loss and the psychological and sociological implications for the towns and villages all over Jamaica.

Despite all of the benefits of emigration, consideration needs to be given to the children who were sent off in the formative stages of their lives, when they were forming deep emotional attachments and indeed, affirming social ties to immediate and extended family members. I suggest that these children have suffered tremendous loss. Their capacity to love themselves has been harmed, as were their abilities to establish deep and meaningful relations with their families in Canada. An untold consequence was the loss or, at the very least, the impairment of their identities as Jamaicans. I consider myself among Jamaica's "lost children," or, as the case may be, those who are lost to Jamaica; I am not sure which it is but suspect a bit of both. Whatever the case, some of us will soon have to find our way back home to care for aging parents who are a part of Jamaica's reverse flow — expatriate seniors who had always imagined they would return home. For Jamaica's lost children, those immigrant children who retained their cultural identity and the senior expatriate parents alike, it will be interesting and important to chronicle the implications of this complex return process.

Child psychologist Eleanor Maccoby has pointed out that "the quality of a young child's affection is not the same as an adult's — it is more demanding and less giving, and it is built on the child's needs and the parents' ability to gratify these needs" (1980: 47). Therefore, for children to be bereft of primary attachments and placed into intimate but unfamiliar family arrangements is to set in motion a broad range of psychic adaptations, and sometimes mal-adaptations, into adulthood—the consequences of which could be aggression, loss of self-esteem, lack of trust, mental instability, dependency and so on. Children are without question resilient, and thus, they accommodate and adapt. The nature of that accommodation and adaptation in the face of continued stress, in this case the immigrant experience, especially marked by the constancy of White supremacy and anti-Blackness, which has been noted for some time to have negative consequences in the lives of African Canadian children and youth (James 1994; Kelly 1998; Roberts-Fiati 1996; McClain 1979).

To what extent are many of the social problems experienced by children in the Jamaican-Canadian community traceable to this dual process of alienation — i.e., disrupted childhood attachment and immigration? The McMurtry/Curling Report is unequivocal that a source of acting out and violence among African Canadian youth is traceable to alienation produced by the macro-aggression of racism. How many of these troubled youth have parents who, like me, had their childhood attachments disrupted? How many of the youth themselves are immigrants who have been torn from nurturing environments and have had to confront racism in schools, on the job and in confrontations with police? These questions cannot be addressed here, but they do suggest serious examination of immigration as a costly and hostile experience for young people.

Schooling and Social Experiences

The schooling experiences of many of us who immigrated in the 1970s have had a profound impact on how we came to understand both ourselves and Canada. For example, being set back a grade or two was a common feature of the experience of many immigrant Jamaican children. Consider that just after independence, in addition to having one of the highest valued currencies in the world, as part of the British Commonwealth, Jamaica had one of the highest standards of education. That mattered little for we were routinely put back in our new school or even sent to "remedial" classes, which functionally stopped our educational progress.

What amounted to an informal policy of racial discrimination in public schools was hard on me and contrasted with my childhood educational experience in Jamaica. I could read at age three, and, for the time I was in Jamaica, at least three of my aunts and uncles were teachers; even my maternal great-grandmother was a teacher. Significantly, my paternal grandparents, with whom I lived, as was the case for my maternal grandparents, were highly literate. When I was five years old, my youngest aunt, who was only two years older than me, would drill me on the alphabet, writing, arithmetic and how to speak North American English. I loved school — the open air classrooms, the uniforms and teachers of great intelligence and strict discipline. No bigger than a stump at age six (my nickname was "false stump"), I walked the five miles to school each day, though most of it was piggy-backing on my uncles or being held aloft on their shoulders. School was in many ways an extension of the home: our teachers were often our aunts, cousins and family friends. This does not mean the relations between students, their families and teachers were conflict free, but on the whole it meant schooling was an extension of the wider network of relations found in the community.

The fact is, in the 1970s and 1980s, as many Jamaican youth progressed through the Canadian educational system, we were routinely shunted into vocational training high schools. While vocational training has much to recommend it, more often than not those schools were seen as "dumping grounds." Not all to be sure, but many White teachers and guidance counsellors imagined African Caribbean youth to be incapable of understanding the more abstract subjects offered in high school. I was, however, among the lucky ones. To this day I remember my mother's defiance in the meeting with the grade eight guidance counsellor. The purpose of the meeting was to chart the next stage of my educational progress. In view of a disastrous grade seven year and a grade eight year that was not shaping up any better, the guidance counsellor thought it wise that I go to a vocational school. As the guidance counsellor pressured my mother to sign the form that would smooth my way to vocational school, my mother shot to her feet, arms akimbo, leaned forward and spontaneously uttered in the rawest patois I ever heard from her: "Yuh nah sen 'im gaw ah nuh vocational school." Case closed. I knew of other students, who though quite capable, never went to high school. It seems their parents never fully altered the traditional view that teachers knew best. As a result of their disempowerment, some Jamaican parents were unable to appreciate the role systemic racism would play in limiting their children's life opportunities. High school in Scarborough wasn't much better than all the other years of schooling in Toronto. At least in high school though, for the males at any rate, like other guys I had utility as an athlete: no matter how perverse, it felt good to be wanted for something. "Coming out for the track team this year, Denton?" was a question that brought us out of invisibility — much like Ralph Ellison's "invisible man," who could only be imagined within a racist narrative of what it should mean to be seen by the White "Other." Ironically, while my mother spared me from the guidance counsellors, she could not do so for my youngest brother, a gifted mechanical engineer. He was diagnosed, labelled and shunted from school to school. To this day, one of the smartest people I know, my brother has not fully recovered from this injury to his self-esteem and psyche. Aside from broader pedagogical issues, we had to contend with racism in the playground and in the society more generally.

So alienated are some Jamaicans I know who immigrated as children and who were separated from their primary caregivers that they have never returned to Jamaica. They don't deny being Jamaican but they just do not make it a point to articulate this as central to their identities. There are also those of us who do not wish to, and thus will never have to, confront the ambivalence of identity nor come to terms with the harms we experienced as immigrant children in Canada. As an example, I know of two Jamaican teenagers who committed suicide between 1982 and 1984: one a female friend and the other a male acquaintance. In both instances, I know these young people bonded with grandmothers or aunts who raised them the whole or part of their formative years in Jamaica. How many more of Jamaica's lost immigrant generation have committed suicide in their teens, I don't know. I suspect, however, their melding into Canada's national youth statistics helps to numb the stigma their families bear as well as undermine a broader discussion of the costs of immigration borne by immigrant children. The absorption of my friend's and acquaintance's suicides into national statistics may well conceal a deep crisis experienced by some Jamaican families and the problems that Jamaica's "lost children" confronted in Canadian society.

Conclusion

"No social study," C. Wright Mills (2000: 4) observes, "that does not come back to the problems of biography, of history and of their intersections within a society has completed its intellectual journey." This chapter is an effort to come to terms with the devastating experience of being torn away from affective ties as a young child in Jamaica in the early 1970s. Nothing, it is said, occurs in isolation; thus, I suggest my experience is far from unique, though this particular group of Jamaicans who immigrated to Canada is. I believe a great deal can be learned and a tremendous amount of healing can arise by taking the experience of this group not only seriously but as emblematic of the price Jamaica and its people have paid for "progress."

But, if my family is any indication, Jamaicans are a reserved lot when it comes to publicly sharing intense and troubling emotional experiences. There is an implicit understanding among Jamaicans in Canada that some issues cannot be called by name: the injuries some of us suffered in Canada and the loss of our supportive ties in Jamaica are, I think, among these. I have had some personal breakthroughs and have become closer to my parents by sharing my experiences with them. The key to these conversations is to address my parents' guilt and responsibility for injuries their children suffered in childhood. How could they and other parents have known the often emotionally barren, if not hostile, landscape into which we were placed when the immigrant is so highly celebrated? Parents, such as my mother, may not have known the particularities of my trauma save for my outward signs of emotional distance and poor performance in school. They knew enough though that what they were experiencing at work and in society was not isolated to them. Caribbean parents in the know connected their children to affirming culturally, emotionally, intellectually and spiritually fortifying milieus, which were like oases in a White Anglo-Celtic sea that was at times hostile and culturally alien. In the case of me and my siblings that took the form of the Black Education Program, the Harriet Tubman Centre and later, the Scarborough night and summer school program, and of course the church. Between 1975 and 1980, my exposure to culturally informed educational programming played no small part in helping me to find the strength within to transcend obstacles I would later encounter.

Most certainly, Canada has offered me, my family and other Jamaicans opportunities to make good — but at a steep price. I think is necessary to recognize and talk about the loss without losing sight of the gains of immigration. The next ten to twenty years will prove to be a significant sociological period for all Jamaicans in Canada. Jamaica's "lost children" and others who were immigrants in the late 1960s into the 1970s are now approaching membership in the "sandwich generation" — middle agers sandwiched between our children and aging parents. Given issues of social exclusion and the experience of loss I describe, this social location will have significant implications for all Jamaicans. No doubt the relevance of this position for those whose parents remain in Canada will be clear. But for those whose parents have returned to Jamaica, the occasion for their re-acquaintance with the land of their birth will present some difficult and novel challenges. With my parents a part of this returnee cohort, along with my siblings, I will have to re-establish ties with Jamaica and in the process come to where my life's journey started. After Jamaica's fiftieth year of independence, it is an open question what role Jamaica's lost immigrant children can and will play at the mirco and macro sociological levels in Jamaica. But, as some of our parents return, we will also have to return to rediscover and renew ties to a country from which some of us were so violently taken. In the process, I hope all concerned will create a new understanding that helps Jamaica heal and forge a stronger future.

Postscript

I recently (May 2012) visited Jamaica with my son, Jelani, like I did the previous year with my daughter, Adisa. Interestingly, elder family members and strangers alike are quite taken by the idea that I am bringing my children back to "know the country." By taking my young adult children to experience Jamaican culture, to introduce them to their relations and to see the burial sites of their paternal ancestors, I seem to be fulfilling a patriotic and moral obligation highly esteemed by Jamaicans. Because of their gender they have different stories to tell, but the acceptance they received and the idealization of their light skin and hair texture are matters of curiosity and discomfort. In all, this experience and the opportunity to write this reflective essay has given me a new perspective on and transformed my relationship to Jamaica.

Acknowledgement

I would like to thank Andrea Davis, Katerina Deliovsky, Carl James, Paula Madden and Brenda Conroy for reading various incarnations of this essay. I am also indebted to Heather Whipple at Brock University's James A. Gibson Library for helping me access the obscure Statistics Canada data

References

Bobb-Smith, Y. 2003. *I Know Who I Am: A Caribbean Woman's Identity in Canada.* Toronto: Women's Press.

Eaton, G.E. 1999. "Jamaicans." In P. R. Magocsci (ed.), *Encylopedia of Canada's Peoples.* Toronto: Published for the Multicultural History Society of Ontario by the University of Toronto Press.

Flynn, K. 2011. *Moving Beyond Borders: A History of Black Canadian and Caribbean Women in the Diaspora.* Toronto: University of Toronto Press.

Foster, C. 1995. *Sleep on, Beloved.* Toronto: Random House of Canada.

Gramsci, A. 1992. *Selections from the Prison Notebooks.* Edited and translated by Quintin Hoare and Geoffrey Nowell Smith. New York: International Publishers.

James, C. 1994. "'I Don't Want to Talk about It': Silencing Students in Today's Classrooms." *Orbit — Anti-Racist Education: Working Across Differences* 25(2).

Kelly, Jennifer. 1998. *Under the Gaze: Learning to be Black in White Society.* Halifax: Fernwood Publishing.

Maccody, E.E. 1980. *Social Development: Psychological Growth and the Parent-Child Relationship.* New York: Harcourt Brace Jovanovich.

McClain, Paula. 1979. *Alienation and Resistance: The Political Behavior of African Canadians.* Palo Alto, CA: R and E Research Assoc.

Mills, C. Wright. 2000. *The Sociological Imagination.* New York: Oxford University Press.

Prince, A. 2001. *Being Black: Essays by Althea Prince.* Toronto: Insomniac Press.

Roberts-Fiati, G. 1996. "Assessing the Effects of Early Marginalization on the Education of African Canadian Children." In K.S. Braithwaite and C.E. James (eds.), *Educating African Canadians*. James Lorimer.

Said, E. 1979. *Orientalism*. New York: Vintage Books.

Simmons, A., D. Plaza and V. Piché. 2005. "The Remittance Sending Practices of Haitians and Jamaicans in Canada." Expert Group Meeting on International Migration and Development in Latin America and the Caribbean. Population Division Department of Economic and Social Affairs United Nations Secretariat Mexico City, 30 November–2 December 2005. <http://www.un.org/esa/population/meetings/IttMigLAC/P01_ASimmons.pdf>.

Statistics Canada. 2007. Profiles of Ethnic Communities in Canada: The Jamaican Community in Canada (Catalogue no. 89-621-XIE-No. 12). Compiled by Colin Lindsay. Social and Aboriginal Statistics Division. <http://www.statcan.gc.ca/pub/89-621-x/89-621-x2007012-eng.pdf>.

Appendix

Country of Last Permanent Residence, Age Group and Sex of Immigrants

Year	0–4		5–9		10–14		0–14 Total	Total Jamaican immigrants
	F	M	F	M	F	M		
1973	149	189	360	386	343	340	1,767	9,363
1974	271	253	612	633	660	583	3,012	11,286
1975	219	219	754	792	899	845	3,728	8,211
1976	164	137	644	689	778	748	3,160	7,282
1977	188	168	453	488	584	544	2,425	6,291
1978	104	83	272	239	346	339	1,473	3,858
1979	51	58	182	177	341	329	1,138	3,213
1980	56	57	124	136	350	296	1,019	3,240
1981	35	35	96	85	247	236	734	2,688
1982	30	37	78	91	245	246	727	2,593
1983	26	21	87	49	175	236	594	2,423
1984	23	19	74	62	213	166	557	2,479
1985	26	20	85	82	193	204	700	2,922
Total	1,342	1,296	3,821	3,909	5,464	5,202	21,034	65,849

Country of Birth by Age Group and Sex

Year	0–4		5–9		10–14		0–14 Total	Total Jamaican immigrants
	F	M	F	M	F	M		
1980	57	57	126	134	354	300	1,028	3,161
1981	35	33	94	84	248	238	732	2,553
1982	32	36	79	92	242	245	726	2,711
1983	25	20	89	49	236	176	595	2,478
1984	23	19	73	62	213	167	557	2,519
1985	26	19	85	82	193	207	612	2,981
Total	198	184	546	503	1,486	1,333	4,250	16,403

All data are Immigration Statistics collected by Manpower and Immigration (1973–1976) and Employment and Immigration Canada (1977–1985). See MP22-1/1973 to Cat. No.: MP22-1/1985.

5. THE TRANSFORMATIONAL INFLUENCES OF JAMAICAN NURSES ON THE CANADIAN HEALTH CARE SYSTEM

Joan Samuels-Dennis, Melanie York and Dwight Barrett

Nursing has had a long history in Canada and has helped to shape our world-renowned health care system. The website of the International Council of Nurses (2010) defines nursing as follows:

> Nursing encompasses autonomous and collaborative care of individuals of all ages, families, groups and communities, sick or well and in all settings. Nursing includes the promotion of health, prevention of illness, and the care of ill, disabled and dying people. Advocacy, promotion of a safe environment, research, participation in shaping health policy and in patient and health systems management, and education are also key nursing roles.

Registered nurses are the single largest group of health care professionals in Canada (Office of Nursing Policy 2006). As such, our practice is diverse and our impact over the past hundred years has been extensive.

Conventional narratives of the history of nursing in Canada concentrate almost exclusively on the white female — with males and non-white females generally omitted. Yet Black women, and specifically Jamaican women, have worked as nurses since the profession's infancy (Rappaport 2005). Mary Seacole, a Jamaican nurse, and Florence Nightingale, a British nurse, cared for soldiers in the Crimean War of the 1850s. Queen Victoria honoured both for their service, yet today, only Nightingale's contributions are remembered, and we suspect that other significant contributions have been erased from nursing's history. The failure to recognize these contributions leaves Jamaican nurses today with little information about their professional background and historical position. In this chapter we provide an overview of the significant contributions of Jamaican nurses to the Canadian health care system, while also contextualizing these contributions within the rise and decline of colonization.

To tell this unique history of Jamaican nurses' contribution to the Canadian health care system, we use historical documents (meeting notes, manuscripts, biographical nursing text, newspaper articles and popular media coverage, sketches, correspondence and documents produced for imperial and other purposes) and interviews from twenty first- and second-generation Jamaican Canadian nurses. Our focus in this chapter is to begin to reconstruct nursing's historical discourse such that the historical and contemporary contributions and struggles of the Jamaican nurse are highlighted, with the hope that the historical place and value of Jamaicans to nursing within the Canadian health care system will be better understood and appreciated.

The Pioneering Work of Jamaica's Mary Seacole

In nursing schools across Canada, England and the United States, Florence Nightingale is generally introduced as the most significant figure in modern nursing and the pioneer of nursing theory and research. Florence Nightingale's position in nursing is established through her work in the Crimean War, during which she directed a hospital devoted to the care of injured soldiers (Nightingale 1860). Today, a number of historical sources have revealed that Mary Seacole, a Jamaican nurse also provided care to injured soldiers.

Mary Seacole was born in 1805 in Kingston, Jamaica. Inspired by her mother, who was a reputable "doctress," or healer, Mary developed a passion for helping those who were ill and required medical treatment. On reflecting upon her lifetime contributions, she identifies her work in Panama between 1851 and 1852 as her most significant contribution and calls herself the "greatest foe" of cholera in the Cruces (Seacole 1857: 37). Using knowledge gained from the cholera outbreak in Jamaica and a post-mortem examination of an infant who died from cholera in Panama, Mary Seacole became an expert in the treatment of the disease. Her nursing expertise was matched by a strong desire to go wherever she could aid the sick and dying. In 1854, this strong moral imperative led her to travel to Balaclava, Ukraine, to support the British soldiers fighting in the Crimean War. Over several weeks she submitted formal requests to the British army to join them in caring for injured soldiers but was denied. She next approached Florence Nightingale about volunteering at the army hospital. But even with all of her experience, her services were again refused because of race/culture.

Mary Seacole's disappointment is reflected in her autobiography: "Was it possible that these American prejudices against colour had some root here? … Did these ladies shrink from accepting my aid because my blood flowed beneath a somewhat duskier skin than theirs?" (83). At her own expense, she established Springhill Hotel, where she provided nursing care to injured soldiers on the battlefield. She gained a tremendous reputation in Crimea, and a number of non-military sources suggest that between 1856 and 1869, Seacole was awarded the British Crimea, the Turkish Medjidie and the French Legion of Honour (Rappaport 2005; Buss 2011; Ramdin 2005). Mary Seacole is perhaps one of the greatest unsung heroes of nursing. Her caring, non-regimented, culturally rooted and open approach to nursing resembles what nurse theorists of the twenty-first century call the "ideal nurse."

Transformational Influences from the 1930s and the mid-1950s

From the 1930s to the mid-1940s, several political and social events made it possible for Jamaicans to migrate to England, Scotland, the United States, Canada and other Caribbean islands. In 1929, the world experienced the start of the Great Depression (Garraty 1987), and given the interconnection of the various countries through trade, services and governance, its effects quickly spread to almost every part of the globe. In Canada and Jamaica the economic fallout of the Depression resulted in, among other things, lost businesses, high levels of unemployment, poor health and general despair (Bernal 1988). In an attempt to address the deplorable conditions in Jamaica — which precipitated civil unrest and riots — the West India Royal Commission Committee (WIRC) was established under the direction of Lord Moyne during the final years of the Depression (1938–1939). The investigation set about to understand the impact of the "crash" on the colonies (Barbados, British Guyana, British Honduras, Leeward Islands, Trinidad and Tobago, Windward Islands and of course Jamaica) with regard to their social, economic and health conditions (Guerre 1971) and to develop plans that would improve living conditions. In addition to identifying problems in education, employment, juvenile delinquency, infant mortality and the political system, the WIRC also focused on problems in health care. Its recommended reforms facilitated the development of the West Indies School of Public Health in Jamaica (WISPH) (McCaw-Binns, Moody and Standard 1998). The WISPH (now called University of Technology) opened its doors in 1943 and serves as the institution in Jamaica where formal nursing training begins.

Nita Barrow was a significant contributor to the formal organization of nursing in Jamaica. After completing a certificate in Public Health Nursing (1944) and Nursing Education (1945) at the University of Toronto, Nita Barrow recognized the stark differences between the training of nurses in Jamaica and abroad. Compared to the Canadian nurses she noted the absence of a structured curriculum, a high reliance on informal education and the inability of Jamaican nurses to apply theory to practice. Working with several colleagues, including Gertrude Swaby and Julie Syms, she established the Jamaica General Trained Nurses Association (JGTNA) in 1946. The goal of the JGTNA was three fold: "First to set up and maintain a register of nurses; second to set a syllabus of hospital training and to conduct examinations;

third to respect and recommend to the central board of health, hospitals suitable as training schools for nurses" (JGTNA 1946).

While the standardization of practice was beginning in Jamaica, two events occurred in Canada that set the stage for the movement of Jamaican nurses into Canada. In 1947, Marisse Scott, an Ontario high school student who graduated with honours, was refused entry into eight Ontario nursing schools, including the Owen Sound General and Marine Hospital Nursing School (Unknown 1947a). The refusal letter, which included the statement, "Sorry, we don't accept coloured girls," incited a long civil protest led by Reverend Allan Ferry, the Scott family, the mayor of Owen Sound and supporters from across Canada (Avery 2001). Eventually, J.A. O'Reilly, pastor of the church of Our Lady of Guelph, requested that Mother Superior of Guelph St. Joseph Hospital accept Marisse into their school of nursing (Unknown 1947b). Scott became the first black nurse to graduate from a school of nursing in Canada. This opened the door for other black nurses to enter training programs in Canada and become employed as nurses. Following suit, St. Joseph's hospital in Toronto became the first hospital to employ newly immigrated Jamaican nurse in the late 1940s and the early 1950s.

In 1952, Ottawa refused rn Beatrice Massop's application to be accepted as an immigrant from Jamaica. Massop contacted Black community leader and chair of the Negro Citizenship Committee, Don Moore, and asked the Negro Citizenship Association (nca) to intervene on her behalf. Fourteen months later, the Immigration Branch recognized Massop as a worthwhile immigrant and allowed her to enter Canada through Malton Airport under the "exceptional merit" category. The Registered Nursing Association of Ontario aided Massop's efforts by sanctioning her credentials, and the new Mount Sinai Hospital in Toronto offered her a position on its nursing staff (Jane Turritin, Centre for Equity in Health and Society).

Jamaican Nurses Are Exported

Between 1948 and 1952, several policies were introduced that facilitated the migration of Jamaican nurses to England and the Americas. The *British Nationality Act* 1948 created the new status of citizen of the United Kingdom and Colonies for people born or naturalized in either the United Kingdom or one of its colonies. As a result, people of the colonies had the freedom to attain citizenship from other Commonwealth-affiliated countries with choice and ease (British Nationality Law 1977). It was anticipated that the act would solve the demand for unskilled and cheap labour. Among all British colonies, Jamaica became the largest exporter of labour to the United Kingdom, the United States and Canada. Within the same period, the Canadian and British governments rolled out universal health care, creating an even greater need for nurses and other health care professionals in Canada and Great Britain.[1]

In 1949, the British Ministry of Labour, Colonial Office, General Nursing Council and Royal College of Nursing developed a policy that permitted the recruitment of un-skilled workers with the intent to train them as nurses in the recruiting country. Based on advertisements like the one presented here, many non-nurses and nurses left Jamaica believing they would be formally educated and/or achieve their de-served ranking in the field of nursing on the basis of their certification. Participants of this project and other sources (Flynn 2011) report that Caribbean nurses obtained nursing positions of the lowest ranking, and due to a number of restrictions, some never had the opportunity to become trained nurses. The remain-der of the chapter uses interview data to report on the contributions of Jamaican nurses who arrived in Canada after 1952; some came directly from Jamaica while others came from Britain, where they were trained.

Contributions to the Canadian Health Care System

To identify the significant contribu-tions of Jamaicans to the Canadian health care system from 1952 to the present, we interviewed twenty first- and second-generation Jamaican nurses, also asking them about the challenges they faced and the ways in which they overcame these

REGISTERED NURSES
YOUR FARE TO CANADA
ARE YOU INTERESTED IN
RELOCATING IN CANADA?

An area that offers the attrac-tions of both summer and winter resort life? If so, then Ste Agathe des Monts, located in the heart of beautiful Laurentian Mountains 55 miles north of Montreal may be the place you are looking for. Mount Sinai, a non-sectarian 115-bed fully accredited hospital spe-cializing in diseases of the chest, has vacancies for registered nurses with Part 1 Mid-wifery. Modern nurses residence offer-ing full accommodation (private room with private or semi-private bathroom) available at $25.00 per month, 37.5 hour work week, 4 weeks annual vacation with full pay, 11 paid statutory holidays. 2 weeks accumulated sick leave benefits per year. Starting salary $390.00-494.00 per month, according to experi-ence and qualifications. Excellent additional fringe benefits and opportunity for advancement.

Your fare to Canada will be advanced interest-free, reim-bursable in monthly payments. One-way transportation paid by the hospital, on completion of 15 months of service.

APPLY TO:
DIRECTOR OFNURSING
MOUNT SINAI HOSPITAL
P.O. BOX 1000
STE AGATHE DES MONTS,
P.Q. CANADA

struggles. Because we wanted to acknowledge both the traditional and non-traditional ways in which people contribute, we began each interview by asking nurses how they define contribution.

Filling the Gap

One of the most significant ways in which Jamaican nurses contributed to the Canadian health care system, particularly in the early years, was by taking on positions that helped Canada to overcome its nursing shortfall. Many of the individuals we interviewed spoke to the fact that Jamaican nurses often took on unpopular or unwanted roles and responsibilities that were nevertheless vital. It has been reported elsewhere (Flynn 2011, 2009) that Black nurses occupied the lowest ranked positions in nursing and were often offered jobs in hospitals for the chronically and mentally ill. Enid Collins, a celebrated nursing educator who immigrated to Canada in the early 1960s, reflected on the flexibility and tenacity of the Jamaican nurse even in these circumstances.

> I think that Jamaican nurses brought the willingness and flexibility to go into different areas … I have known people who came [to Canada] — my sister's friend for example — and they've gone up North to work … and worked up there for many years when people from Canadian schools were not going up there when the [Canadian health organizations] were desperately looking for nurses to go up [North] … We came as people who had never even lived and worked in a cold climate but were willing to go up North … There weren't a lot of Jamaican nurses in those days [early 1950s] … But a few were around, and a few of those few were willing to take the challenge to go work in the North. I think that speaks to a spirit of adventure.

Being Advocates, Initiating Change

Male and female Jamaicans alike are known for their vibrant and assertive personalities. Our historical position as once enslaved people has created a keen instinct for recognizing and eliminating social injustice. A number of nurses spoke about their role as advocates and change agents within clinical, community and academic settings. Una Ridley, who immigrated in 1954 and ended her career as the dean of the School of Nursing at the University of Lethbridge, played a central role in developing a nursing program specifi-cally tailored to Aboriginal students. The program was established so that Aboriginal nurses were available to provide nursing services to their own communities. She recalled:

> Saskatchewan has a large Aboriginal population that is extremely disadvantaged … They live in poverty, lack the necessary education … and in nursing there are very few [Aboriginals] or there were

very few registered nurses to work with their own people ... I was concerned about this because when I came to Saskatchewan, I would hear comments that were derogatory to Aboriginals from one person or the other ... Now I was not alone ... I'm never alone in these things, there were always other people. But I made it a bit of my mission to do something to promote nursing among Aboriginal people. Eventually, we established a program where Aboriginal students came to the University of Saskatchewan for a year and did a sort of a pre-nursing program and then they applied to different schools around the country.

Not only did Ridley lead the University of Lethbridge in developing this tailored program she also approached nursing schools across Canada to partner with her in creating seats specifically dedicated to Aboriginals. Although the program no longer exists, it served the important role of developing a pool of skilled health professionals who could return to their own communities with the skills necessary to enhance the health of all who live there.

Lorna Ferguson, who was trained at University College Hospital in Jamaica and migrated to Montreal in 1956, was a pioneer of family centred maternity (fcm) care. Now a standard approach, fcmrevolutionized how mothers and babies were cared for in the post-partum period. Ferguson spoke humbly about her contributions and recalled it in the following way:

> I introduced [a process] whereby one nurse would take care of both mother and baby ... I also instituted rooming-in, where the baby would stay with the mother in her room for the majority of the day ... The purpose was to [allow] the mother to get used to caring for the baby before she went home ... I also made it possible for husbands or rather fathers to be present in the delivery room during the delivery ... At that time that was a big no, no..., but to me these things were not special ... They were practical and they just made sense.

For the past thirty years, Lillie Johnson has quietly taken on the task of supporting individuals and families who suffer with sickle cell anemia and ensuring that health care providers appropriately screen for and treat the disease. A former teacher in Jamaica, Johnson began her nursing education in Edinburgh, Scotland, in 1954 and immigrated to Canada in the 1960s. In Canada she held various staff and leadership positions with Health Canada, the Victorian Order of Nurses and Toronto Public Health. In the early 1980s she established the Sickle Cell Association, an agency which has played a key role in having all newborns screened for this disease.

Culture, Caring and a Great Sense of Empathy

Although not always verbalized, we sensed a desperate yearning for everyone to be recognized as Canadian, not separate or distinct parts of the Canadian mosaic. For example one nurse stated the following:

> In my opinion … we're here in Canada and we're not really think-ing about Jamaica … I guess we should … we don't. I think we're [more likely to think] about what we have here and what we're seeing in front of us, which is Canada and Canadian nurses … It doesn't matter [which] ethnic group you're from."

When asked about the contributions of Jamaican nurses to the Canadian health care system, there was a resounding agreement that Jamaican nurses bring to their practice cultural awareness and sensitivity, a nurturing and empathic way of being and a natural determination, all of which makes them compassionate and amazing nurse. Annette Bailey, who immigrated to Canada at age seventeen and who is currently an assistant professor in the Nursing Department at Ryerson University, makes the following connection between culture, caring and determination:

> I have worked with quite a few Jamaicans through the years, and they were the ones that did not take no for an answer. And I started to wonder about that because other nurses would say, 'okay doctor if that's what you say.' But I have found that Jamaican nurses, when they want something for their patients, they're not going to stop until [they get it]… That dogged determination, I think is rooted in [our] culture.

The Challenges

Practising in Canada was not without its challenges. A number of the nurses recalled experiences undergirded by racism, discrimination, hierarchical oppression and the constant imposed idea that they were not good enough. The following are some of their comments:

> Because you have an accent you are not considered to be smart or taken seriously or people dismiss you.

> I don't want any Black people touching me.

> [You have] feelings of almost like you are not needed.

> Some physicians think nurses in general are not knowledgeable … have to keep validating that you are a competent nurse to physicians.

The nurses who came here in the early days and paved the way for many other Jamaican nurses to work in our hospitals and other health care facilities could be considered pioneers. For the most part, they reported experiencing less discrimination and fewer problems with upward professional mobility than the current generation. They attributed this to their self-confidence, carried over from the prestige associated with being a nurse in Jamaica, and the fact that their numbers were so few in Canada. As pioneers, they were more likely to say, "Canada has been good to me," or "I was very lucky."

In terms of professional mobility, several nurses discussed concerns that Jamaican nurses tend to remain predominantly in "front line" or in general nursing positions, which often means caring for the patients with the most challenging illnesses. They had difficulty acquiring advanced practice roles, which would provide them the skills and experiences for professional advancement. Some nurses currently practising in hospital settings stated that some physicians overlook their suggestions but did not do the same with nurses of other races. In the face of these struggles, Jamaican nurses have used a number of strategies to resist or overcome these circumstances. For instance, after being denied a passing grade in her clinical course on the final day of her practicum, one nurse recalled her resistance:

> Well I got really mad ... because I don't think I've ever failed at anything. And I thought to myself, 'Oh my God I don't want to do this anymore' ... because it was so hard ... But I just thought, 'You know what ... use it as an opportunity.' [That instructor] made me more determined to succeed because if you tell me I can't, well I have to prove you're wrong.

Jamaican nurses have used both formal and informal channels to resist the numerous forms of racism they experienced. Jane Turritin, Research and Advocacy Coordinator for the Centre for Equity in Health & Society (cehs), commends Jamaican nurses for their bravery in formally bringing charges in connection with discriminatory practices within health care organizations, even though their nursing organizations have failed to act when these injustices were brought to their attention. Two significant cases are worth referencing.

In 1990, a group of nurses took their complaint of discrimination in employment and harassment to the Ontario Human Rights Commission, citing being fired, forced to resign, denied access to professional development and subjected to harassment and discipline because of their race. When they had applied for jobs at the Northwest General Hospital, they were told there were openings only in long-term care, while their white counterparts were offered jobs in their practice specialty. Following mediation, in May 1994, the seven nurses were awarded $320,000 in compensation, and the hospital was instructed to reinstate, remove adverse reports from their files, provide further training and transfer them to new positions (Centre for Equity in Health and Society 2010).

In another case, Jamaican-born Claudine Charley, who worked as a surgical nurse at Toronto General Hospital, filed a grievance alleging that she had been deliberately set up for failure by a white colleague with regard to her delivery of patient care. The case went to arbitration, and she was supported by a small volunteer group, Nurses and Friends against Discrimination. During thirty-nine days of hearings, testimony revealed what the white nurse had done and Charley was vindicated. In 1996 Charley received $250,000 from the hospital (Centre for Equity in Health and Society 2010).

Hopes and Aspirations

At the end of our interviews, we asked each individual about their hopes and dreams for nursing, Jamaican nurses and the Canadian health care system. Their responses were rich and hopeful but demonstrate a desire for continual growth and change.

> My hope is we will continue to put caring at the forefront [of nursing]. But I would also hope to see more Jamaican nurses stepping forward … because as you know, Jamaicans man the [front lines] of hospitals … So I would like to see more coming forward … I think it will happen through education … more and more nurses are getting advanced degrees, but I would like to see a lot more … I think a lot of it will come through research and publication.

> I hope we can coexist together without looking at the barriers like the skin, the accent … so cohesive that you don't even know there are difference races … I'm hoping that at some point somebody will either start an organization or just get the ball rolling to give back to some of these really poor Jamaican communities that lack just basic nursing needs.

> I hope that as nurses we become independent … work closely with doctors, while also educating them that nurses are a vital part of health care.

> We need more caring … Too often we are taken away from the patient and placed in front of computers …. nursing experience is lacking, and it's the experience that makes you caring and knowledgeable … we only get experience by being with the patient, working with other nurses and understanding health conditions.

Conclusion

Nurses represent the single largest group of health-care professionals in Canada. We have a long and varied history. However, the telling of this history often omits the contributions of men and non-white women. At key transitional points in our country's history, Jamaican nurses have contributed significantly by helping Canada to overcome its nursing shortfall and by committing to work in places and positions that Canadian-born nurses were reluctant to pursue. In general, we found that Jamaican nurses have approached their practice with much commitment — rarely seeking recognition and often shrinking from the spotlight. Jamaican nurses have played the key role of advocate and change agent by shining a light on social injustice and developing educational and clinical programs directed at enhancing the health of those most marginalized in Canadian society.

Notes

The research which supported the development of this manuscript was funded by the Social Sciences and Humanities Research Council of Canada. Correspondence concerning this article should be addressed to Joan Samuels-Dennis, School of Nursing, York University, 4700 Keele Street, Toronto, ON, M3J 1P3, (416) 736-5271, E-mail: jsdennis@yorku.ca.

1. In 1949, the Ministry of Labour, Colonial Office, General Nursing Council and Royal College of Nursing developed a policy that permitted the recruitment of unskilled workers with the intent to train those individuals as nurses in the recruiting country.

References

Avery, R. 2001. "Rejection Still Troubles Nurse." *Toronto Star*.

Bernal, R.L. 1988. "The Great Depression, Colonial Policy and Industrialization in Jamaica." *Social and Economic Studies*.

Buss, J. 2011. *Black Nightingale: Mary Seacole, Hero of the Crimean War.* Lexington, KY: David Millett Publications.

Centre for Equity in Health and Society. 2010. *Nursing Equity Pioneers.* [Brochure]. Toronto, ON: Jane Turritin.

Flynn, K. 2009. "Beyond the Glass Wall: Black Canadian Nurses, 1940–1970." *Nursing History Review* 17(1).

____. 2011. *Moving beyond Borders: A History of Black Canadian and Carribean Women in the Diaspora.* Toronto, ON: University of Toronto Press.

Garraty, J.A. 1987. *The Great Depression: An Inquiry Into the Causes, Course, and Consequences of the Worldwide Depression of the Nineteen-thirties, as Seen by Contemporaries and in the Light of History.* Anchor Press/Doubleday.

Guerre, J.L.A., 1971. "The Moyne Commission and the West Indian Intelligentsia, 1938–39." *Journal of Commonwealth & Comparative Politics* 9(2).

International Council of Nursing. 2010-last update. "Definition of Nursing." At <http://www.icn.ch/about-icn/icn-definition-of-nursing/>.

JGTNA (Jamaica General Trained Nurses Association). 1946. *Meeting Minutes Novermber*

27 1946.

Mccaw-Binns, A.M., C.O. Moody, and K.L. Standard. 1998. "Forty Years. An Introduction to the Development of a Caribbean Public Health." *West Indian Medical Journal* 47 (supl. 4).

Nightingale, F. 1860. *Notes on Nursing: What It Is, and What It Is Not.* New York: D. Appleton-Century.

Office of Nursing Policy. 2006. *Nursing Issues: General Statistics.* H21-281/6-2006E. Ottawa: Health Canada.

Ramdin, R. 2005. *Mary Seacole.* London, UK: Haus Publishing.

Rappaport, H. 2005. "The Invitation That Never Came: Mary Seacole After the Crimea." History Today 55, 2 <iupui.edu/~histwhs/h364.dir/SeacoleHistToday.pdf>.

Seacole, M. 1857. *Wonderful Adventures of Mrs. Seacole in Many Lands: With Introduction by W.H. Russell.* London, UK: Penguin Group.

Unknown. 1947a. "Colored Girl Trains in St. Joseph's." *Elora Express.*

___. 1947b. "Owen Sound Negro Girl Leads Her Nursing Class." *Owen Sound Sun Times.*

6. THE PLACE OF CULTURE IN DOCTOR-PATIENT ENCOUNTERS

Maxine C. Clarke

I arrived in Canada in 1978 to pursue a residency in pediatrics. This was the first time I would be living away from home and my first trip to Canada. I had travelled frequently to the United States and Britain, but Canada was an unknown entity. I remember being accepted to the program in Vancouver and having no idea where this city was located. I knew about Toronto, since this was a popular travel destination for Jamaicans, but Vancouver was new. I decided to find it on the map and realized it was on the west coast of the country — miles away! When I discussed it with my pediatric consultant, he reassured me that of all the cities in Canada, this was probably the best place to live, in terms of weather. The idea was that they had very mild winters and no snow. Of course, he did not mention that they had rain for most of the year!

I remember the flight from Toronto to Vancouver and the amazing views of the Rockies. That was when I realized just how far away I was going to be from my family and friends. I arrived safely on June 30 and started my residency program on July 1.

In planning to leave home for training, there is always a sense of uncertainty about how one will cope in the "first world" medical system. Although I knew I had received excellent medical training at University of the West Indies, there was a bit of anxiety about entering a system which was more technologically advanced. I soon realized that although I had a lot to learn about the technology, I had been very well trained in clinical medicine and for certain conditions, I actually had much more clinical experience. This allowed for a sharing of knowledge, not just a one-way street as I had feared.

I have always known I wanted to be a pediatrician. My mother reports that even as a young child, when asked what I wanted to be when I grew up, I would say "pediatrician." I have no idea why I was so convinced of this path. I had very little contact with the medical system and I certainly did not know any pediatricians. In those days mothers were the main "doctors" in the family; one only went to see a doctor or visited a hospital for what was considered an extremely serious ailment. No child would be taken to a doctor for the usual childhood illnesses — fever, measles, chickenpox. It was usual that children would be diagnosed and treated at home with the arsenal of remedies passed down the generations.

As a resident, I remember being surprised at the number of children who would be brought to the Emergency Room for conditions which, back home, would not be thought to need a doctor's assessment. This was my introduction to the differences in cultural practice in the area of health care. Over the years, I have become very interested in the relationship of culture and health care, particularly as it relates to medical school curricula.

For the majority of my time in Canada I have lived in cities which did not have a lot of visible diversity. I realized however that culture and diversity encompass many more features than the readily apparent race and ethnicity. Culture may be defined as the sum of language, customs and beliefs considered characteristic of a particular group of people. With this definition, each of us has a culture which is essential to the way we live our lives. Health issues are a very important part of the cultural framework, and the influence of culture on health is well recognized.

I have seen many examples of the difficulties which may arise in the doctor-patient relationship when cultural issues are not appreciated or understood. The clinical encounter is always one of a power imbalance between the physician and the patient. This power imbalance is exaggerated if other factors — such as race, ethnicity, gender, different health beliefs — are present. Information flow and a physician's attitude and behaviour during the encounter influence patients' satisfaction, their trust in the physician's competence and the level of stress they experience. When patients perceive that physicians care about them and are interested in them as persons, they are likely to provide more information, be more actively involved in and more satisfied with the visit and be more compliant with management plans (Veist and Nuru-Jeter 2002). Patients who are perceived as "different" are more at risk of having their contribution dismissed and of not benefiting fully from the clinical encounter.

Each of us would like to be comfortable with our health care provider and confident that we will be respected, understood and involved in the decision-making process. This was brought home to me by the number of times patients enquired if I would be willing to become their child's pediatrician. These patients were all racially and ethnically similar to me and felt they would be much more comfortable with me as their child's physician. There was a sense of familiarity and the feeling that I would understand their health care beliefs and needs. Unfortunately, as a hospital-based neonatologist, I am unable to accommodate them. It was an honour, however, to receive these requests.

During a period when I did a brief stint as a locum general pediatrician in Toronto, I remember a Jamaican mom who was very concerned about her little girl in hospital and was very happy to see me as the physician. Over several days we had many conversations about the little girl's health and several other topics. A few days into our relationship she decided to ask me a question that had been troubling her all along. She wanted to know if someone had done something to her daughter to cause this illness. I knew immediately what she was concerned about and reassured her that the illness was due to an infection and nothing else. She was relieved and explained that she knew she could ask me that question because she knew I would understand. Thinking about this later, I recognized that she would not have voiced this question to someone she thought would not understand. She would continue to be worried and distressed about this possible cause of her daughter's illness.

Cultural issues have a significant influence on health care and have been identified as one cause of health disparities. Reports of health care disparities relating to socio-cultural factors have emphasized the need for medical schools to integrate diversity teaching into their curricula. To ensure that all members of the society receive appropriate health care, physicians must be prepared to accept, appreciate and accommodate cultural differences in the doctor-patient relationship. In this regard, in 1993, the General Medical Council for the United Kingdom included socio-cultural issues in the standards for the U.K. undergraduate medical curriculum.

On the same basis, in 1999, following reports of health disparities as a result of racial and ethnic factors, the United States Congress commissioned the Institute of Medicine (IOM) to study the issue of racial/ethnic disparities in the health care system and to provide recommendations to alleviate these issues. In March 2002, the IOM published its final report (Smedley, Stith and Nelson 2002). The following were its major findings:

- racial and ethnic disparities in health care exist and are associated with worse health outcomes;
- racial and ethnic disparities in health care occur in the context of broader historic and contemporary social and economic inequality, and there is evidence of persistent racial and ethnic discrimination in many sectors of American life;
- many sources contribute to racial and ethnic disparities in health care, including health care providers and patients; and
- bias, stereotyping, prejudice and clinical uncertainty on the part of health care providers may contribute to racial and ethnic disparities in health care.

The IOM pointed out the need to eliminate health care disparities in the areas of patient care, education and research. Specifically, in terms of education, the report recommended that cross-cultural education be integrated into the training of all health care professionals

The Liaison Committee on Medical Education, the organization responsible for setting accreditation standards for undergraduate medical education in the United States and Canada, has included cross-cultural education in its list of standards. To achieve full accreditation, all North American medical schools must demonstrate diversity teaching in their curricula. In Canada, the literature relating to health care disparities on the basis of race and ethnicity is sparse, but the issue persists. Health Canada, which recognizes culture as a determinant of health has stated that, in an environment determined by dominant cultural values, some groups face health risks stemming from a "lack of access to culturally appropriate health care and services" (Public Health Agency of Canada 2001.

A small number of Canadian studies have found that Aboriginal and foreign-born Canadians face barriers to health care access (Reime et al. 2007). These barriers include culture, poverty and caregiver attitudes (Guilfoyle, Kelly and St-Pierre-Hansen 2008). With the importance of education in addressing health care disparities related to socio-cultural issues clearly being recognized, there has been an increase in the number of programs developed as a component of the undergraduate medical curriculum aimed at producing culturally sensitive physicians.

But there is more to be done, and educating physicians to work in an increasingly diverse society is a particular interest of mine. I am currently completing a survey of Canadian medical schools to determine if they have specific curricula related to cultural diversity and to chronicle the results of these interventions. I plan to use this data to develop a comprehensive, integrated diversity curriculum for my home medical school. My dream for the future is a physician workforce prepared to accept, appreciate and accommodate cultural differences in all doctor-patient encounters.

References

Guilfoyle, John, Len Kelly, and Natalie St-Pierre-Hansen. 2008. "Prejudice in Medicine." *Canadian Family Physician* 54.

Institute of Medicine Report. 2002. *Unequal Treatment: Confronting Racial and Ethnic Disparities in Health Care.* (Edited by Brian D. Smedley, Adrienne Y. Stith and Alan R. Nelson.) <nap.edu/openbook.php?isbn=030908265X>.

Public Health Agency of Canada. 2001. *Towards a Common Understanding: Clarifying the Core Concepts of Population Health* — Appendix E: Culture as a Determinant of Health. At <http://www.phac-aspc.gc.ca/ph-sp/docs/common-commune/appendix_e-eng.php>.

Reime, B., A.W. Tu, and S.K. Lee. 2007. "Treatment Differences between Aboriginal and White Infants Admitted to Canadian Neonatal Intensive Care Nurseries."

Canadian Neonatal Network. *Pediatric and Perinatal Epidemiology* 21(6).

Veist, Thomas A., and Amani Nuru-Jeter. 2002. "Is the Doctor-Patient Race Concordance Associated with a Greater Satisfaction with Care?" Journal of Health and Social Behavior 43(3).

7.   TAKING A PIECE OF THE PAST WITH US

Jamaican-Canadian Fruits of Migration
in Makeda Silvera's *The Heart Does Not Bend*

Sharon Beckford

Jamaican-born Makeda Silvera migrated to Canada in 1967 at the age of twelve. She was the co-founder, managing editor and co-publisher of Sister Vision: Black Women and Women of Color Press, which provided an outlet for the publication of women's writing. Her own non-fiction text *Silenced: Talks with Working Class Caribbean Women about Their Lives and Struggles as Domestic Workers in Canada* details the experiences in 1980s Canada of Caribbean domestic workers who, because of fear of being deported or further marginalized in society, were unable to speak freely about their oppression. This book remains popular, especially in the social sciences and humanities, evidenced by the many times it is quoted from and listed in bibliographies for academic studies on the West Indian/Caribbean experience in Canada. In her short story collection *Her Head a Village*, Silvera portrays aspects of Jamaican experiences across time and location. The title piece recounts the psychological struggle of a Black female protagonist and her attempts to write her own story and the stories of her ancestors, but who feels voiceless living in a society that privileges men. Silvera's characters' identities are marked by their Jamaican diction; orality strongly marks the text. Her writings help explain what it means to live as a Jamaican Canadian or a Caribbean immigrant in Canada; thus, Silvera advances cultural knowledge that importantly aids the relationship between Jamaica and Canada. As a Jamaican Canadian, Silvera has made a significant contribution to Canadian culture through the medium of literature.

As a Jamaican Canadian female, I offer a reading of Silvera's novel *The Heart Does Not Bend* that is informed by my own migratory experience. I recognize how faithfully Silvera captures a specific but common migratory experience that represents what it means to be a Jamaican immigrant living in Canada and what that individual must do, over time, to survive in a strange land. Although the story reflects the lives of fictional characters, nevertheless it is relatable to many Jamaican immigrants in Canada, who, like me, appreciate the story's depiction of the human condition in ways that will become evident throughout this chapter. Silvera imbues her narrative with a specific Jamaican flavour, and using food as a literary trope, she serves her fictional account as a special meal itself, making more explicit the literary and symbolic relationship between food and storytelling. In engaging questions of Jamaican/Canadian identity through fiction, Silvera taps into aspects of Jamaican culture that folks like me rely on to recapture a sense of home when we feel alienated in Canadian society.

The Heart depicts a Jamaican Canadian diasporic experience through the lives of five generations of the Galloway family. The story is told from the perspective of the naïve narrator Molly, the granddaughter of Maria Galloway, who is affectionately called Mama. The novel opens in Jamaica at the reading of Mama's will, making the will a significant symbol of Jamaican Canadian *citizenship* through inheritance, as the family members are now living in Canada but part of the estate is in Jamaica. In her representation, Silvera merges Mama's assets in both Jamaica and Canada, and through the act of bequeathing she portrays what it means to be entitled to a Jamaica Canadian identity. In this way we are reminded of how important it is for many Jamaican Canadians to inherit property from their ancestors. In the novel Mama's four children, Peppie, Glory (Molly's mother), Freddie and Mikey are in attendance and so are her granddaughter Molly, grandson Vittorio (Freddie's son), great granddaughter Ciboney (Molly's daughter) and her great great granddaughter Maud (Ciboney's daughter). They gather to listen to Glory reading the will. It is then they discover to everyone's surprise that, except for Vittorio and Ciboney, who were born in Canada, they have truly been disinherited. Mama has bequeathed her estate to Vittorio and her hope chest to Ciboney because the others, though they were born in Jamaica, had shown no interest in their Jamaican heritage while living in Canada. In taking this position, Mama, after death, signals her hope for Vittorio and Ciboney to, at the very least, claim some part of her past.

Silvera appears to be suggesting, in this foreshadowing, something that is perhaps even more important: that in helping her *"pickney dem"* (145, emphasis added) to immigrate to Canada, Mama had perhaps unintentionally psychologically disinherited them, leaving the generation of Jamaicans that followed her deracinated, cut off from the true sources of their authenticity. Only Vittorio and Ciboney seem to have caught the embers of the culture that gave them a sense of identity and a true meaning to life even in a foreign land. And for Silvera, as a civilizing and humanizing trope, this authentic culture is in a real sense the Jamaican food — not only the materials they would naturally consume in Jamaica but how the characters even mechanically create the dishes that are the meals that sustain them in the culturally

strange and alienating place. To me this is a major contribution to the discussion of how Jamaicans have survived at home and in the diaspora in the
half century since political independence. I contend that Silvera sees this
survival as analogously a struggle for sustenance not only of the body but
of the human spirit — typified by a rummaging around to find the right
provisions in an unknown land and then having the fire to make the sparse
findings fit for human consumption and therefore survival. *The Heart Does
Not Bend* suggests this struggle is even at the level of what and how Jamaicans
physically eat to keep themselves whole as a people; it is a narrative of how
and what they do to maintain any hopes for a cultural authenticity, whatever
Jamaicans like Mama in the novel might consider that to be.

While living in Jamaica, Mama established a familial structure that ensured her family's survival. She migrates to Canada when she suffers failed
relationships and personal disappointments and desires a change. She is
searching for a sense of home. Mama's experiences parallel those of many
Jamaicans who relocate under similar circumstances; this story reflects a
common diasporic journey that charts the cyclical movement from Jamaica
to Canada and the (hoped for) return. As Andrea Davis (2004: 68) observes,
"Like so many Caribbean immigrants, Mama returns to Jamaica to die,
but cannot find her way home." This journey often leads to reunification
for many diasporic families, but that reunion is often fraught with tensions.
Mama epitomizes the importance of the journey and the cultural baggage
in suitcases rather than concentrating solely on the arrival, on an outcome
that might very well turn out to be less than ideal if not a downright disappointment and failure, as was the case for so many of those domestic workers
Silvera wrote about earlier.

After Mama's death, Molly reflects on her earliest childhood memories
with Mama in their home on Wigton Street in Jamaica: "The kitchen smelled
of mouth-watering sweet cakes, puddings, spicy Jamaican foods. I never ever
wanted to leave that house, but I mustn't blame you" (13). Molly and Mama
develop a close bond during the moments they spend together while Mama
prepares a meal or bakes. In one of her reminiscences of happy childhood
moments, Molly observes: "The smell of burnt molasses, fresh-ground nutmeg, slivers of fresh ginger floated in the air. I loved to watch Mama turn
plain white flour into plantain tarts, gizzadas with sugared coconut inside,
totos, bulla cakes, molasses almond tarts and rose-apple cupcakes with yellow
icing on top" (26). Clearly food and, importantly, the memories associated
with food are central to Molly's relationship with Mama. They are equally
important to the structure of this novel and to our understanding of the
characters and their histories. Silvera employs food to plainly show how
important Jamaican dishes are to identity. This is one of the aspects I love
about Silvera's novel: when I read it, I recognize all the foods, I remember

Jamaica, I want to cook all the meals. If I cannot, I taste them just by reading about them.

In *Heart*, Silvera invites readers to consider what it means for Jamaicans to travel from Jamaica to Canada and to experience a sense of belonging by taking with them a piece of their past. Significantly, Silvera introduces readers to the Jamaican national dish of ackee and saltfish the day Mama's son Freddie migrates to Canada, leaving one nation for another. In a typical scene that reflects the experience of most Jamaicans about to migrate, Silvera textures the narrative with local colour, featuring the members of the community gathered at Mama's home and at the airport. Importantly, as Molly points out, "Maria Galloway did not go to [the Kingston] Palisadoes Airport to see her son Freddie off. She never went to airports, not even when her son Peppie left in 1958 and then her daughter, Glory, in 1960" (16). However, other family members and friends accompany Freddie to what in an independent Jamaica is now called the Norman Manley International Airport, bidding him tearful farewells with talk "full of promises" (17). Mama remains at home preparing a meal for them. Upon their return, Mama welcomes them with "roasted yellow-heart breadfruit and yam, ackee and saltfish and golden-brown flour dumplings" (18), reaffirming the idea of national unity through the Jamaican national dish(es). The community, which significantly extends beyond mere blood relations, partakes of this meal while discussing what they would miss most now Freddie is gone. The event parallels a wake, to celebrate the life of the departed; a wake as a method of celebrating, remembering and consoling that is itself based seamlessly on a cultural memory of continental African origins. We will again see a similar occurrence later in the book, but this time in Canada and with a physical death.

Through the community's partaking of the meal and reminiscing about Freddie, we learn about cultural tradition. While Mama raises her concern about Freddie and his philandering ways in the midst of the recollections, Joyce, Mama's sister, expresses fond memories of Freddie as "a sharp dresser, and a ladies' man" (19). Mama, however, disagrees: "If dressing was all dere was to life and having whole heap of 'oman, him would be king.... Ah only hope him remember poor Monica and de baby" (19). But Molly reminds Mama of another aspect to Freddie's character, by asking, "Mama, yuh won't miss him for de crab season?" (20). The question introduces a discussion about a Jamaican cultural pastime. The crab season represents one of the most enjoyable community social activities during the rainy season. Freddie's absence reminds them of his contribution to their lives in social and economic ways. Ruth owns a restaurant that relied on Freddie to provide the crabs for her specialties: "de crab soup and de crab fritter" (20). This loss is augmented by the meal Mama serves and the memory of the social crab cookout — an event at which Freddie's presence was central. As Molly recalls: "During crab season, we ate crab so often we forgot the taste of other meat" (21). Freddie provided the main ingredient that fuelled this pastime that truly connects the Wigton Street community. For me, Silvera intimates that this meal and the discussion about crab season suggest that identity is about the food we eat and about the community we inhabit and reinforce through the breaking of bread together.

If we observe the points at which particular conversations within the Galloway family households occur, we will notice that controversial discussions take place and difficult decisions are made at some of these gatherings and that food is usually the stimulant. When Mama is socializing and having a drink of rum — intended by Silvera as symbolically a national beverage with seeming religious overtones — readers are also served up dishes comprising character traits, desires and ways of life.

While Mama is primarily shaped by her domesticity, Mama is not crippled by it in quite the same way as women have been depicted in patriarchal societies. In Silvera's text, Mama's domestic realm is a powerful feminist one: "[it] demonstrate[s] not only the importance of women's relationship with meals but also the peculiarly creative power of this relationship" (McGee 2001: 150). As with her other works, Silvera is quite concerned to make spaces available for women to voice their experiences. With this novel, she claims space as a writer documenting the experiences of characters whose lives she portrays as worthy of literary expression. McGee's discussion on the role that male modernism played in the exclusion of "women's writing in the realm of high art in part, at least, because of what content was defined as acceptable art," is useful here, for she argues that women modernist writers who have structured their novels around women's domestic activities bring "another perspective." She further points out: "The fact that the gender of the writer and the server of the meal is the same adds an important dimension to [the] fiction" (150). Viewed this way, Silvera's novel, then, creates a space for fiction that depicts Jamaican folkways through the women characters.

Jamaican Canadian identity is taken to another level when Mama and Molly migrate to Canada to reunite with Glory and her husband Sid, continuing a tradition: several pieces of the past become uprooted from Jamaica and transplanted in Canada, beginning with the migration of Peppie, Glory and later Freddie. But food also makes the journey — first, when Freddie migrates, Mama sends "escoveitch fish" and "fruitcake" (29) for Peppie and Glory. When she and Molly arrive they bring "fried fish, roasted yam and breadfruit, cassava cakes and baked goods for everyone, as well as fever grass, dried cerasee, leaf of life and other herbs for medicinal purposes" (88).

Mama intends to transport as well her former lifestyle as the matriarch, although she has not occupied that status in her children's lives since they migrated to Canada decades earlier. She does so by performing her Jamaican identity in a *Canadian* household. As Molly reports: "The moment we arrived Mama assigned herself the post of housekeeper, cook and adviser.... Uncle Freddie and Uncle Peppie came around a lot to see us and ate with us *every Sunday evening*" (emphasis added, 90). The Sunday dinners became a ritual, a reassembling of the *nation* or tribe: "*Every Sunday we had a full-course Jamaican dinner* complete with rice and peas, fried chicken or curried goat, coleslaw salad and freshly made carrot juice. Uncle Peppie, Aunt Val, Uncle Freddie and whatever woman he was seeing at the time would join us for dinner" (emphasis added, 92). Molly's report opens a window to Freddie's new life and to Mama's attempt at re-establishing her Jamaican cultural ritual — the family Sunday dinners. However, this version of the family tradition soon changed when the location of the family Sunday dinners shifts to Peppie and Val's home, leaving Mama feeling alienated and unwanted by her family. In this scene, Silvera represents the experiences of Jamaicans who migrate and join a wider Canadian family but who find it difficult to adjust to their new life, and while the immediate family and the wider society may tolerate the individual's identity as Jamaican, before long the individual must make the effort to transition into Canadian society and accept a *new* identity. Mama is experiencing having to make a similar shift. The heart does not bend, however, for it is incapable of being other than its true self.

The role of matriarch and the status it affords raise tensions within the Galloway clan. Upon migrating, Mama realizes her status has changed. She feels powerless within the family, and the family is her community in Canada. Without this power and status Mama suffers an identity crisis and becomes alienated from her Jamaican *self*. Not everything Mama takes with her from Jamaica is welcomed and accepted, especially by the women in her family, who have already established their home in Canada and prefer to maintain the status quo: Val, Peppie's wife, "hovered protectively around Uncle Peppie," Molly observes; "that might have been why Mama took an instant dislike to her" (89). Silvera uses this dislocation in family status to give new meaning to the idea of a *food fight*, or rather fighting over food.

Mama's dislike for Val becomes evident when Val first establishes her family ritual around Sunday dinners at her and Peppie's house. "The food was good," as Molly recounts: "Aunt Val cooked much the same food as Mama.... That was the first time I'd eaten macaroni and cheese, and it was delicious" (102). When pressed by Val for her opinion of the macaroni and cheese, Mama grudgingly responds: "Mi never care too much for it, too dry. Dem things suppose to be moist wid 'nuff cheese and milk" (103). Mama insults everyone — Peppie's wife Val (and Peppie too), Glory and Sid, Freddie and his new girlfriend Joanne, and Molly — by openly criticizing Val's cooking and undermining her success at preparing a delicious family meal. She is isolated in the family. After leaving Peppie and Val's home, Glory admonishes

Mama, but Mama remains unapologetic; she laughed: "'What yuh want mi fi do, lie? De something dry like cork; as fi de chicken wid all dis barbecue sauce fi gravy.' Mama laughed louder." Mama refuses to relinquish her status as the best cook: "Unnu always bet pon de wrong horse, so yuh want to come cuss wid mi now because of Val?" (104). This response discloses Mama's inner fear, provoked by the tenuous nature of her position at the centre of the family; in her absence new rituals have been formed; Canadian sensibilities seem to be overtaking those *authentically* Jamaican, food is still the centre of the rituals but the organizer has shifted. Molly states: "Mama and I didn't go back to Aunt Val's for quite a while, for even though we were invited, Mama had no desire to go. Our Sunday meals balanced themselves on one foot. Sometimes Sid and Glory ate with us and other times they went to Aunt Val's, where they were joined by Uncle Freddie and Joanne" (104). This disagreement signals a major change in family tradition as a result of migration. It also parallels the experience of the immigrants relocating and attempting to re-establish their life — in effect balancing themselves — in a multicultural Canada. Instead they usually experience a sense of dislocation and thus withdraw, remaining alienated from the wider society and unbalanced as if standing on one foot

Mama doesn't readily adjust to her Canadian life. In the early days she and Molly visit the neighbourhood park to get out of the apartment and see something of the new landscape. Once, Mama meets an Italian man, Paolo, who is attracted to her. Thereafter, he brings her flowers and one day makes a traditional Italian meal for her: "pasta primavera in a Pyrex dish.... Mama was very impressed, said she found it tasty" (107). Paolo invites Mama to his home, but she declines. When Molly presses her for a reason, she responds: "Yuh nuh understand yet, but mi know him daughter would a laugh when him tek mi home.... Mi like him, but too much obstacles. Me black, him white." And later she comments: "Well, ah never think ah would see de day when a man cook fi me.... Nuh man never really cook fi mi except Mikey" (107), and as we will see she does not think Mikey much of a man. Could Silvera be suggesting this typifies a danger for Jamaicans: that of being afraid to adjust, especially when one is not at the heart but in the periphery of the diaspora? For maybe there are times when the heart can, indeed, bend, and still be the same *self*.

Mama does not tell Glory and the other family members about Paolo, and this is particularly significant because it registers Mama's sense of alienation from culture, place and *race*. It also shows Mama's awareness of racial and ethnic positioning as a social aspect that can unbalance the best of us because she mentions her feeling that Paolo's daughter would reject her. While she enjoyed Paolo's meal, a symbol of sexual intimacy, she also recognizes their racial shadings: "Ah know you cyan always look at things in colour, but some things just is. And as much as mi think some a dem black man can learn a thing or two from white man, like how fi treat woman, mi nah tek di chance…. Molly, in life yuh learn dat black man is a necessary evil. Mi know dat, for mi live wid dat poison all mi life" (107). Her keen awareness of gender, racial and cultural difference further alienates her in this multicultural setting, where even human desires rarely overcome racial obstacles. At this point, Mama's sense of belonging or feeling a sense of balance is challenged by her struggle to firmly root her Jamaican *self* in the Canadian landscape, establishing a home and successfully transplanting her own rituals that will bloom in time. Elsewhere in the novel Mama speaks of her dream about Glory owing a house one day. Finally, she moves into Val's uncle Mel's house, as a move to survive the cooped up life and a way of establishing a sense of belonging through property ownership. In Silvera's representations of belonging, property ownership is central and it symbolizes one's identity as Jamaican or Canadian. To own property in both countries further grounds one's identity through place and in both places.

Belonging, for Mama, also means to be needed; as Molly states: "She needed to be needed, but she also needed to show her independence" (108). It is important for immigrants to feel needed, to feel a sense of belonging in their new home and to be financially secure. Without this independence, too, Mama is powerless; her identity becomes destabilized. She resorts to nostalgia, especially through the memory of food and eating back in Jamaica, expressing a longing for the days of the Chinese pastry shops, Ruth's restaurant and her home on the dead end street: "Nothing like yuh own house, wid yuh things surround yuh" (108). In Mama's view, recognition comes through her culinary skills and these skills provided her ticket to independence. In her new land she cannot bake pastries and transport them on foot to restaurants and Chinese pastry shops. Silvera shows how difficult it is to transition from one identity to another without losing one's independence.

Some habits die hard, and they, too, accompany immigrants to their new homeland. In Mama's case, it is her drinking binges. As a way of coping with the news of the death of her estranged husband back in Jamaica, Mama succumbs to a habit that she had developed while living in Jamaica. Eventually, in an effort to keep an eye on Mama, Peppie takes Mama from Glory's apartment to live with him and Val. It isn't long before the women's relationship is tested, however. Soon Mama complains to Glory, "One evening mi cook some escoveitch fish wid scotch bonnet pepper and de woman nearly go mad. 'Peppie don't like too much pepper.'… What she know 'bout him?" Val, too, expressed her issues with Mama, raising them with Glory when the family met for dinner one Sunday, "Glory she's a handful. There is nothing I can do right. I don't even recognize my own kitchen. She has to cook every meal, changed up my kitchen completely." Glory empathizes with Val and comments: "The short time we live together, ah realize is not de mother mi think mi did know." And Molly overhearing their criticisms of her grandmother concludes: "Ungrateful bitches" (122). Here the *new Canadianized* women see Mama, the older generation and an outsider from Jamaica, as threatening, interfering or plain out of place.

Living in this contestatory environment further alienates Mama from the women in her family. She has a reprieve when her mother Mammy dies and she returns to Jamaica to attend her funeral. Upon her return to Canada, Mama and Molly become trapped by one of Canada's famous magazine advertising *scams*. This new distraction offers a way for Mama to bend a bit and try to become socialized as *Canadian* through the content in specific magazines: "*Homemaker's, Chatelaine, Canadian Home and Garden, McLean's*"; Mama is enticed by the offer of free sample issues, as Molly explains, "If you were satisfied you could continue to receive the magazines." Mama decides: "Ah going send fi dem. Dem will give Glory some decorating ideas when she and Sid buy dem house, and the days when mi home alone, mi can catch up on more Canadian news" (125). The magazines are important socializing tools and they help Mama to understand her new "homeland" and to learn *Canadian* recipes. Upon receiving the first set of magazines, Mama cuts out some of the recipes: "Mek mi try a few of dem dishes. We can't just eat island food — sometime mi get tired of cooking di same thing" (126). It is clear that Mama desires to adjust to a new way of life as typified by her interest in an assortment of meals, other than Jamaican cuisine, for variety. If we are what we eat, Mama's willingness to eat Canadian meals affirms her desire to become Canadian. She now has the recipes to form a new hybrid identity — Jamaican Canadian — emerges but at heart it is Jamaican in a true Canadian multiculturalism way. Mama's identity is now evolving; she is becoming more outgoing, showing interest in Canadian culture.

Mama continues to explore Canadian culture and she learns to cook Italian dishes from her son Freddie's new girlfriend, Bella. Mama, in turn, teaches Bella how to cook Jamaican dishes, in an act of cultural exchange, another example of Mama's embracing another *Canadian* ethnic/cultural identity. Mama is willing to negotiate cultural difference through the female, unlike her earlier refusal to embrace Italian culture, by rejecting Paolo's overture through his pasta primavera dish.

One Christmas, Mama prepares a lavish holiday dinner that symbolizes her old self but also her new identity as now a true Jamaican Canadian. Molly observes: "There was enough food for three holiday feasts. Mama really outdid herself." She describes the Christmas dinner setting:

> The table was laden with sliced, honey-marinated ham garnished with grilled pineapple slices, roast turkey served with English pota-

toes, fried chicken with fried plantains, curried goat, steamed snapper in ginger and thyme sauce, gungo peas and rice, coleslaw salad,
potato salad, Aunt Val's macaroni-and-cheese pie, cornbread, and
a baked sweet potato dish. A large selection of beverages occupied
a side table: fresh carrot juice, ginger beer, sorrel drink, eggnog,
rum punch, punch à creme. And finally there was Mama's black
Christmas cake and plum pudding. (136)

Notably, Aunt Val's macaroni-and-cheese pie has pride of place among
Mama's feast, another sign of Mama's willingness to embrace change and to
recognize the *Canadianized* version of this dish in the Jamaican meal. Molly
declares: "We couldn't have asked for a better Christmas" (136).

One of the most important traditions that informs my Jamaican
Canadian identity is Christmas. I must perform the ritual of preparing and
baking Jamaican Christmas cake and making sorrel drink or it wouldn't be
Christmas; I must include Jamaican foods even if I prepare other cultural
dishes. Silvera uses this tradition to make an important statement about the
significance of the passing down and carrying forward of cultural traditions
and the implications of doing so to one's progeny. I believe that rituals such
as this affirm one's identity and allow successive generations to carry forward
an important part of their cultural heritage even when they do not or have
never lived in the original homeland. Although my son was born in Canada,
he knows what a Jamaican Christmas dinner should be, and he and his wife,
born in Canada of Filipina descent, learn how to cook Jamaican meals and
do so quite often even though they may experiment or use a recipe book
that I bought for them in Jamaica. They also insist on having their wedding
in Jamaica and on having Jamaican dishes on the menu so that his wife's
family can experience Jamaican culture — in fact my son said, "Mom, we
want the wedding cake to be like the one we get at Jamaican weddings, the
kind that taste almost like Christmas cake." Silvera represents a similar ritual
at Christmas time in a scene prior to the Christmas dinner party discussed
previously. Mama prepares the traditional Jamaican Christmas cake and
sorrel drink. She hands down her family tradition of Christmas baking and
preparations to Molly. While Molly sees this baking ritual as a return to
"Wigton Street, except for the cold and the snow outside" (131), it is more
than that. Subsequent factors suggest it is perhaps the central transitional
ritual in this text that also defines a Jamaican identity.

Pointedly Mama decides to pass on to her granddaughter Molly —
symbolically the *balanced* Jamaican Canadian — a tradition that was handed
down to her by her mother Mammy, rather than passing on the tradition to
the next in line, her daughter Glory. The handoff takes place in a strange
land, where, perhaps, Molly was in greater need of this tradition than her

mother, whose coming of age was in Jamaica. Molly remembers her time spent baking with Mama, but Mama interrupts that reverie and tells her to write down the recipe, and Molly does so "in [her] best handwriting" (132). During this process, Mama reminisces, telling stories about her childhood in Port Maria, giving Molly not only a baking lesson but a history lesson as well. The details of this family's history are punctuated by recipe instructions for Jamaican Christmas cake and sorrel drink. All this, Mama does to reinforce the importance of tradition and family rituals. Yet, Mama does not hand down the recipe to Glory, skipping a generation of the clan. For the heart does not mend. It breaks and then starts anew.

Soon after this baking lesson, Mama receives a letter from Ruth advising her that the Wigton Street property is in dire need of repairs. Mama calls a family meeting at which she appeals to the family for suggestions on what to do about the property. However, all her children suggest that the property be sold. There should be a clean break. Their suggestion is an indication of how distance and time have so alienated them from their homeland that they have no longer any sentimental feelings for the property. Molly recounts the details:

> "Mama, me out of de picture," Glory said. "I don't hold no great attachment to de place, and is Canada we is now and we have to look to de future, not wallow in de past."
>
> Mama glanced away and made to spit into her handkerchief, but thought better of it. Instead she said, "Then is forget, unnu forget so quick? Is amnesia unnu come down wid? Freddie, yuh don't remember de dead-end street? … de crab season? … Glory, yuh forget de baking in dat house? De pastries and catering that pay yuh passage to come Canada"? …
>
> My grandmother laughed bitterly, and now she did spit in her handkerchief. "Nobody want to remember where dem come from.… "ah won't sell it.… One day when de house rotten down, ah will donate de land to charity, mek dem build a orphanage for all de pickney dem dat don't have fish nor fowl to mind them." (145)

Mama expresses her bitterness at their rejection, vowing to disinherit them from that day. They will be cursed to return to the status of having no culture, just like the fish and fowl, for they would no longer be Jamaican with an authentic culture and even civilization. Here, it is important to recall the baking ritual performed by Mama, passing down the traditional Jamaican Christmas cake and sorrel drink recipes to Molly. What would have happened in this scenario had Mama passed on the tradition to Glory instead of Molly?

Mama directs her care and attention to the younger generation, and after Mel's death she completely dotes on them while relying heavily on Molly for her care. When she dies, she leaves her estate to Vittorio and her hope chest to Ciboney. They will remain in the house that she inherited from Mel and live as the *Canadians* they are. Importantly, however, they will still retain their Jamaican heritage: Mama's beloved Wigton Street home, despite Molly thinking: "How could Mama do this? How? I was her only granddaughter. I was there. I was always there. Vittorio never was, and what did he know of Wigton Street?" (7). It's again useful at this point to recall Mama's words when she declared that rather than sell Wigton Street, she would donate the property to "de pickney dem dat don't have fish nor fowl to mind them" (145). Vittorio fits this description. Vittorio and Ciboney have become the fruits of migration, the new hybrid Jamaican Canadians, but Canadians nonetheless.

The Jamaican Canadian fruits of migration as presented through Silvera's narrative of the Galloway family constitute a continued history framed by family rituals. All this uprooting, transplanting and grafting of selves in a new location not only nurture and bloom new Jamaican Canadian identities but also lead to self-awareness for all partakers. The meals reinforce the notion that national identity is significant; we are what we eat and food helps us overcome challenges and deal with loss, while giving us a sense of self and even belonging when we feel alienated. Indeed, Silvera seems to be asking, as creatures in a particular time and space, metaphorically, are we not all consuming life as much as we are consumed by time itself? We are the food we eat, and we end up eating ourselves by the way we bend to life challenges.

Molly, however, will have the legacy of Mama's recipes and may continue to develop a new tradition in her new cultural landscape, Canada. The novel closes with Molly and Ciboney in Port Maria, Jamaica, having partaken of a meal of "fried snapper and hard-dough bread, washing it down with lemonade" (262). This is a fitting ending because it recalls Mama and Molly's last meal with Mammy just before they migrated to Canada, and it reinforces a continuation of a tradition by Molly's and Ciboney's return to the *motherland*, both Jamaica and Mammy and Mama's hometown, Port Maria; Molly introduces the *motherland* to Ciboney, in effect carrying forward the tradition, reaffirming cultural identity, prefaced by the ritual of a meal (263–64).

References

Beckford, Sharon Morgan. 2011. *Naturally Woman: The Search for Self in Black Canadian Women's Literature*. Toronto: Inanna Publications.

Davis, Andrea. 2004. "Diaspora, Citizenship and Gender: Challenging the Myth of the Nation in African Canadian Women's Literature." *Canadian Woman Studies/ les cahiers de la femme* 23, 2.

Mannur, Anita. 2010. *Culinary Fictions: Food in South Asian Diasporic Culture*. Philadelphia:

Temple University Press.

McGee, Diane. 2001. *Writing the Meals: Dinner in the Fiction of Early Twentieth-Century Women Writers.* Toronto: University of Toronto Press.

Silvera, Makeda. 1983. *Silenced: Talks with Working Class Caribbean Women about Their Lives and Struggles as Domestic Workers in Canada.* Toronto, ON: Williams-Wallace Publishers.

___. 1994. *Her Head A Village.* Vancouver: Press Gang Publishers.

___. 2003. *The Heart Does Not Bend.* Toronto: Vintage Canada.

PART THREE – LANGUAGE AND CULTURE

8. PATWA
Its Power, Politics and Possibilities
Annette Henry

> Persons belonging to national or ethnic, religious and linguistic mi-
> norities (hereinafter referred to as persons belonging to minorities)
> have the right to enjoy their own culture, to profess and practise
> their own religion, and to use their own language, in private and in
> public, freely and without interference or any form of discrimination.
> —Declaration on the Rights of Persons Belonging to National or
> Ethnic, Religious and Linguistic Minorities

In Praise of Jamaican Language

I had the pleasure of my mother living with me for the last six years of her
life. Now that she has passed on, my one constant link to Jamaican language
and culture has also departed from my life. Our elders are living archives;
they link us to an intergenerational cultural memory. As I would come home
and slip into my most comfortable clothes, so was the feeling of hearing my
mother's Jamaican speech — the affect, inflections, the pet names for every
family member, the gestures, such as kissing her teeth, the plural markers
(di bwoy-dem) and the particular tones of voice and rhythms germane only
to Jamaicans and, dare I say, Jamaican mothers. I'll miss the duplication —
"kete-kete," or "long, long time," the unique vocalizations — "eh-eh!," the
discussion of dreams in the morning and the stories of duppies and rolling
calves. Even her laugh! A Jamaican laugh rises up from the depths of the
lower belly, full, joyous and unapologetic! Ah, the metaphors, the everyday
creativity and the poetry of the language! The use of sayings, proverbs and
other Jamaicanisms — as cockroach nuh business inna fowl fight[1] — are
significant cultural ways of theorizing. The joy of hearing a Jamaican talk
is like biting into a sweet mango, juices running down your chin and onto
your hands.

Language and Identity

About six months after her retirement, my mother confessed, "I'm so glad I don't have to speak Standard English anymore!" This utterance was a surprise. Always eloquent, always articulate, she never gave the impression that the Standard English varieties of Britain and Canada, places where we lived, were an imposition, that she longed to relax into a more personalized form of speech, even though it was the language of home, her family, her feelings, her heart.

In raising her children, my mother emphasized the reality that Black people are judged the moment we open our mouths. My parents knew, without reading the research, that in the U.K. and Canada, Black/Jamaican students are often stereotyped as deficient because of their language and sometimes erroneously placed in remedial classes or embarrassed by teachers in front of peers. The languages we speak are implicated in society's view of us, and our views of ourselves. Once I heard some Latina friends debating whether one could be a "real" Latina if she didn't' speak Spanish. I wondered, can one call herself a Jamaican if she doesn't speak "patois?"[2]

Across social classes, many children of Jamaican descent are raised to disregard or dismiss Jamaican language. Attitudes regarding the use of Jamaican Creole vary according to region, social status, age and gender (Jamaican Language Unit 2005). Indeed, our foreparents who received a particular kind of British colonialist education were taught that patois was an illegitimate vernacular. In Caribbean countries, contemporary efforts to establish Creoles as national languages and languages of instruction have been welcomed by some but scorned by others, even met with great suspicion and accusations of "keeping our children back." In Jamaica, opponents argue that Jamaican Patois should remain the language of the home and other informal settings. It is now widely accepted in practice and in research (Bialystock 2001) that speaking one's home language does not inhibit literacy development in the wider society.

However, the ideological biases against Caribbean Creoles are deeply entrenched in the dominant society and in our cultural memory of shame and inferiority vis-à-vis an imposed British standard. My parents had some Jamaican Canadian friends in Ontario in the 1960s. The husband introduced himself and his wife with an affected "British" accent: "My wife is Jamaican and I am British West Indian," he explained. I was only nine years old, yet I remember being struck by the discrepancy between this man's thinking and his actual language practice. A Native American colleague once confessed that he never writes on the board while teaching because he sometimes makes spelling mistakes while speaking and writing simultaneously. He feared that his students would think, "That Indian can't even spell!" These examples reflect the weight of a colonialist past that lingers into the linguistic present. Language discrimination—linguicism –and the pressures to attain an uncomfortable standard of language use affect our sense of identity, sense of competence and our perceptions of success in the wider world.

The Meanings of Patwa

Jamaican Creole, or Patois, or Patwa, can represent a secret language, a language of power, of self-determination, of pride, of resistance, of comfort, of inclusion, of solidarity, of struggle and of voice. We may joyously dip and slide along the socio-linguistic continuum of Standard English and Patois sometimes with intention, for rhetorical or stylistic purposes, and at other times almost unconsiously. When I was a school teacher, I would witness students codeswitching between English and Patois with great delight when they didn't want the (White Canadian) teachers to understand, when they wanted to show solidarity and when they wanted to defy the social norms of Eurocentric Canadian schooling that stress a particular "standard." Canadian youth who are not Jamaican often perceive the language as "cool." Popular culture, music and the media have helped to enhance this "coolness." Language frames our desires, subjectivities and social and cultural worlds.

Language, by nature, is ever evolving. Jamaican Creole in Jamaica and beyond reflects a colonialist past where languages, cultures and histories have struggled and melded and are constantly created anew in a postcolonial present. Contemporary Jamaican Standard English (JSE) is influenced by other Englishes (especially American), and in this globalized and postcolonial world, influenced by the Internet, social media and transnationalism. The language of Jamaica and Jamaicans represents processes of hybridity, cross-fertilization and syncretism. Jamaicans in Canada and in Jamaica speak a language of multiple locations and borders.

Poets Theorizing Language

Poet and essayist Marlene Nourbese Philip (1989: 11) has written copiously about "the anguish that is English in Colonial societies." She writes:

> ... and english is
> my mother tongue
> is
> my father tongue
> is a foreign lan lan lang
> language
> l/anguish
> anguish...
> (56)

Philip feels that she has no choice but to use English as the base from which she works, but it is a father tongue for her — an international, written language, rather than a mother tongue — a localized and personalized one. Father tongues, rather than mother tongues (Creoles), remind us in some sense of a pervasive "master discourse" (Davies 1995), a language which categorizes and positions us in a discourse "that reflects the realities of those who must *speak through more than one language/culture at once*" (Chancy 1997: 11, emphasis added). Consider Grace Nichols (1984: 63), one of many Caribbean poets who captures this multiplicity:

> I have crossed an ocean
> I have lost my tongue
> From the root of the old one
> A new one has sprung.

These poets express how we embrace the world with an insider/outsider linguistic consciousness. Loving Jamaican language and culture involves a recognition of the colonialist past as well as of the challenges of living in an ever-changing global society. This "new tongue" that has "sprung" has necessarily been embroiled in dissent and controversy.

Articles in Jamaican and international newspapers regarding the Patois Bible translation project, for example, reflect some of these debates. For example, consider the cartoon from the *Jamaican Gleaner* (July 1, 2008) in which the prime minister expresses his sentiments. The Jamaican Creole translation

Cartoon copyright Las May, used with permission.

project describes its sole aim as one of providing Jamaicans the Bible "in their heart language."[3] The entire New Testament is scheduled to be launched to coincide with the fiftieth anniversary of Jamaican independence. Online commentaries of ordinary citizens worldwide reveal a range of reactions to this project. Some believe that it makes a mockery of God and spirituality; one person referred to it as a "Joke Bible" (Ade-Gold 2008). Another wrote on Jamaicans.com that when people will hear the parson read from the patois Bible, "Nuff people ago dead wid LAUGH" (Dennis 1998). Since the launch of the Book of Luke, parishioners have claimed that it creates a relationship with a more intimate God; the *Daily Mail Reporter* (2010) cites a Jamaican pastor who says, "People feel liberated. They say they are able to visualize the Bible better." The Rev. Courtney Stewart, general secretary of the Bible Society of the West Indies, goes on to argue: "The Scriptures have the greatest impact when you hear it in your mother tongue. So this translation to Creole is affirming the Jamaican speaker's language, and it is very, very powerful."

Despite the fundamental right to use one's own language in private and public (*Declaration on the Rights of Persons Belonging to National or Ethnic, Religious and Linguistic Minorities*), the King James Version of the Bible has been intricately interwoven into everyday Jamaican culture and music. It is an ingrained part of Jamaican life for the unschooled and erudite alike. Indeed, as some argue adamantly in favour of its literary value, Lindsay Johns (2011), who describes himself as a "staunch atheist," writes to the *Daily Mail Reporter*:

> Nothing can compare with the rich, mellifluous and hypnotically beautiful cadences of the magisterial King James Version and the cultural and literary touchstone it has now become. The phrases, allusions and imagery are ... an acknowledged masterpiece of literature in its own right.

What Does It Mean to be Literate in the Twenty-first Century?

Post-independence musicians, writers and other artists have been instrumental in redefining and concretizing Jamaican national and diasporic identities through literary and social texts. Some Jamaican educators and linguists have been grappling with the complexities of envisioning Jamaica as a bi-lingual country (English and Jamaican Creole) amid resistance. They have been working out practical matters such as standardizing orthography and finding suitable curricula and pedagogy for bi-literacies in Jamaican schools (See Devonish 2010; Moren and Moren 2007). These efforts are cloaked in debates of how best to prepare children with the necessary twenty-first century literacies. Opponents question the appropriateness of Jamaican Creole in the curriculum as a tool in preparing global citizens; some even point to the contradiction that the very people who advocate formalizing Creole in schools received a traditional Eurocentric education and send their own children to elite preparatory and secondary schools. These issues of Jamaican language as the medium of instruction are not unrelated to Canadian debates of culturally relevant curricula and pedagogy for Jamaican Canadian students and how to validate and build upon the non-dominant language practices that they bring to the classroom.

Students in Jamaica and abroad can benefit from formally learning Creole and learning about Creole. They will appreciate its history and hybridity (Cooper 2011; Kouwenberg et al. 2011). This learning is part of what Vèvè Clarke named "diaspora literacy" (1991), which involves people of African heritages understanding their languages and cultures from informed, indigenous perspectives. Understanding and validating one's linguistic heritage contributes to sustaining an intergenerational cultural memory and involves understanding correspondences with West African languages and the social and political history of languages in contact. Indeed, Caribbean languages are cloaked in histories of exile and slavery and reveal a people's creative strategies for linguistic and cultural survival.

Since 2008, the United Nations General Assembly has recognized the necessity to preserve and protect all languages of all peoples. In her message for International Mother Language Day 2012, Irina Bokova, Director-General of UNESCO, emphasized: "The language of our thoughts and our emotions is our most valuable asset. Multilingualism is our ally in ensuring quality education for all, in promoting inclusion and in combating discrimination." As the *Declaration of Rights* underscores, people have the right to conduct their daily lives in their mother tongue. Learning Creole in school does not impede English literacy; in bilingual education, children's literacies increase in both languages. Let us not be overly romantic about teaching Jamaican in school, whether in Canada or in Jamaica. Importantly, we need to recognize and appreciate the spectrum of language practices in various social and cultural contexts in Jamaica, the Caribbean and internationally (Youssef 2004). An inclusive curriculum can contribute to understanding the rich cultural and political histories of the Caribbean and of Caribbean Canadians. Educators need to ensure equitable access to a quality *"both/and"* education for students of African heritage (Henry 1998), an education that allows students *both* to understand their lives, histories and languages, and dream about their futures from their own informed, indigenous perspectives; *and* an education that affords students equitable access to twenty-first-century knowledges with the required critical literacies to participate as confident, competent international citizens in a globalized, transnational world.

Notes

1. Don't meddle in things that don't concern you.
2. Linguists would call Jamaican language a "Creole," whereas the everyday Jamaican would refer to it in a range of ways: Patois, Patwa, Jamaican and unfortunately, "bad " or "broken" English. Creoles are languages with origins in one or two other languages, as Grace Nichols expresses in her poem in this chapter. For the purposes of this chapter, I use Jamaican Creole, Patois, and Patwa interchangeably. Creoles have their own rule-governed grammars and sound systems. Much of the vocabulary of Patwa is English-based, a reality that has helped to promote the notion that it is a corrupt, inferior form of English. The lines of demarcation between dialects, creoles and languages are often geopolitical. For example, a dialect of a particular language might have less similarity than two distinct languages.
3. Historically, the Bible has always been translated into people's vernaculars, and this Creole project is no exception. A team returned to the original Greek, and compared with English translations and translated the ideas in culturally appropriate ways. (See <http://jamiekanbaibl.org/lib/runPeople.php>) and CBC Sunday Edition <http://www.cbc.ca/thesundayedition/shows/2010/12/19/december-19-2010/>.

References

Ade-Gold, Christine. 2008. "Patois Bible, A weh yuh a seh!" *Jamaican Gleaner Online,* June 23. At <http://jamaica-gleaner.com/gleaner/20080623/news/news9.html>.

Bialystok, Ellen. 2001. *Bilingualism in Development: Language, Literacy and Cognition.* Cambridge: Cambridge University Press.

Bokova, Irina. 2012. "2012 International Mother Language Day: Mother Tongue Instruction and Inclusive Education." At <un.org/en/events/motherlanguage-day/>.

Chancy, Myriam J.A. 1997. *Framing Silence: Revolutionary Novels by Haitian Women.* New Brunswick, NJ: Rutgers University Press.

Clark, Vèvè. 1991. "Developing Diaspora Literacy and Marasa Consciousness." In H. Spillers (ed.), *Comparative American Identities.* New York: Routledge.

Cooper, Carolyn. 2011. "Governor General Gives Throne Speech in Patois." *The Gleaner online,* November 6. At <http://jamaica-gleaner.com/gleaner/20111106/cleisure/cleisure3.html>.

Daily Mail. 2010. "Di ienjel go tu Mieri…': Jamaican Church Creates Patois Gospel of Luke after Congregation Fails to Grasp King James Bible." *Mail Online,* December 21. At <http://www.dailymail.co.uk/news/article-1340185/Jamaican-church-creates-patois-Bible-congregations-struggle-understand-standard-English-version.html#ixzz1qX5yFu5n>.

Davies, C. 1995. "Hearing Black Women's Voices: Transgressing Imposed Boundaries." In C. Boyce Davies and M. Ogundipe-Leslie (eds.), *Moving Beyond Boundaries Vol. 1: International Dimensions of Black Women's Writing.* New York: New York University Press.

Dennis, Leslee. 1998. "Di bible in patois." Jamaicans.com, August 20. At <http://www.jamaicans.com/culture/jatimes/bible.shtml>.

Devonish, Hubert. 2010. "Interview: Professor Hubert Devonish, Advocate for Jamaican Patois as a Language." Jamaicans.com, January 1. At <http://www.jamaicans.com/speakja/patoisarticle/JamaicanPatoisLanguage-2.shtml>.

Henry, Annette. 1998. *Taking Back Control: Black Women Teachers' Activism and the Education of African Canadian Children.* New York: State University of New York Press.

Jamaican Language Unit. 2005. *The Language Attitude Survey of Jamaica.* Department of Language, Linguistics & Philosophy: University of the West Indies, Mona, Jamaica. At <http://www.mona.uwi.edu/dllp/jlu/projects/Report%20for%20 Language%20Attitude%20Survey%20of%20Jamaica.pdf>.

Johns, Lindsay. 2011. "Lord Have Mercy! Jesus, Unno Ready Fe Dis?......," *Daily Mail*, December 19. At <http://johnsblog.dailymail.co.uk/2011/12/lord-have-mercy-jesus-unno-ready-fe-dis.html>.

Kouwenberg, S., W. Anderson-Brown, T. Barrett, S. Dean, T. Lisser, H. Douglas, amnd J. Scott. 2011. "Linguistics in the Caribbean: Empowerment through Creole Language Awareness." *Journal of Pidgin & Creole Languages* 26, 2.

Morren, Ronald, and Diane Morren. 2007. "Are the Goals and Objectives of Jamaica's Bilingual Education Project Being Met?" Summer Institute of Linguistics International Electronic Working Papers 2007–2009.

Nichols, Grace. 1984. *The Fat Black Woman's Poems.* London: Virago.

Philip, Marlene Nourbese. 1989. *She Tries Her Tongue: Her Silence Softly Breaks.* Charlottetown: Ragweed Press.

Youssef, Valerie. 2004. "'Is English We Speakin:' Trinbagonian in the 21st Century." *English Today* 20, 4.

9. MEMORIES HAVE TONGUE

A Conversation with Afua Cooper

Lisa Tomlinson

Afua Cooper's contributions to African Canadian history and the creative arts, as well as her political and community engagement, make her a truly renaissance woman. In 2005, she was chosen by the editors of *Essence* magazine as one of the twenty-five women who are shaping the world. She currently holds the position of James R. Johnston Chair in Black Canadian Studies at Dalhousie University in Halifax, Nova Scotia.

Cooper was born in Westmoreland but grew up in Kingston, Jamaica. She attended St. Michael's Primary School, Camperdown High School and Excelsior Education Centre. In 1980 she migrated to Canada, where she completed a doctoral degree in African-Canadian history at the University of Toronto. Her publications in African Canadian history include two co-authored volumes, *We're Rooted Here and They Can't Pull Us Up: Essays in African Canadian Women's History* (1994) and *The Underground Railroad: Next Stop, Toronto!* (2002). Her acclaimed book *The Hanging of Angelique* was published in 2006. Two recent children's novels, *My Name is Henry Bibb* (2009) and *My Name is Phillis Wheatley* (2009), received the Social Studies Trade Book Award for Young Children and the Beacon of Freedom Award respectively. Her books of poetry include *Memories Have Tongue* (1992), *Utterances and Incantations* (1999) and *Copper Woman and Other Poems* (2006). She has received several awards, including the Harry Jerome Award for Professional Excellence, the Planet Africa Renaissance Award, the African Canadian Achievement Award and the Premier of Ontario Award for Excellence in the Arts.

Situating Afua Cooper's Work

In his 1995 article "Borrowed Blackness," Trinidadian Canadian Andre Alexis (1995) maintains that diasporic Black culture is overwhelmingly influenced by an African American aesthetic. He goes so far as to suggest that Black Canadian culture is merely an imitation of African American creative production, complaining that "no one, Black or white, has yet accepted the fact and history of our [African Canadian] presence, as if we thought Black people were an American phenomenon that has somehow crept north" (18). He argues further that our admiration of African American figures such as Malcolm X and bell hooks only reinforce this United States hegemony.

Alexis' anxieties about Black Canadian culture are understandable. Indeed, Canadian culture is often overlooked in African diasporic discourse. Gilroy's (1993) celebrated Black Atlantic frame, for example, fails to take into account Black Canadian histories and experiences, barely acknowledges Caribbean art and aesthetics, and presents African American cultural production as the singular template for Black diasporic cultural identity. Ironically, in the articulation of his concern, Alexis himself overlooks the compelling tradition of Black Canadian writers and scholars, like Afua Cooper, who in integrating a Caribbean sensibility within the specificity of the Canadian environment have created a uniquely Black Canadian aesthetics. Indeed, the breadth, depth and vitality of Afua Cooper's work challenge Alexis' assertion that Black Canadian culture does not exist separately from African American culture. Cooper, in fact, repositions the path of the Black Atlantic to include the rich legacy of Black Canadians, including the unique feature of cultural exchange between Canada, her native Jamaica and the wider Caribbean.

Afua Cooper has located much of her work within the Canadian landscape, with a focus on class, race and issues of concern to the Black community. As a historian and dub poet, her work has been instrumental in recovering a Black Canadian presence long pushed to the margins and/or ignored in Canada's national narrative. Her poem "African Wailin'," for example, speaks about the significant issue of police brutality against African Canadians. Many of her poems also reflect on the specific realities of Black women living within a male-dominated white Canadian society. "Oh Canada," provides a powerful critique of the negative impact the West Indian Domestic Scheme has had on the lives of Caribbean Canadian women. Her seminal and prize-winning book *The Hanging of Angelique* records the life of an African woman who is alleged to have burnt down a large portion of the city of Montreal in protest against her enslaved status. More recently Cooper's children's books, *The Young Phillis Wheatley* and *The Young Henry Bibb* have captured the lives of enslaved children, a perspective rarely covered.

Much of Cooper's work can also be situated in Jamaica. She proudly celebrates her early upbringing in the hills of rural Westmoreland, demonstrating an appreciation for the local cultures of her fore-parents. The cultural aesthetics of Jamaica (language, African-centred religion, orality etc.) are central in her texts. Her poetry collections *Memories Have Tongue* and *Copper Woman*, for example, echo early Jamaican writer Claude McKay in their integration of the Jamaican language and indigenous Caribbean themes and symbols. Cooper, however, also offers a pointed analysis of her homeland in her critique of the Jamaican colonial education system and its valorization of colonial conquest.

What follows is a conversation between Afua Cooper and me that took place in fall 2011 in which she reiterates many of the early concerns in her scholarship and poetry and introduces new ones. The interview gives us some sense of the overwhelming significance of her contributions to Canadian society and the Jamaican influences that have guided her life and work.

Tomlinson: I have observed in some of your works, your poems "O Canada II" and "Atabeyra" for instance, reference to Aboriginal/First Nation Peoples of Canada and Jamaica. What are your reasons for these inclusions?

Cooper: Yes, while African Canadian people are central to my work, I have included the experiences of Aboriginals to a lesser degree. I have included their stories because there is an unspoken question on how we negotiate space with Aboriginal people. Black people must have a consciousness of the marginality of Aboriginal communities and understand that they have also suffered from land loss, identity and so forth. Within our collective struggle we must therefore also pay attention to theirs. Unfortunately, many Black people have bought into the idea that Canada is not their land [not the land of the First Nations peoples] and we see them through the lens of White racists. We don't see their struggles as parallel to ours. I have heard Blacks referring to the Aboriginals they see downtown as drunkard and lazy, not fully understanding their history. Given the history of geography in this country, as a writer I cannot turn a blind eye to the oppression of other marginalized communities. And the fact that there are over 2000 land claims before the courts is a testimony to the unfair and inhuman treatment of our First Nation community. Unfortunately, many Caribbean Canadians have not engaged the history of the Canadian landscape to include the Native people of Canada.

The same thing can be said for Jamaica. When I went to school in Jamaica, we were not taught the full history of the first people to have inhabited the land. Instead we were taught about our conquerors. For example we were taught that Christopher Columbus "discovered" Jamaica in 1492. Nothing about their way of life or even the genocide of these people was really taught.

Tomlinson: Your creative writing has obviously been shaped by the Canadian landscape and culture, e.g., slavery in Canada, and as we have just spoken about in the previous question, the Aboriginal peoples. Can you speak to the ways that the Jamaican cultural landscape has similarly shaped your work?

Cooper: Jamaica has very much shaped my work. The ways in which I talk about the Jamaican landscape, the people, historical events and my family experiences are all a part of my Jamaican cultural experiences. I gained my global consciousness of Black people by living in Jamaica —Rae Town, Kingston. From my early years, I knew there were Black people oppressed everywhere. I used to be boggled by Apartheid and asked myself how this could be — that a country that was dominated by Blacks was ruled by a White minority under such humiliating conditions? It wasn't until the men on the street corner, who would be playing dominoes, educated me about Apartheid, that I fully understood what was really happening. These men were the font of knowledge. They also educated me about global issues involving Black people's struggles and triumphs. They were the griots of the community, you can say. I also had the privilege of having two of the teachers who Walter Rodney taught at UWI, which accounted for their Black consciousness. I can also remember when historian and writer Kamau Braithwaite visited my drama class to do rehearsal. These were defining moments for me. I have poems written about the Rodney Riots, "Kingston Bun Down," while the "True Revolution" makes mention of Kamau Brathwaite. In addition to Jamaica and Caribbean history, diaspora experience has also contextualized how we thought of ourselves. My early childhood spent in Westmoreland and family members who played significant roles in my child rearing are all captured in many of my poems. I have a poem about my grandfather, for instance, whom I never knew. But I still wrote about him, in a fictitious way of course, and it is based on the information my family provided.

Tomlinson: Can you share that poem and speak to how any of your works have any autobiographical elements?

Cooper: Oh yes, my grandfather was known as a grand figure in the family who everyone spoke about. He drank rum a lot, so in the poem, I have him spew rum in my face, a kind of baptism I suppose [laugh]. Of course, he never did that but based on the stories I heard of him, it is something I can imagine him doing [we both laughed]. A lot of my other poems about my family are partially fiction. You know, family mythology, as I just shared with you about my grandfather. Even though I left Westmorland and moved to Kingston at age eight, I would go back there for summer vacation. My childhood was happy—that's why we grew up so confidently.

Tomlinson: The Jamaican landscapes seem to have had a significant influence on your work. I gather from the way you spoke that the local cultures and history of the country have always been of great interest to you. However, the path you have taken in terms of documenting history has been to focus on Canada. Why study Canadian history and not Caribbean?

Cooper: First of all, since I was fifteen years old, I knew I wanted to be a historian. Having being exposed to a rich cultural heritage through my surroundings, I actually came into the academy thinking that I was going to study African history, but I switched over to Canadian history, which soon made greater sense to me. How can I live in Canada and not explore the experiences of Black people in this land space? The resources were already there; the archival documents, the oral stories. So for me it was urgent for me to do this work. Besides, I was comfortable in my Caribbean skin. I had no anxieties around being a Jamaican. I had already gotten that cultural nurturing from family, teachers, my environment.

Tomlinson: You've spoken about how your Jamaican cultural background has helped to shape your academic and creative work. Can you see these aesthetics in the works of other first- and second-generation creative writers and/or cultural producers?

Cooper: I see younger Caribbean artists attempting to use a Caribbean aesthetics. Some of the younger generations of poets, for example, do a good transition of this where they are able to fuse reggae, dancehall rhythms and use Patwa quite nicely. But memory is sometimes used quite superficially. I don't mean that in a bad way. What I am trying to say is the shift from Canada to Jamaica and the Caribbean, per se, by some of the younger artists is not fully there. I think this is because many of these younger artists are still trying to negotiate spaces between their Jamaican backgrounds and Canadian identity, which is quite natural living in a diasporic space.

Tomlinson: What would you say is the role of African Canadian writers in the continued development of Black literary culture in Canada and beyond?

Cooper: Canada is the place where Black literature is happening. Look at what has happened here for the last two decades. It has also been fertile grounds for Black female writers. Dionne Brand just won the prestigious Griffin Poetry Prize, and her work has garnered many other literary awards. Many of these writers have Caribbean background and they say their muse is the Caribbean. Jamaican writer Olive Senior, for example, continues to maintain links with Jamaica and Canada, and this is vividly expressed in her work. There is also literature coming from other parts of the diaspora, for example, Ghanaian writer, Esi Edugyan writing from out of British Columbia. Check her out. Her book *Half Blood Blues* won the Scotiabank Giller Prize in November 2011. She is the hottest thing in CanLit right now!

Tomlinson: Yes, I have also noticed that the creative works by Black Canadian writers are appearing more on university reading lists — I rarely saw this happening in the nineties.

Cooper: Oh yes, Black Canadian writers are being included on course reading lists a little more so now. I went on the Internet a while back and saw that my book *Angelique* was the required text for about two hundred courses. I was amazed! Oftentimes Canadians are not remembered so something such as including Black Canadian writers on course lists puts Canada on the map. This especially gives visibility to the Black Canadian population because Canada as a country is perceived around the world as just White people. This inclusion speaks to the diverse narratives and experiences of Canada. I am Jamaica and am Black. I am a Canadian writer, and I write about Black people and their experiences. As writers we have something to share and it must be valued.

Tomlinson: What about at the high school level? Do you see these changes?

Cooper: Unfortunately, this is not the case for the high school or elementary level. Definitely, more work needs to be done here. Literary and history texts are still centred on Anglo and French experiences, "the founding peoples." These two groups continue to represent the central discourse of what constitute the nation. So there is still the question of what a nation is and whose stories are worthy to be told. Why not replace Mark Twain's *Huckleberry Fin*, a text that has been used for so many years now in the curriculum, with Gabriel Garcia Marquez.

Tomlinson: *The Hanging of Angelique* was a ground-breaking history book because of the way it not only uncovers what has been denied and omitted from Canadian history, but also because it offered a female narrative. Is there a figure in Jamaican history that you would you like to recover into a historical non-fiction of this sort and why?

Cooper: Queen Cubah — she was one of the leaders of Tacky Rebellion of 1760 — or should I rephrase and say, she was symbolic to the rebellion. We are not certain whether she was really a crowned queen taken from Africa or whether it was a title given to her in the New World. Apparently Queen Cubah was crowned prior to the rebellion and her crowning initiated the rebellion. With the exception of Nanny of the Maroons, not many of our enslaved women are spoken about or remembered in our national history of slavery. We know of male figures like Tacky, Paul Bogle, Cudjoe, Nanny's brother and more contemporary figures like Marcus Garvey. Enslaved women have resilience and never allowed their circumstances to hold them down and were very instrumental in many of the revolts and gaining freedom.

Tomlinson: I want to shift the interview now to your work. I am very interested in folklore and African spirituality. My doctoral thesis explores these particular aesthetics in the creative writings of African Jamaicans, including many of your poems. What are some of your sources for these aesthetics in your poems?

Cooper: I came to African spirituality in a number of ways. When I lived in Westmoreland I went to Shiloh Holiness Church — a church where people get into spirit. There was also a pocomania church down the road which always aroused my curiosity. This church was referred to as "bad" and we weren't into that church. We were supposedly "better" than them.

During the nineteeth century many Yoruba people settled in Whithorn and Logwood, Westmoreland, where I grew up. These Yoruba fused Orisha spirituality with Christianity and created a new religion. Shepard Kirlew's church came out of that African based spirituality. Shepard had managed to maintain some of this West African tradition. The women wrapped their heads with colourful scarves. The backyard was set up with all sorts of paraphernalia. Then there was the gere, an African dance. I used to see my cousins dance this in Kumina.

When I moved to Kingston, my aunt wanted to please my mother so she just continued to send me to church. It didn't matter where I went, as long as I went to a church. I went to an Anglican Church and later Methodist. Camperdown, the high school I attended, was founded by the Presbyterian Church so I occasionally attended that one. I found these churches boring because they weren't the same as the previous churches that I was used to attending, the holiness and the pocomania churches down the street from us. The hand clapping and the singing were absent from the services and the getting into spirit, you know the excitement! [We both laughed]. But growing up in east and central Kingston always exposed me to some form of church — you know, the roadside preaching. I enjoyed those because it captured the spirit of the Jamaican culture. I later got into yoga, where I leaned about Hinduism and was introduced to other different kinds of faith. Rastafarian became appealing to me because it came with culture and history. I later on became a Muslim.

Tomlinson: In an interview with Kwame Dawes you said that reggae was a major influence in the writing of Jamaican writers coming out of the seventies and early eighties because it provided writers, including yourself, with confidence. Do you see dancehall providing this inspiration to dub poets today?

Cooper: I do think if there was no reggae music we would not have dub poetry, because dub came out of the music. And I was introduced to dub poetry in a very direct and personal way. After I left high school and doing the Rasta trad I lived with dub poet Mutabaruka and his then wife Yvonne. Muta and I used to write poetry and discuss it in great detail. We even decided to do a book together but then I did not want to deal with the Babylonian capitalistic aspect of publishing so the book never materialized. Instead, he did that project with Faybienne Miranda. Later, I went to Excelsior Community College (EXED) to pursue teacher training, and one of our guest speakers for our language arts class was Oku Onoura, aka Orlando Wong. He had just come out of prison then. His brand of dub poetry was burning up Jamaica. He was a great inspiration. Our professor Keith Noel brought Oku to EXED and what a treat that was! I saw more possibilities for my writing, especially in regards to sound, rhythm, voice and music.

Both Muta and Oku were influenced in different ways by the music. On the other hand, I am also a literary person — a page poet, a print poet. I was first introduced to poetry by my primary school teachers, and we read poems from books, though occasionally we would dramatize some of those poems, and the use of the voice was of clear importance. Our teachers also entered poetry choirs in the Festival speech competition and, again, voice was paramount. Some of the poets that were introduced to us as children were Kamau Brathwaite, Nicolas Guillen, Derek Walcott, Claude McKay, Louise Bennett, William Wordsworth and of course, verses and chapters from the King James Bible. We did not read a lot of women Caribbean poets because, to be honest, there were not many in English, with the exception of Bennett and Una Marson, for Jamaica at least. Though later there was Olive Senior and Velma Pollard. I loved reading poetry. It brings me immense satisfaction. It allows for a kind of reflection one does not necessarily find in the spoken word. And my first training was in a kind of literary poetry so that stays with me. Writing poetry was a purely literary endeavour, paying attention to both form and content. But for me, the poetic tension is to combine the voice and the print, the literature and the orature, the written word and the spoken word, and to write dub and make it jump off the page.

Tomlinson: How then would you say your work reads parallel to early and contemporary Caribbean writers and how has it diverted?

Cooper: My work is postcolonial with a strong sense of history, of place, of culture, of family, of concerns with identity. I think Kamau Brathwaite has been an enduring influence on me and my work. He is a historian, he is a poet… I don't know if I unconsciously patterned myself off him. But we all have role models. What I know is that his poetics is very much rooted in concerns of history and culture and politics and displacement. Mine likewise. Later I would discover the lyrical eroticism of Pablo Neruda (in politics, revolution and love!). I see similarities with my work and that of St. Martin poet, Lansana Sekou. But yes, my work has to divert and be on its own path because as writers we have our own uniqueness. I think my concern with both the esoteric and exoteric, with spiritual exploration happening alongside erotic exploration, is another way my work has diverted. Actually, also being an embodiment of diaspora in motion is another way. I am Jamaican now living in different places in Canada, and living and creating a Black Canadian experience is another way. I just came back from Ethiopia and going to Sierra Leone shortly. You see this movement in my poetry.

Tomlinson: I can recall when you were featured in the 2005 *Essence* magazine as one of the top women shaping the world. This ranking was alongside the Honorable Portia Simpson Miller, who has just become Jamaica's first elected female prime minister. I remember being so excited to see two women of Jamaican heritage being featured among this list. How did you feel to be included in such a list with Simpson Miller and now this being almost a decade and both of you are serving in such influential roles?

Cooper: How did I feel? It was fantastic to be included in such a stellar list and to have the lead story! To be named as one of the women who are shaping the world was simply extraordinary. When I was told I was chosen by the editors for such an honour I was mighty pleased, to say the least. For me, it meant that my work was being recognized far and wide. I was very honoured to be placed with the Hon. Portia Simpson. I was proud that both of us were there as Jamaican-born women. I was sort of in awe to be honest, because Portia is a lion lady, and I admired her a lot. She has won the recent election in December 2011, and this shows that she is a formidable woman. She is now the prime minister of Jamaica, the first woman to hold that position and I wish her the very best. I am sure she would wish me the same in my new role as Johnston Chair.

References

Alexis, A. 1995. "Borrowed Blackness." *This Magazine* 2.

Bristow, P., D. Brand, L. Carty, A.P. Cooper, S. Hamilton, and A. Shadd. 1994. *We're Rooted Here and They Can't Pull Us Up: Essays in African Canadian Women's History.* Toronto: University of Toronto Press.

Cooper, A. 1992. *Memories Have Tongue.* Toronto: Sister Vision Press.

——. 1999. *Utterances and Incantations: Women, Poetry and Dub.* Toronto: Sister Vision Press.

——. 2006. *Copper Women and Other Poems.* Toronto: Natural Heritage Book.

——. 2006. *The Hanging of Angelique.* Toronto: HarperCollins.

——. 2009. *My Name Is Henry Bibb.* Toronto: KidsCan Press.

——. 2009. *My Name Is Phillis Wheatley.* Toronto: KidsCan Press.

Edugyan, E. 2011. *Half Blood Blues.* Markham: Thomas Allen Publisher.

Gilroy, P. 1993. *The Black Atlantic: Modernity and Double Consciousness.* Cambridge, MA: Harvard University Press.

Shadd, A., K. Smardz Frost and A. Cooper. 2002. *The Underground Railway Next Stop, Toronto!* Toronto: Natural Heritage Books.

10. I REMEMBER

Naila Keleta-Mae

i remember long before i paid $1200 a year for a gym membership so i could run in place, jog in place, walk in place, step in place, climb in place, row in place … before i began to think that surely these hips could defy gravity and fall in space.

i remember when patsy & barbara & monica & gloria were all my mommy's best friends so i had to behave myself on the city bus; couldn't cuss and scream like my purely canadian friends 'cause i knew if any one of my polite caribbean aunties saw me misbehaving, when i got home i'd have to do some explaining.

i remember every september thinking classrooms were heavens where everything was constructed by white. new crayons & markers & pencil sets; hb 10 with a pink rubber eraser, maybe a new g.i. joe action figure for lunch time and breaks … and we used hi lighters as markers (that was before we had to become academic textbook readers).

i remember yellow lunch boxes with cabbage patch kids on the side. a can of coke, before there was diet, fruit roll-ups and nutella sandwiches on white wonder bread (i'm lying. that was kelly's lunch. i had a thermos with warm milk, cut up carrot sticks for snacks and a ham and cheese sandwich on dempster's 100% whole wheat bread).

we traded marbles and stickers. drew hopscotch on sidewalks with chalk. we made friendship pins and bracelets out of gimp.

we were the self-declared "cool girls from the grade 4 & 5 split class."

recuerdo también cuando solamente me preocupaba de lo que me llevara a mi escuela, sin pensar en el salud de mi familia o mis amigas. (i remember when i only knew two languages and didn't need to show off like i just did, but please don't check for grammar i'm one of those new latin culture appropriators.)

i remember when i took health for granted, when nobody i knew died. pills? pregnant? abortion? gay? flavoured condoms? we would have thought those were candies and tried to buy them with a nickel at the corner store where gummy bears cost a penny and red lollipops too much at a dime.

i remember when kissing was such a big deal we pretended to kiss while playing kissing tag. when sex was for bees and honey (or was it bees and birds? it really didn't matter 'cause we really didn't care).

i remember when i took memory for granted and could remember everything. when birthdays were at mcdonalds with big cakes and few candles and 27 invitations for every single kid in the class (i always wanted to invite the teacher. that always made my dad laugh).

i remember
when i never tried to see myself through others' eyes
when walking down the street i didn't see the passers by

i remember when johnny & suzy & suzette & ann-marie were all my bestest of best best friends. when playing was the priority and the biggest threat was "you can't come to my birthday party" and we all knew that was a lie. when tying shoe laces was complicated and zellers sold runners with two velcro straps and we all wore sikes not nikes and luma tracksuits 'cause puma was too expensive and it really didn't matter 'cause we really didn't care

i remember

i remember

i remember
when my reality changed

when perception began to alter how i saw those around me and unknowingly began to construct new philosophies that would prohibit me from playing in innocence
when friendship making became a viable networking tool and dinners were served in soup kitchens 'cause community work looks good on résumés. soon thereafter the in crowd became the out crowd and the once out crowd became the cool crowd 'cause now they were critically analyzing all the other crowds

when wearing brand names and labels meant you were "consumed by commercialism," no longer signs of fashion but those of selling out

i remember when having money wasn't cool 'cause it meant you subscribed to the system. who would have thought (definitely not our parents) that being poor would become a badge of honour. exchanging second hand store shopping finds. when permed hair meant processed and fake so it had to be wrong and not just a hair style. when kinky nappy natural hair suddenly gave me "conscious sistah" clout

i remember when we smiled at police officers and thought they'd save us from the bad guys, until we realized that in their minds that meant our brothers, fathers, uncles, cousins and even aunt gloria's cute son jamal. and so we branded those uniformed men beasts, 5-0, pigs upholding fascism. convinced they were only there to serve and protect and break a brotha's neck. we decided we were wiser with a better understanding of the system. changed first names to something more african-sounding – johnny became ade kunle zimbabwe – and everyone bought into consciousness, maybe they sold it at convenience stores with pendants, copper bracelets, dashiquies, egyptian musk incense and more. and everyone became an artiste 'cause it meant you could create and find ways to articulate anger and hate.

legitimize hate
masquerade it
package it
compartmentalize it into

        word spoken abstract
        intellectual prose
        that / and / …
lies

'cause poetically you can be "conscious" and still say nigga and call anyone a devil or a swine. chastise, mock or criticize, legalize it with poetic justice and the audience will clap and fall in line.

now i never talk to my once four best friends. last i heard suzy was a married single mother raising their three kids. suzette was pregnant with a baby father on permanent pregnancy leave from her. ann-marie was telemarketing part-time finishing her degree in political science (don't have to be a rocket scientist to know she ain't gonna get paid with that). johnny, sorry, ade kunle zimbabwe, i heard he's a mechanic at canadian tire and me too, i'm canadian and tired of living in this cold place. on the outside and on peoples' inside, feeling like a stranger in my birthplace.

now i've adopted a jamaican patois in just these last few years. clutching on to any semblance of heritage, wishing i could adopt that sweet immigrant language of "back home." romanticizing the freedom of "back home." ungrateful, wondering why my parents ever left home.

now it seems i remember too much from books read over the last few years. it seems i remember too much from critical analyses around pot luck dinners and sunday brunches. it seems i remember too much from lectures and workshops and conversations with new friends. it seems i remember too much from krs-one, common sense, roots and me'shell ndegocello lyrics. it seems i remember too much from reasoning with sisterens and muslims and christians and bald heads and rastas. now it seems i remember too much to continue to live in peaceful numb in babylon.

some might say i remember too much.

Note

"i remember," *T-Dot Griots: An Anthology of Toronto's Black Storytellers,* Karen Richardson and Steven Green (eds.) (Victoria: Trafford Publishing, 2004).

PART FOUR – THE DIASPORA

11. THE GWANNINGS

Mark V. Campbell

"Eh, wha a gwan my yout?" is a greeting one might expect to hear on the streets of August Town or in a basement party in Scarborough. In 2012 Toronto, one should not be surprised to hear these words coming out of the mouths of Tamil, Phillipino or Vietnamese youth. It is an interesting conundrum that the expressive culture of Black youth often becomes popular culture, yet innovative Black youth are still disproportionately devalued, criminalized and systemically marginalized from fruitfully and holistically contributing to the betterment of Canada society.

The process of youth identity development for Black males in what may be the world's most politely racist city is sandwiched between fear of Blackness on one hand and intrigue over our "coolness" on the other. The context in which we young Black males attempt to survive is both hopelessly contradictory and violently dismissive of our humanity. The institutional environment is one in which the police services have a long history of murdering young Black males; the schools consciously seek to push out Black male teenagers, sometimes eagerly awaiting our sixteenth birthdays to refuse to let us back into school; the popular media mimics the American media and criminalizes us; and jobs are unavailable for any young Black male who is uninterested in moving furniture or sell running shoes. Entering the information technology sector is as easy as becoming a pop star, and financial institutions will hire only the most sanitized versions of Black males — which means having as little hair and accent as possible.

The words of Martinican psychologist Frantz Fanon (1967) continue to ring true, somehow in the Western context, I am "beaten down by tom-tom drums" (Fanon 1967). The tiny, well controlled box in which Blackness is allowed in Canadian society is a crushing, static space, packed with European colonialists' fear, with little to no ventilation. Shad K, a London, Ontario, based emcee said it best in his 2009 lead single, "Brother (Watching)":

> After a while, it sort of starts naggin at you/The crazed infatuation
> with Blackness/That trash that gets viewed/And the fact that the

tube only showed Blacks actin' the fool/And I was watching...

Shad explains in the chorus, "saturated with negative images and a limited range of possibilities is strange..." Imagine fifty plus years since Fanon's declaration, several continents and countries away, Eurocentrism remains doggedly persistent. Shad's lyrics could very well have been a verse from Aime Cesaire's 1972 classic text *Discourses on Colonialism.*

It is in this context that we find aspects of Jamaican identity and culture dominating the ways in which Black male identity operates in Toronto. The context and the environment in Toronto are clearly oppressive and lack a healthy public dialogue around the various issues that work hard to contain and control Blackness. For youth, in the midst of the crisis we call identity development, Jamaica and its cultural dominance (from Marcus Garvey to Usain Bolt and from Patois/Patwa to rudebwoys) become a heavily relied-upon resource to negotiate the treacherous landscape. In fact, I argue that Afro-Jamaican identity both unconsciously operates as, and it is consciously utilized as, a defence mechanism for marginalized youth seeking to resist the media's mainstream marginalization of non-White individuals. Throughout this chapter I identify and elaborate how Afro-Jamaican identification practices operate as a common tool for oppressed and marginalized Black youth's battle against institution-led disempowerment.

It is not just Black youth and Afro-Jamaican youth you'll find creatively taking up some of the vestiges of a Creolized Jamaicanness. Members of many other ethnic groups take up Jamaican Patois/Patwa and sometimes other forms of self-fashioning as they battle their own marginalization. It is important to observe some of the Creolized Jamaican identification traits amongst Fillipino, Somali, Tamil and Vietnamese youth because this allows us to recognize the similarities across all these ethnic group members.

In what follows, I detail three distinct ways in which Afro-Jamaican identity is utilized in the Toronto context and effectively Creolized to meet the needs of local youth caught in the midst of racial profiling and schools that "push them out." These three ways include the use of creative Creolized Patois/Patwa, an engagement with, and consumption of, local non-American hip hop, and the use of chupsing as both a cultural continuity and a form of resistance. While undoubtedly, there are several other forms of resistance, such as dress, pronunciation and comportment, I focus on these three inter-related forms of Black expressive cultural forms of resistance in hopes of drawing some parallels between contemporary and historical expressions of Afrodiasporic cultures under duress.

Before delving into an analysis of Jamaican identity and culture in Toronto it is critical to remember that there is no one "Jamaican culture." I am cognizant that from Rastafari to Seventh Day Adventist to Maroon rural culture, Jamaica is vastly more diverse than television and newspapers lead us to believe. Although the dominant media try to sell us a homogenized idea of what Jamaican is, the term encompasses a diversity of identities. Here, I focus on the youth-related popular forms of identifications connected to musical cultures, urban vernacular and modes of dress. Before doing so, in the section that follows, I look back into our history in order to draw some critical parallels.

Akanness

During the period of the slave trade in Jamaica, the Akan ethnic group was often identified, by local planters such as Edward Long and Bryan Edwards, as being central to a number of rebellions and uprisings in Jamaican planta-tion society (such as the 1673 rebellion in St. Ann's, the 1690 rebellion in Claredon and the 1760 Westmoreland uprising) (Schuler 1970). This is not unique to slave societies in the diaspora as the Muslim Hausa were rebellious leaders in Brazil and the Fon were central in Haiti's (what was at the time called Saint Dominique) revolution.

The Akan and GA/Adangme speaking people, (also called Koromantine, Koromanti, Coromantine in the Caribbean context) consisted of an amal-gamation of various ethnicities from modern-day Ghana's coastal regions. Once these various groups reached the Caribbean, "Koromanti" became a dominant label for imported individuals from the Gold Coast. Jamaican planters from the time would often marvel at their strength and at the in-fluence enslaved Akan would have over other imported West Africans. In many instances, enslaved individuals from the Gold Coast were preferred by Jamaican planters, which explains their large importation numbers. Due to the consolidation of the Asante/Ashanti kingdom in West Africa, pris-oners of war and other soldiers became captives ripe for shipment to the Americas. These enslaved individuals were often highly skilled in militaristic endeavours and thus helped form the core of several uprisings in Jamaican plantation society. In fact, the Akan have been identified as setting the course of cultural development of the Maroons, whose successful rebellions led to several British treaties that helped to protect Maroon land in the island's interior. It has been estimated that around the year 1750 almost 40 percent of people of African origin in Jamaica spoke Akan/Coromantee as their mother tongue (Schuler 1970).

What is clear from the historical records is that many people who were caught up in some form of rebellion and born in Jamaica, with Creole roots, continued to subscribe to an Akan ethnic label or use Akan as a lin-gua franca. This means that enslaved individuals and Maroons who had never stepped foot on African soil continued to identify with Akanness. In addition to Creoles' identification with Akan ethnicity or "Akanness," some historical evidence suggests that Yoruban and Igbo individuals identified as Akan, particularly in connection with an uprising or rebellion. Part of the difficulty with the historical records, besides the inherent bias of the planter's first person accounts, is that the ethnicity of enslaved individuals in Jamaica is oftentimes only illuminated in connection with rebellion or religion. Thus we learn about ethnic identifications only at certain times of social crisis, times in which ethnic labels might come under duress or ethnicities become adaptive means of survival.

What we have then in Jamaican plantation society, from the 1650s up until at least the end of the slave trade in 1807, is not just a predominance of Akans but an identification with Akanness and Akan culture among people of different ethnic origins. One might go as far as to say that being Akan was synonymous with rebellion, particularly from the planter's perspective. From the perspective of the enslaved individual, Akanness may have offered forms of protection or social status by virtue of their ability to frighten their oppressors in the plantation system. While some scholars reject the "dominance of the Akan culture in Jamaica" thesis, the predominance of Anansi stories from the Ashanti oral tradition and other facets of Maroon society continue to suggest an intimate connection between rebellion in Jamaican slave society and Akan ethnic culture (Kopytoff 1976; Kouwenberg and Singler 2008).

Clearly, from the Maroon Wars to the revolutionary ideas of Marcus Mosiah Garvey, to the Rastafari movement, to Robert Nestor Marley's poetics of protest, Jamaica has a long history of rebellion, protest and anticolonial sentiment. In fact, I would argue that a rebellious spirit is in fact cultural capital for elements of Jamaican society, both those living on the island and those in the diaspora. Particularly in the case of migrant workers in Cuba, both Garveyites and non-Garveyites alike appealed to the British Crown once they felt discriminated against (McLeod 1996). Undoubtedly, willingness to protest, critique and rebel has been a part of the Jamaican diaspora in a number of cities and countries. Toronto has not been an exception.

Akanness in Toronto in Terms of Patwa?

Returning to the reality of living in Toronto as a Black male, I argue that Jamaican vernacular innovation in this context demonstrates one of the ways that protest and protection manifest for Black youth with limited access to power. Masculinized terms of endearment amongst Jamaican males in Toronto, which include "badman, rudebwoy, don and top-shotta," become limiting and at times problematic forms of empowerment. As both extensions of patriarchy and as terms of endearment, to be a "badman" is not seen as a liberating, revolutionary persona in mainstream society. These terms combat the mirco-aggressions of daily racism and devaluation, but, like the

Maroon societies of Jamaica's interior, they have limited influence over the transformation of the system/society.

These masculinized terms of endearment all suggest that protest and rebellion are, if not solely forms of cultural continuity and thus protection, forms of social capital when protest is considered a valued trait. It is easy to look at these terms of endearment and think they are all connected to outlawed actions or an illegal existence, but this is not entirely the case. Specifically, if we turn back to the rudebwoy phenomenon in Jamaican society just after independence, these youth were distinguished by dress and comportment, not solely by illegal activity. If social critique, protest and a critical socio-political disposition are assigned value (social capital) by Jamaicans and this positively correlates with Jamaica's histories of rebellion, then referencing terms that highlight one's social critique becomes central to the identification process of what it means to be Jamaican, particularly in a diasporic context.

As a Black male of Jamaican ancestry born in Toronto, to be called a rudebwoy was and still is a compliment for two reasons. First, it is only like-minded individuals that can invoke the term rudebwoy; a person who is familiar with Jamaican popular music and social culture can make the connection between the oppression found in Toronto and the oppressive regime of Jamaica's neocolonial governing system, particularly for the lower classes. The use of rudebwoy signals that the user is aware of the less-than-ideal living conditions for Jamaicans in the diaspora. Second, and more important, is that individuals who address Black males using the terms of endearments previously listed demonstrate their value of Jamaican forms of protest and rebellion as both historical/cultural continuity and as an equity-seeking activity.

It is not only these terms of endearment that pervade the Toronto cultural context. A slew of other words have migrated north, allowing Jamaican migrants in Toronto to feel some continuity. I use continuity loosely here; a term like transformation should also be thrown into the discussion to help address the complex ways in which Jamaican culture exists in the Toronto context. The day my mother corrected me for asking my friend "What's gwanning?" was the first time I paid attention to the very creative ways in which the Patois/Patwa word "gwan" has been transmitted into the Toronto context. Originally meaning "to go or move," as well as "what's going on," gwan has entered the lexicon of Toronto's non-White youth (largely, not exclusively). Gwan, in being treated like a standard English word, has somehow acquired an "ing" ending.

To someone born and raised in Jamaica, gwanning is an incorrect usage of the word gwan. For a youth born in Canada, with limited firsthand exposure to the daily usage of Patois/Patwa by the entire society and without the lived reality of being Jamaican in Jamaica, gwanning is correct in a blissfully innocent and ignorant way. There are no Saturday morning classes for youth to accurately learn how to use Patois/Patwa. Furthermore, there are even fewer baby boomers who have taken an interest in learning and preserving Jamaican Patois/Patwa as it still operates as marker of class distinction. This means there is no clear direction of how to maintain, extend or engage with Jamaican Patois/Patwa for youth in Canada. Given this situation, popular culture becomes the learning tool, the default teacher of Patois/Patwa, as Jamaican deejays such as Bass Odyssey, Stone Love and Black Chiney lace mixtapes with the latest terminology. While this opens possibilities for some kind of loose cultural continuity, it also means that in the age of the Internet anyone can access Jamaican language and cultural notions directly from the island.

Hip Hop's Caribbean Twang

Far from being solely a reggae-related phenomenon, Jamaican Patois/Patwa is learned by Toronto youth from locally produced hip hop music. As early as 1989 hip hop artists Rumble and Michie Mee were both recording in Jamaica (as well as London, New York and Toronto) and included in their music the current vernacular in their songs. For example, Rumble's track "Booyaka" and Michie Mee's "Jamaican Funk" significantly influenced the cultural arena in Toronto. With production from a young Junior Reid and backup vocals from emerging stars (at the time) Shabba Ranks and Patra, the songs created by Michie Mee and Rumble were absolutely key in circulating and popularizing Jamaican Patois/Patwa to a Canadian-born population of Black and "othered" youth.

I can clearly remember a young Filipino neighbour of mine in Scarborough asking me, with a clear sense of pride, if I knew what booyaka meant. According to him, he was in the know and proud of it. Importantly, the fact that he was not part of the dominant culture was and remains significant. Besides instilling a clear sense of pride to an already strong Jamaican diasporic consciousness, Michie Mee's "Jamaican Funk" featured her styling out in both Patois/Patwa and Canadian English on a hip hop track. Hip Hop in the late 1980s and early 1990s in Toronto attracted a mainly Caribbean youth population, so for the St. Lucian, the Kittitan and the Vincentian, Jamaican Patois/Patwa was easily accessible in the public sphere at local jams and at home via music videos, particularly those aired during the VJ slot of Master T.[1]

By being part of popular culture, Jamaican Patois/Patwa seeped into the consciousness of Caribbean youth, many of whom could not pass as members of the dominant ethno-racial group and were thus excluded from some of the more common identity categories connected to being Canadian.

Importantly, for many of the Caribbean youth in Toronto in the midst of identity formation there was limited, if not regular, access to images of the Caribbean, such as satellite television and radio stations in the late 1980s and early 1990s.

Since remnants of Jamaican culture found its way into Toronto's local hip hop music, for those youth who did not easily fit into the dominance of rock, Italian culture and eventually Whiteness, hip hop's creative stylings became one way to gain value and social capital for non-White youth. Hip hop's origins are both Afro-Caribbean and Latino, which provides a space for identification of a variety of non-White youth, especially when the language used is localized and accessible. For my Filipino neighbour, hip hop's creativity and innovative vernacular provided a space for him to explore his identity as he eventually became a b-boy and more deeply involved with hip hop culture.

In 2001, Kardinal Offishal, a Toronto-born emcee of Jamaican ancestry dropped his wildly successful lead single, "BaKardi Slang." The song, in a very humorous and accurate way, chronicled all the ways in which the Caribbean diaspora in Toronto speak in a localized, Creole way. Terms such as "carn," "shotta" and "crepe" and phrases like "wheel and come again," "jam done" and "dat nah mek it!" flavoured the track, distinguishing Toronto's hip hop culture from America's version. Part of the popularity of the track was not only that it visually provided viewers with access to some of the city's more Caribbean locales, the song's lyrics documented the integral part Caribbean vernacular plays in how locally born youth creatively articulate their belonging to Toronto's multicultural fabric.

BaKardi Slang reflected the city's Caribbean vernacular continuities, and it also provided youth with an extended vocabulary. Common phrases from Trinidad circulated in the same vocabulary as common phrases from Guyana and Jamaica, extending the ways in which Caribbean-descended and others evoked a sense of belonging outside of Canada's dominant images of Whiteness as Canadian.

Chupse

An important part of Kardinal's video is a section where a club-going woman loudly kisses her teeth, overriding the song's lyrics and beat. Kiss-teeth has been defined as "an interactional resource used to negotiate moral positioning among speakers and referents" (Figueroa 2005: 76). It is an embodied paralinguistic, paralexical oral gesture, also known in the Eastern Caribbean as chups(e) or suck teeth in North America. It can signify a range of emotions from frustration to disrespect to indifference (Cassidy and LePage 1980/2002; Figueroa 2005). There are three kinds of kiss teeth: a long liquid vibrating chupse, which expresses defiance; the "thin hard chupse of disdain" and "the effortless chupse of indifference" (Figueroa 2005: 73). Within a track designed to valourize Toronto's Caribbeanness, Kardinal intentionally focuses on highlighting chupsing as a strategy of empowerment and cultural continuity in a diasporic context.

Chupsing is an important oral tool of specific use to Afrodiasporic populations, whose linguistic diversity sought to find an effective way to convey meaning under the most oppressive conditions of enslavement. Kardinal's willingness include a scene of a woman's kiss-teeth or chupse in the middle of his video re-inscribes this Afrodiasporic inheritance, not solely as a defiant countercultural activity but as an important cultural mechanism by which disempowered diasporic youth might assert their belonging to the Canadian nation state.

For the significant proportion of non-White youth in Toronto, hip hop culture — as a form of popular culture — operates as a way for young people to acquire social capital and a sense of worth. Since Toronto's local hip hop music has been so deeply intertwined with the city's children of the Caribbean diaspora, we find, from the days of Rumble in the late 1980s to the lyrics of Kardinal in the early 2000s, a dynamic Toronto Creole indebted to the vernacular ingenuity of the Caribbean and its diapsora.

Interestingly enough, a significant proportion of Toronto's earliest emcees were of Guyanese heritage,[2] yet we do not find common phrases from that region integrated into Toronto's hip hop music. Instead, we find an abundance of Afro-Jamaican vernacular. Consequently, rather than solely and simply being a reflection of Jamaican cultural continuity, the popularity of Jamaican language and culture in the Toronto context is also a reaction to the processes of "othering" that mark all non-White bodies in Canada as not-belonging. For Vietnamese, Filipino and continental African youth alike to evoke Jamaican Patois/Patwa is both to acquire by positive association a "coolness" connected to popular culture and simultaneously an act of belonging. For a non-White body within a country and city that overly values its Whiteness and its European heritage, Patois/Patwa — more accurately T-Dot Creole — operates as a lingua franca of resistance.

Conclusion

Just like the clear centrality and usefulness of Akanness in Jamaican plantation society, racialized youth in Toronto gravitate towards and utilize a locally Creolized form or strand of Jamaican culture. In the Toronto context it is not uncommon to hear Tamil, Somali, Vietnamese and Indo-Guyanese youth using Jamaican Patois/Patwa in their Toronto-based (aka T-Dot) Creole. Not all youth engage or have knowledge of Jamaica's extraordinary histories of rebellion when they chose to express themselves in this vernacular. But what these youth have in common is the desire to belong in a country that "other-

izes" non-White people. These youth, as T-Dot Creole users, also access this
form of vernacular expression as a way to empower themselves within the
context of disempowerment cultivated by various local institutions.

As a highly accessible part of popular culture, particularly as circulated
by local Toronto hip hop music and culture, T-Dot Creole allows diasporic
youth to speak directly to and beyond the various forms of power that daily
circumscribe our lives. It is Jamaica's centuries of rebellion, survival and
protest that serve as forms of social capital within the crushing realities of
marginalization, racism and structural barriers that coat the Canadian experience with an unsavoury residue of Eurocentrism. It is within this reality
that T-Dot Creole as "Akanness" in 2012 Toronto remains an intriguing and
important mechanism for survival.

Notes
1. Master T, also known as Tony Young, was a video jockey on Muchmusic (a
    Canadian music video channel) for seventeen years. He is responsible for ensur-
    ing there was a visual outlet for various forms of Black music.
2. I am thinking specifically of Maestro Fresh Wes, Butch Lee and Lady P.

References
Cassidy, Fredrick Gomes, and Robert Brock LePage. 1980/2002. *Dictionary of Jamaican English*. Kingston: University of the West Indies Press.
Cesaire, Aime. 1972. *Discourses on Colonialism*. New York: Monthly Review Press.
Fanon, Frantz. 1967. *Black Skin White Masks*. New York: Grove Press.
Figueroa, Esther. 2005. "Rude Sounds: Kiss Teeth and Negotiations of the Public Sphere." In S. Muhlelsen and B. Migge (eds.), *Politeness and Face in Caribbean Creoles*. Dublin: University College.
Kopytoff, Barbara. 1976. "The Development of Jamaican Maroon Ethnicity." *Caribbean Quarterly* 22, 2–3.
Kouwenberg, Silvia, and John Singler. 2008. *The Handbook of Pidgin and Creole Studies*. London: John Wiley & Sons.
McLeod, Marc. 1996. "Garveyism in Cuba, 1920–1940." *Journal of Caribbean History* 30, 1–2.
Schuler, Monica. 1970. "Akan Slave Rebellions in the British Caribbean." *Savacou* 1, 26.

12. BLACKGROUND

Kevan "Scruffmouth" Cameron

SCENE 1   EXTERIOR   ESTABLISHING   FADING INTO THE FOREGROUND

I am
a bwoy.
See di bwoy deh?
See di foreign bwoy deh?
Is spoil 'im spoil up a foreign
'mus a 'im mudda what mek 'im stay dat weh.

Boy
It's good to be home
even though it's cold
at least I can be invisible again
and I don't like bami or breadfruit.

Dance a yard before yuh dance abroad

So I danced with Eskimos and oil tycoons
before I remembered the pirates and Maroons
who raided for booty and freedom
shaking the slave ship bashment
or shuffling up on deck.
My house is a bungalow
And my field is a prairie.

SCENE 2   INTERIOR   JAMAICA ASSOCIATION FUNCTION

Beggy-beggy nuh picky-picky
Whappen?
Yuh too foreign fi know betta?
At leas 'im speak di Queen's properrr English

Come pickney, mek mi teach yuh some patois.
Mommy Miss Lou
"What di _____claat… Don't make mi cuss bad word!"
Non-Jamaican Friend
"Why do your parents speak with an accent?"
Which accent dat?
I mean, what accent are you referring to?
JAMAICAN
Well I don't think my parents have an accent.
"You are used to it, just like you are used to the cold."
Yuh eva 'ear bout a ting call *Negro Chill Factor*?
Based on my research, it is 50 percent colder for Black folks than it is for white folks in subzero temperatures.
"Whatever, you were born here, just like me."
Yes, I was born here.
No, I am not like you. (I would say you suck like bag juice, but this dis is too sweet to be wasted on your flavourless eardrums.)

SCENE 3   INTERIOR   INTROSPECTIVE MONTAGE

I like ackee an' I pick out di saltfish – 75/25 is my preferred mix.
I listen to Brooklyn hip-hop and reggae music,
I dance like Reggae Boyz and track stars,
I run like Reggae Boyz and track stars,
I watch Reggae Boyz and track stars on Canadian televisions manufactured by Japanese name brands playing broken records like disgruntled soundbwoys before di alarm get ring.
I watch *Shottas* and *Dancehall Queen* while drinking *Ting* with a sting.
I grow up looking young for my age writing dub poems for the page and stage.
I dread my likcs like the blood beat and chop them off like a Rastaman in colonial streets.
I am an invisible Ellisonian protagonist
fading into the blackground
while shadow actors play my role.

SCENE 4   INTERIOR   BUNGALOW BASHMENT

"But wait. Wha di backside! If I told you once, I told you a million times! Don't make me cuss bad word!"
The time it took for her to get the belt from the closet was my headstart.
Mother is legendary like her national heroine – Queen Nanny Koromanti.
If my math was incorrect, or my act full of slackness or whackness, my maternal disciplinarian would stop stirring the dutch pot cauldron and my aforementioned backside would pay the price (so I learned to play nice).

This is the reason I am so fast
All spiced cornmeal porridge and interdisciplinary sprints.
Nutmeg?
"Yuh mus 'e a nut meg yuh a gwan so…"
Cinnamon?
"O lawd, please cinn a mon to teach this child a lesson."
My mom is tough-loving, detail-oriented and strict.
But,
My dad is straight up postal.
Original top-ranking badman from Kingston pon di couch
Shooting channels for target practice – weapon handy around his waist.

SCENE 4   INTERIOR   (CONTINOUS)   LIVING ROOM

There is no headstart when my father dished out discipline like rice & peas, fried plantain, boiled yams and stew beef on any given Sunday family dinner. There is no pause in the action as he would catch his prey in full stride, one hand on my trembling arm, while the other skillfully unhooked the belt and flung it off on the backswing as he followed through on the back of my side – stinging my childish pride.
I cry.
Sometimes I go run and hide because as much as I try
I can never turn invisible around my folks
So I put certain things aside between broughtupsie and dropping legs
I find a middle ground on the soccer field.
Football pitch a wha we call it!

SCENE 5   EXTERIOR   BUNGALOW BACKYARD

Black kid run up and down to stay warm
Foreign bwoy from abroad when yuh go back a yard.
But my backyard grow apple tree and play street *Hockey Night in Canada*
My backyard is shooting hoops and netball, navigating limbs as I adeptly ascend big trees that have no coconuts to fall but is rooted same way.
Yes, I am first generation of this toque-wearing nation, but my genetic re-memories are thick with Akashic humidity
I clap with relief as Air Jamaica drops its legs on tarmack and not the Caribbean Sea.
So tell
Coconut Willy, Mango President (wherever Man go, Woman follow), Jack Fruit & his wife Passion that my maroon house is a bungalow and my golden/emerald pitch is a prairie fire that burns like a flag held by the Rocky Mountain Lion of Judah.
And I am
JAMAICAN

Born on northern snow plantations
My nom de guerre traded like canerows of hair for gravity defying afros.
Revered by my peers for its epic woolly mammoth like proportions.
I use a pick rather than a shear so I can dig for my roots as I search for self
In between machete versus machine.
Seen?

SCENE 6   EXTERIOR   BACK A YARD

"Numba 3! Why yuh neva play fuh Jamaica?" asked Speedy Gongardes – the
best striker Jamaica never had.
Good question, I reply invisibly.
If I played for my Isle of Springs
I would lose myself in the Cockpits
And find myself on Blue Mountain pinnacle
I have a North American attention span and African hands
With poetic bloodlines that drift like continents
And clench like justice.
I learned to dance a yard before I danced abroad because I was born with
this rhythm.

SCENE   END CREDITS   FADE TO BLACK

13. CHARTING JAMAICA'S CONTRIBUTIONS TO CANADA'S SUCCESSES IN SPORT

Carl E. James, Desmond Miller and Robert Pitter

No discussion of the contributions that Canadians of Jamaican descent have made to the society would be complete without mention of the significant role they have played in helping to build Canada's reputation in the area of sport. The world of athletics provides one of the most ready and broad stages for countries, including Canada, to display their prowess and national fortitude in front of a global audience. Jamaican Canadians have dutifully represented Canada for close to a century and continue to do so, with many rocketing Canada to international acclaim. Indeed, a country's reputation in sports contributes to its sense of national pride, and Jamaican Canadian athletes have contributed to this pride, maintaining what might be called the Jamaican tradition of excellence in athletics.

Chart 13.1 presents a sampling of the Jamaican Canadian[1] male and female athletes who have contributed to Canada's success in sports such as track and field, hockey, cricket, jockeying, boxing, field hockey, netball, basketball and bobsleigh. As the chart shows, as early as the turn of the century, young male athletes of Jamaican descent were playing hockey in the Colored Hockey League of the Maritimes. And putting aside Herb Carnegie's significant contribution to the sport in the mid-1900s, the noticeable presence of Jamaica Canadians in the sport did not occur again until the 1990s. In fact, it was not until the 1980s, that we see a visible presence of Jamaican Canadians participating in national and international sporting events (e.g., the Olympic, Commonwealth, Pan American, World Championship and other Games) and winning medals, thereby contributing to the respect that Canada has garnered, particularly in track and field.

Chart 13.1 mostly includes athletes from the 1970s to the present day, with a few from the mid-twentieth century and much earlier. Given limited time and space,[2] we present this list with the hope of filling in some of the gaps in Canadian sport history and that others will be inspired to add the many athletes — even themselves –we have missed. Please do not consider any glaring omissions a slight on our part but rather the limitation of the works we consulted. Indeed, we very much want to bring the stories of Jamaican Canadians from the margins of history. On the special occasion of Jamaica's fiftieth anniversary of independence, although this chapter celebrates the achievements of athletes of Jamaican descent, we recognize that other individuals of Caribbean heritage have also made many contributions to sports in Canada.

Contrary to the stereotype of the "natural" abilities of Black athletes — and in this case, Jamaicans, whose representation in track and field raise questions about their "fast running" — their positioning in relation to the social, cultural, economic and political conditions in which they are expected to live, learn and "fit in" has much to do with their attraction to, participation in and attainment in sports. In Canada, many immigrant and second-plus generation youth have used sports to negotiate, navigate, acculturate and/ or cope with the hurdles and barriers of racism and discrimination that they encounter (James 2005; Abdel-Shehid 2005; Issajenko et al. 1990; Carnegie and Payne 1997). Indeed, as the stories of many African Canadian athletes reveal, in their efforts to be accepted, recognized and respected and to equally *participate* in Canadian society and its institutions, they take to the sporting field not merely for the enjoyment, sociality and peer group solidarity but for what they have been able to gain as a result. The popular thinking is that sport is an arena where anyone can excel based solely on hard work, dedication, ability and talent and that who a person is, or where they are from, does not matter. In this sense athletics is seen as providing a level playing field, one that is accessible to all who desire to participate and succeed on merit — by what they are able and willing to put in to do so. Sport is viewed as a space to transcend inequalities and discrimination. But while we might be brought to the edge of our seats rooting for the "underdog" or sit back in awe at the incredible feats of superstars, the stories beyond the playing field and behind the camera tell much more than the superficial, meritocratic, "hard work equals success" narrative we are given. We need only to look at historical accounts to understand the challenges and struggles that many African Canadians in general, and those of Caribbean and Jamaican descent in particular, have endured to reach the heights they have achieved both on and off the field.

For this chapter we chose to sample athletes from track and field, hockey, cricket, jockeying, boxing, field hockey, netball, basketball and bobsleigh (discussed in that order) because our research revealed these to be the sports in which men and women of Jamaican descent have participated at national and international levels. This is not to suggest that they do not participate in other sports, but as indicated earlier, limitations of time and space have necessarily restricted our focus.

The visible presence of Jamaican-descent athletes in Canadian sports

Chart 13.1 Jamaican Canadian Atheletes

Athlete	Sport Event	Performance	Event	Year
ATHLETICS				
Angella Taylor-Issajenko	100m women	17th	Summer Olympic Games	1988
	4x100m relay women	11th	Summer Olympic Games	1988
	4x100m relay women	6th	World Championships	1987
	60m women	Silver	World Indoor Championships	1987
	100m women	Bronze	Commonwealth Games	1986
	200m women	Gold	Commonwealth Games	1986
	4x100m relay women	Silver	Commonwealth Games	1986
	100m women	8th	Summer Olympic Games	1984
	4x100m relay women	Silver	Summer Olympic Games	1984
	100m women	Gold	Commonwealth Games	1982
	200 women	Bronze	Commonwealth Games	1982
	4x100m relay women	Silver	Commonwealth Games	1982
	4x400m relay women	Gold	Commonwealth Games	1982
	200m women	Gold	Liberty Bell Games	1980
	Athletics	DNP*	Summer Olympic Games	1980
	100m women	Bronze	Pan American Games	1979
	200 women	Silver	Pan American Games	1979
Anthony Wilson	200m men	31	Summer Olympic Games	1992
Atlee Anthony Mahorn	4x100m relay men	Bronze	World Championships	1993
	200m men	20	Summer Olympic Games	1992
	200m men	Bronze (NR)	World Championships	1991
	200m men	5th	Summer Olympic Games	1988
	4x100m relay men	7th	Summer Olympic Games	1988
	200m men	8th	World Championships	1987
	4x100m relay men	4th	World Championships	1987
	200m men	Gold	Commonwealth Games	1986
	200m men	Silver	Universiade	1985

Athlete	Sport Event	Performance	Event	Year
Ben Johnson	100m men	15th	Summer Olympic Games	1992
	100m men	DQ	Summer Olympic Games	1988
	100m men	Gold	Commonwealth Games	1986
	100m men	Gold	Goodwill Games	1986
	200m men	Bronze	Commonwealth Games	1986
	4x100m relay men	Gold	Commonwealth Games	1986
	100m men	Gold	World Cup	1985
	60m men	Gold	World Indoor Championshisp	1985
	100m men	Bronze	Summer Olympic Games	1984
	4x100m relay men	Bronze	Summer Olympic Games	1984
	100m men	Silver	Commonwealth Games	1982
	4x100m relay men	Silver	Commonwealth Games	1982
	Athletics	DNP*	Summer Olympic Games	1980
Carl Folkes	4x400m relay men	15th	Summer Olympic Games	1988
Carline Muir	400m women	6th	Commonwealth Games	2010
	4x400m relay women	Bronze	Commonwealth Games	2010
	400m women	Bronze	Summer Universiade (FISU)	2009
	4x400m relay women	6th	World Championships	2009
	4x400m relay women	Gold	Summer Universiade (FISU)	2009
	400m women	20th	Summer Olympic Games	2008
	400m women	15th	Pan American Games	2007
	4x400m relay women	6th	Pan American Games	2007
	400m women	Silver	Pan American Junior Championships	2005
Charmaine Crooks	800m women	18th	Summer Olympic Games	1996
	4x400m relay women	4th	Summer Olympic Games	1992
	800m women	10th	Summer Olympic Games	1992
	400m women	15th	Summer Olympic Games	1988
	4x400m relay women	8th	Summer Olympic Games	1988
	400m women	7th	Summer Olympic Games	1984
	4x400m relay women	Silver	Summer Olympic Games	1984
	400m women	Gold	Pan American Games	1983
	Athletics	DNP*	Summer Olympic Games	1980

Athlete	Sport Event	Performance	Event	Year
Donovan Bailey	100m men	40th	Summer Olympic Games	2000
	100m men	Silver	World Championships	1997
	4x100m relay men	Gold	World Championships	1997
	100m men	Gold (WR/NR)	Summer Olympic Games	1996
	4x100m relay men	Gold	Summer Olympic Games	1996
	100m men	Gold	World Championships	1995
	4x100m relay men	Gold	World Championships	1995
Eric Spence	110mH men	22nd	Summer Olympic Games	1984
Foy Williams	4x200m relay women	cr		2004
	400m women	14th	Commonwealth Games	2002
	400m women	28th	Summer Olympic Games	2000
	4x400m relay women	12th	Summer Olympic Games	2000
	400m women	9th	Commonwealth Games	1998
	4x400m relay women	Bronze	Commonwealth Games	1998
George Wright	Triple Jump men	19th	Summer Olympic Games	1988
Hugh Fraser	4x100m relay men	8th	Summer Olympic Games	1976
	100m men	6th	Pan American Games	1975
	200m men	5th	Pan American Games	1975
	4x100m relay men	Bronze	Pan American Games	1975
Karen Clarke	100m women	36th	Summer Olympic Games	1992
	200m women	7 h3 r2/4	Summer Olympic Games	1992
	4x400m relay women	4 h1 r1/2	Summer Olympic Games	1992
Keturah "Katie" Anderson	100mH women	23rd	Summer Olympic Games	2000
	100mH women	29th	Summer Olympic Games	1996
	4x100m relay women	13th	Summer Olympic Games	1996
	100mH women	19th	Summer Olympic Games	1992
	4x100m relay women	11th	Summer Olympic Games	1988
	4x100m relay women	6th	World Championships	1987
Leighton Hope	4x400m relay men	4th (NR)	Summer Olympic Games	1976

Athlete	Sport Event	Performance	Event	Year
Mark Boswell	High Jump men	Gold	Commonwealth Games	2006
	High Jump men	7th	Summer Olympic Games	2004
	High Jump men	Bronze	World Championships	2003
	High Jump men	Gold	Commonwealth Games	2002
	High Jump men	6th	Summer Olympic Games	2000
	High Jump men	Gold	Pan American Games	1999
	High Jump men	Silver	Universiade	1999
	High Jump men	Silver (NR)	World Championships	1999
Marvin Nash	Athletics	DNP*	Summer Olympic Games	1980
	4x100m relay men	8th	Summer Olympic Games	1976
	4x100m relay men	Bronze	Pan American Games	1975
Milt Ottey	High Jump men	Bronze	Commonwealth Games	1990
	High Jump men	17th	Summer Olympic Games	1988
	High Jump men	7th	World Indoor Championships	1987
	High Jump men	Gold	Commonwealth Games	1986
	High Jump men	6th	Summer Olympic Games	1984
	High Jump men	9th	World Championships	1983
	High Jump men	Gold	Commonwealth Games	1982
	Athletics	DNP*	Summer Olympic Games	1980
	High Jump men	Bronze	Pan American Games	1979
Molly Killingbeck	4x400m relay women	8th	Summer Olympic Games	1988
	400m women	9th	Summer Olympic Games	1984
	4x400m relay women	Silver	Summer Olympic Games	1984
Philip "Phil" Granville	10kmW	8 h1 r1/2	Summer Olympic Games	1924
Robert Esmie	4x100m relay men	Gold	World Championships	1997
	4x100m relay men	Gold	Summer Olympic Games	1996
	4x100m relay men	Gold	World Championships	1995
	60m men	Bronze	World Indoor Championships	1995
	4x100m relay men	Bronze	World Championships	1993
Robert Pitter	High Jump	Gold	Candian Interuniversity Athletics Union	1981

Athlete	Sport Event	Performance	Event	Year
Tony Sharpe	100m men	8th	Summer Olympic Games	1984
	4x100m relay men	Bronze	Summer Olympic Games	1984
	Athletics	DNP*	Summer Olympic Games	1980
Yvonne Saunders (Mondesire)	800m women	Gold	Liberty Bell Games	1980
	Athletics	DNP*	Summer Olympic Games	1980
	4x400m relay women	8th	Summer Olympic Games	1976
	800m women	4th heat5 r1/3	Summer Olympic Games	1976
	400m women	Gold	British Commonwealth Games	1974
Aaron "Pa" Carvery	Hockey		Colored Hockey League of the Maritimes	1922
Anthony Stewart	Hockey	Gold	World U18 Championships	2003
	Hockey	Silver	World Junior Hockey Championships	2004
	Hockey	Gold	World Junior Hockey Championships	2005
Chris Stewart	Hockey	5th	IIHF World Championship	2011
Frederick Carvery	Hockey		Colored Hockey League of the Maritimes	1922
Graeme Scott Townshend	Hockey		First Jamaican born NHL Player	1989
	Hockey		IHL Man of the Year	1995-96
	Hockey		WPHL Man of the Year	1998-99
Herb Carnegie	Hockey		1st Black Player offered to play in NHL	1948
James Carvery	Hockey		Colored Hockey League of the Maritimes	1899-1922
James R.F. Johnston	Hockey (league official)		Colored Hockey League of the Maritimes	
Jason Doig	Hockey	Gold	World U17 Hockey Challenge	1993
	Hockey	Gold	World U18 Championships	1994
	Hockey		World Junior Hockey Championships	1997
	Hockey	Silver	Spengler Cup	2007

Athlete	Sport Event	Performance	Event	Year
Nigel Dawes	Hockey	Silver	World Junior Hockey Championships	2004
	Hockey	Gold	World Junior Hockey Championships	2005
Oscar Johnson	Hockey		Colored Hockey League of the Maritimes	1898
P.K. Subban	Hockey	Gold	World Junior Hockey Championships	2008
	Hockey	Gold	World Junior Hockey Championships	2009
Paul C. Jerrard	Hockey	Coach		
Richard Carvery	Hockey		Colored Hockey League of the Maritimes	1900-22
William Carvery Jr.	Hockey		Colored Hockey League of the Maritimes	1922
William Carvery Sr.	Hockey		Colored Hockey League of the Maritimes	1899-1904
Franklyn Anthony Dennis	Cricket	8th	Cricket World Cup	1979
	Cricket	2nd	ICC Trophy Cup	1979
George Joseph HoSang	Jockey	Champion	Prince of Wales Stakes	1979
	Jockey	Champion	Breeders Stakes	1981
Chris Johnson	Boxing (middleweight)	3T	Summer Olympic Games	1992
	Boxing (middleweight)	Gold	Commonwealth Games	
Howard Grant	Boxing	Gold	Commonwealth Games	1986
	Boxing	9T	Summer Olympic Games	1988
Lennox Lewis	Boxing	5T	Summer Olympic Games	1984
	Boxing	Gold	Summer Olympic Games	1988
Lisa Lyn	Field Hockey women	6th	Winter Olympic Games	1988
Sandra Levy	Field Hockey women	4th	Womens Hockey Champions Trophy	1987
	Field Hockey women	6th	Summer Olympic Games	1988
	Field Hockey women	7th	Summer Olympic Games	1992
Sharon Butler	Netball		Candian National Team	2007
	Netball	3rd	Nations Cup Tournament	2009
Sheryl Thorpe	Netball	3rd	Nations Cup Tournament	2009
	Netball (coach)	Gold	Canadian National Netball Championship	2009

Athlete	Sport Event	Performance	Event	Year
Tiffanie Wolfe	Netball	3rd	Nations Cup Tournament	2009
Jodi-Ann Robinson	Football	18th	Summer Olympic Games	2008
Brody Clarke	Basketball men (Cadet)	Bronze	FIBA Americas Championship	2011
Julian Clarke	Basketball men (Junior)	11th	FIBA U19 World Championships	2011
Michael Meeks	Basketball men	7th	Summer Olympic Games	2000
Norman Clarke	Basketball men	6th	Summer Olympic Games	1988
Tony Simms	Basketball men	4th	Summer Olympic Games	1984
Tristan Thompson	Baskeball men (U18)	Bronze	FIBA U18 World Championships	2008
Howard Dell	Bobsleigh	15th	Winter Olympic Games	1988
Lascelles Brown	Bobsleigh (four-man)	Bronze	World Championships	2005
	Bobsleigh (four-man)	4th	Winter Olympic Games	2006
	Bobsleigh (four-man)	Silver	World Championships	2007
	Bobsleigh (four-man)	Gold	Winter Olympic Games	2010
	Bobsleigh (two-man)	Gold	World Championships	2005
	Bobsleigh (two-man)	Silver	Winter Olympic Games	2006
	Bobsleigh (two-man)	15th	Winter Olympic Games	2010
Shelley-Ann Brown	Bobsleigh (women's two)	Silver	Winter Olympic Games	2010

*DNP=Did not participate. Canada boycotted the 1980 Olympic games in Moscow, Russia in protest of the Soviet Union's invasion of Afghanistan.

started in the 1980s, which corresponds approximately to a decade following the peak of Jamaican immigration, a time when women who had come as domestic servants would have settled and sent for their children to join them. The young people's representation in sports also indicates the role that sports played in their settlement in Canada, having had their start (as well as their interest, skills and abilities) in competitive sporting activities in Jamaica. For example, Angella Taylor Issajenko, a three-time Olympian, indicates in her book *Running Risks* that she came to Canada as a teenager to join her mother (who had immigrated years earlier) and that she had participated in and won many track and field competitions in Jamaica. She writes that in high school in Jamaica, she dedicated a lot of time to running "not for any working-class dreams or lofty aspirations. It just made me feel good and at school I was beginning to feel that my life was taking shape" (1990: 14). Rob Pitter's contribution, in the next chapter, provides a reflection on the experience of an athlete — now coach and scholar — for whom, starting as early as grade four, sports played an instrumental role in his achievement.

Sports, Games and Performances

Why do Jamaicans run so fast? It's the question Asafa Powell most often gets asked. This is also a question that countries like the United States, Canada and scores of others across the globe have been trying to figure out. A more general question also often asked is: Why are Jamaicans so good at sports? Spectacular sporting feats have proliferated ever since members and their offspring of this small Caribbean island have been involved in world sporting events. Jamaican fast bowler Michael Holding (ESPN cricinfo 2012) helped the famed West Indian cricket team of the seventies and eighties to a fifteen-year undefeated streak in test matches and "the longest unbeaten run in test history (twenty-seven matches from 1982 to 1984)" (*Test Cricket Ratings Service* 2003 in Griggs 2006) — and by any nation in an international sport (Riley 2010).

More recently, we see Jamaicans dominating sprint athletics on the world stage. Performances of Jamaica's men and women at World Championships frequently blew away the field. In fact, on July 8, 2011, "Jamaica became the first country to hold the gold medal title in the men's 100m across all groups" (Reid 2011).[3] And at the 2008 Beijing Olympics, Jamaica took home six gold, three silver and two bronze medals (SI.com 2008) — an astonishing, almost mystifying achievement considering the country's comparatively lesser economic resources, population and size in relation to many of its competitors

This question, "Why do Jamaicans run so fast?", is taken up in the documentary film (with that title) by Nando Garcia-Guereta and Miquel Galofré, which was released in 2009. Following the path of several contemporary Jamaican sprint athletes leading up to, during and following the 2008 Olympics, the filmmakers went to Jamaica in search of answers. Featuring prominent Jamaican musicians, artists, politicians, community leaders, coaches, citizens and the athletes themselves, we find almost as many answers as there are people in the film. And while opinions are divided, several narratives emerge.

From participants in the film, we heard that it is the food that Jamaicans eat — yam, carrots and other all-natural ingredients — that provides the energy to be so speedy. Some contend that the trans-Atlantic slave trade had a part to play. The hypothesis goes that Jamaica was the first stop of the slave ships during the Middle Passage and Jamaica was where the slave traders dropped off the "baddest" slaves (the ones who gave them the most trouble). Hence, in Jamaica there are strong bloodlines of determined, tough people of African descent. Others believe that it is what is on the inside that counts. Jamaicans have the will and the heart — much more so than comparatively larger nations like the United States which have lots of money and great training facilities but which lack the spirit Jamaicans possess in abundance.

Coaches interviewed in the film said that it is a combination of natural athletic talent, a long institutional history of successful girls and boys clubs and the increasing availability of a high level of coaching and guidance. And one cannot forget, as one citizen pointed out with a smile and flash of his gold tooth, that "Jamaicans love gold." While everyone seems to have their own theories on the long-argued "nature versus nurture" debate, there is no clear consensus and no conclusive answer. The viewer is left to mull over the opinions and decide for themseves or simply enjoy the compelling underdog story.

Although Jamaicans have long had a predisposition toward excellence in sports, in the Canadian context, young men and women have had to struggle against the institutionalized racism and discrimination manifested through colour bars and the glass ceiling. Nevertheless, many of them have managed to play an instrumental role in bolstering Canada's national pride in sports on the international stage. And importantly this discussion allows us to challenge the popular misconception that the only thing Jamaicans can do is run fast.

Track and Field

Most Canadians will recall Donovan Bailey lighting up the track in the men's 100 metres at the 1996 Atlanta Olympics. He surprised his competition en route to claiming the title "World's Fastest Man," setting a then World and Olympic record time of 9.84 seconds.[4] Achieving such a feat on the soil of our southern neighbours made this victory all the sweeter. His record-breaking 100 metres win was only enhanced by the gold medal he would help win with fellow Jamaican Canadian Robert Esmie, as well as Carribean athletes Bruny Surin[5] and Glenroy Gilbert.[6] Today, Bailey may be a well-known Canadian figure but he is neither the first nor will he be the last of Jamaican Canadians to represent Canada on the world stage.

Bailey's rise to prominence came eight years after that of Ben Johnson, who, in his own right, was a forerunner who helped to establish Canada's standing in sprinting. In their article "Pride and Prejudice: Reflecting on Sport Heroes, National Identity, and Crisis in Canada," Jackson and Ponic (2001) note that having beaten U.S. sprinter Carl Lewis's world record at the World Championships in Rome, it was Johnson's record-setting performance at the Seoul Olympics that established him as a Canadian hero and international superstar. They argue that the national and international significance of the race had to do with a combination of the 100 metre sprint being the premier event of the Olympics, that Johnson was the first Canadian to win a medal in this event since Percy Williams, that people had never before witnessed such extraordinary performance and that Johnson's victory was symbolic of the "prevailing Canadian anxiety in anticipation of its post-free-trade agreement future" (51). In the aftermath of Johnson's unfortunate exit from competition, which saw him, in media reports, go from Canadian to Jamaican Canadian to Jamaican in a matter of days, Black athletes and Jamaicans in particular, according to Jackson and Ponic, "lived under a microscope" (56), causing some, like Bailey, to "deliberately and strategically proclaim a dual identity as both Canadian and Jamaican" (56).

Although maybe not in a spectacular fashion by today's standards, Philip "Phil" Granville competed in equally exciting events of his day. At a time when endurance events were all the rage Granville burst onto the scene in the 10 kilometre race walk, representing Canada in the 1924 Olympics in Paris (Sports Reference 2012). A Jamaican immigrant residing in Hamilton, Ontario, Granville, in the absence of complete historical records, may have been the first Canadian athlete of Jamaican descent to represent Canada at the Olympics. Four years later Granville took part in the 1928 Footrace Across America. "The Bunion Derby," as it was also called, was a grueling eighty-four-day 3,400 mile endurance event from Los Angeles to New York City (Williams 2007). Enduring harsh environmental conditions and even harsher treatment from spectators throughout the racist American south, Granville outlasted most of the fifty-five men remaining from the 199 who lined up at the starting line, capturing third place and a $5000 purse.

Chart 13.1 shows an increase in track and field participation in the 1970s and 1980s, which suggests that this was a watershed period (although not necessarily for other sports). The reasons for this may be political action by sports people in support of human rights, evidenced by the Black Power salute by American sprinters John Carlos and Tommie Smith on the podium at the 1968 Olympic Games in Mexico City and boycotts of Apartheid South African sport teams. And, as mentioned earlier, changes to immigration policies allowed parents who had come to Canada to work years earlier to send for their children (see Angella Taylor Issajenko's book *Running Risks*).

There may also be something to the accessibility and measure of possibility for athletes that makes track and field so appealing for those experiencing discrimination. The sport requires little equipment, and it is thus a relatively inexpensive activity, a plus for newly immigrated and working-class families. Also, in track and field, measurements of distance and time are difficult to falsify. With many team sports, where selection is based on subjective opinion, it was easier to dismiss great non-White players or offer them less than their White counterparts. (Herb Carnegie comes to mind as an example; see his book *A Fly in a Pail of Milk*, 1997). With advancements in timing technology taking place all the time and the desire of competitors to not only race against but beat the best, Black people who were discriminated against in the 1980s are now more likely to participate on a playing field where a winning performance is more difficult to deny.

Hockey

What some might consider an oddity at first, there is nothing aberrant about the significant contributions of Canadians of Jamaican descent to hockey. The National Library of Canada's website describes ice hockey as "Canada's game." Roche Carrier (2003) writes: "Hockey is also the history of Canadians. The game reflects the reality of Canada in its evolution, ambitions, character, tensions and partnerships." Within this context, the presence of Jamaican Canadians at the highest levels has been at best limited, especially in comparison with other sports such as track and field. In hockey's early days non-Whites were kept on the sidelines, at least as far as competing against Whites was concerned. Early regulations concerning amateurs denied non-Whites the opportunities of competing in mainstream sport activities with or against Whites. This did not prevent Blacks in Canada's Atlantic region from organizing their own leagues, which thrived between 1895 and 1928. Some of the players in these leagues were descendants of the Maroons, the first Jamaicans to settle in Canada (Frosty and Frosty 2008). Gradually, access to hockey for African Canadians improved to the point where today it is no longer rare to see Blacks playing hockey at the highest levels. We can credit Herb Carnegie, the son of Jamaican immigrants, for making some of this possible. Carnegie is well known in some communities as the first Canadian of Jamaican descent to play ice hockey at a professional level in Canada. He played in the Quebec Provincial League on a line with his brother Ossie and with Manny McIntyre. Carnegie earned the title of most valuable player in three consecutive years (1947–49), playing alongside John Béliveau, who went on to become a hockey legend while playing for the Montréal Canadiens. Carnegie refused to sign with the New York Rangers, who offered him a contract that would have required him to take a pay cut, which he was not prepared to do. After his retirement from playing hockey, Carnegie, who has yet to be inducted into the Hockey Hall of Fame, despite the acclamations and calls by his contemporaries who have received the honour, founded Future Aces, one of the first hockey schools in Canada.[7] He later became a golfer, winning several Canadian seniors golf titles.

Carnegie paved the way for Black hockey players like Willie O'Ree to become the first Black player in the National Hockey League, and these days it is not uncommon to see Black players — some of Jamaican descent — take to the ice in the NHL or play on Canada's national teams. Many of those who now play are second- and third-generation Jamaican Canadians, like the Stewart brothers, Chris and Anthony, who have represented Canada on the world stage and now play in the pros. But these brothers' rise to the NHL was not without its challenges. Growing up in Scarborough, Ontario, in a family that wasn't always able to afford expensive hockey equipment (Rosen 2009) and transportation to and from the arena, the brothers were assisted by the kindness and friendship of another hockey family (Featherstone 2010). It is possible that we could be seeing more African-Canadian youth of Caribbean descent playing hockey were it not for racism and discrimination (we still hear about racial slurs [Richards 2012] and bananas peels being thrown on the ice [Canadian Press 2011]), which contribute to the alienation of many racialized youth, who experience similar racism in the minor and novice leagues (Allen 2010; CBC News 2011). P.K. Subban is one rising star making waves in the NHL. A skilled defenceman, Subban helped Canada win a gold medal at the 2008 and 2009 World Junior Hockey Championships while working his way up from the minors. Now at the age of twenty-two, he is a solid contributor for the Montréal Canadiens, even making it into the history books by becoming their first rookie defenceman to register a hat trick (Montréal Canadiens 2012). And with younger brothers Malcolm and Jordan catching the eyes of pro scouts, they may not be far off from joining P.K. in the NHL.

Cricket

Cricket is both a popular sport in Jamaica and one which, as mentioned earlier, has brought the island much acclaim. Originally a game the British used as a colonizing tool to "civilize" indigenous populations, countries like Jamaica have used cricket to beat the colonialists on the sporting field. One great cricketer featured in Chart 13.1 is Franklyn Anthony Dennis. Coming from Kingston in the early 1970s and having played cricket growing up in Jamaica, through the sport Dennis was able to make an impact in Toronto, where he settled. He is perhaps best known for two impressive performances for Canada. In 1975, his batting skills enabled his Eastern Canada team to defeat the then powerhouse Australian team, with Dennis scoring fifty-seven in the five-wicket victory (Boller 2012; Bolter 2002; ESPN cricinfo 2012a). Later, in 1979, Canada achieved a berth in the World Cricket Championships, where Dennis made quite a showing against another powerhouse, England, scoring twenty-one runs — almost half of Canada's forty-five all out (Waring 1975). Since then Dennis has stayed involved in cricket and coached at the local, provincial and national levels while still participating in cricket recreationally (Toronto and District Cricket Association 2002).

Part of the legacy of Jamaican Canadian and other Caribbean athletes is the transportation of the sport with them to Canada. And while the sport wanes in popularity for future diaspora generations in favour of other sports like athletics and basketball, a shorter version of cricket, called Twenty20, may help encourage the participation of future generations in Canada for years to come.

Jockeying

With the dominance of Black Jamaican Canadian women and men in Canadian sports, we often forget about the ethnic diversity of Jamaicans. Possibly not so well known by many people other than Chinese Jamaicans is the contribution of George Joseph HoSang to jockeying in both Jamaica and Canada. Immigrating to Canada in 1976, HoSang continued the streak of successes he started in Jamaica, winning the 1979 and 1981 jockeys championships and finishing his career in 1998 with nearly 1400 wins (*Jamaica Gleaner* 2002). In 2002, he was awarded the None Such Award (for lifetime achievement in racing) for his many accomplishments as a jockey, competing for both Canada and Jamaica, with many considering him "legendary" (*Jamaica Gleaner* 2002).

Boxing

Boxing has a very long history that dates back to before the birth of Christ and was part of the ancient Olympic games (Zeigler 1998; Boddy 2008). Boxing's rules, popularity and legality fluctuated until the mid-1920s, when it became a mainstream spectator sport in the United States and elsewhere (Boddy 2008). In *Race, Sport, and Politics: The Sporting Black Diaspora,* Ben Carrington (2010) argues that boxing is the most dramatic example of how sport became a mechanism through which, for some people, racism is lived. The defining moment occurred in 1908, when American Jack Johnson became the first Black to win the World Heavyweight boxing title by defeating Canadian Tommy Burns. Burns himself was the first White boxer to agree to fight a Black opponent for the world title and thus break the colour line established by his predecessors. Johnson's defeat of Burns challenged the then belief that Blacks lacked stamina and endurance and were generally inferior to Whites. The door that Burns opened to boxing allowed the careers of athletes like Chris Johnson, Howard Grant and Lennox Lewis, who won gold at Commonwealth and Olympic Games.

Field Hockey

While not as popular as other sports, field hockey, nevertheless, has a small and dedicated following in Canada and has its share of athletes who have represented Canada in international games. In fact, Lisa Lyn and Sandra Levy played on the Canadian Olympic women's field hockey team in the 1980s to the early 1990s. The sport, which was introduced to colonial Canada by the British Army in the nineteenth century and has had a low profile over the years, has benefitted from the consistent contributions, support and performance of athletes from its immigrant communities.

Netball

While not as widely known or as popular in Canada as basketball (its relative), netball travelled to Canada from the Caribbean, including Jamaica, where it is still quite popular. This game with colonial roots has produced solid players, like Sharon Butler. Having immigrated to Canada in the 1980s, Butler played basketball at the University of Toronto under the tutelage of storied coach Michele Belanger. While growing up in Jamaica, Butler had also played netball, and in 2007 she represented the Canadian National Netball Team. She even came out of retirement in 2009 to assist a rising Canadian team at the Nations Cup in Singapore in an attempt to qualify for the 2011 World Netball Championships (Fanfair 2009). Today, Butler coaches the women's basketball team at George Brown College in Toronto and has a strong record as a coach. She brought home the East Division Coach of the Year Award for the 1996–1997 season, in 2009–10 led the George Brown College Huskies women's basketball team to an East Division Championship with a 15–1 record (George Brown College Huskies 2011) and most recently, guided the women's Huskies team to a bronze medal in the Ontario College Athletic Association championships (George Brown College Huskies 2011a).

Basketball

One would think that with stereotypes of Black people being good at basketball, we would see more basketball players listed in the chart. Unfortunately, the archivists of Canadian basketball history, from James Naismith to Jamal Magloire, have not kept the best records so it is difficult to say how many more players there have been. But we know that in recent times Tristan Thompson is making history. The highest ranked Canadian-born draft pick to the NBA since 1953,[8] Thompson was selected fourth in 2011 (Thompson 2011). He grew up with his Jamaican-born mother in Brampton, Ontario, before taking his talent south to the United States, where he became a McDonald's All-American, the fifth Canadian player to ever receive the honour (QHoops. net 2011). During high school, Thompson helped Canada to a bronze medal at the 2008 International Basketball Federation (FIBA), America's U18 Championship for men. After a one-year stint with the University of Texas Longhorns, Thompson has been showing his skills and talent with the Cleveland Cavaliers. At only twenty-one, he is already paving the way and modelling possibilities for the next generation of Jamaican Canadian ballers in the NBA, working hard and being rewarded with the consistent minutes — even being selected for the Rising Stars Challenge at the 2012 NBA All-Star Weekend (National Basketball Association 2012).

With Thompson, the Clarke family and others like Summer Olympians Michael Meeks and Tony Simms helping to pave the way, the future of

Jamaican Canadians in the NBA looks bright. The Clarke family's involvement in the sport is one of note. Norman Clarke grew up in Toronto with parents who emigrated from Jamaica. It is reported that they worked hard to provide for Norman and his siblings — instilling in Norman a work ethic that fostered his desire to get an education and therefore make a better life for his children. Norman played basketball in the National Collegiate Athletic Association (NCAA) for St. Bonaventure University, where he was on a scholarship. He went on to captain the team (Lankhof 2010). Norman also represented Canada in the 1988 Olympics in Seoul, which he cites as his greatest thrill. Today, he coaches at his old high school, Oakwood Collegiate in Toronto (NorthPoleHoops.com 2012). He helps to coach local teams that participate in the Ontario Basketball Association and assists Basketball Canada in developing promising basketball players. Norman's sons, Julian and Brody, have bright basketball futures. Julian has an athletic scholarship and is now at Santa Clara University. In his senior year he managed a 91.6 percent average and led his high school team to the provincial championship (Lankhof 2010). He also had the honour of representing Canada at the FIBA U19 Championships in 2011 (International Basketball Federation 2011). Little brother Brody, while only in grade eleven (Durack 2011), helped Canada's Cadet Men's Basketball Team to a bronze medal in the 2011 FIBAAmericas Basketball Championship (Basketball Canada 2012).

Bobsleigh/Bobsled

Contrary to the stereotypes that Black people are afraid of cold and ice, many athletes who make the move to bobsleigh (commonly from athletics or football) have demonstrated that they have the tools to succeed.[9] Two Browns (no relation) who played a big role in Canada's success at the 2010 Winter Olympic Games are perfect examples. A multi-medal winner at both the World Championships and Olympic Games, Lascelles Brown helped propel Canada towards a bronze medal and its goal to "Own the Podium" at the Vancouver Olympics. Born in May Pen, Jamaica (Olympic.ca 2012), Brown competed for the Jamaican bobsled team and set the Jamaican push-start record in 2002 (Bobsleigh Canada 2012) before emigrating to Canada in 2005 to compete in bobsleigh. Amid some controversy,[10] Brown received his citizenship only two weeks before the 2006 Turin Olympics, allowing him to compete for Canada. A world-class brakeman, Brown's two-man bobsleigh team also won a silver medal at the 2006 Winter Olympics.

Unlike Lascelles, Shelley-Ann Brown had no prior bobsleigh experience before first competing for Canada in 2007, but her prowess in track and field made her a fit for the sport. Born in Scarborough, Ontario, to Jamaican parents (Kennedy 2010), Shelley-Ann competed for the University of Nebraska, garnering All-American Honours in the hurdles. The explosiveness, power and speed she possessed, necessary for sprints, translated well to bobsleigh, which requires equal measure of these abilities. She too blasted her sled to the podium at the Olympics in Vancouver, finishing with a silver medal behind fellow Canadian teammates.

Players and Builders

This exercise has been a revealing and interesting one for us. While we were of the opinion that athletes of Jamaican descent were well represented in Canadian sports — particularly at the national and international levels — we were not sure exactly what we would find. Indeed, the complied list is impressive, showing the depth and breadth of Jamaican Canadians' involvement in sports and many great athletes — some of whom we had not heard of. As we watch and celebrate today's players, we cannot forget the foundational athletes or builders who weathered the challenges of racism, xenophobia and discrimination to establish the legacy we have today. Herb Carnegie started the Flying Aces, giving many the opportunities to participate in and learn the fundamentals of sport, in turn allowing them to become productive and engaged citizens. Sharon Butler's sentiments, which appear on the George Brown College Huskies' website, "I don't only coach for basketball, I coach for life"(George Brown College Huskies 2011), are likely shared by many of the athletes who have turned to coaching to pass on their expertise to the next generation. Paul C. Jerrard went on to coach in the NHL after a career in the minors and a five-game stint in the NHL (Sherrington 2011). Molly Killingbeck now helps Athletics Canada develop sprinters across the country using her experience from her successful track and field career, in which she won silver with Canada's women 4x400 metre relay team at the 1984 Olympic Games (Athletics Canada 2012). Charmaine Crooks, once a successful 400 and 800 metre runner for Canada is now a key part of the Canadian Olympic Committee, which continues to push for sporting excellence in Canada (Charmaine Crooks.com 2012)

As we look forward to the many other athletes of Jamaican descent who will mesmerize us with their speed, athletic talent and record-breaking performances, we need to remember the racist context in which they will be doing so. Recent events in Toronto and Montreal remind us that racism remains an issue with which Blacks generally have to contend, and in the Canadian imagination, Blackness is often conflated with or gets translated to mean and hence represented as Jamaican. Take, for instance, racist Halloween costumes: in 2009 University of Toronto students donned black faces to imitate the Jamaican bobsled team from the popular Disney movie *Cool Runnings*. And in 2011, with reference to an athletic themed event, students of the Université de Montréal affiliated École des Hautes Études commerciales de Montréal (HEC Montreal), covered in blackface paint, dressed up as Jamaican track athletes (supposedly referencing Usain Bolt) and carried stuffed monkeys saying things like, "Smoke more weed"(CBC News 2011a). On the one hand, these racist acts and stereotyping suggest that the presence and athletic performances of Jamaicans are not going unnoticed. On the other hand, they indicate how racism — certainly not based on benign ignorance — has historically been used and continues to be used to undermine the efficacy of Jamaican's contributions to sports nationally and internationally. We sincerely hope that this sampling of the contributions of Jamaica Canadians to Canada's sporting successes and reputation helps to bring some awareness.

Notes

1. We use the term Jamaican Canadians for convenience to refer to individuals of Jamaican descent. This is not to suggest that everyone we discuss identify themselves as Jamaican Canadians or might recognize their Jamaican heritage. Nevertheless, we refer to them because the records show that they, their parents or grandparents were born in Jamaica. Further, we are conscious of the ethnic, racial, class and generational (i.e., first-, second-plus generation) diversity of the Jamaican Canadian population, so to the extent that we have a significant representation of Jamaicans of African origin, is representative of what the data show and likely of the individuals who, through sports, negotiated, settled and established themselves as Canadians.
2. The challenges in developing this list may speak to the power imbalances in Canadian sporting history. Who writes the history books? Who decides what is important and what is not? And what gets cast to the margins in the process?
3. Lerone Clarke was the Commonwealth Games champion, Odean Skeen won the Youth Olympic Games, Dexter Lee won the World Youth Championships, and Usain Bolt held the champion title for both the IAAF World Championships and the Olympic Games.
4. Bailey still holds the Canadian National Record along with then teammate Bruny Surin.
5. Bruny Surin is Haitian-Canadian <http://www.olympic.ca/en/athletes/bruny-surin/>.
6. Glenory Gilbert is Trinidadian-Canadian <http://www.olympic.ca/en/athletes/glenroy-gilbert/>.
7. Carnegie's death on March 9, 2012, brought forth an outpouring of tributes from Canadian and American press but not without some quiet controversy. The *Toronto Star* and others published several retrospectives on the career of this Canadian legend, and most had an obituary ready for the Monday paper following his death on the Saturday. As sociology of sport scholar Mary Louise Adams noted in an email to the North American Society for the Sociology of Sport, list-serv newspapers often prepare obituaries in advance for individuals considered of importance. The *Globe and Mail*, Canada's so-called national newspaper, only had a notice of his death, saying that an article would be forthcoming. As Adams notes, this misstep, in light of even the *New York Times* writing an article, "tells us a lot about who and what makes up the mythologies around Canada's 'national' game."

8. Bob Houbregs was drafted third overall by the Milwaukee Hawks in 1953 (Eskenazi 2011).
9. The first Jamaican bobsled team debuted at the 1988 Calgary Olympics and became immortalized in the Disney produced movie *Cool Runnings*, which is loosely based on Jamaica's first crack at the sport.
10. Then teammate Pierre Leuders expressed frustration in not knowing if Brown would be eligible to compete. And, not surprisingly, Jamaican officials were upset with Brown leaving to compete for Canada and are quoted as suggesting some type of compensation be doled out for the time and resources spent developing him (CBC Sports Online 2006). This instance is emblematic of the "brawn drain" that countries like Canada are able to perform on less economically wealthy countries. It is also interesting to note for whom and under what circumstances the immigration process is expedited.

References

Abdel-Shehid, G. 2005. *Who Da Man? Black Masculinities and Sporting Cultures*. Toronto: Canadian Scholars' Press.

Allen, K. 2010. "Hockey Coach Faces Ban for Opposing Racial Slur." At <http://www.thestar.com/news/article/900955--hockey-coach-faces-ban-for-opposing-racial-slur>.

Athletics Canada. 2012. "Coach Profiles." At <http://athletics.ca/page.asp?id=128>.

Basketball Canada. 2012. "Senior Team Alumnus: Norm Clarke, Keep It in the Family." At <http://www.basketball.ca/senior-national-team-alumnus-norm-clarke-keep-it-in-the-family-p148922>.

Bobsleigh Canada. 2012. "Lascelles Brown." At <http://www.bobsleigh.ca/AthleteBio.aspx?BiosID=KCf/hPAKpJg=>.

Boddy, K. 2008. *Boxing, a Cultural History*. London: Reaktion.

Boller, K. 2012. "The History of Cricket Canada." At <http://gocricketgocanada.com/history>.

Bolter, K.E. 2002. "A Batsman for Big Occasions." At <http://www.cricketstar.net/tdca/index.jsp?page_id=DENNIS2>.

Canadian Press. 2011. "Man Charged in Banana-Throwing Incident at NHL Game." At <http://www.thestar.com/sports/hockey/nhl/article/1061091--man-charged-in-banana-throwing-incident-at-nhl-game>.

Carnegie, H., and R. Payne. 1997. *A Fly in a Pail of Milk: The Herb Carnegie Story*. Oakville, ON; Buffalo: Mosaic Press.

Carrier, R. 2003. "Backcheck: A Hockey Retrospective." At <http://www.collectionscanada.gc.ca/hockey/index-e.html>.

Carrington, B. 2010. *Race, Sport, and Politics: The Sporting Black Diaspora*. Thousand Oaks, CA: Sage.

CBC News. 2011. "Racist Slur Directed at Minor Hockey Player." At <http://www.cbc.ca/news/canada/ottawa/story/2011/09/30/ottawa-racism-minor-hockey-player.html>.

___. 2011a. "Montreal University Students Dawn Blackface." At <http://www.cbc.ca/news/canada/montreal/story/2011/09/15/blackface-universite-montreal.html>.

cbc Sports Online. 2006. "Bobsledder to Get Canadian Citizenship, Say Sources." January 20. At <http://www.cbc.ca/news/canada/story/2006/01/20/

bobsledder-citizenship060120.html>.

Charmaine Crooks.com. 2012. "Biography." At <http://www.charmainecrooks. com/bio.html>.

Durack, S. 2011. "Oakwood Players Chip in at FIBA Americas." At <http://www. insidetoronto.com/sports/article/1036125--oakwood-players-chip-in-at-fiba-americas>.

Eskenazi, D. 2011. "Wayback Machine: Bob Houbregs and the '53 Final Four." At <http://sportspressnw.com/2011/03/wayback-machine-bob-houbregs-the-53-final-four/>.

ESPN cricinfo. 2012. "West Indies/Players/Michael Holding." At <http://www. espncricinfo.com/westindies/content/player/52063.html>.

___. 2012a. "Canada/Players/Franklyn Dennis." At <http://www.espncricinfo. com/canada/content/player/23768.html>.

Faculty of Physical Education & Health. 2010. "There Can Only Be One? The Natural Black Athlete Student?" Panel Discussion. University of Toronto, February 25.

Fanfair, R. 2009. "Netball on the Move in Canada." At <http://archive.sharenews. com/sports/2009/07/01/netball-move-canada>.

Featherstone, B. 2010. "From Scaborough to Stardom." At <http://www.torontoob-server.ca/2010/11/24/from-scarborough-to-stardom/>.

Frosty, G.R., and D. Frosty. 2008. *Black Ice: The Lost History of the Colored Hockey League of the Maritimes, 1895–1925.* Halifax, NS: Nimbus Publishing.

Garcia-Guereta, N., and M. Galofré. 2009. *Why Do Jamaicans Run So Fast?* Nice Time Productions.

George Brown College Huskies. 2011. "Coaching Staff." At <http://athletics. georgebrown.ca/sports_index.asp?info=w_basketball_coaches>.

___. 2011a. At <http://athletics.georgebrown.ca/news_index.asp?info=womens_ basketball_medals>.

Griggs, G. 2006. "Calypso to Collapso: The Decline of the West Indies as a Cricketing Super Power." *Journal of Sport & Social Issues* 30 (3).

International Basketball Federation. 2011. "Group Standings." At <http://www. fiba.com/pages/eng/fe/11/fu19m/p/group-standing.html>.

Issajenko, A., M. O'Malley, and K. O'Reilly. 1990. *Running Risks.* Toronto: Macmillan of Canada.

Jackson, S.J., and P. Ponic. 2001. "Pride and Prejudice: Reflecting on Sport Heroes, National Identity, and Crisis in Canada." *Culture, Sport, Society* 4, 2 (Summer).

Jamaica Gleaner. 2002. "HoSang ges None Such Award." At <http://jamaica-gleaner. com/gleaner/20020302/sports/sports3.html>.

Kennedy, B. 2010. "Scarborough School Shares in Silver Spotlight." *Toronto Star,* February 25. At <http://www.thestar.com/mobile/gta/article/771620>.

Lankhof, B. 2010. "The Clarkes Reach for the Top." At <http://www.torontosun. com/sports/columnists/bill_lankhof/2010/03/30/13416941.html>.

Montreal Canadiens. 2012. "P.K. Subban." At <http://canadiens.nhl.com/club/ player.htm?id=8474056&view=bio>.

National Basketball Association. 2012. "Griffin, Irving, Rubio Headline Rising Stars Roster Pool." At <http://www.nba.com/2012/allstar/2012/02/08/shooting-stars-roster-pool/index.html>.

NorthPoleHoops.com. 2012. "Oakwood, Scouting Report and Game Analysis." At

<http://northpolehoops.com/schools/oakwood/>.

Olympic.ca. 2012. "Lascelles Brown." At <http://www.olympic.ca/en/athletes/lascelles-brown/>.

QHoops.net. 2011. "Birch, Chery, Osse on McDonald's List." At <http://www.qhoops.net/articles/article.jsp?aId=1289>.

Reid, P. 2011. "Todd Completes Perfect 100m Cycle for Ja." At <http://www.jamaicaobserver.com/sports/Todd-completes-perfect-100m-cycle-for-Ja_9162704>.

Richards, G. 2012. "Panthers' Barch Suspended One Game for Comment to Subban." At <http://www.thestar.com/sports/hockey/nhl/article/1111278--panthers-barch-suspended-one-game-for-comment-to-subban>.

Riley, S. 2010. *Fire in Babylon.* WIB Productions.

Rosen, D, 2009. "Stewart Showing He Belongs in Colorado." At <http://www.nhl.com/ice/news.htm?id=411334>.

Sherrington, K. 2011. "Heika: Stars' Jerrard Downplays Unique NHL Status as Black Coach." At <http://www.dallasnews.com/sports/20110723-heika-stars_jerrard-downplays-unique-nhl-status-as-black-coach.ece>.

SI.com. 2008. "Medal Tracker: Total Medals by Nation." At <http://sportsillus-trated.cnn.com/olympics/2008/medals/tracker/>.

Sports Reference. 2012. "Phil Granville." At <http://www.sports-reference.com/olympics/athletes/gr/phil-granville-1.html>.

Thompson, A. 2011. "How Did GTA Star Tristan Thompson Get to the NBA? Ask Mom." At <http://www.thestar.com/sports/basketball/nba/article/1014995--how-did-gta-star-tristan-thompson-get-to-the-nba-ask-mom>.

Toronto and District Cricket Association. 2002. "Franklyn Anthony Dennis." At <http://www.cricketstar.net/tdca/index.jsp?page_id=DENNIS>.

Waring, E. 1975. "Boundary Belter Dennis Leads Canadians to Surprise Victory Over Aussie Cup XI". At <http://www.cricketstar.net/tdca/index.jsp?page_id=DENNIS1>.

Williams, G. 2007. *C.C. Pyle's Amazing Foot Race: The True Story of the 1928 Coast-to-Coast Run Across America.* Emmaus, PA: Rodale Books.

Zeigler, E.F. 1988. *History of Physical Education and Sport.* Champaign: Stipes Publishing Company.

14. ALWAYS HAVE TO BE TWICE AS GOOD

Reflections of an Athlete, Coach and Academic

Robert Pitter

I was born in Canada to Jamaican-born parents, who separated when I was very young. I was mostly raised by my mother, who came to Canada around 1955 either as part of the West Indian Domestic Scheme, initiated by the government in 1955, or a similar strategy for Caribbean nurses of "exceptional merit" (Calliste 1993: 91). To be eligible for the Domestic Scheme, women had to

> be between 18-35, single, have at least a grade 8 education, and be able to pass the medical examination. Final applicants [were] interviewed by a team of Canadian immigration officials who visit[ed] the islands once a year specifically for this purpose. On arrival in Canada, the women [were] granted landed immigrant status and [were] placed in a home for a period of one year. (Henry 1968: 83)

Writing about the experience of the sixty-one women who participated in her study in 1968, Henry noted the majority "expressed disappointment in the Canadian people with whom they came in contact, finding them unfriendly, ignorant and prejudiced" (86). I am confident my mother shared that disappointment.

My mother must have been one of the very first women to immigrate to Canada from Jamaica under these schemes. She first worked as a practical nurse, caring for newborns and training their mothers, and later she spent some time working in a number of Toronto hospitals. My father came to Canada to attend school. He went to the agricultural college in Guelph, which would later become the University of Guelph.

Because my mother worked as a practical nurse who often stayed with her clients, I was boarded out from age four to eight. At first I stayed in the home of a woman I remember as "Nurse," whom I just recently learned is the mother of a celebrated Jamaican-born Canadian civil rights leader. I left Nurse at the age of six and spent the next two years with a White couple and their two children, who were younger than me. During these years I would only see my mother on the occasional weekend or during the summer holidays for a couple weeks.

My mother came to Canada seeking a better life with the understanding she would integrate into the prevailing Canadian culture if she wished to stay. She also had little love for popular Jamaican culture and customs. She disliked Jamaican Patois, and she scolded me when my behaviour reminded her of people back in Jamaica. In keeping with her commitment to integration, my mother always encouraged me to "fit in" and adopt what I interpreted to be a Canadian way of life. In this she succeeded, for more than one person has told me I am the most Canadian person they have ever met.

I remember being the only Black person in the many communities I grew up in and in the schools I attended. I went to five different elementary schools. This was not easy, considering how I was often bullied during those years. I remember that in grade four on the first day of school in North York's west end I heard the word "nigger" for the first time. Soon after, on my way home, I was stalked and attacked by other students, who thought I deserved a beating. But there was also the time when one of my neighbours, a boy around my age, took me aside and taught me the rules of hockey, baseball and football so that I could play with the other kids in the field behind the apartment building where we lived. I fell in love with ball hockey and begged my mother to allow me to play organized ice hockey like my peers did. My father sent me the money I needed to purchase the required equipment.

When I reached junior high school, I realized that athletic prowess (physical capital) rather than intellectual prowess (cultural capital) was the better form of capital to exert if I wanted to be accepted by my peers. I was horrible at sports when I first began playing. I was constantly ridiculed and demeaned for my lack of skill, and of course, I was always picked last when it came to forming sides. However, by the time of puberty, when I reached junior high, I began to be competitive in the running games and sports we played, and as a result I felt more respected. I tried out for track and field, basketball and football and was chosen to represent my junior high school as a member of its all-star football team, which was made up of top players from the school's intramural football league.

When I completed junior high school, my family moved from North York to Etobicoke, where I attended a brand-new high school. This was a completely different experience. The most significant difference was that my high school was much larger, with about 1,500 students — almost twice the size of my junior high — and for the first time in my life, I was not the only Black kid in the school. There were about twenty other Blacks in the school throughout grades nine to thirteen. I got to know most of them and now had friends whose skin was the same colour as mine. I believe most of the Black students at my high school were not born in Canada — some had moved directly to Canada from Jamaica, and others had come to Canada via England. So we were a mixture of Jamaican-born, Canadian-born and British-born Blacks at the school. Most of these Black friends had parents who were originally from Jamaica. Not all of the Black students participated in sports, but the majority of the males did. I don't have any memory of the girls doing sports.

Moving into a new community is always an opportunity to establish a new identity. And I took advantage of this at my new high school. No one there knew of my early failures in sport, and I felt immediately accepted as a skilled member of the athletic community. I was encouraged to participate in several sports at my high school and I did. In grade ten, I played basketball at the bantam and midget levels, and I qualified for the Ontario Federation of Secondary School Athletics (OFSSA) track and field championships in the high jump. I had to give up playing my favourite sport, hockey, when I grew out of the equipment. It was just too expensive for my mother to replace. By the time I reached high school, my mother was unemployed because of health problems and lived on a combination of social assistance and the per diem she received for looking after at least four foster children at a time.

I seemed to fit in better at my high school than I had at any of the schools I attended previously. I am not exactly sure why. Apart from my new athletic celebrity, it might also have been due in part to the fact that the people at the school had already had experiences with people of colour and were comfortable and did not feel threatened by us. But I can say with some confidence that had it not been for my involvement in sport, my circle of friends and acquaintances at the school would likely have been smaller.

In grade eleven, I quit basketball to focus on track and field since my initial hope was to become a top class 400 metre runner. I appreciated the challenge of competing head-to-head on the track more than the turn taking that took place in the field events. I especially relished the relay races, particularly the 4x400 metre event. It was more of a shared experience.

As part of the mid-1970s through 1990s track and field community, I watched and admired Jamaican Canadian athletes such as Yvonne Saunders, Hugh Fraser and Marvin Nash, who represented Canada in the 1976 Olympic Games in Montreal. They would be followed by other Jamaican notables, including Ben Johnson, Angela Taylor and many others. I also remember hearing debates about whether their successes were due to being Black — suggesting some kind of genetic advantage. I always questioned these presumptions. I was Black but was not nearly as fast as the top sprinters in this group despite my efforts to improve my speed.

I do not remember early on competing against very many Black athletes in high jump. Certainly the proportion of Black high jumpers was much smaller than the proportion of Blacks in the more popular sprint events — especially the 100 metre and the 200 metre. In fact, I can only remember competing against a few Blacks in high jump. It was almost entirely a White person's event, despite the adage that "White folks can't jump." The Blacks that I did compete against in high school did not compete beyond high school, although that eventually changed.

I turned to high jump mainly because the harder I tried to improve my performance in the 400 metre event, the more I improved my performance in the high jump. I won two titles at the OFSSA championships in grade eleven and twelve, setting records both years. In grade thirteen, my graduating year, I was elected president of the Boys Athletic Council — the first non-White to take that position at my school. The person who followed after me was another Black student.

I saw my involvement in sport as a way to develop social capital. My hope was that I could open doors to many opportunities through sport that I would not or might not otherwise have. And I believe that my participation in sport was crucial for that. Had I not participated in sport, I doubt that I would have been admitted to the University of Toronto after I graduated from high school with mediocre grades. It was my experience as a student athlete at university that ultimately led me to become the academic I am today. In addition to the time I spent competing and winning medals at provincial, national and international competitions while at the University of Toronto, I also spent time visiting schools doing track clinics with my teammates and coaching the women's basketball and ice hockey teams in my residence.

I think my approach to sports was different and perhaps a little bit more realistic than that of many of my Black friends of that time, most of whom were of Jamaican descent. I had one friend who believed that sport was his one and only way to achieve success. He was so dedicated to a dream that equated success with sport that he believed if he did not become a player in the Canadian Football League, his life would only be seen as a failure. I am not sure exactly where this perception came from. But I do remember that at the time, there seemed to be a similar expectation of me –that I should be looking for success in, and only through, sport. I think this largely came from my mother's non-Jamaican White friends and perhaps some of my schoolmates and their parents.

After graduating from university, I thought seriously about continuing my involvement in sport as a coach but felt there really was no room for another high jump coach in the Toronto area. There were only two major clubs with high jump coaches, and both were very successful. I was also interested in attending graduate school and thought about the possibilities of becoming a sport administrator or an academic. I continued to pursue my goal of becoming a member of Canada's national team after leaving Toronto and coached myself. A few months after arriving at the University of Alberta for graduate studies in the field of physical education and sport studies, I was approached by a former Ontario high jumper to join her in forming a track and field club. We founded the Arctic Coast Athletics Club, which lasted for about three very successful years. I coached two women to gold medals in national championships, one in high jump and the other in long jump.

My new Ontario friend, Laura, became a White ally, an essential conduit through whom my ideas would be delivered for others to accept. Together, we coached and ran our club, organized two national championships and challenged the provincial association to better serve its members. I eventually served as the association's vice-president and a Canada Games coach. Few of these things would have been possible without Laura's endorsement or sponsorship.

I always felt that some of the athletes I coached — like some of the many sport administrators I worked with– had doubts about my qualifications to be a coach and that those doubts were largely based on the colour of my skin. But I have no way to know for sure. During one fall training season in Edmonton, I hosted a successful German jumps coach. I offered to take him to the Rocky Mountains in exchange for him conducting a clinic with the athletes I was coaching. I was a little bewildered when, after the session, several athletes relayed their astonishment that this foreign expert used the same techniques I had been using with them for years. I wondered if some of these individuals could not see beyond the colour of my skin to the credentials I had earned, such as my degree in physical education, the outstanding mentors I'd had as an athlete (including the foreign coach), my proven skills in the area of learning and teaching new skills, and my outstanding performance as a graduate student. I felt that sometimes I had to be twice as good as my White counterparts in order to receive the same recognition from many athletes and some coaches.

After obtaining my PhD, I coached sporadically. During my six years of teaching sport management courses at the University of Memphis, I worked with the high jumpers on the women's track and field team for a year. Janeen Gooden won the indoor and outdoor conference titles that year, 1995. But when she was refused a larger scholarship, she left the team and so did I. Today, my time is devoted mainly to teaching courses that examine social and political issues related to sport at Acadia University, where I have been for twelve years. On occasions, I have coached kids at the local junior and senior high schools.

I have two sons. Both are fair skinned. Neither has an interest in competitive or high performance sport. I am happy about that. They can see sport as an end in itself rather than as a means to an end. This will make it much easier for them to flow in and out of sports as they grow up and eventually pursue their careers. I found the means-to-an-end motivation that underpinned my involvement as an athlete to be very stressful. I often felt powerless, kind of like an addict — it was never an easy decision to leave sport for other pursuits. In reality, "choosing" to pursue sport because you feel it's your only path to success really means you feel you have only one option. The truth is having only one choice means you don't have any choices. A person without options has very little power or opportunity to exercise choice. I want my sons to realize they have real options — they have better life chances than I did. I want them to discover and pursue their passions on their own terms.

References

Calliste, A. 1993. "Women of 'Exceptional Merit': Immigration of Caribbean Nurses to Canada." *Canadian Journal of Women and Law* 6.

Henry, F. 1968. "The West Indian Domestic Scheme in Canada." *Social and Economic Studies* 17, 1 (March) At <http://www.jstor.org/stable/27856309>.

15. THE ROLE OF THE CHURCH IN THE DIASPORA

Kenneth O. Hall

I wish to congratulate the organizers, especially the Consul General S. George Ramocan, Nigel Smith and other members of the planning committee, for organizing this conference, with its special focus on the leaders of the church. It is my considered view that the leaders have an un-paralleled opportunity to be involved in the relationship between Jamaica and its diaspora who live in Canada. The central theme of my presentation is that the churches have a unique opportunity to influence and to provide leadership for the Jamaican community in Canada as we continue the process of strengthening those bonds.

This conference is taking place at a strategic crossroads in the relationship between Jamaica and its diaspora as we prepare to celebrate the fiftieth anniversary of our independence. The Jamaican diaspora is defined as persons who migrated from their homeland as well as second- and third-generation persons born in the countries to which their parents migrated. The essential element for inclusion in this group is the maintenance of Jamaican identity, values and culture. These are the characteristics that have shaped the interaction between Jamaicans abroad and Jamaicans at home and give rise to the opportunities for the churches to play a significant role.

It is estimated that there are over 300,000 Jamaicans living in Canada, and according to Statistics Canada, the growth rate of that community is faster than that of the overall population. Unlike the diaspora communities in Great Britain and the United States, the vast majority of Jamaicans in Canada became residents in the past thirty years. Indeed, less than 2 percent of Jamaicans living in Canada arrived before 1961. Pivotal to today's discourse is that the large majority of Jamaican Canadians belong to religious denominations. Despite the important role of the churches in the diaspora it is noticeable that until very recently there were no significant roles played by them in the strengthening of the relationship between Jamaica and its diaspora. We are aware that in 2008, at the third diaspora conference, one of the workshops was devoted to the role of the church.

A network of church leaders has been established amongst the Diaspora.

It was established in recognition of the "potential of the Christian community to provide visionary, inspirational and positive contributions toward the moral and cultural renaissance of the nation." The significance of this initiative derives from the potential to elevate the work of the churches in local communities to that of leadership in the transformation, not only of the Diaspora, but of Jamaica itself.

The prospects of successfully engaging in the transformation of the local Diaspora communities and Jamaica, are greatly enhanced by the existence of close connections between the churches in Jamaica and those here. It is well known that the Diaspora community, through remittances, philanthropic contributions to schools and churches and the exchange of skills makes a significant impact on the quality of life for thousands of Jamaicans at home, yet the impact of those activities on building peace and development programs are often limited because of the specificity of the contributions and the absence of a mechanism to pool those resources and allocate them to have an enduring impact on the long-term development of the country. It is this absence of a framework to optimize the use of the resources that provides the churches with one of its greatest opportunities to have a strong impact on the future of Jamaica.

Put another way, given the characteristics of the community in Canada, with wide church membership, geographical dispersion and a strong desire to contribute to peace building and development, an initiative to provide leadership by the churches to mobilize the efforts of the Diaspora is desirable. What is needed is for the church leaders to recognize their unique position of influence to provide constructive intervention to improve the quality of life in local communities. They can become the defenders of the Jamaican population and the spokespersons for the unrepresented in addressing a range of issues that affect the local community. The churches have another unique characteristic which could be helpful. They are not susceptible to the political divisions that often characterize other community organizations.

How this enormous potential is utilized should be a central focus of this gathering. They can continue to address and be devoted to the needs of their local communities and their membership, or they can articulate a vision of upliftment and hope for Jamaicans at home and in the Diaspora and establish a network to harmonize these efforts to ensure sustainability and effectiveness.

In proposing a new mission for the churches in the Diaspora, account must be taken of the efforts being made by the government, private sector and academic institutions in Jamaica on the one hand, and the organizations among the Diaspora communities here in Canada to foster a new relationship over the past few years. The significance of the Diaspora to Jamaica has gradually been acknowledged. This is demonstrated in the increased role being played by remittances. It is estimated that remittance flows have reached US$1.9 billion in 2007, and even though there has been a decrease during the recession since 2008, those inflows have remained in the area of US$1.5–1.6 billion. To understand the importance of this to Jamaica, estimates of net receipts remaining in Jamaica were less than the total of Jamaica's top ten foreign exchange earners in 2005, namely bauxite/aluminum, tourism, coffee, sugar, rum, bananas, apparel, cocoa, pimento and yams.

In addition, the charitable initiatives of Jamaicans, including those in Canada, have provided tangible relief from the pressing social needs of the population. Numerous schools have been assisted, hospitals equipped and children's and senior citizen's homes refurbished. For many parents and children, the barrels of goods provided before schools reopen in September of each year and before Christmas are essential for maintaining a decent quality of life.

For the business sector the export of Jamaican products to the Diaspora has expanded to become a sizable part of their operations. Management of the remittances has also led to the creation of new businesses and significant expansion of some existing financial institutions. For our artistes and performers, the frequent staging of concerts in the Diaspora has emerged as an essential part of their income.

For these reasons the government of Jamaica in 2002 identified Diaspora relations as deserving of a ministerial portfolio. Through that ministry four conferences have been organized, beginning in 2004, with the support of the business community and the local universities. Institutions such as the Diaspora Foundation and the Diaspora Institute in Jamaica and the Jamaica Diaspora Canada Foundation have been established to foster this relationship.

The dialogue that was developed through these activities and the increased attention paid to the Diaspora have no doubt strengthened the relationship. Yet as Delano Franklyn, former Minister of Foreign Affairs with responsibility for Diaspora affairs concluded:

> The increased efforts of Jamaica, since 2002, to broaden the discourse with the Jamaica Diaspora have clearly proven that without the establishment of workable organizational linkages, the strengthening and deepening of the ties necessary to achieving a greater and more co-ordinated, mutually beneficial working relationship will not materialize.

It is the need for these workable organizational linkages that provides the strongest argument for involving the churches as essential ingredients in building a mutually beneficial relationship between Jamaica and the Diaspora. Few organizations in the Diaspora can match the depth of the churches in the community and the potential to mobilize the Diaspora to articulate its needs with conviction to the authorities here in Canada and at home in Jamaica. The opportunity to fill this void should not be missed at this critical time. The churches and their leaders should therefore see as a part of their mission the need to create new avenues for linking the Diaspora and Jamaica. Such a role is not without precedent as in times of crisis and disasters such as hurricanes, the churches have been called upon and have responded successfully to perform organizational functions. In 2007 for instance, after the hurricane, because of the political divisions that exist, the churches were called upon to distribute the relief that was received to assist the population.

One of the more significant challenges for the Diaspora, especially in Canada, is how to maintain the Jamaican identity, values and culture among the youth of the second and third generations. Addressing this issue is of fundamental importance because as we have seen earlier, it is this identity and commitment to Jamaica that have enabled the Diaspora to continue the significant role they have played in the past thirty years. In the absence of that identity, it is unlikely that they will be motivated to continue to send remittances, to invest in enterprises or property, to provide the social interventions which have assisted churches and schools to play such important roles at the local level or to offer their skills and training to assist the areas of deficiency in Jamaica.

For the second and third generations of Canadians of Jamaican descent, it is their Canadian identity that is likely to take precedence. Already, according to the Ethnic Diversity Survey, a substantial majority, over 80 percent of Canadians of Jamaican origin, said they had a strong sense of belonging to Canada. Bearing in mind the sources of identity development such as family, schools, community, peer groups and churches, it will be difficult to maintain a Jamaican identity in the absence of deliberate programs of intervention from groups within the Diaspora. Such identity is maintained now through high school associations, university and college alumni associations, participation in artistic and cultural organizations and churches with significant Jamaican leadership and membership. Of all of these institutions and organizations, the churches are likely to play the dominant role if they are committed to do so in the future.

They are able to organize youth activities and groups, they are able to provide a location for Jamaican activities to occur, they are able to expose young people to Jamaicans of all walks of life through lectures, visits and other church sponsored activities. Moreover, through their relationship with their counterpart churches in Jamaica, familiarization visits to Jamaica can be organized.

It should be evident that there is a distinctive role that the churches can play to sustain the bonds in the Diaspora that link them to Jamaica. This is not a role that needs to be assumed by the church alone, but we believe that in partnership with other groups, the churches and their leaders can shape the Jamaican identity among the youth in measurable ways.

In conclusion, the churches have and will continue to have a central role in shaping the direction, form and texture of the relations between Jamaica and its Diaspora in Canada. Church leaders are being encouraged to recast their activities and their mission to be able to assume positions of leadership in the Diaspora community. Their unique situation among the population positions them to play this pivotal role. The deficiencies in the existing efforts to strengthen relations between Jamaica and the Diaspora create new opportunities for their active participation. Their capacity to influence future generations in the Diaspora will make them indispensible in sustaining the ingredient of Jamaican identity.

Note

This speech was delivered on November 23, 2011, at the conference "Jamaica50 and Beyond: Towards a Developed Nation," organized by Seth George Ramocan, Jamaica's Consul General to Toronto.

PART FIVE –
CANADA FROM EAST TO WEST

16. A CARAVAN OF WORDS

Rachel Manley

My cat got into Canada before I could.

In 1986 it coasted through immigration at Mirabel Airport in Montreal without a hitch. All it needed were the inoculations and a cat kennel required by Air Canada. I first met the scrawny, injured tabby at a Canadian diplomat's home in Barbados. It was on its way to the local pound that very evening. I secretly decided to keep it, for deep in my heart I felt that a Barbadian puss shouldn't meet its end through foreign edict. So I offered to take it to the pound for them. I called the kitten Freda. In time, it became clear that she was a he. So Freda became Fred, and settled into the family.

I, on the other hand, had to wait several months to be allowed in. I married a Canadian who lived in Montreal and applied from Barbados, where I worked to join him under family reunification. The move wasn't straightforward. Unlike Fred, whose name change didn't seem to matter to the Canadians, I first had to change my married surname legally back to its maiden status of Manley to conform to the Napoleonic Code of ancient French law used in Quebec. It was a sign of things to come. For linguistic estrangement more than anything else would make this passage my exile.

I was homesick even before I landed at Mirabel Airport. Knowing that this province only spoke French made it seem even more foreign than the thought of its snow. It reminded me of how I had felt at eleven going for the first time to boarding school far away in the bauxite-red hills of rural Jamaica. There I would wake up every morning to my sadness. But I had a Scottish teacher who explained that if I treated my mind as my home, and my thoughts as my company, I would never feel homesick wherever I roamed. "Make it your caravan," she said in her mellifluous brogue.

So now each morning in Montreal, as soon as I woke, I'd fight the urge to cry and seek once more the company of my thoughts in the safety of what I've come to believe is my mobile home. In there I'd find those waking thoughts which realign themselves like drifting clouds, the mind preparing to reconnect us to the world after the solitude of sleep — thoughts that could make a home of Kingston or Mandeville, Jamaica or England, Africa, Barbados or Canada, first homes or last ones. Home is the mind. Like holding onto a dream, I was able to imagine I was still in the Caribbean and would wake to a world that was warm, its landscape and people familiar. How do we think before we can speak? Thoughts come from anywhere — from any place and any time; they arrive on words, and I'd take those words when I woke and write simple poems, as though putting myself on record, as slowly each truth would return, one by one, like a count of last night's sheep.

Canada is stubborn about rights. One's right to one's health and education, social security and language. It is a country whose personality is otherwise quite without chauvinism, which may be why some people call it bland. Canada is a rare instance of official bilingualism in the new world. English and French co-habit though not always comfortably. Who knows if this bilingualism resulted in a national value of language, but nearly two and a half centuries after this country was established the July international issue of *Newsweek* magazine rated Canada as the top country to live in as a fiction writer. It would remind me that histories are longer than migrations and that our own Caribbean story really begins in the Garden of Eden, not at the point of European arrival at Jamaica's Columbus Cove.

As a Jamaican I come from a region where each island holds on to its own unique character. The official language of Jamaica is English. It has replaced hundreds of small, imported tribal African tongues whose mute echoes are now no more than the rhythm of our music or a distant yearning for meaning we can never quite conjure up. When I was a child anyone with an education was expected to speak perfectly enunciated, uncorrupted standard English, doggedly resisting the drop of an H or putting one on in the wrong place. (Actually, the slaves didn't learn it "improperly" as the English thought — they learned it well enough to mispronounce it cleverly so that their masters couldn't understand them. Derek Walcott and V.S Naipaul would eventually prove that not only in cricket could we beat our masters at their own game!) But nowadays it's fashionable — in fact, viewed by many as nationalistic - to speak the more commonly heard Jamaican dialect known as Patois or the modern Rastafarian I-and-I talk of peace-piped spiritual love. It is proof that one is Jamaican and "rootsy."

As a child of mixed bloods, the colonizers and the colonized, I am a hybrid of different sorrows, and English, in all its evil and its good, is part of me, whether I like it or not. My education was in schools where my teachers were often English or "well spoken" Jamaicans. I was never academic and studied English at university because I have always loved to write. Apart from dutifully learned declensions in Latin and Spanish now forgotten, I can speak only English. Arriving in Canada, I had thought of myself as a poet. But most importantly, all my life language had been my subject, my currency, my consolation and refuge, my inlet and outlet. I was adrift without it. Now faced with this exotic, melodic, acrobatic French tongue, I felt mute and totally paralyzed by incomprehension. I was unable to understand a word of the sounds around me — I might as well have been in Paris or Guadeloupe; in the dark, I couldn't tell the difference.

In addition to this, I was bewildered by this province that was angry with their federation, which had only marginally survived a referendum to separate Quebec from English Canada. Here I was, an Anglophone, in a French underdog province, a position unnatural for me. It felt as though I lay on the wrong side of history. I come from a family who believe in Caribbean federation, an instinct forged of our island's common past. This was quite different. Here federalism was threatened by two very unlike and often competitive European traditions whose countries had opposed each other for the acquisition of Canada, and one had been defeated. I figured that at least in the Caribbean we were all united in kicking out the British.

Montreal is elegantly green, unafraid of sentimental ornamentation, with wide shouldered, robust buildings and parks which brave the slopes of their central mountain. We had moved to Outremont, a largely middle-class area on the side of Mount Royal, away from downtown. Our home was a large, airy top floor flat of a duplex that was always collecting some angle of sunshine, even on the bleakest winter day. We were taking over a lease from a painter who loved its light.

There were two separate duplexes side by side, four flats, two up and two down. In the tenancy of this complex was reflected the conundrum that is Canada. The upstairs flats were linked visually at the front by matching balconies and at the rear by small iron stoops at the top of the fire escapes beyond the kitchens. The next-door upper flat was home to a very tall family we fondly called the Trees, except for the matriarch, who was a comparatively small Italian lady of indulgent heart who worked at an old people's home, and would return after intermittent deaths to the tiny rear enrailment where I'd see her sitting quietly, weeping. Her husband was an American commercial filmmaker. Their two six-foot daughters were what most young Montrealers are today - multilingual, speaking English, French and, in this case, Italian.

Beneath us lived the Joyal family and beside them, Madam Joyal's parents, the Tremblays, who owned the complex. After several weeks of trying to greet the obdurate, wordless neighbours below where we shared an entrance hall, I left a bag of Jamaican Blue Mountain coffee with an introductory note. The coveted beans enchanted not even a smile from them. He would nod without looking at me, and Madam simply held her pretty head down and swished past me like an eel in water disappearing into the shadows of her sanctum. So strange, I thought, coming from islands where culture, size, proximity and temperament make neighbours of us all. These people have no "broughtupsy," I concluded, resorting to a good Jamaican word.

"Perhaps they don't speak English," I suggested to Juliana next door.

"How you mean they no speak Engaleesh!" she declared more than asked the question with her energetic Italian inflection. "They met at Harvard University! No, they *won't* speak Engaleesh."

Meanwhile, we had taken in another stray, a sleek black female cat as company for Fred. We called her Freda. Once again Fred acclimatized immediately, communicating in whatever language Quebecois cats meow or purr in, striking up a loving friendship with his feline counterpart.

I not only couldn't get a decent job or speak to a neighbour, but even if I could be understood, I was in a place I couldn't understand. I was very jealous of this world of my husband's with its fashionable French women and the exotic language he was fluent in, from which I felt excluded. In Montreal, most of the theatres played current English movies, so we'd go out to a film and dinner. In a steak house strewn with sawdust reminiscent of Jamaican dairies, we sat opposite each other at a rustic bench. My husband was facing the door. I drank wine and watched him drink his beer. He could see the door, and suddenly he brightened and waved.

"Allo, Michel," he called out.

I waited for my steak, aware his gaze had followed this Michelle person, checking now and then to make sure she was still there. An old girlfriend, I decided, or maybe a present one. When the steak arrived in its blatantly unpretentious tin plate, charred and yet juicing, I announced a headache.

"I want to go home," I said.

My husband gamely called for the bill, and I enjoyed his unspoken regret. Did he think I was going to sit there while he ogled Michelle?

As we were leaving he waved to a man seated at a far table I could now see.

"Salut, Michel."

Michel he now explained was an announcer from work.

A male announcer.

The gender subtleties of French and its pronunciation were lost on me. Defeated by language again.

Since I couldn't purr or yeowl, I decided I'd better learn French. I joined an extension class at a local university and tried diligently with my teacher, a Monsieur Turgeon. It was by now the January term, and I had hunkered down, making my warm flat home, seldom going outdoors — the winter of 1986 was said to be fierce, but what did I know? It was a world I could not have imagined possible. Mountains of snow that before had been no more than pictures on Christmas cards received while we spent holidays by the sea in Ocho Rios. White can be so pretty on its own, glamorous and silly. I was used to it in lace or the cotton sheets at home — always smelling of khus khus or moth balls. White was almost like its own colour in summer, frivolous in June roses, elegant in orchids. Blank white-lime washed walls and the base of trees, white that so easily showed dirt or a mark or a stain; white pants beware a panty line, white swimsuit sheer when wet. Now this whiteness of snow, monumental and silent. The thing that I noticed first was that snow has no smell at all. It seemed meaningless to me heaped over everything like packaging for some journey. I decided to flop down backwards in my bulky, loud yellow duvet coat to make a snow angel. My husband helped me up and explained about dog pee or worse trapped beneath. For me, not even the snow was understood.

But from my window, winter was not all that daunting. I have never been adventurous or athletic. I hate outdoors and picnics, day trips or sightseeing. As a teenager I loved rainy weekends when my sporty friends couldn't get to the beach to tan or water ski. I am the original kill-joy, the mean indoor spirit that likes to know it's not missing out on anything. So winter's inadvertent malevolence suited me, and the cats and I watched it from the safety of our windows.

I bought French immersion tapes and listened to them at night, sometimes falling asleep to strange sounds my mind unwittingly absorbed. I'd wake with some small exchange stuck in my head.

"Ou est la clay? "

"La clay est ici."

But if I'd found the key, it wasn't opening any doors for me.

I got extra help from the taller of the Tree sisters next door whose face flushed each time she failed to convey the concept of how to make a French verb negative.

"Vous allez a New York?" She'd ask again patiently.

And I never could figure out whether I je ne pas visite, or I je ne visite pas or quite what it was I or Monsieurs Mercier or Durand in my study book did with theirs either.

"Ou est la chat?" asked the Tree.

"C'est mon chat. Mon chat est Fred," I tried to remember what "ou est" meant. "Mon dieu!" I declared in a phrase I did know. The cat had escaped.

Fred returned days later bringing many new friends with him ... ticks, fleas and mange.

Finally, in my tenth week, Monsieur Turgeon, who despaired of my inability to pronounce his sensual vowels, threw down his book on the desk in front of him.

"Madam Manley, you are *murdering* my language," he declared sounding like an anguished Maurice Chevalier.

I stood waiting for the number 129 bus in minus twenty degree weather, too frozen to cry or laugh, my eyes dry with cold, my nose hurting. I was utterly mute. The cars as they passed me seemed to reflect my dilemma on their licence plates: "Je me souviens." I could never forget my past either. I took refuge in the certainty that sooner or later I'd get back home …

"Back to life,

back to reality…"

I sung the melody of this then popular song petulantly, greatly offending my husband. I felt sure there was no place for me in Canada. My electric typewriter provided the only comfort. I found myself needing more room than the poetic frame, lengthening my sentences, explaining my thoughts long-windedly over and over to myself or to the page, eking out breath in an effort to be heard, Fred, unperturbed, asleep at my feet.

My despairing husband persuaded his friendly physician to try hypnosis on me.

"You *vary vary* tired, eyes they *vary* heavy."

Now how was I to be hypnotized when instead I was mentally correcting his English, inserting verbs and definite articles?

Finally, defeated, my husband arranged a transfer to Toronto. We packed up two lifetimes of books and my Jamaican paintings and I left without sentimental farewell.

In Anglophone Ontario I discovered my Canada. At last I was able to speak to people who would listen to me and answer, hear me and understand. Even the annoying invasion of commercial calls on my telephone was now welcome. They spoke in English. They spoke a milder version of American; still a twang, but a less shrill defiance of English reserve.

They say that if America is a melting pot of cultures, then Canada is a mosaic. This is doubly true of Toronto. And language is the outline setting each apart. The brushstroke hieroglyphics of Chinatown mark the windows in black and red along Spadina. The round patterns of Russian along Bathurst and Steeles; the linear lashes and dashes, a scripted flowing hemstitch of Arabic in Mississauga. Each wave of immigrant has their own street festival, their national costumes, their food, their instruments, their sorrow. Yet, against the threat of America's cultural imperialism, Canada often defines itself by what it is not, giving its neighbour more than a simply proverbial cold shoulder.

In the past, I would return from England or America with clothes and shoes, memories of fine theatre and stories of sights I'd seen in my brief escape. But now as a migrant I felt like a traitor. Here I was in the First World, soothing my conscience with placebos: I had married a foreigner whose work was here, in his country, what else could I do? But deep inside I knew I came from a region that had educated me, shaped me in every way from its limited resources, and that I had left without giving anything back. I was filled with guilt.

I holed up in my townhouse at my desk in front of a window framing a maple tree whose seasons I would come to know leaf by leaf, bough by bough, as the neighbours changed in the windows beyond. At my new computer I was evoking my past, telling my story. In brief forays I would brave the city for necessities. My medicare card, my bank, my weekly trip to the supermarket, the post office or the pharmacy. After the gracious avenues of Montreal — the sidewalk cafes and residents whose avant garde demeanour, their dress and how they walked and talked, how they arranged themselves, even their beggars seemed almost artistic — Toronto seemed somehow narrower and more focused, less dissipated on entity, passion and calamity; its roads seemed about direction, its citizenry bent towards purpose, their dress unimportant; panhandlers scruffy and direct in their approach. Or maybe the difference was simply that now I understood what people were saying.

But whether Montreal or Toronto, this was the land of Margaret Laurence and Mordecai Richler, Margaret Atwood and Robertson Davies. It was also the land of Austin Clarke and Dionne Brand, Cecil Foster and Olive Senior. This was the land of the Canada Council for the Arts, of arts grants and prizes. It was a First World land that had turned its heart to literature. It cared that its people read books. It cared that they wrote them in either language.

It would take time, but as a Jamaican Canadian, a citizen of both countries, I would move from my own underbrush of poetry to lawns of prose. And back in my language, it was easier to settle in and write that prose, feeling I now had a potential audience. Here I could unburden myself of my guilt by writing another piece of Jamaica's story. My estrangement from both the past and the present slowly became the pages of a book.

And so, ten years after landing in Canada and four years after coming to Toronto, I was published. Not exactly an overnight triumph, but say it for Canada: a story of my island and its brief two years within a federation, and the memories of ancestors who had made a difference to that cause, held worth for this country's readers. I got grants from the Canada Council, and I even won a Governor General's award with not a single mention of Canada in my story.

But you know, there is always one pivotal moment when things become real, be it a story, a country, a person, a relationship, a place. When what is only a set of dancing ideas suddenly pulls together and makes sense. That moment came for me soon after I arrived in Toronto.

"Yes, Rachel speaking."

"Oh hello. I am calling from the Immigration Court. We need a translator."

"Oh?" I was mystified.

"We understand you speak Ah-da…?"

"Ah-da?" I wondered if this was a joke being played on me by someone who knew I'd long needed a job, so long in fact I'd given up trying.

"The Jamaican language?"

"Why?" I asked.

"A Jamaican refugee has requested an interpreter and by law we must provide one. You were suggested."

Unseen, I rolled my eyes. A Jamaican refugee from what? I saw through the scam.

"We pay seventy five dollars an hour — even if the case isn't heard that day, once you attend court, we will pay you a minimum of four hours."

I thought about this. It made no sense. As a graduate of English at our university, I knew of no language called Ah-da. But I also knew there was no Jamaican I couldn't understand, translate for or explain to, and I needed the money.

"Ok, I said. Let me know when."

A Jamaican friend phoned to ask if I'd received the call. She had given my name.

"But what is Ah-da?" I asked, looking at Fred, who had wandered in as though to take the call. Being a Barbadian cat, he didn't care at all.

"Don't be ridiculous! How you going to interpret Jamaican if you don't know that?"

I was confused. Indeed I had signed on for a language whose very name eluded me.

"When they asked the man if he spoke English, he must have said no, he spoke the ah-da language."

"Oh, the *other*!"

Obvious indeed.

It seems a small thing. In fact I only went once, and the case was postponed, and I never was called to the courts on College Street again. But in the Canadian context, I had found my small place. I still receive the occasional package of guidelines. I believe I'm still the official Jamaican interpreter. A small tile in the Canadian mosaic, my place as a group member, my country represented, my mastery over language, even the one they called Ah-da.

It seems all my life every important concept had come down to language. Slaves, words. Montreal, words. Exile, words. Toronto, words.

Was Canada my country now? Was Jamaica? Was England the land of my language and my other heritage?

More words.

My mind is my home, thoughts are my companions. I lure them out from an alphabet of possibility. I live in a caravan of words.

Note

This essay first appeared in Teresa Toten's anthology. *Piece by Piece: Stories About Fitting into Canada* (Puffin Canada, Toronto, 2010), and is published here with the written permission of the editor.

17. JAMAICANS IN OTTAWA, 1964 –

Ewart Walters

> Four strong winds that blow lonely
> Seven seas that run high
> All these things that don't change
> Come what may
> — Ian Tyson

We landed in Ottawa around midnight, early September 1964. I had long ago rationalized Canada. It would not have the idiosyncrasies of the British, and it would not have the racism of the U.S. Deep South. It would have a little of both but not too much, I told myself, expecting to see Indians but, for some gap in my education, not French-Canadians. My rationalization continued on board the aircraft. A predecessor of Air Canada, it was a four-engine turbo-prop operated by Trans-Canada Airlines. Much too soon I became aware of a vibrating rattle and observed that it was coming from paneling above me that had lost its riveting and was now complaining loudly in protest. Ah, well, I rationalized, I need not worry. Canadian inspection processes would not have allowed that if it were a serious blemish. Besides, this was Canadian technology I was riding on. Besides, a fat lot of good it would have done me to come to any other conclusion. What would I do, jump off? I took a sniff of my fiancée's handkerchief with the scent of the Yardley *Entice* fragrance she had made her own, and calmed myself. Truth is, I was excited and was not about to let a rattle, no matter how persistent, dampen my spirit. I had won a scholarship offered by the Canadian External Aid Office (later to become the Canadian International Development Agency) to study journalism at Carleton University. I was excited at the news. I was going on a plane! I was going to university! I was twenty-four and had been working for five years. I was ready for this two-pronged adventure — Canada and university. The plane stopped in Toronto and then took off again for Ottawa, our final destination. I say "our" because on the flight with me was my Calabar schoolmate Claude Robinson, also going to Ottawa on scholarship to study journalism. And also on the flight, but not with me, was the St.

George's College old boy and captain of the 1962 Jamaica football team, Anthony Hill. Wonder where he was going?

Disembarking in Ottawa I was comforted by the news that the tempera-ture was 55 degrees Fahrenheit. Well, I could live with that, I thought. It could not get much colder, could it? As we walked off the plane onto the tarmac we approached a small shack of a building. This was the Ottawa airport and it made our Palisadoes (later Norman Manley International) airport look good. My other thought that night, both in Toronto and Ottawa, was of the silence of the place, the absence of people in the endless empty corridors, a sort of anaesthesized, semi-modern wilderness that we had to navigate. Finally, Customs and Immigration came and went and we were met by a welcom-ing committee of two students from Carleton University, Russell Davidson and Jackie Larkin. Russell talked between puffs on a pipe and Jackie drove us through a seemingly endless forest between the airport and the university. They took us to the university residence, where we were booked into a room and spent the next week or so, eventually to be told that we were not going to remain in residence but should find accommodation off campus.

We ended up on the three-bedroom second-floor of a home at Euclid Avenue off the city's main street, Bank Street, near the corner of Sunnyside Avenue. It was four or five bus stops and about a twenty-five-minute walk from the university. Of the two rooms available, Claude grabbed the one with what he thought was the better bed, leaving me with what I thought was the better room. We had a fridge and a range where we would cook our evening meals, and we shared a bathroom with the occupant of the third room — a student from Mauritius, who was a year ahead of us at the university. A third-floor attic was occupied by a young married couple. Our landlords, a young German couple, completely dispelled any doubts we might have harboured about Germans. The wife looked after the house in its entirety, changing our bed linen, taking out garbage, replacing toilet tissue and keeping the bathrooms and the rooms clean, while her husband went out to work. We made our beds and prepared our meals. And that led to my first attempt to cook rice and peas. I simply placed the rice and the peas in a pot and set it to boil. After a half an hour or so, the meal seemed ready. But when we tried to eat, the peas were as hard as little stones. Claude remembered that he had seen the peas soaked before they were boiled. I had too. So I put the peas in some water and left it overnight to soak. The next day, I poured the rice on top of the soaked peas, set the pot to boil again and after about 40 minutes removed the cover and shared out the meal in triumph. The darned peas were still rock hard! It then dawned on us that we should make inquiries from the Jamaicans we had met about how to overcome this problem. And that is how we eventually did the right thing, boiling the peas first, before putting the rice in.

Running almost from where the Ottawa River dissects Ontario from

Quebec, past Parliament Hill, all the way down to Morrisburg on the banks of the St. Lawrence River system some sixty miles south, Bank Street is Ottawa's main artery, becoming Highway 31 outside city limits. It is not surprising that the small Jamaican expatriate community of the early sixties grew up near Bank Street, mostly in and around the section of the city known as the Glebe (because of the preponderance of churches). We knew just about everybody then — everybody with Black skin, that is. Bank Street itself became a sort of meeting place. So few and so novel were Black people in Ottawa in those days that it was accurately said, "If you were at the top of Bank Street and saw another Black person at the bottom, you both ran to each other and embraced." And the majority of these people were Jamaicans, mainly women who had come to Ottawa on the government-to-government scheme of the times that brought young women to work in homes as domestic helpers. At least one generation of Ottawans was raised by these West Indian women, who were later able to secure landed immigrant status and take jobs in other areas and enterprises. The arrangement for these helpers varied somewhat from home to home, but all of them got a day off or at least an afternoon off on Thursdays, and they would then go down to the YMCA, where they could talk with each other, exchange information and pleasantries and sometimes meet other West Indians like us students and the few who were actually here working in Ottawa. The other place where we would meet was the International House, an older building downtown that was set up mostly for students to meet Canadians and have parties.

On arrival I found Ottawa to be culturally bereft. I was coming from a Jamaica freed two years earlier from the crippling bonds of colonialism and exploding with creativity. The comparison was stark. By comparison Ottawa was, well, a wasteland. There was a mood there, and it carried over into my first months in this country, walking along the cold silent sidewalks of Ottawa and finding not one gaze that would meet mine. I was … an alien. Or else, the people I saw were aliens. I tried to capture those thoughts in the poem, "Lonely Sidewalks," which I wrote a decade later:

> Lonely sidewalks
> crowded with faces
> White and blank
> Reversed blackboards
> Sterile without the probings
> Of the chalk
>
> Lonely sidewalks
> Crowded with bodies
> In motion and yet Inert
> No movement that enters my soul

Lonely sidewalks
Crowded with the emptiness
Of voices frozen
By a hundred years
Of searching for a culture
That could emerge
Could emerge
But there's no beat
No Drum

Lonely sidewalks
Crowded with longings
Unexpressed
Since I
(One large exclamation mark)
Who punctuate a sterile board
Will make no sense, really
Till I find a word to follow
And that's BLACK
..................*!*

But things changed. One of the reasons for that change was cricket.

Cricket

Jamaica established its High Commission in Ottawa as soon as it became independent in 1962, and this was a real connection for me and others. Visits to the High Commission usually meant contact with Jamaica through reading copies of the *Daily Gleaner*. But these visits also meant I got to learn about the small Jamaican community and meet some of them, including Ivor Mitchell, who had been at Calabar High School with me and with whom I worked in my first job, at the Ministry of Housing and Social Welfare. He was now on the staff of the High Commission. What is more, I discovered they played cricket in Ottawa. And Mitch was the captain of the West Indian team, known as the Coral Reef Club. Never having heard anything about cricket in Canada, I had left my whites and my bat in Jamaica. Now I yearned for them even though, with winter approaching, there were only two matches to be played. My khaki pants would have to do! And that is how I got launched on to a cricket career in Ottawa that led me to become not only captain of my team but also president of the Ottawa cricket league and a director of the provincial cricket association in Toronto. Long before that happened, however, I had made my stand against racism in cricket in Ottawa.

Cricket in Ottawa was played at Rideau Hall, the governor general's grounds, and four teams — Ottawa Cricket Club, New Edinburgh Cricket Club, Christ Church Cathedral Cricket Club and Defence Cricket Club — played there. A fifth team, the Canadian Forces Cricket Club, played at another venue, an old airbase at Rockcliffe. These five teams played competitively in the Ottawa league. The West Indians in the Coral Reef Cricket Club played friendly games as a club, but while any of the five clubs above from time to time would invite individual Coral Reef players to supplement their teams, there was strong resistance by the Ottawa cricket league to having a group of Black guys play as a team in their league. The exception to this resistance was the Canadian Forces Cricket Club, and along with four or five other West Indians, I played as a regular member of the Forces team when Coral Reef was not engaged. Soon enough, however, the matter came to a head. Coral Reef applied for membership in the Ottawa league and was turned down. But Coral Reef had its origins in the Jamaica High Commission and the counsellor, the first secretary and the accountant as well as Mitch were members. When the High Commissioner Vin McFarlane heard about this, he had a quiet word with the Canadian governor general. In no time, Coral Reef received a letter from the dons of the Ottawa league inviting us to a meeting.

The meeting was held in the pavilion at Rideau Hall one evening, and Coral Reef was represented by Eric Samuels, a Jamaican working in the federal public service; Hugh Bonnick, the wicket-keeper and High Commission accountant; and me, a student. We went in and sat down, and I was taken completely by surprise when the dons opened the proceedings by asking, "Well gentlemen, what would you like to do?" I lost it. "What!" I exploded. "We applied for membership; you turned us down flat, now you call us to a meeting and ask what we have to say? You need to tell us what you plan to do!" Under the table Bonnick's bony knees bumped mine as he whispered, "Take it easy Ewart, take it easy." But I felt I was right. The nerve of these guys!

The governor general had told them in no uncertain terms that he would withdraw cricket privileges unless they accommodated us. "No Blacks, no cricket," was the quote I was told. Clearly they had heard it too. But if I expected they would just acquiesce I was wrong. "Listen," they said. "We will admit you to the league but you will have to find your own grounds; you cannot play here at Rideau Hall because with the four teams playing and practising here, there is no more room for a fifth team." And that was that. We had won, but we hadn't won everything; we had some work to do. It was then left to Eric and me to find a suitable place, and then it was only me because he went off to Rome on an assignment. And yes, I did find a place near the corner of Baseline Road and Woodroffe Avenue, and Coral Reef Cricket Club — renamed the Bel-Air Cricket Club after a road adjacent to our ground — began playing competitive cricket in Ottawa while continuing its mission of welcoming new West Indian immigrants to Ottawa by still playing friendly games. Bel-Air was to become the best team in the league, winning the competitions over several years.

Overcoming Culture Shock

Several of the Jamaican students had taken to driving taxi to supplement their funds, and in the summer of 1966 I joined them. We rented the taxi for twelve-hour shifts, paying the company a certain amount and keeping for ourselves anything that was left over. To me this was great adventure, and it was also a widening of my education as regards human nature and behaviour as passengers spoke about many things or, as in one case, tried to escape without paying. I also got to know the city and its environs very well. One of the first things I did was to purchase a radio. I could not in those days find a short-wave radio in a store anywhere in Ottawa. This meant I was cut off from the BBC news and therefore from the world, and I had to settle for an AM-FM radio. It immediately became my main window to the city and to the country. But as the days went by I found Ottawa and Canada to be very parochial. There was no real window to the world as there had always been in Jamaica. No news from the BBC. No news from Voice of America. No stories really of international news or culture or sports, just Canadian football and ice hockey (of course, here they simply call it hockey). Even football, the real football (soccer), played a far distant cousin to Canadian football. And on Sundays I really missed the line-up of religious programs and music that adorned Jamaican radio. And the popular music! That was something else again. So, okay, I got to like Roy Orbison, the American singer that Ottawa radio adopted and whose "Pretty Woman" was very well produced and very popular. And I certainly loved Herb Alpert and his Tijuana Brass, but he was another American.

As Canadians, Ian and Sylvia Tyson with their Country offering "Four Strong Winds," were all right. And I was exposed to Hootenanny and sitting round a campfire singing Canadian folk songs. But after you'd listened to Lucille Starr sing "Jolie Jacqueline" ten times you wanted something else. The Canadian singer who caught my attention and earned my respect was Gordon Lightfoot with songs like "In The Early Morning Rain," "Rich Man's Spiritual," "Go-Go Round" and "Black Day In July." And I did occasionally hear The Drifters' "I Can't Bear To Go On Without You" and Diana Ross and The Supremes' "Stop In The Name of Love" and much later Aretha Franklin's "I Say A Little Prayer For You." Still, I did not hear the hits of Nat King Cole or Sam Cooke, or Fats Domino, or Smiley Lewis, or Ivory Joe Hunter, or Brook Benton, or Mickey and Sylvia, or Gene and Eunice, or even the Platters. Worse, Jamaican popular music had just burst forth in the Ska, which had become wildly popular in Jamaica and the Caribbean, and was even beginning to make a mark in the U.S. But not in this Great White North! No Toots and the Maytals, no Desmond Dekker, no Byron Lee and the Dragonnaires, no Derrick Morgan, no Stranger Cole, no John Holt, no Melodians, no Ethiopians, no Jimmy Cliff, no Bob Marley. Not even Sparrow! How could we be ignored? If I felt that way about it I was sure the other Jamaican and West Indian students were in the same boat. I had to do something to overcome the numbing effects of this cultural desert! I had to let Ottawa — if not Canada - know that there was a world, a bright pulsating world, beyond the Rideau Canal.

I'd brought a few records with me from Jamaica and now as my first Jamaica Independence Day in Canada drew near, I wrote a half-hour radio program of Jamaican music and took it down to radio station CKOY on Richmond Road, where Bill Lee was glad to see me and arranged for it to be recorded. He asked me if I was a broadcaster and when I said well, I was a journalist. He said they could not pay me for the program but it would be broadcast nevertheless. I suppose he would get paid for it as he would also be on air as the host. No matter. I was glad the music was being played! Then I went out and phoned my colleagues and friends to tell them about the coming event. By this time I had acquired my musical pride and joy — a tiny Phillips stereo portable record player with speakers. On moving to an attic apartment on Carling Avenue, I threw open the windows, placed my speakers in them and gave passers-by on the road below a small taste of good music. That Christmas I arranged with the CBC to have Jamaicans come to their studios to send greetings back to family and friends in Jamaica at no cost. And, finally, I took my little portable record player to the dining room at Carleton University, which we had rented for a dance, placed the speakers in front of a microphone and performed the duties of Ottawa's first Jamaican DJ. Thank God for the West Indian parties; they kept us warm and alive whether in living room or basement. And while Vin McFarlane was High Commissioner for Jamaica, the basement of his residence was frequently opened to us for parties. So on the cultural side, the drought was not prolonged or permanent. Moreover, my own sense of adventure at being in this new place helped me overcome the shortcomings it presented.

The other thing that helped to decrease my culture shock was that I bought a car. To accomplish this I visited a bank.

Encounter with the Bank

I'd always been fascinated with cars. So the first chance I got I bought one. I purchased my first car in November 1964 in Ottawa. It was a green 1958 Volkswagen, and it cost a princely two hundred dollars. I had not planned to buy a car. Indeed I was lucky to have found living quarters so close to Carleton University for my first year of university and my first Ottawa winter.

The bus service in Ottawa has always been good, and it served me well. But that late October morning when the temperature dipped dangerously and the winds blew belligerently on me waiting at the bus stop, it seemed as if the bus was taking forever. As I gritted my chattering teeth and shivered in the autumn cold, I reminded myself grimly that it was not even winter yet. Worse was to come! Well, I'd be prepared. I would not be standing outside in this malevolent weather waiting for any bus. I was going to get me a car.

Just a few blocks up Bank Street from Euclid, at the corner of Second Avenue, there was something that might just do. Morton Motors, a Volkswagen dealer, had a used-car lot, and while there were three or four cars that looked attractive enough, only one came near to the purchasing power of an expatriate student who had not planned to buy a car. The sticker price was $200, and I thought I could get them to come down a little bit. After all, I would have to buy insurance too. But, no go. Two hundred dollars was what they insisted on. The days passed and still it was two hundred bucks. So, screwing up my courage, I walked into the Bank of Nova Scotia on Bank Street just south of Sunnyside and spoke to the manager about securing a loan.

"How much do you want," he asked.

"$400," I told him.

"What can you offer as collateral? "

"Well, there is the car itself… " I began. But he cut me off. The bank would not take so old a car as collateral on a loan. Was there anything else?

"Well, " I offered brightly. "I have a typewriter and my books. "

The manager struggled to maintain his banker's face and suppress a smile. But it was a losing battle and a little smile eventually broke through his resistance. I suppose he must have remembered his own penurious student days. Besides, I had hastened to indicate that the Bank of Nova Scotia was well known and well respected in Jamaica and that I had done business with them. Maybe he thought I had an honest face. Whatever it was, I got the loan. By the time a drunk driver drove through a stop sign on Percy Street and crashed into me one night, nearly a year later, the loan had been fully repaid. The little Volkswagen was my pride and joy. I drove everywhere and got to know the city. I got to know how to drive in the snow.

Snow

You can't live in Ottawa and not learn to contend with snow. I used to sit in my room and just watch the snowflakes waft their way to the ground and wonder how many of those would accumulate to the depth of one inch, or fill a shovel, or a snow plough for that matter. I just sat and watched them fall, the first flurries of late October not completely captured by gravity. By the time they had morphed into the thick, heavy snowfalls of January and

February of course, I had had enough of watching. Nevertheless, my first act of wrestling with snow came during my first Christmas. On leaving a party hosted at the home of Stuart McKinnon, the lead singer of the Fourth Avenue Baptist Church choir, I got back to my trusty Volkswagen, only to find that it was not going anywhere — snow had accumulated above the hubcaps. What to do? There was no traction. No matter what I did, the wheels would spin in the snow but the car would not move. I started the car and put it in first gear. Leaving the engine running with the first gear engaged and the wheels spinning, I jumped behind it and pushed. The car rolled. And then I had to run a little behind it and spring into the seat before it went too far without a driver. Fortunately the snow was acting as a brake so the car did not get too far.

The second snow incident was with my Austin A-60 Cambridge, and it had less to do with the snow itself than with the regulations governing snow and snow clearance. One of the things that I found amazing in Ottawa was the street-parking rules. Compared to Kingston, which operated for decades with no-parking signs but without parking meters, this vastly spread out city of Ottawa had parking meters almost everywhere — and Green Hornets (traffic attendants) to enforce them with tickets. Where I lived on Powell Avenue there were no parking meters, but the overnight parking regulations would be in force on all streets in the city. Between November 15 and March 15, the City of Ottawa regulations apply ticket sanctions to cars parked for more than three hours between 1 a.m. and 8 a.m. in order to make it easier for the snow crews to clear snow from the roadways in time for the workday. This affected me because there was no garage or laneway space for me where we lived. There was an empty lot nearby and that is where I normally left my car but this night in early March I was doing an all-night study session with a group of guys and I left the car on the street across from the house, having determined that we would avoid the ticket by driving the car around the block before parking it again just before 4 a.m. and again around 7 o'clock. This we did. And so I sallied forth in high spirits at 8.30 to take my ride to work at the Civic Hospital and go on to school.

To my astonishment there was a ticket on the windshield. After all the trouble I had taken the ticket was for contravening the overnight parking regulations. The quick flash of anger turned quickly to disappointment and then to determination. Well, this one I would fight! Indeed, the ticket had several errors of fact on it. First was the name of the roadway, which it listed as street instead of avenue. Then it had my name wrong, and there was something else which I don't recall now. But I knew from my days in the courts in Kingston that these could work very strongly in my favour, perhaps even get me off. So off I went to court — a student in a strange land — to fight my overnight parking ticket. One week early!

So eager was I to try out my knowledge of courtroom procedure that I'd followed the day and not the date listed on the ticket. Ah, well, a whole week to wait! On the correct date I turned up again at the court. A man met me and inquired what I was there for. When I told him, he asked what I planned to do. On learning that I was going to fight it, he suggested that my plan would likely not work. I suppose I seemed to resign myself to my fate and he left me. When my case was called I was shocked to see that the Crown counsel was no other than the man who had questioned me at the door! Ah, I thought. The sneak! But as I would learn later that was how things are done here. Now came my moment. I told the judge that I had some preliminary objections, but when I listed them he smiled softly and observed that the City had thirty days to make the corrections and re-issue the ticket. Did I have anything else? Well, I said, drawing myself up to my full fighting height, I am here to testify on oath that I did not commit the infraction stated on this ticket.

The judge, still a bit bemused, ordered me to be sworn and called on the Crown to bring his case against me. The man looked slightly flustered. Based on our earlier conversation, he was sure I would not fight the case and he had sent the policeman away since he thought he would not need him. He told the judge his witness was not there and asked for a postponement.

"No," the judge said. "This gentleman is here today. Put on your case."

The Crown tried again but the judge, no longer bemused, was resolute. I was free to go. I left that courtroom glad that I won but somewhat sorry that I did not have a chance to put on my own properly prepared defence. Ah well, you win some, you lose some.

A third thing that helped dissipate the sense of alienation was the sense of community we developed.

Organizations

In 1964, my first year, we began a student organization at Carleton called the West Indian Association of Ottawa. It comprised mainly Jamaicans and Trinidadians at the start, the leading Trinidadian dropping out when he heard that the RCMP was keeping a watch on us and indeed had invited him to do a little spying on the group. It was not long before the idea for a conference on West Indian affairs was born. Carleton students Anthony and Robert Hill, along with Barry Myers, all Jamaicans, stoked the idea into fruition in consultation with Montreal Jamaicans Alvin Johnson, a journalist with the *Montreal Star*, and Jamaican student Hugh O'Neil. Others who assisted were Montreal students, including Roosevelt (Rosy) Douglas (Dominica), Franklin Harvey (Grenada) and Anne Cools (Barbados), at whose home many of the meetings were held. Again I was excited. A conference on West Indian affairs! A conference that we students arranged from the ground up and did not have to seek permission to stage, a conference we could not likely have put on in the West Indies.

And so it was that in the fall of 1965 the first Conference on West Indian Affairs was staged at McGill University, with notable Barbadian author George Lamming as the guest speaker. A cultural session led by Trinidadian dancer Jeff Henry was arranged by a team led by Franklin Harvey. The conference came off very well. We were proud of ourselves. The conference was repeated the following year with Trinidad and Tobago's C.L.R. James as guest speaker, and the next with Orlando Patterson of Jamaica. The year after that, 1968, it morphed into the Black Writers' Conference, which was what Guyanese University of the West Indies (UWI) lecturer Walter Rodney was returning from when he was declared *persona non grata* by the Hugh Shearer government in Jamaica and refused re-admission, an act that triggered the biggest ever student demonstrations in Kingston, with the UWI students leaving campus and marching downtown and to the prime minister's official residence. One early spin-off from the conference was the decision to build the West Indian Association of Ottawa into a larger entity that would include the domestic helpers and the other Jamaicans in the city. And so was born in 1967 the Jamaica Canadian Association (Ottawa Chapter), which later became the Jamaica Ottawa Community Association.

In the late 1970s the Third World Players appeared. This was a theatrical group launched by Lloyd Stanford, Karl Gordon, Jennifer Hosten-Craig, Ricardo Smith and David Craig. Its first production, *Slices of Life*, mounted with the assistance of the Penguin Theatre in April 1979, set the tone of the mutlilingual, multicultural repertoire that has been characteristic of the group. The selections made by Karl Gordon included pieces in French, Haitian Creole, standard English and Jamaican Patois. The group worked in stage, television and radio productions, using established talent and un-earthing new ones. A now famous "graduate" is noted actor, playwright and television host Andrew Moodie. An early production for television was called *Accents Shakespeare Never Knew.*

Since November 1980 the group has been doing on radio station CKCU-FM a regular broadcast *Third World Players Present,* a program of rehearsed readings from Third World literature and interviews with writers from the Third World, including those resident in Canada, as well as critics. These broadcasts have included a series of "literary portraits" of Argentina, the Bahamas, Barbados, Brazil, Chile, Columbia, Cuba, Guyana, Haiti, India, Jamaica, Pakistan, Sri Lanka and Trinidad and Tobago; broadcasts on seasonal themes like summer and autumn, and festive or religious occasions like Easter, Thanksgiving and Christmas.

As president Lloyd Stanford says, it is significant that through these broadcasts and its stage presentations, the group introduced the radio audience and the general public to the work of four Nobel Prize winners from the Third World *before* they became laureates — Chinua Achebe, Wole Soyinka, Gabriela Marquez, Derek Walcott — and to the work of Michael Ondaatje much prior to his Booker and Governor General's awards.

Black History Month Ottawa

In 1986 ten organizations came together and agreed that Ottawa should join hundreds of cities in the United States and Canada to mark February as Black History Month. The Barbados Association used to celebrate a Black History Week, but that had faded. So, Black History Month celebrations in Ottawa were held for the first time in 1986. As we continued, year after year, we learned many things; we learned to sing the Black National Anthem; we learned about our martyrs, our trail-blazers and our heroes, here in Canada and across the Diaspora. We learned about each other; our diversity was paraded in its different geography, customs, clothes and cultures. We brought in speakers from far and wide who widened our horizons about Canadian and other Black historical facts and situations. We conducted most of those early opening ceremonies in the West Wing of our Parliament, precisely because we wanted to demonstrate that it was *our* parliament. We began the talent show called BlackMusicFest and thus provided an artistic launching pad for many young people. We faced many challenges, not least of which was the oft repeated complaints about the deep cold of February. But out of all that diversity, we brought ourselves together.

In launching Black History Month we wanted:

- to create and foster an awareness of Black presence and achievement, not only among white Ottawans but also among Black people;
- to sensitize Canadians in the National Capital Region to the contributions Black Canadians have made to Canada;
- to provide Black youth with role models and to inculcate a sense of dignity regarding their heritage;
- to involve the wider Canadian majority in the history of Black Canadians and to continue to bridge the gap between the majority and those Canadians who are distinct by reason of colour, thereby promoting multi-racial and multi-cultural integration. And yes, we did focus on history; and
- to encourage schools and the school board(s) to include books on Black history and achievement in the curriculum.

Over the last several years Ottawa's Black community has grown and grown. Already, the most recent group of Black immigrants — the Somalis — number some 17,000. When added to the other groups, they push the overall total to somewhere between 50,000 and 70,000. And Black History Month has taken a central place in the activities of the City of Ottawa because that is where the opening ceremonies are being held, year after year, with the mayor in attendance to read the proclamation.

Someone has noted that African Americans, through their oral history, kept the story of the descendants of Thomas Jefferson and Sally Hemmings alive while "official" history denied this fact. In that vein, Lucille Clifton, a Black American poet, strikes a note of resilience in the poem, "Why some people be mad at me sometimes."

> they ask me to remember
> but they want me to remember
> their memories...
> And I keep on remembering mine.

Most Whites do not know Black history. But neither do most Blacks. Without knowledge of the positive achievements by the many outstanding Blacks in Canada, the U.S., Africa and all over the world, many people are left to assume wrongly that Blacks have done nothing worthwhile. So the City of Ottawa has been culturally enriched by the coming of the Jamaicans and the West Indians. When the National Black Coalition of Canada (NBCC) was snuffed out in 1982 a void was created that lasted a few years. Eventually, this void was filled by Harambee Centres Canada, and that whole process began right here in Ottawa. One night after a meeting of the National Barbados Association of Canada in Ottawa, a group of West Indians got together in a hotel room, and their discussion resulted in the launching of a new national organization that would offer "culturally sensitive services" to the Black communities of Canada. This effort became known as Harambee, and it led to one of the most innovative fundraisers ever seen in Ottawa. At the suggestion of Mairuth Sarsfield, the Black Orpheus Ball was staged. It was a two-part affair, the first part being a formal dinner at somebody's home, for which attendees would pay a ticket price of something like $40. There were several of these celebrity dinner hosts. After dinner, everybody made their way to the splendidly decorated West Block on Parliament Hill for the Black Orpheus Ball, and the city's Black glitterati and their colleagues from across Canada were in elegant attendance. The next year the ball was held at the National Gallery, and it featured speeches from octogenarian Carrie Best of Nova Scotia and Ontario Lt. Governor Lincoln Alexander. The funds raised from these events went to the establishment in Toronto of Harambee Centres Canada.

Today

I have to say that Ottawa has changed. Today I find it to be a delightful city, easy to get around and culturally rich not only with the music of my native land but also the cuisine. No longer do we think about alienation; we see Ottawa as home, as a good place to bring up our kids. Fortunately, it is still not the kind of creeping metropolis that Toronto has become and, hopefully, never will be. But the capital city has grown in many ways, including the musical fare that one hears on radio, largely due to the pioneering work of volunteers at university radio stations. First there was Junior Smith, a Jamaican mathematics student at Carleton University who began his Saturday afternoon program, *Reggae in the Fields*, on Carleton's CKCU-FM in the mid-seventies. Indeed, I helped him cement his show by writing and co-producing seven programs on the history of Jamaican music. Then he was followed by another Jamaican, Richard "Papa Ritchie" Connell, with his show *Rockers* on the University of Ottawa's CHUO-FM, also heard on Saturdays. The movement began long before them, however. It started with Byron Lee and the Dragonnaires coming up to Montreal and performing for Expo 67.

In a very real way the changing Ottawascape also took sustenance from Pierre Trudeau, who as justice minister and later prime minister helped lift Canadians' self-image by placing the country firmly and positively on the international agenda and domestically propounded a goal of trying to achieve the "Just Society." In the meantime, Jamaican food began making an appearance. The ubiquitous patty was not yet for sale in shops or supermarkets and the Toronto patty factories had not yet been constructed. One student occasionally baked a few and distributed to us. Then "Spicy" Luke Campbell, a Jamaican chef who operated his own Canadian Chef restaurant, began baking patties. And Eric Samuels, along with his friends Rawle Scott and Henry Cadogan, opened a Jamaican grocery where one could buy yams, sweet potatoes, plantains and canned black mangoes among other products. Then came Canada's big incursion into track and field, courtesy of a string of Jamaican-born sprinters. This was followed by the growing popularity of soccer — an international game if ever there was one — which again lifted Canada out of the limiting confines of hockey, its current national sport.

18. A CONVERSATION WITH A CHINESE YARDIE ABOUT LIFE AS A JAMAICAN CANADIAN

Leanne Taylor

I arrived at Carol Wong's home in Markham, Ontario, with a box of Chinese pastries and buns in one hand and my laptop computer in the other. It was during Chinese New Year celebrations and the ushering in of the Year of the Dragon. The pastries were, in part, a way of marking the ongoing festivities. However, they also reflected what my Jamaican father, relatives and godparents had always told me: "Never arrive at someone's house empty handed." This was also what my parents had always referred to as "good broughtupsy" (good manners) — a Jamaican expression they used anytime they felt they needed to emphasize Jamaican culture and tradition to their Canadian-born children.

Although Carol had known my parents for over forty years, we had only met personally a few times, and not for several years. I had received her contact information from relatives, whom I had approached a few weeks earlier and had explained that I would be writing a piece for an anthology of Jamaican Canadians — a book to mark Jamaica's fiftieth anniversary of independence. I told her that Carl James, one of the editors, had asked about getting an essay about the experiences of Chinese Jamaicans in Canada. Without hesitation, my cousin said: "You need to speak with Carol Wong." Carol, she added, was not only a friend of our family but had been heavily involved in the Jamaican Chinese community, had access to numerous resources and would likely be able to share a range of experiences. "Trust me," she said, "Carol is the one you want to talk to." I called Carol right away, explained the project, asked if we could meet, and within two weeks I was walking down the hall, through her living room toward her kitchen and sitting down to what became a three-hour conversation.

As we approached the kitchen table, it was clear that Carol had prepared for my visit. Displayed on the table were numerous books, pamphlets, newsletters and photo albums documenting the histories of her own family and those of many other Chinese Jamaicans residing in Canada and in the

United States. Among these resources was a book entitled *The Shopkeepers: Commemorating 150 years of the Chinese in Jamaica, 1854–2004 (Chen 2005)*. In this book, Carol had published a personal essay called "Among the Cane Fields of Westmoreland," in which she detailed her experiences and memories growing up in Jamaica. Most impressive was that much of what she presented was compiled through her own research, which she had conducted "with intention" (as she put it) over the years in search of her family's Hakka Chinese roots. During the three-hour visit, we drank Chinese tea, ate buns, pastries and fresh fruit, and talked about Carol's life history, her experiences in Canada, her involvement in various Toronto-based Jamaican and Chinese organizations, her perspectives on Jamaican Chinese identity and her vision of Jamaica in the future.

From "the Cane Fields of Westmoreland" to Canada

Carol Wong was born Carol Williams in 1941 in Glenislay District, Westmoreland, Jamaica and grew up in Savanna-la Mar and Petersfield District. She attended Wolmer's High School for Girls in Kingston, where, as a boarder, she "received an excellent foundation of British discipline and education." Carol's Hakka Chinese parents, Nathan and Gladys Williams, migrated to Jamaica over a hundred years ago, originally settling in the parish of Westmoreland. The name "Williams," Carol explained, was the Romanization of the Chinese name "Wei," which had been changed on the "whim of the immigration officer" when her first ancestor migrated.[2]

In 1965, Carol moved to Montreal with her husband, Edward Wong (a civil engineer), to pursue a career in fashion designing. Although Montreal in the late 1960s was "swinging during that era," Carol, Edward and their young son (born in Montreal) returned to Jamaica, where they remained until 1978 helping with the business of Edward's father. They returned to Montreal — having memories of Toronto as "so British and so WASPY" and feeling "not too fond of the U.S." — with the hope of raising their now three sons. However, they quickly discovered that it was not the Montreal they remembered.

> It was our misfortune that when we got to Montreal things had changed and the Separatist movement had started. Levesque won in the year we came up and so all the kids would have had to go to French school ... and letterbombs in the postbox and stuff. It was different ... and so we didn't even unpack the trailer. We headed over to this dead British Toronto.

Shortly after settling in Toronto, a three-year engineering assignment sent Carol, Edward and their three sons to Hong Kong, until they returned to

Canada for good in 1981. By this time, Toronto "while still WASPY" had seen an influx of immigration and was "not so bad" as they had remembered. Settling first in the Toronto suburbs of Scarborough, they eventually decided to move to a more northern suburb:

> *Carol*: I just thought I would get my children out … and we figured we were going to integrate into the Canadian society. We were surrounded by apartments and we figured let's get out into the suburbs … So when it started getting overpopulated we figured we should move out of town because I had three children. So I happened to drive up to Unionville and liked the main street and so we came up here. But we were the only Chinese family in Markham.

> *Leanne*: What was that like?

> *Carol*: Well, my Scottish girlfriend wrote back home at that time to her family and said "I met a real life Chink," referring to me. We're still friends but this is what she told me she wrote when she first met me … These were some reactions.

As "the only Chinese family in Markham" at the time, reactions like these were not uncommon. However, Carol made it clear that when faced with these experiences, she tried to see them not as challenges but as opportunities — a perspective she attributed to her Jamaican heritage and cultural upbringing. Throughout our conversation, Carol spoke of her desire and commitment to sharing her experiences and knowledge of Jamaica with those who may be unfamiliar with the island. This dedication informs much of her ongoing interest in and passion for volunteerism, a passion she developed in Canada but which was also passed down from her mother, who had been heavily involved in local charity groups in Jamaica.

"I Was Awakened"

Given Carol's strong ties to Jamaican culture, her involvement in the Jamaican Chinese community, her love of Canada and her desire to have her children integrate into Canadian society, I asked her how she would identify or what she would say if someone asked her where she was from. Without hesitation, she explained: "At this point, I would say I am Hakka Chinese." Of course, Carol did not arrive in Canada with this identity or connection to the Chinese and Hakka community. Rather she explains that this understanding of herself was "awakened" by "a sequence of events" or even "destiny" — the most significant being her unfolding involvement with the Hakka Chinese community.

In Canada, Carol has held membership in countless organizations and has taken on key roles in many of them — including serving as president of the Unionville Tennis Club for five years. However, much of her work has involved Chinese and Caribbean organizations. Carol worked with the Toronto Harbourfront Centre several years ago as part of the Island Soul Festival to represent the Chinese in Jamaica. And, in 2001, Carol joined the Tsung Tsin Association of Ontario (TTA) where she has been president since 2008. She explained that throughout her involvement in the TTA, she works to address the cultural needs of the membership. Carol sees this cultural attention as significant since

> Ninety-nine percent of their members are Jamaican Chinese im-
> migrants, whose elders, upon arriving in Toronto, pooled their
> resources and built a meeting place for the Hakka community to
> come together in this new homeland — Ontario, Canada ... [The
> organization] just kept together while we were bringing up our fami-
> lies ... and we have kept it going and have maintained the building
> and taxes. Plus, we're bringing in our Jamaicanness now.

The association produces a newsletter four times each year advertising activities and festivals happening in the Hakka Chinese community and organizes ongoing "Jamaican-type functions like 'Reggae Night' and 'Fry Fish Night' with skits and performances by the Heritage Singers." This creates the opportunity for get-togethers, which, as Carol explained, "replaces the nostalgia for their birthplace, and a great camaraderie continues to be developed among their membership, Jamaicans and Canadians at large." The association (currently with thirty-eight board members) is also branching out now to involve younger generations through youth-focused activities such as Karaoke nights, kids parties and summer festivals.

However, it was at the association's first Hakka conference, held in 2000 in Toronto, that precipitated Carol's "awakening."

> After going to the first conference in 2000, the Hakkaness awak-
> ened. All the time my father used to tell me that I'm so Jamaican
> and not Chinese. Because we were comfortable being Jamaican and
> "jumping up" etc. He wanted us to be more Chinese. But I would
> tell him, but I was born in Jamaica! Meaning that if he wanted me
> to be more Chinese, he should have stayed in China. I was a very
> mouthy child as well. So it's that 2000 conference that awakened
> my Hakkaness. Before that I wasn't so Hakka. And then, when we
> had that conference, the then president of the association decided to
> invite us — our generation — to the association to have a meeting.
> And I said that after this conference, I'm so Chinese now! So he in-
> vited us and we said, let's continue the conference and have a cultural

development association. We can include a little more of culture with our generation because we're so Jamaican. So that is what we did. We started having talks by people, like Dr. Anne Marie LeLoy, who gave this talk about children being sent from Jamaica back to China. We asked her to come to the association in Scarborough, and we had a chat room and we had Chinese people from South Africa come and talk about what it was like being Chinese there. And the Indians and the people from Mauritius also talked about how it was when they were growing up. That is how we learned what happened to the Chinese during apartheid — how they're not Black, they're not white.

Carol has since been involved in each of the Toronto Hakka conferences (2004, 2008) and works in various capacities to support and preserve Chinese culture and heritage in Toronto. Being involved in the Hakka Association has helped her to understand and express her Hakka Chinese heritage and identity, while also helping to "keep the Hakka community together, preserve our heritage and culture."

"Are You Hakka?"

Carol's sense of her Hakka heritage has also been formed in relation to and against Canadian non-Chinese and other non-Hakka Chinese groups living in Toronto. In fact, she spoke of how her Hakka Chinese attachments and Jamaican culture have not always allowed for an easy blending into the broader Chinese community in Toronto. She explained how her Caribbean ties and Jamaican cultural heritage combined with her relatively new understanding of her Hakka culture and community have led to Carol feeling "outsiderness" among other Chinese groups. Take for example Carol's experiences of engaging and interacting with Hong Kong Chinese in Toronto.

> They might see us as "less Chinese" because in their view if you don't speak the language, you are not even Hakka. You know they will say "are you Hakka? You can speak Hakka?" And so I'll always tell them I can understand but cannot speak.

I asked Carol about her experiences at Pacific Mall, a large Asian mall located in Markham. Its vendors and customers are predominantly Hong Kong Chinese or from other parts of China.

> *Leanne*: When you go there, do you find you blend in easily? What is the understanding of Chinese Jamaicans there?
>
> *Carol*: There is an understanding of Chinese Jamaicans and also

even in downtown Chinatown. But, when we first came, if you ordered a knife and fork, they would grumble and throw down the plate and they would just grudgingly serve you; and the pastry shop the same thing again. The problem was saying "one of this, two of this" rather than naming it. But they had to make money ... But over the years, they have realized that we are good customers. In the pastry shops now, we have been buying a box of this, a dozen of that. So then they are, hi! Hi!

Leanne: So they indulge you because you are good for business?

Carol: Yes, good for business ... And so I know some Cantonese now to tell them. And they say then "oh my grandma is Hakka too!" They wouldn't say it before.

But there are still challenges and Carol must constantly do the work of "convincing" others — a challenge she takes on willingly rather than dismissing it as discrimination. For example, at the moment, she is taking a Cantonese class. She explained how it was initially difficult to break into the predominantly Cantonese group of women.

Carol: And then at this Cantonese class too, I found out who could speak English. They wouldn't speak English — they are so rude, they would speak English among themselves although they know I can't speak Cantonese. But eventually I would find who could speak a little English and I would talk to them. And now they are calling me to dim sum — they want to practise their English with me now.

Leanne: So are you teaching them Jamaican words too?

Carol: [Laughter] No I'm speaking proper English — the Queen's English now! At Wolmer's school, where I went in Jamaica, we were taught proper grammar which they don't teach in the schools here ... So for me, what I always found interesting is that I never look at it as discrimination. I look at it like a challenge. Because now I want to learn Cantonese, so I can explain to them that I cannot speak it because I'm from overseas or "waa kew" — which means overseas.

Identifying as Hakka Chinese has also meant that Carol has worked to educate her children on their Chinese heritage, especially now that she sees the importance of passing on her newfound knowledge to another generation — her grandchildren.

But I'm glad that through me, my children are learning about that part of their culture. You know, we don't have a Bob Marley in the Chinese part, but it is such a conversation piece. But my grandchildren are talking about their blend of the Chinese and the German — one daughter-in-law is German, one is French-Canadian and English, and one is Chinese but from Seattle, she is Toisan.

"I Don't Want to Give Up My Jamaican Accent"

Nowhere is Carol's Chinese Jamaicanness more evident than in her language — specifically, her accent. Indeed, accents, like language, are key components of identity and are points of identification. They allow us to recognize who belongs, who doesn't and with whom we feel we can relate. It fosters the expression of culture and tradition and helps us find shared understanding of stories, expressions and history. Carol's Jamaican accent fulfills similar purposes and is just as strong today as when she arrived in Canada more than forty years ago. When I asked her about it and how others respond, she told me that her accent holds significance on multiple levels: it connects her to community, creates opportunities for her to educate others about her Jamaican heritage and facilitates her attempts to insert Chinese experiences into the public story and understanding of Jamaica and its diaspora.

> Yes, and this is my conversation piece — when they hear my accent they look at me and say: "How come you're Chinese?" And so that is why I don't want to give up my Jamaican accent. There are lots of Jamaicans here who do that. Though whenever I speak to Canadians I am a little bit not as relaxed as I am with you. But I like my Jamaican accent and it's an identification too because as soon as I speak it's as if, "oh, but you're one of us!" and then the other reaction from the Canadians is "Oh, but you're not Black!"

She shared one of the first times she experienced this "You're not Black" reaction — something she continues to face, although to different degrees today.

> *Carol*: In 1965. I phoned up for a job, either at Eaton's or the Bay in Montreal ... and of course I first made the appointment on the phone and then I went down. And when it was my turn for the interview, I went up but they called my name again. Coming from Jamaica I just stood there politely. You know, and eventually when they called a third time, I said "I'm Carol" (at the time Williams) and they said, "Oh, but you're not Black."

> *Leanne*: They said that to you?

> *Carol*: Yes, oh yes and especially because I didn't have an identifiable Chinese name and then with the accent — Yes, the accent. [Laughter] And now that we have multiculturalism, in Toronto people are more aware that people have migrated and travelled and that there are Japanese here. But in the 1960s, a lot of Canadians weren't very educated about Jamaica and Jamaicans.

> *Leanne*: Do you find that even with multiculturalism, people in Canada are still uninformed about places like Jamaica?

> *Carol*: Oh no, now they're telling me: "Oh I have a Jamaican friend." And they're telling me: "Oh my neighbour speaks like you!" They are quite aware now. We Jamaicans are great that way; we make an impression. We make an impact. I always say, you know, if there is a quiet lineup anywhere, the first person to break a silence is a Jamaican. And they're going to say, "but wait! Why we have to wait so long?" I tell you, we are such a colourful people!

Carol explained that she has actively sought to preserve her accent as a way of maintaining connection to the Jamaican community. Thus, rather than see her accent as contributing to her difference -- and possibly experience forms of discrimination, she sees her accent as an important source of identification and belonging among Jamaicans. As she put it, "If I open my mouth, it's like, 'Yes you're one of us'." However, even though Canada's multicultural programming and practices may mean that people are more informed now than they were when Carol first arrived, she feels an ongoing need to make certain cultural experiences known — especially those that might tend to fall off the radar.

An example of these efforts, as Carol shared, was about six years ago (2006) at the funeral of the Jamaican cultural icon, poet and commentator Louise Bennett-Coverley (Miss Lou).[3] Carol was one of those who spoke at the memorial service in Toronto. She recalled meeting Miss Lou in Toronto at the sesquicentennial anniversary event celebrating the arrival of Chinese in Jamaica. Miss Lou was the guest of honour along with dignitaries from the Jamaican Consulate.

> *Carol*: And then at Miss Lou's funeral, I went and gave the eulogy to let people know that there were Chinese in Jamaica. Yes, there were other Chinese people there, but I was the only Chinese who went up. And when I spoke everybody laughed for about a few minutes, for a long time…

> *Leanne*: What were they laughing at?

Carol: Well, it was very hot in there and everyone went up and they talked and talked and talked. And then I went up and before I said my little piece I said, "If Miss Lou was here, she's have said, 'Lawd, what a heat!'" And everybody laughed because they didn't expect it to come from this Chinese face. And everybody went up and spoke nicely. I was the only one that went up and spoke Patois. And it was just my first language.... "Miss Lou would a seh, Lawd, what a piece a heat!"

Leanne: Given that Miss Lou featured Patois as part of her storytelling, it is interesting that people would not have expected you to use Patois in honouring her. What do you think of that?

Carol: But that is what Jamaicans are. When they go out, they like to make a good impression, so they speak nicely — it's only when we are together that we break out into our Patois. I was amazed by the reaction — and everybody sort of lightened up too. Maybe the reaction was because I'm not Black — after all most of the people there were Jamaicans — I feel I can get away with not behaving the usual way or the proper way. My headmistress at Wolmer's wanted us to behave the proper way or else we would get detention. We would get a detention if we didn't speak proper language or we didn't wear our school beret, or did not act like proper ladies.

Carol is keenly aware of the importance of language and would use it not only to express her sense of belonging but also as a way to educate others about the diversity and complexities of Jamaicanness. As Carol put it:

It's the Jamaican in me, I was not like the Hong Kong people who kept to themselves. I was going to tell them about Jamaica. So we played tennis and I joined the tennis club. And every chance I get, I was telling people about Jamaica. Once you talk, they will listen. And I'd say, "I'm Chinese from Jamaica." And they would say: "I didn't know Jamaica had Chinese." And I'd say, "Oh yes, 97 percent of the population is Black but there are 3 percent Chinese, Indian and Syrian." And by the time they got to know me at the tennis club, I let them know that I left a big house in Jamaica and we had maids and gardeners, because they started looking down at me thinking we are so backward and underdeveloped.

Carol was also cognizant of the importance of *who* gets to speak *which* language and *when*. There are different perceptions attached to language and accent depending on the speaker. Although Patois operates as a point of connection among Jamaicans, Carol's experiences suggest that it remains a form of expression among friends and family and not something expected to be used in public. Carol felt that she could "get away with" speaking Patois at Miss Lou's service because she was not Black and presumably would not perpetuate racialized stereotypes of Black Jamaicans as "backward" or "unrefined." However, while she sees her use of Patois in some contexts as complicating understandings of Jamaicanness (and asserting her identity as a Chinese Jamaican), in other contexts, Carol consciously chooses to use "proper" English (as she learned through her British education at Wolmer's) in order to challenge people's assumptions about Jamaica, reflecting her desire for Jamaicans to be understood as educated and as making important contributions to society.

At this point, I shared with Carol my own observations of people's reactions to Chinese Jamaicans speaking Jamaican Patois. Several years ago, in the days following my father's funeral, local friends and acquaintances visited our family home to pay their respects. They remarked, with interest, on the large numbers of Jamaicans in attendance at the funeral and commented on the Jamaican accents they had heard — something that, while somewhat familiar because of their friendship with my father, was not something they were used to hearing en masse, given the town's (Cornwall, Ontario) homogenous population. However, as I told Carol, what completely *puzzled* them, were the Jamaican accents among the Chinese visitors: "Are they Jamaican? Why do they have those accents? How do they know Garth (my father)?" This has continued to confuse many of our friends, who, when at gatherings with large numbers of Chinese Jamaicans, are forced to question their assumptions that being Jamaican means being Black. Carol had already given this quite some thought. Aware of such assumptions, she carefully explained how she always takes time to enlighten her Canadian friends about the nuances of Jamaican culture.

> Well, when my Canadian[4] friends here meet with Jamaicans not only do they not understand, they say we are very "insultive." So I explain to them that Jamaicans we just say what we like because the other party can tell us if they like it or don't like it. We never heard the word "political correctness." We pay compliments but it's like a backhanded complement but it's taken in good humour because the other party understands that a Jamaican would understand. And if they don't like it they will tell you "fi gway" [to go away]. You know? Or we have it out and it's all over. But to a Canadian, it's like we're insulting each other, they didn't get that type of humour.

For Carol, language is important, and her stories demonstrate the ways in which certain languages and accents get shaped as having a "time and a place" within certain parts of Canadian society. So, challenging assumptions and speaking Patois help challenge assumptions about Jamaica but also Chinese stereotypes. She told me that as Jamaicans,

> we bring that outgoingness up here too. Chinese are supposed to be demure and doll-like. But not Chinese Jamaicans. Especially because we grew up in the country too. We could roam freely all over the place. And any adult Jamaican will scold you or discipline you as your parents would. This subscribes to the idea that it takes a village to raise a child. This was how it was when we were in Jamaica. I don't know what it is like now.

"We Have Helped Build These Foreign Countries"

Towards the end of our conversation, I asked Carol what she would really want people in Canada to understand about Jamaica and Jamaicans. She framed her response through a vision of hope for the country and a sense of responsibility.

> Well, I always say that Jamaica is the most beautiful place in the world. I've been to Bali and the Isle of Capris and all over. And boy, nowhere as beautiful as Jamaica. It's such a great country. I would like people to know that Jamaica was a British Colony, that Jamaicans were well educated and that basically Jamaica is very friendly and accepting of people and situations and very, I guess, flexible. I don't know what you'd call it. But because of the political problems that they went through in the seventies, there was a brain drain and hardship for a lot of people. But Jamaica is, because of the exodus of Jamaicans, we have helped the foreign countries. We have helped build these foreign countries, and so now because of our experience and probably progression, we are now going to give back to build the country again. And now we're able to do it. Before, we were just going away to seek a better life for our children. But our children are grown up now, they have done well for themselves, and they can be left here. And they know we are in a position now, a generation is in a position now, to help Jamaica build again. Because it needs good political guidance. We now have a female prime minister. This is the second time for her. I have great confidence in women leaders. Gandhi, Margaret Thatcher and Bhutto. So hopefully, although our prime minister is new at this, she didn't grow up in a political family like the Manleys and Bustamantes, you know. Hopefully Jamaica will be on the up because it really did slide when all the productive people left. Jamaicans always go back. No matter how they bad-mouth the country. Oh yes, in our

association, they all gravitate back there. Because we all have people back there too — our friends.

Clearly, Carol has a desire to make Jamaican Chineseness known — not just to Chinese and non-Chinese Canadians but to her own family as well. It emerges from her experiences growing up, her struggles and challenges moving to Canada and her work raising three children in Toronto. As she put it:

> We use the term down there: "We're just a group of Chinese Yardies⁴" because of the way we speak, the way we think, the way we do things. Even when we are doing things in the association ... No matter how old we are, because we're older we're seeking our roots, this Hakkaness or Chineseness. But basically, we're still Jamaican ... I have been going around merrily being Jamaican Chinese and different and shocking people — and they marvel about how we can dance and have rhythm, Jamaican rhythm!

It would seem that being a Hakka Chinese Jamaican in Canada carries certain responsibilities. An email from Carol, some time after our interview, directed me to the broader contribution of the Jamaican Chinese and their involvement in Canada and abroad. She wrote:

> Something came to mind to let you know that although I have directed my volunteer time to preserving our Hakka culture at Tsung Tsin Association, other Jamaican Chinese have directed their energies to fundraising for their respective high schools in Jamaica, and families like mine have also formed other charity groups like the Westmoreland Basic School Service to adopt the basic schools, where most of us had attended as children, and unlimited funds have been generated by all from various events held up here in Toronto to be sent back to the island of our birth.
>
> Needless to say that Jamaican Chinese have also jumped in when disasters strike like the aftermath of hurricanes and through the Chinese Benevolent Association in Kingston, raised funds to repair the Chinese Cemetery and environs.
>
> Not sure if I had mentioned that at past Toronto Hakka conferences, achievement awards were presented in the field of medicine, business, science and arts, and awardees included Raymond Chang, Michael Lee Chin, Dr. Herbert Ho Ping Kong, Dr. Karen Chang, Prof. Emeritus Albert Chung, Ronald Chung, Anthony Chen, researcher Moo Young, photographer Ray Chen, music icon Byron Lee etc.

While Carol's identity is distinct, it is not static. It is connected with/to Jamaica and Chinese Hakka heritage however that is being constructed or understood at the time. But it is also asserted as a way of protecting and preserving both. To be a "Chinese Yardie," at least for Carol, seems to be about balance, a dance and a form of/opportunity for education.

Reflections: How Race, Ethnicity and Class Travels

Following our conversation, I started thinking about my father, his similar sense of national pride and his attempts to ensure that my brother and I understood our Jamaican heritage. Like Carol and her husband, my father and mother decided to raise their children in Canada rather than in Jamaica. Eventually settling in a small town in eastern Ontario, they wanted their children to excel but felt an added pressure to develop our appreciation and respect for Jamaica. My father was no different than Carol in this regard and encouraged us to partake in a range of Jamaican activities. We visited friends and family in Jamaica every year and regularly attended Jamaican functions in Ottawa and Toronto. We came to understand many of the nuances associated with Jamaica, particularly music, language and food. My mother had learned to cook most Jamaican food soon after she was married, and my father ritually baked rum cakes each Christmas — these cakes were a family recipe and a significant memory of his baker parents in Montego Bay. Each year we were made to memorize the recipe and replicate it under his watchful eye.

I found myself wondering what my father would have said if he were part of my conversation with Carol. What questions might he have asked? Although I can only speculate on his specific reactions, I think he would have related to many of Carol's experiences and views. Not only was he of the same generation as Carol, but they shared the goals of many immigrant parents who seek to create opportunities for their children while recreating a sense of "home" that they do not want to be forgotten. And in Canada, the elements of Jamaica they emphasized were inevitably mediated by popularized assumptions of Jamaica relating to globally popular musicians such as Bob Marley and exotic tourist attractions such as the hedonistic Sandals resort, and at the same time, make every attempt to counter mainstream media portrayals of Jamaica as plagued by gangs, drugs and violence.

How individuals read Jamaica depends on how they are situated and situate themselves across race, ethnicity, class, gender, language, accent, age, period of immigration and place of residence. As a Black man in Canada, my father's Jamaican identity was rarely questioned. His accent was always expected — it seemed to fit some people's assumptions about Jamaicans. As a doctor, his racial experiences were tempered by his class position and the prestige associated with his profession; however, his class position, education and profession also challenged ideas of Jamaicans as uneducated and underdeveloped. Thus, while his Jamaican heritage may not have been in question, his role as a doctor often was. In contrast, although Carol's identity as a Jamaican might have been questioned, there were certain privileges based on race and class that she was able to call upon to assert her Jamaicanness, as in her volunteer work and social activities. Though each were differently located, both Carol and my father challenged stereotypes by presenting an image of Jamaica as relatable, stable and ultimately positive.

While unique, Carol's story affords an opportunity to examine the ways in which Jamaican identity travels and takes hold in different contexts. In what follows, I offer some final thoughts on how we might read Carol's story in ways that open up a discussion of Jamaican Canadian identity beyond essentialist understandings of music, food and language, and illuminate the role of various privileges in racial and ethnic constructions of Jamaicanness.

In Canada, where multiculturalism is a federal state policy, the narrative of national belonging remains superficial and often problematic — given its focus on distinct and separate cultures serves to "other" some ethno-racial groups while normalizing the practices, values and perspectives of the dominant group. Understandings and expressions of a Jamaican Canadian culture and identity inevitably get linked to particular performances, festivals (e.g., Caribanna), cultural associations and other group activities. Such expressions are undeniably important to one's sense of belonging and cultural identification. But as Carol's story indicates, in the Canadian context, expressions or representations of her complex Jamaican Canadian identification remain a difficult task. Her experiences highlight an ongoing effort, as with other Chinese Jamaican Canadians, to position and represent themselves as "from" Jamaica and to counter the idea that Jamaica is a "space that excludes Chineseness" (Lee-Loy 2010: 116). Lee-Loy further writes:

> To "be seen" as West Indian means to "be not seen" as Chinese, and to choose to participate in those cultural signifiers that are particularly associated with an Afro-Euro creole West Indian culture. Thus, in such articulations of national belonging, Chineseness remains uncommon in the common culture.

Lee-Loy also contends that "such representations of nationhood suggest that Chinese West Indians ironically repeat 'what they seek to overthrow' — that is, a limited concept of nation enclosed in ethnic boundaries." What this indicates, is that the upheld images of Chinese Jamaicans can be considered a "strategic attitude" — a term Lee-Loy borrows from theorist Rey Chow to indicate the ways in which Chinese assert their sense of belonging in the context of Jamaica and the Caribbean.

The multicultural discourse in Canada constructs boundaries between cultural groups in ways that make it difficult to imagine certain bodies as part of particular groups, since they seem not to "match" essentialized notions of those groups. Accordingly, the idea that Jamaicans can be anything other than Black or that those racially identified as Chinese may have a Jamaican identity is viewed as uncommon and gets called into question. Part of Carol's attempts to "make common" or insert Chinese Jamaican identification and related culture into a Canadian national imagination is reflected in her work with the Hakka Association. This work is clearly an important part of Carol's life and seems to represent, as Li Minghuan (1999: 1) suggests, an attempt to forge a sense of ethnic identity:

> Ethnic migrants in alien surroundings often forge a sense of collectivity. Despite individual differences in training and experiences before and after their arrival, they have identified themselves, and are always identified by non-Chinese people by their shared ethnic background. To ensure a better future in their receiving country, the immigrants organize themselves through visible and invisible links. The emergence of associations is recognized as an important collective symbol.

For Carol, it was her identification as a Hakka Chinese[5] that was important. Chang Bohr (2004: 49) explains the connections among Hakka Chinese in the diasporic community:

> Unlike those living in China, overseas Hakka have a powerful pride in their migratory history, as well as a strong identification with Chinese culture. This migratory tradition has had a strong impact on the Chinese in Jamaica since many of them also identify with, and take great pride in, their history.

This feeling of pride in Hakka history is informed not only by a long historical Hakka presence in Jamaica, but also by their various labour and cultural contributions to the island. In referencing her Hakka Jamaican roots, Carol is reminding us of her ancestral history and its significance to Jamaica's development. Understandably with this history comes pride — particularly in relation to her race and class background — even in the Canadian context. She was able to make choices of when and where she might call upon her Jamaican identification or cultural attributes. Take, for example, her decision to "shock people" with her use of Patois at Louise Bennett's funeral — something Carol admits she could "get away with." Reflecting on this, I thought of my father, whom I cannot remember using — and likely never would use — Patois to re-assert his Jamaican identification in public spaces but would largely limit its use to the household and to family gatherings. So, while both Carol and my father each enjoyed a range of privileges, those privileges differed in relation to race, class and context.

Overall, my conversation with Carol extends and helps to represent the diverse and complex identities and connections to home, the complexity of Jamaica and Jamaicans and the multifaceted ways that Jamaicans understand their relationships with and to Jamaica and other Jamaicans. I see her story as allowing us to understand how race, ethnicity, class and gender might travel, how they might travel differently when represented in different bodies and how people might differently make sense of those bodies and ideas of belonging and nationhood in the Canadian context.

Notes

1. Through Carol's historical research and compilation of her family tree, which went back eighteen generations to 61 BCE, she learned that the Wei families who moved to Trinidad kept their name as Wei, while in Guyanna, it changed to Ngai. The inability of English immigration officers to pronounce the name meant that, in the Jamaican context, they were just given the English name Williams.
2. Louise Bennett Coverley (Miss Lou) (1919–2006) was well known for her poems, many written and spoken in Jamaican Patois, which captured the philosophy, culture, traditions and everyday experiences of Jamaicans. She has been de-scribed as "the only poet who has really hit the truth about her society through its own language" and her poems are often touted as "valid social documents reflecting the way Jamaicans think and feel and live" <http://louisebennett. com/bio.asp>. She lived in Canada for the last decade of her life and died in Scarborough, Ontario. See also Chapter 21 in this volume.
3. It is important to note that Carol's reference to Canadian friends signals how she, like most Canadians, is unconsciously informed by the discourse of Canadian meaning white.
4. While this word has had different applications, it is most commonly used to refer to people who are natives of Jamaica or of Jamaican descent.
5. Yamamoto (2008: 171) explains the Hakka migration history: "In Jamaica, most Chinese are Hakka and their origins are traced to Chinese laborers who came to the island in the late 19th to early 20th centuries. Seventy-five per cent of those who were dispatched to the British West Indies were sent to British Guiana in the late 1800s, although many moved to Jamaica later. Ninety-six per cent of the Caribbean-bound Chinese immigrants came from a small region of Kwantung on the Pearl River Delta." However, Patrick Lee, in *Canadian Jamaican Chinese* (2000) suggests we may need to question such ties, explaining the history and sig-nificance of Hakka Chinese in the Caribbean in the following way: "The Hakka are a migratory people. We move outwards on the tides of history. Most of us have relatives in Surinam, Panama, the British West Indies, as well as Singapore, Malaysia and other parts of South-east Asia. After several more generations in Canada, will it still be significant that we sojourned for a few generations in Jamaica? For now and as far we can see, that is how we identify ourselves, and that is also how we are perceived by the wider Canadian community.... In this generation we became part of a North American community, with significant

concentration in Miami, New York, Toronto and other U.S. and Canadian cities and even London, England, as well as Hong Kong and Taiwan."

References

Chang Bohr, A. 2004. "Identity in Transition: Chinese Community Associations in Jamaica." *Caribbean Quarterly* 50 (2).

Chen, Ray. 2005. *The Shopkeepers: Commemorating 150 years of the Chinese in Jamaica, 1854–2004.* Kingston, Jamaica: Periwinkle Publishers.

Lee, P. 2000. *Canadian Jamaican Chinese 2000: A Pictorial History of Jamaican Chinese Families Spanning Five Generations.* Toronto: Huntsmill Graphics.

Lee-Loy, A. 2010. *Searching for Mr. Chin: Constructions of Nation and the Chinese in West Indian Literature.* Philadelphia, PA: Temple University Press.

Minghuan, Li. 1999. *"We Need Two Worlds": Chinese Immigrant Associations in a Western Society.* Ambsterdam: Amsterdam U Press.

Yamamoto, S. 2008. "Swaying in Time and Space: The Chinese Diaspora in the Caribbean and its Literary Perspectives." *Asian Ethnicity* 9 (3).

19. "COME MEK WE WHEEL AND TUN, GAL"

Snapshots of life in Jamaica and Calgary

Cecille Marie DePass

Time: Early March 2011. Place: A Small University of Toronto Classroom

"Come mek we wheel and tun"[1]: Three of us, like-minded professors from two Albertan universities, are attending an international conference in Toronto. We enjoy meeting some of the participants and keynote speakers and actively network. For our panel, we intend to present perspectives which explore different but complementary components of the historical and contemporary, colonial educational agenda still evident in Canadian and Jamaican schools. In my paper, for example, I plan to use music from Bob Marley's song "Redemption Time." Marley's encouragement to his listeners to liberate themselves from mental slavery is particularly appropriate when considering the widespread reliance on what Paulo Freire (1970) aptly describes as "banking," or transmission, models of education, which are still the dominant teaching strategies nationally and internationally. To stimulate interest, I plan to play samples of Marley's music, as part of the introduction to our panel presentation. To begin, I put in the CD. Bob Marley's popular music quickly fills the air and wafts into the corridor, since the classroom door is still ajar in order to allow participants for the seminar to enter the room. I am amused when a very Jamaican woman's voice exclaims from the corridor: "What is Bob Marley's music doing here!" "Yes, yes, indeed," I thought. Such small incidents have influenced my inclusion of Jamaican Creole and music in a few of my recent writings and conference presentations (e.g., DePass 2008 and 2006). As importantly, the use of Jamaican Creole has helped to influence the celebratory tone of writing this chapter, prepared as a small contribution for the fiftieth anniversary of Jamaica's independence.

In a telephone discussion with Carl James and while further thinking seriously of contributing some of my Calgary experiences for his edited book, I realized that to present a more comprehensive picture, I needed to begin with a few stories of my Jamaican youth, in order to better situate some of my adult immigrant experiences within larger contexts. To do so, this chapter draws on memory, a strategy used by some people to ensure that their alternative explanations of local and regional history and events are not erased fully by the dominant culture's narratives and interpretations of the world in which we live (e.g., Brown 2010; Manley 1997; Hyatt 1989). Growing up I heard stories from my grandmother and her sisters regarding generations of my mother's family. (One great aunt, Dor Robertson (2002), herself a secondary school teacher, collected family oral histories and researched and wrote the family's history and its diaspora). Since my extended family was very large and employment opportunities in the island were fairly limited, I heard stories regarding branches of the family which had migrated and established themselves in the United States, England and more recently in Canada. I also heard somewhat different versions of Jamaican and West Indian history from my teacher great aunts to those I learned in school (Black (1961) and Augier et al. (1960) are two examples of the history texts used in high school).

This chapter is conceptualized as a series of snapshots of my childhood experiences in Kingston, Jamaica, which I contrast with adult encounters associated with living in Calgary, after my Jamaican husband and I migrated. During the late 1970s in Calgary, for instance, I realized that we were stared at often by Euro-Canadians when we walked along the main streets in the city's downtown core. (Admittedly, at that time, the visible minority, immigrant population from the South was very small, and the African Caribbean population was perhaps only a few thousand people). I still remember a few unsettling events quite vividly. For example, one day, when three of us, my husband, a Jamaican male friend and I were entering a convenience store, we were cursed soundly by a Euro-Canadian male who pushed quickly between us. Also, from time to time, the derogatory phrase "paki, paki" was shouted at me from a passing car, when I was standing alone, waiting to cross the street. From such irritating encounters, it was obvious that if individuals did not appear to be white, such persons were labelled and fitted into the category of unwelcome, unwanted strangers or "Others." In moving from presenting personal experiences to a broader societal critique, academics such as Carl James (2000) have demonstrated the significant difficulties associated with minority life in Canada. James analyzes dominant responses to racial and ethnic differences. As importantly, his book traces important contradictions underlying assumptions inherent in claims of equality, equity, colour-blindness, multiculturalism and diversity in Canada.

The first part of this chapter highlights a few stories of my early life in Jamaica, summarizing memories of the 1960s, when the emerging Jamaican culture (demonstrated in popular music, dance and use of Creole) was being created and gaining larger acceptance. During this period, the folk culture was re-vitalized and reclaimed from its roots in African Caribbean enslavement associated with a plantation economy. The second part of the chapter spotlights some amusing and somewhat troubling Calgary experiences. It is deliberately conversational, written as if I am relating these events to my mother in Jamaica. As importantly, at strategic points, Creole phrases are inserted in the text in order to bring the bi-dialectic quality of "Jamaican talk" to the forefront (conversation with Pamela Mordecai, well known Jamaican author, spring 2007).

Memories of Independence Celebrations and of Cultural Developments Post-Independence

During the 1960s, I attended a secondary girl's school in Kingston which was supported actively by one of the established churches. Memories of the pageantry associated with the first independence celebrations are still vivid pictures in my mind. Specifically, I remember sitting excitedly with my family in the bleachers of the new National Stadium for the official ceremonies, which marked the end of almost three hundred years of English colonial rule.

"A fe we time now." [It is our time, at last]: While eating our picnic supper, which was probably slices of freshly baked, hard dough bread, and the main event, delicious, very peppery, escovitch fish, we watched the closing ceremony at which the outgoing English governor, resplendently dressed in his formal regalia, solemnly handed the symbolic baton of the country's governance to the first Jamaican prime minister, Sir Alexander Bustamante. I remember that Princess Margaret, who was representing her sister Queen Elizabeth II at the independence celebrations, had arrived earlier. She was cheered by the crowd when, wearing a fabulous outfit, she stepped from the governor's car. After fifty years, understandably, I do not remember any of the speeches but I do remember that we watched eagerly as the Union Jack was lowered and the new Jamaican flag unfurled, and that we struggled with singing the unfamiliar words of the new national anthem. My family and I attended several independence festivities, often with spectacular displays of food from the parish and national cooking contests. For these competitions, Jamaicans were encouraged to use local food, fruits and vegetables and to create original dishes. We listened to and learned the words of the popular independence songs and of course, we danced at the first independence street fêtes.

As a very curious teenager, I remember reading avidly the *Daily Gleaner*'s reports about the first Jamaican diplomats who were sent to London, New York and the United Nations to establish diplomatic offices. In terms of the rapidly emerging popular culture, I remember reading about and seeing demonstrations of the ska by the well-known radio announcer Neville Willoughby and his glamorous sister, Judith Willoughby. I was also intrigued to read of educational successes of young Jamaicans. For example, I cheered when I read that Noreen Barrett was awarded a scholarship to study music in England. (In later years, she became a well-known classical concert pianist and went to live and work in Germany.) I was thrilled too, to read that Anne Hickling had received a major scholarship to study at a university in either Hong Kong or Singapore. She returned to teach in Jamaica and much later migrated to Australia. (In the early to mid-2000s, while attending a university conference in Halifax, Nova Scotia, I was delighted to learn that Dr. Anne Hickling Hudson had become the president of the World Council of Comparative Education Societies).

Most of my teenage memories of the 1960s are of the growing nationalistic sentiments and of the people who blazed a trail on the national and international, educational, cultural and economic fronts. During this period, a new national culture was being imagined, re-invented and created in which, for the first time, representations of the folk culture assumed central importance in the visual and performing arts. There was, for instance, the pleasure and pride with which our family attended Boxing Day performances of the annual pantomime at the Ward Theatre. Pantomimes such as Busha Bluebeard and Queenie's Daughter, featuring Louise Bennett, Ranny Williams and Lois Kelly Barrow, were particularly memorable events for a youthful teen with a vivid imagination. The pantomimes presented a welcome contrast with the dominant culture. At that time, virtually all of the representations of cultural activities in which we were immersed, such as movies, books and written materials, were stamped made in England or the United States and concentrated on life in the major metropolitan centres.

The emerging popular culture of Jamaica presented an alternative which deliberately resisted reliance on the colonial culture (Ashcroft et al. 2001). The shift to acceptance of a local culture was most obvious perhaps in the growing inclusion of Creole/Patois in plays and in the emergence on the public stage of folk, mento and reggae music. Traditionally, as part of the well-established colonial education mission, individuals were forced to speak and write Standard English in schools, in mainstream churches and in the workplace, particularly when doing business with representatives of the colonial institutions. Furthermore, as a child, I learned that Creole speakers were regarded as uneducated. Accordingly, at the pantomime it was thrilling to watch a play written and performed by Jamaicans and to hear Creole used unabashedly as the official language. The annual pantomime through humour, song, dance and story, held a mirror up to society's foibles and focused on historical and contemporary events. It ridiculed the affectations and pretensions of all social classes. The middle and upper classes, who had long adopted affected English accents and arrogant behaviours as markers of dominance, were especially ridiculed. The audience laughed at the adventures of the trickster. This was the Anansi character, usually played by Ranny Williams, who plotted and used what Jamaicans call "ginnalship" strategies to outwit and triumph over oppressive, brutal characters (like Busha Bluebeard) and who found ways to survive unjust and unequal social and economic conditions. It was through such plays and through folk music, as a child, that I learned of the significant societal disparities. Such critical learning experiences were reinforced when my sister and I accompanied my father, a senior social worker, on his visits to rural villages.

With my family, I enjoyed attending performances of the newly established Jamaican Folksingers, founded by Olive Lewin. We listened to and learned a wide range of folk songs, which depicted, often with humour, the harsh everyday, working-class life, as well as celebratory events. We sang along with digging songs, ring games, songs of courtship and songs which made fun of rivalries between men and women (e.g., "Woman a Heavy Load"). Increasingly too, Jamaican and Caribbean folk music and songs were broadcast on the two radio stations. Each year, on the dance scene, I eagerly anticipated the next season's performances of the National Dance Theatre Company (NDTC) at the Little Theatre. One year, I especially enjoyed watching the NDTC performance of some of Jimmy Cliff's rude boy, reggae music. (This was well before the reggae film *The Harder they Come* was released). Without realizing, I learned important lessons, specifically that cultures, in the broadest sense, are neither fixed nor static, nor divinely created,but are social constructs developed by men and women.

"Come mek we dance and sing": On passing the Cambridge advanced level examinations, I attended the Mona campus of the UWI in order to study for a bachelor of arts degree. I was very happy to be surrounded by and to make friends with students who came from across the English speaking Caribbean. For the first time, the Caribbean countries which I had learnt about in McPherson's geography text *Caribbean Lands* came to life through the men and women that I met on campus. It was when I lived on campus that some students from either Trinidad or Guyana occasionally teased me by stating that I did not look like a typical Jamaican. However, since, my family's roots were very deep, I used to laugh and not take their teases seriously. It was also at UWI, at the Student's Union and Carnival fetes, that I danced happily to the calypso and jump up music of Trindad and Tobago's Mighty Sparrow.

Snapshots of Migration and Life in Canada

"Honour your partners: Learning to dance in western Canada": My husband and I migrated directly to Calgary, primarily to join his brother's family, who had lived in western Canada since the 1950s. Like many other immigrants, particularly immigrants from the South, whilst learning to dance in western

Canada, initially we encountered such systemic problems as difficulties of finding jobs commensurate with our educational qualifications and previous work experience in Jamaica. Before migrating, I had studied in New Zealand and completed a master's degree in economic geography. Furthermore, I had also taught at a Jamaican postsecondary institution for several years and completed a diploma in education at UWI. To my surprise, when applying for jobs, I found out that only my New Zealand university qualifications were accepted. (Non-recognition of academic credentials could be regarded as exemplified in the folk song "Carry Me Ackee Go a Linstead Market.")

In Calgary, I was hired by an urban planning company financed primarily by the private sector and the city to coordinate a large comparative research project. The overarching objective of the project was to identify key factors facilitating decentralization of major head office functions and the office-warehouse service sector in Calgary. To my chagrin, I later found out that because of the demanding nature of research skills required to complete this project, no one else who was interviewed was willing to accept the relatively low salary being offered by the company's president. I suspect that, like many other immigrants, I seized this project as a way to break into the Canadian workplace at a level comparable with my previous formal education and training. I completed such an exceptional project that in progress report meetings, I was commended by the city's urban planners for the high calibre of research. Interestingly, a few years later, I was asked to explain my research methodology and strategies more fully to a doctoral student at the university who wished to conduct a similar research project for her dissertation.

While working as a researcher, one interesting incident illustrates best some of the gender stereotypes which existed concerning the types of jobs and levels of responsibility that women and men were considered capable of fulfilling in the high education sector of the paid labour market.

Time: Early 1980s. Place: Large Office Building, Suburban Calgary
"Can I speak with Mr. Cecil DePass?": One morning, one of the senior secretaries called me on the internal telephone. She stated that a client demanded to speak with Mr. Cecil DePass. She informed the client that there was no one called Cecil DePass at that office but that he needed to speak with Mrs. Cecille DePass. The client refused to accept her statements. When she connected me, the client stated that he needed to speak with Mr. DePass who had signed the report which he was reading. I replied that I had written and signed the report in question. I do not remember the rest of the conversation. In retrospect, it was probably easier to believe that in an engineering and urban planning company the writer of a report should be a man. The next snapshot demonstrates that there tends to be some confusion concerning my

racialized identity when an outsider with little knowledge of the Caribbean attempts to label me and usually errs.

Time: Early 1980s. Place: Downtown Core, Calgary
"Which Native reserve are you really from?": One day, while with Carol Rousseau, a First Nations friend who worked as a human resources officer with a major Canadian company, she introduced me to one of her First Nations male friends, who was visiting from Ontario. As we headed for lunch in a nearby restaurant, Carol and her friend fell into an easy conversation. Since we could not walk three abreast without blocking the sidewalk, I went a few paces ahead.

Within a short time Carol, called out: "Hey Cecille, we are talking about you, you know!"

I replied with surprise: "Why is that?"

She chuckled and stated: "Charles and I are discussing you. We know that you are a Native woman. We are now trying to decide which Native reserve in Canada you really belong to."

I laughed, thinking this was a hilarious joke. I reminded Carol that a few years ago we had met at a Carifest event at Prince's Island Park. I reminded her also that John, a mutual friend from St. Lucia, had introduced us. She replied that Charles and herself were really convinced that I must be a Native woman.

This vignette is an example of the process of labelling someone who does not appear to fit within preconceived, stereotypical notions of what a Black person from the English-speaking Caribbean should look like. Amusing, troubling and sometimes problematic situations can be created when someone who is not from the Caribbean tries to label me and determine my identity by using superficial, erroneous cues. The dilemma associated with problems of relying solely on physical appearances to determine someone's identity is also illustrated in the next snapshot.

Time: Early 1990s. Place: Downtown Head Office
of a National Company, Calgary
"Who is that woman? What is she doing here!": When I was working as a research consultant on a provincially funded project to identify and classify some of the early types of employment equity initiatives in federally regulated industries, I remember distinctly an incident which occurred prior to one of the research interviews with a senior manager in the head office of a major company. While I was waiting for my interview in the large reception area, quietly reading a magazine, I noted that after a considerable time a Euro-Canadian man and woman were engaged in a friendly conversation just outside an office door. I continued reading the magazine. I heard when

the man approached the receptionist and was shocked when his angry voice shouted. "Who is that woman? What is she doing here?" There was no one else in the reception area. I close my reminiscences with a snapshot of another critical incident.

Time: A Spring Day, Late 1990s. Place: Small Cafeteria, Calgary
"Aunt Cecille, why is everyone staring at us?": During late spring one year, on a bright sunny day, my sister and her two sons were visiting from Jamaica, and we went for a walk in the park around the city's reservoir. We decided to have lunch in the cafeteria in the shopping centre adjacent to the reservoir. As we sat enjoying our soup and scones, my nephew David, who was then twelve years, suddenly turned to me and said: "Aunt Cecille, am I wrong, why is everyone staring at us?"

Over the years I had become accustomed to being stared at in Calgary. I put down my scone and looked around the room slowly. I turned and scrutinized my sister and her two sons, then responded in an ironic tone: "David you are quite right. People are staring at us because they are wondering why these Indians from the nearby reserve have dared to eat in this cafeteria."

In Retrospect

In an attempt to provide a more balanced view of my life in Calgary, I should rapidly explain that in the big picture, my life and work experiences have been extremely positive ones. Canada is well known internationally for its acceptance of immigrants and refugees who during the past thirty years have come increasingly from countries in the South. Since our arrival in the 1970s, we have established a strong circle of friends from several countries who have supported us during good times as well as during serious life changing events, such as the deaths of our parents. In turn, in keeping with Jamaican and Caribbean traditions of creating a family from friends, we have become surrogate aunts and uncles for several of our friends' children. We have celebrated small and large events with them, have helped actively in the organization of a few of their children's weddings and also have become godparents.

Shortly after migrating, I returned to university and completed a doctoral degree, and I have taught at the municipal university for many years, establishing a solid career. Still looking at the big picture, I have gained tremendous life and work experiences on and off campus. These experiences have been invaluable in terms of my continuing personal, academic, professional and spiritual development. In terms of family and Jamaican traditions of giving back to the community in which one lives, for more than thirty years, I have been an active and well-appreciated volunteer with several community and academic organizations. Most recently, I was absolutely astonished when I was nominated and then placed as a finalist in the Immigrants of Distinction Awards.

Given my successes, why then are the relatively irritating encounters remembered and put into print in a book designed to celebrate the wide range of contributions of Jamaicans in Canada? Admittedly, some of the incidents could be attributed to mainstream ignorance of visible minorities; however, perhaps more importantly, such incidents represent lived experiences of far larger, systemic, structural issues of life in a society in which inherited colonial patterns of dominance and subordination have been accepted and normalized (see Carr and Lund 2007; James 2000; Steinberg 2008 for fuller discussion). Since the late 1970s, with the significant increase in numbers of immigrants and their children from countries in Asia, Africa, Latin America and the Caribbean who now live in Canada's major urban centres and who, in some cities, like Toronto, constitute a statistical majority, there is increasing recognition of their vital contributions to all aspects of social, cultural and economic life. In light of these changes, it will be interesting to see the ways in which these cosmopolitan dancers and their children continue to succeed in breaking down structural barriers and continue to build a Canadian society in which each of us is truly valued.

Happy Fiftieth Birthday Jamaica!

Notes

1. "Come mek we wheel and tun, gal" can be translated as "Come and dance with me" and is taken from the well-known Jamaican folk song "Dis long time gal, me neva see yu…," which was made popular in the 1960s.
    This chapter is dedicated to Louise Bennett, Olive Lewin and Fay Simpson, who through the arts have fostered a pride in and affirmation of being true to one's self. After independence, interest in Jamaican folk culture was fostered by groups such as the Jamaican Folksingers, founded by Olive Lewin, and through Louise Bennett's Creole poetry. Perhaps one of her best known anthologies is *Jamaica Labrish* (1966). Her anthology has influenced the title, tone and spirit of this chapter.

References

Ashcroft, B., G. Griffiths, and G. Tiffin. 2001. *The Empire Writes Back: Theory and Practice in Post-colonial Literatures*. New York: Routledge.

Augier, R., S.C. Gordon, D.G. Hall, and M. Reckford. 1960. *The Making of the West Indies*. Harlow: Longman Caribbean Limited.

Bennett, L. 1966. *Jamaica Labrish*. Kingston: Sangster's Book Stores.

Black, C. 1961. *The History of Jamaica*. London: Collins.

Brown, Y.S. 2010. *Dead Woman Pickney: A Memoir of Childhood in Jamaica*. Ontario: Wilfred Laurier University Press.

Carr, P., and D. Lund (eds.). 2007. *The Great White North: Exploring Whiteness, Privilege and Identity in Education*. Rotterdam: Sense Publishers.

DePass, C. 2006. "'Independence Is We Nature': Growing Up in a Post-Colonial Caribbean Country." *Journal of Contemporary Issues in Education* 1(2).

___. 2008. "'Rock Stone Under River Bottom…': Memories of a Caribbean Childhood." In A. Abdi and G. Richardson (eds.), *Decolonizing Democratic Education: Trans-Disciplinary Dialogues.* Rotterdam: Sense Publishers.

Freire, P. 1970. *Pedagogy of the Oppressed.* New York: Continuum Publishing.

Hyatt, C. 1989. *When Me Was a Boy.* Kingston: Institute of Jamaica Publications.

James, C.E. (ed.). 2000. *Experiencing Difference.* Halifax: Fernwood Publishing.

Manley, R. 1997. *Drumblair: Memories of a Jamaican Childhood.* Toronto: Vintage Canada.

Robertson, D.E. 2002. *The Harrison's of West Portland.* Kingston: A Family Publication.

Steinberg, S. 2008. *Diversity and Multiculturalism.* New York: Peter Lang.

PART SIX – INFLUENCES THEN AND NOW

20. MARCUS GARVEY AND THE UNIA IN CANADA

Contextualizing Black Canadians
in the History of the African Diaspora

Jamil Jivani

As a Toronto-born African Canadian of Kenyan, Irish and Scottish descent, I have cultivated my own identity using Jamaican culture as one of my primary influences. Many of the Black Canadians I grew up with and have built communities with are of Jamaican descent. Much of the music that provided the soundtrack to my childhood and the words I use to express myself are rooted in Jamaican culture. For me and many other Black Canadians of varying cultural and ethnic backgrounds, Jamaica is of great significance because of the rich contributions Jamaicans have made to Canada and the prominent role Jamaican culture has had in shaping Black identities in Canada and across the world.

Perhaps no better example of Jamaica's influence over Black identities across the world is the work of Marcus Garvey and the Universal Negro Improvement Association (UNIA). In my quest to better understand my own identity in Canada—a country that is home to many Black diasporas—Garvey's efforts to take ownership of his culture, to build relationships between Black communities around the world, and to imagine a more equal world across racial divisions deeply resonate with me. This chapter describes how my journey of self-discovery deeply intertwines with Jamaican history and reflects the rich and diverse history of ideas and experiences from which I have drawn inspiration as a young African-Canadian.

In September 2009, as a York University undergraduate, I presented a version of this chapter at the U.S./Canadian History and Genealogy Conference in Buxton, Ontario, home to one of Canada's oldest Black communities. To this day that presentation remains one of the highlights of my life because of how fortunate I was to converse with descendents of UNIA members from the 1920s and 1930s and see different generations of Black Canadians react to Garvey's ideas. That presentation also saw Black Canadians of all different ethnic, national and linguistic backgrounds come together as part of a united community to discuss important moments in Canadian Black history noting what that history means for Canada's future. And, as on other occasions, I hope this essay will inspire future conversations.

Setting the Context

Black people have been referred to as "invisible people" in Canada's national narrative due to the exclusion of Black experiences in dominant representations of the country (Este and Kuol 2007: 29). This invisibility encourages the neglect of Black Canadians in discussions of the history of the wider African diaspora in the Americas. Indeed, Afua Cooper (2006: 68) describes Canada's engagement with the transatlantic slave trade as "Canada's best kept secret, locked within the national closet." But the fact remains that Black Canadians have long settled in Canada, some of the earliest communities being Black Loyalist settlements in Nova Scotia and those established through the Underground Railroad, which was used to flee the United States to Ontario. Canada is also home to what David Austin (2007) has termed a "Black radical tradition" that has inspired political movements — such as Pan-Africanism and Black Nationalism — through which members of the community have pursued racial equality and have managed to change their social, political and economic conditions. Throughout history Canadians have connected to and played a meaningful role in political movements to empower Black communities in the African diaspora and Continental Africa.

Of the political movements in which Black Canadians have engaged to advance Black communities, perhaps none have been as transnational as Marcus Garvey's UNIA, which helped create a following for Pan-African and Black Nationalist philosophies across the world. Like many of the transnational Black movements pursuing racial equality that found a home in Canada, such as the Caribbean Conference Committee and the Congress of Black Writers, the UNIA, established in Canada during the mid-twentieth century, resulted from the migration of Blacks from the Caribbean to Canada, reflecting the diverse composition of Canada's African diaspora. Through UNIA city divisions, conferences and other activities, Garvey was provided a platform to engage Black Canadians and promote his unique brand of Pan-Africanism, achieving varying degrees of popularity throughout the country. Examining the history of the UNIA and Garvey in Canada serves as a window into Canada's tradition of Black political movements and contextualizes Canada within the African diaspora. This chapter also discusses the legacy of Garvey in Canada and how his efforts toward racial equality continue to be relevant to Canadian multiculturalism today.

The UNIA and Black Canadian Experiences

The UNIA was founded in 1914 as a response of Marcus Garvey to the destitute conditions plaguing "the fallen of the [Black] race" in the early twentieth century, reducing them to "the level of a peon, a serf, or a slave" (Garvey 1925: 24) the world over. In declaring the UNIA's core objectives, the organization made specific references to its goals in its home nation of Jamaica but ultimately understood that the conditions facing Black communities, like racism, poverty, illiteracy and oppression, were transnational problems requiring transnational solutions. According to Garvey, "the cause of this prejudice against Black people is because the sober-minded white people believe that the Black people have contributed nothing to the civilization they want to enjoy co-equally with them, and that is where the prejudice comes; not so much because you are Black, but because we have achieved nothing in comparison to what they have achieved" (Garvey 1921, in Hill 1995: 192). In this context, the UNIA was conceived of as a universal Black confraternity to "rehabilitate the Negro race" (Cronon 1962: 17) and through Pan-Africanism and Black Nationalism to establish "the Black man's Government[,] his King and his kingdom[,] his President, his country, and his ambassador, his army, his navy, his men of big affairs" (Garvey 1923, in Wintz 1996: 171).

Although Africa became the grounds for Garvey's proposed "rehabilitation" of the Black "race," philosophically through "Back to Africa" rhetoric and practically through initiatives like the Liberia Project and the Black Star Line, the UNIA provided the foundation for Garvey's rehabilitative political movement:

> For want of a sovereign territorial base, Garvey effectively substituted membership in the UNIA — this was the form of political authority that institutionalized the universal rights of the Pan-African nation. Indeed, it was through the UNIA's shipping company — the Black Star Line — that Garvey sought to concretely establish commercial and industrial links between the Black Diaspora and the African continent that would build the "sinews of power" even in the absence of sovereign territory. (Shilliam 2006: 397)

The UNIA's founding documents do not make any references to Canada, but the organization's observations of the challenges facing Black communities are reflected in Canadian Black history. For instance, in one of the UNIA's founding documents, the 1920 "Declaration of Rights of the Negro Peoples of the World," the denial of equal wages to Black workers and underfunding of Black schools were emphasized. At the same time the Declaration was written, Black workers in Alberta were being exploited as a source of cheap labour by railway companies (Este and Kuol 2007: 35). And in the nineteenth century Black teachers in Ontario were underpaid, and segregated Black schools — established as a result of exclusion from public institutions — were under-funded (McLaren 2008: 73).

These examples of Garvey's and the UNIA's work reflected in Canadian Black history are a few of many and highlight the transnational resonance of Garvey and the UNIA's discussion of Black experiences. Still, Garvey and the UNIA's brand of Pan-African solutions to the challenges facing Black communities are not as common in Canadian Black history. Unlike in the U.S., in Canada Garveyism did not have the high profile philosophical predecessors of a Martin Delany or Booker T. Washington, who advocated for Black self-help on a national scale. Thus, the UNIA's expansion into Canada offered a significantly different alternative to political thought as compared to Canada's homogenous Black political agenda of racial integration.

Garvey and the UNIA in Canada in the 1920s and 1930s

In addition to the shared experiences between Black Canadian communities and the wider African diaspora, two other factors were influential in the UNIA's expansion into Canada. The first was the influx of Black immigrants to Canada from the Caribbean, where the UNIA and the philosophy of Garveyism began and built its foundation of supporters and believers. The second was Canada's proximity and close relationship to the United States, where the UNIA had established its international headquarters in New York City by 1916.

The first recognized and best documented Canadian division of the UNIA was established in Montreal in 1919. Leo W. Bertley (1982) credits the establishment of the division to Caribbean-born Blacks who were versed in Black radical thought as past affiliates of Panama's Association of Universal Loyal Negroes. The founders of this division were motivated by an "inspiring lecture" given by Garvey in Montreal just two years before (Bertley 1982: 10). Eventual chief executive officer and secretary-treasurer of the division, Dillon C. Govin served as the catalyst for the UNIA's expansion to Montreal after approaching the UNIA's international headquarters with interest in leading the new division.

The Montreal division's membership and popularity peaked in 1922, when seven hundred people joined throughout the year (Bertley 1982: 94), and membership varied throughout the early and mid-twentieth century, impacted by such events as the Great Depression, two world wars and the imprisonment of Marcus Garvey on charges of mail fraud. Much of the division's activities took the form of social and fundraising events for Montreal's Black community. The UNIA Montreal division also engaged in advocacy around continental African politics by pressuring the Canadian government to address its political concerns in South Africa and Ethiopia (Bertley 1982:

222). Moreover, the Montreal division had a concerted interest in working with youth, as "the majority of [the UNIA's] programs were designed to give young blacks a sense of identity and to prepare them for the struggle they would face as adults" (Este 2004: 13). Bertley (1982: 442) also notes that the Montreal division "made important and memorable contributions to the development and survival of the UNIA as a whole" in the form of international conference participation and UNIA governance.

The strategic value of the Montreal division to Garvey and the UNIA was highlighted following Garvey's imprisonment and eventual deportation from the United States in 1927, when Garvey used Montreal as an intermediary point to speak to his followers in the United States and maintain his influence in the country. During the 1928 U.S. presidential election, Garvey spoke in Montreal, urging African Americans to support Democratic candidate Alfred E. Smith. Following his advocacy for Smith from Montreal and a complaint from U.S. authorities, Garvey was arrested and asked to leave Canada (Fax 1972; Cronon 1962: 250). In response to the incident, Garvey revealed that no specific charge was laid against him, and rather he was made to "promise on [his] word that [he] would not say anything on the elections" while in Canada (*Toronto Daily Star* 1928: 12). This instance of collaboration between Western governments to stifle the efforts of Garvey was not an isolated incident, as the U.S., British and French governments also joined forces to stop the UNIA's purchase of land from the Liberian government in 1924 (Christy 1931: 525; Akpan 1973: 122).

Detailed information on other divisions of the UNIA in Canada is scarce, and such scarcity underscores the need for additional scholarship on Black history in Canada, particularly Black political movements. Bertley (1982: 39) notes a peak in 1922 of twenty-eight UNIA divisions across Canada, many of which were short-lived, as only fifteen remained by 1925. The UNIA's Toronto division was established in 1924 and purchased its first physical space in 1925 (Marano 2010: 253). The Toronto division was active in UNIA governance and hosted a variety of conferences and conventions in the late 1930s, including the inauguration of Garvey's School of African Philosophy in 1937 (Garvey 1939, in Hill 2006: 684) and in 1938 the UNIA's eighth convention, which was the final UNIA convention in Garvey's lifetime (Asante and Mazama 2005: 458). Garvey also gave a series of lectures at UNIA meetings across Ontario (Fax 1972: 270; Cronon 1962: 163–64). Alberta was home to two UNIA divisions, in Edmonton and Amber Valley, which served as incubators in the 1920s and 1930s for other Black political organizations, such as the Negro Welfare Association of Alberta and the Negro Political Association (*Alberta Source* n.d.). Moreover, several UNIA divisions were based in Nova Scotia in the 1920s and 1930s, with Sydney's Caribbean-born Black population leading most documented UNIA activity in the province (Marano 2010: 252).

Problems Appealing to Black Communities in Canada

As previously noted, the UNIA was ushered into Canada by an influx of Caribbean immigrants in the early twentieth century. Blacks of Caribbean heritage generally remained at the helm of Canadian divisions and comprised the vast majority of the UNIA's membership in Canada. Robin W. Winks (1971) attributes the inability of Garveyism and the UNIA to appeal to non-Caribbean Black communities in Canada to two main factors: Garvey's notion of racial purity and the back-to-Africa doctrine. Garvey was deeply committed to the idea of a "pure Black race," going so far as to refer to the intermixing of "races" as "evil" and the variations of skin colour among Blacks as a "curse" (Garvey 1925: 29). Further, Garvey viewed "light-skinned" Blacks and "mulattoes" to be enemies to Blacks (Winks 1971: 415). As Elliot M. Rudwick (1959: 423) notes, Garvey's references to a "Black-mulatto schism" reflected Jamaican racial dynamics that W.E.B. Du Bois criticized for being irrelevant and promoting disunity in the U.S. context. Such a schism is not widely prevalent in Canadian Black history, perhaps because Black Canadians are a small minority in terms of population size compared to Jamaica, with its Black majority population. Further, Blackness in Canada has been inclusive of people of various shades and racial admixtures; thus, Garvey's notion of racial purity had little relevance to Black communities made up of "considerable intermixing with Indians and whites" (Winks 1971: 415).

Garvey's back-to-Africa doctrine, which referred to the movement of the most highly trained Blacks back to resettlements in Africa (Williams 1997: 59) but often manifested itself as a call for all Blacks to return to Africa, also challenged a definitive characteristic of many Black communities in Canada: the desire to integrate into Canadian society at large. The desire was evident from British Columbia, where Blacks "have been resolutely integrationist in political tendency" (Compton 2007: 291) since the first Black settlements there in 1858, to Toronto, where the threat of segregated schooling was fended off in the nineteenth and twentieth centuries in favour of policies of integration (McLaren 2008: 71). In fact, in many other examples, the framework of integration greatly informed Black activism in Canada. Thus, Garvey's emphasis on Africa did not find a significant audience among non-Caribbean Black communities.

The openly opinionated Garvey also had trouble appealing to non-Caribbean Blacks in Canada due to ideological differences between his particular brand of Black self-help and other competing self-help ideologies in the country. For instance, in Montreal, Garvey's focus on race-based activism was met by a counterpart in African American Asa Philip Randolph's focus on class mobilization. Many supporters of Garvey left his movement for Randolph's unionization movement in the mid-1930s. Dorothy W. Williams

(1997: 59) attributes Randolph's greater appeal to the fact that Randolph's approach was more responsive to the struggles Blacks faced in their non-unionized workplaces, noting a disconnection between Garvey's emphasis on "race" and the most pressing issues facing Black workers in Montreal. Randolph's success in mobilizing Black communities in Montreal around class interests is another example of Black Canadians' historical disposition toward integration — in this case integration into labour unions — as opposed to Garvey's more racially divisive approach to community development.

Garvey's persistent emphasis on "race" also alienated the followers of Father Divine, also known as George Baker, an African American preacher, who had developed a strong following in Canada, particularly in British Columbia. Divine conscientiously chose to "not speak in racial terms" and did not approach community development with "race" as a central organizing principle (Winks 1971: 353). Divine built his following by providing "food and spiritual sustenance for the confused and world-weary" during the Great Depression. His popularity posed a threat to Garveyism in Canada, as the two were diametrically opposed on how the issue of "race" should be approached. Thus, Garvey strongly criticized Divine for the religious and non-racial nature of his work, describing Divine as "a common swindler and under the control of scheming whites" (Satter 2003: 572). Garvey's attacks on Divine and subsequent alienation of Divine's followers contributed to Garvey's inability to appeal to many non-Caribbean Black communities in Canada.

Furthermore, Garvey's issues with Divine were indicative of a broader frustration Garvey felt as a result of his followers being "too religious" (Winks 1971: 416). Although the UNIA in Montreal had been closely intertwined with the city's Union Church (Este 2004) and the UNIA had used "biblical prose" in its written materials to attract members (Bertley 1982: 93), Garvey had become increasingly frustrated with how much his followers relied on "God." Garvey promoted his own religion, the African Orthodox Church, a fusion of Black Nationalism and Christianity built around a Black deity. In Garvey's frustrations lies another conflict between his approach to Black self-help and that of many Black communities in Canada, as the Black church has been central to Black self-help efforts in Canada, dating back to the Black Loyalist settlements in Nova Scotia (Walker 1980). As David Este (2004: 21) concludes, Black churches have served to preserve Black culture and address injustices facing Blacks in Canada. In many ways, Black churches in Canada already fulfilled the role Garvey had hoped the UNIA would occupy in Black communities by providing a Black-owned meeting space, community bonds and a space for social events. Therefore, Garvey's efforts to separate Black radicalism from the tradition of the Black church in Canada failed and resulted in a limited audience for his organization, largely confined to Blacks of Caribbean descent. Due to their more recent arrival in Canada, many Caribbean immigrants were less attached to the established Black churches and, thus, more likely to respond to a movement like the UNIA, which they were familiar with because of the organization's significant presence in the Caribbean.

The difficulties the UNIA and Marcus Garvey had in appealing to segments of the African diaspora in Canada provide significant insight into the complexities of the Black radical tradition in Canada and the diversity of Canada's African diaspora. The inefficacy the UNIA experienced in its secular activism underscores the long-standing history of Black activism in Canada through Black churches, and the organization's emphasis on "race" conflicted with Black Canadians' prioritizing of class interests. Also, Garvey's struggle to appeal to Canadian-born Blacks reveals some of the defining characteristics of Black communities in Canada, namely the unstated application of the "one-drop rule" in defining Blackness and the predominant political tendency toward integration.

Garveyism and Canada in the Twenty-First Century

Despite Garvey's and the UNIA's inability to build a significant following among non-Caribbean Blacks in Canada, his legacy in Canada is significant. Nova Scotia is home to the Glace Bay UNIA Cultural Museum, which continues to serve as the headquarters of the Glace Bay UNIA division (*Glace Bay UNIA*). Additionally, the Marcus Garvey Centre for Unity continues to operate in Edmonton as a meeting space and Honorary Consul for the Jamaican High Commission in Canada (*Jamaican High Commission*). In Toronto, the Marcus Garvey Centre for Leadership and Education provided community services for over a decade in Toronto before closing in 2009 (*National Post* 2009). Recent Black History Month celebrations, however, continue to honour the UNIA's history in the city for the important role it played in Toronto's Black communities (*Archie Alleyne Scholarship Fund* 2012). Beyond material representations of Garvey's impact on Canada, however, is the legacy of Black pride, Black organization and mobilization, and transnational Black unity that continues to inform efforts toward Black progress in Canada to this day. Many current efforts to advance the cause of racial equality for Black communities in Canada, such as Toronto's Afrocentric schools programs, are faced with a challenge similar to Garvey's—that of creating a coherent and inclusive Black Canadian identity that transcends ethnic, national and linguistic differences for the betterment of Black Canadian families.

Garvey's ideas and the UNIA's work also resonate beyond Black political movements, as his efforts to address the domestic interests of Black communities while remaining connected to his homeland of origin speaks to Canadian multiculturalism. Canada is a nation comprised of various diasporas and through a multicultural philosophy encourages its residents to maintain connections to their homelands. Canadians of all diasporas continue to remain connected to their homelands by sending remittances, celebrating their cultural backgrounds and advocating for international political issues. Garvey and the UNIA cultivated an identity and culture that connected both the past and the present to pursue a future of greater equality. In a nation with so many resources and opportunities, Canada has the potential to contribute a great deal to the international community by continuing to embrace Garvey's challenge of normalizing the principle of bettering the world at home and abroad.

References

Akpan, M.B. 1973. "Liberia and the Universal Negro Improvement Association: The Background to the Abortion of Garvey's Scheme for African Colonization." *The Journal of African History* 14/1.

Alberta Source. n.d. "Alberta's Black Pioneer Heritage: Glossary." At <http://www.albertasource.ca/blackpioneers/resources/glossary.html>.

Archie Alleyne Scholarship Fund. 2012. "Archie Alleyne Presents Syncopation: Life in the Key of Black." February 5. At <http://www.aasf.ca/syncopation/>.

Asante, M.K., and A. Mazama. 2005. *Encyclopedia of Black Studies.* Thunder Oaks, CA: Sage Publications.

Austin, D. 2007. "All Roads Led to Montreal: Black Power, the Caribbean, and the Black Radical Tradition in Canada." *The Journal of African American History* 92/4.

Bertley, L.W. 1982. *The Universal Negro Improvement Association of Montreal, 1917–1979.* Ph.D. Thesis, Concordia University. Ottawa: National Library of Canada.

Christy, C. 1931. "Liberia in 1930." *The Geographic Journal* 77/6.

Compton, W. 2007. "Hogan's Alley: Mapping Vancouver's Lost Black Neighbourhood." In David Divine (ed.), *Multiple Lenses: Voices from the Diaspora Located in Canada.* Newcastle: Cambridge Scholars Publishing.

Cooper, A. 2006. *The Hanging of Angélique: The Untold Story of Canadian Slavery and the Burning of Old Montréal.* Athens, GA: University of Georgia Press.

Cronon, E.D. 1962. *Black Moses: The Story of Marcus Garvey.* Madison, WI: University of Wisconsin Press.

Este, D.C. 2004. "The Black Church as a Social Welfare Institution: Union United Church and the Development of Montreal's Black Community, 1907–1940." *Journal of Black Studies* 35/5.

Este, D.C., and W.M. Kuol. 2007. "African Canadians in Alberta: Connecting the Past with the Present." In David Divine (ed.), *Multiple Lenses: Voices from the Diaspora Located in Canada.* Newcastle: Cambridge Scholars Publishing.

Fax, E.C. 1972. *Garvey.* Cornwall, NY: Cornwall Press.

Garvey, Marcus. 1921. "Speech by Marcus Garvey." In Robert A. Hill (ed.), *The Marcus Garvey and Universal Negro Improvement Association Papers: Africa for the Africans June 1921 — December 1922, Volume IX.* 1995. Berkley and Los Angeles: University of California Press.

___. 1923. "The Negro's Greatest Enemy." In Carry D. Wintz (ed.), *African American Political Thought, 1890–1930: Washington, Du Bois, Garvey, and Randolph* [1996].

Armonk, NY: M.E. Sharpe.

___. 1925. "Dissertation on Man." In Amy Jacques-Garvey (ed.), *Philosophy and Opinions of Marcus Garvey*. New York: Universal Publishing House.

___. 1939. "Article by Marcus Garvey in the Black Man." In Robert A. Hill (ed.), *The Marcus Garvey and Universal Negro Improvement Association Papers: Africa for the Africans 1923–1945, Volume X* [2006]. Berkley and Los Angeles: University of California Press.

Glace Bay UNIA. "Cape Breton's Only UNIA Museum-Hall." At <http://unia.webs.com/>.

Jamaican High Commission. "Contact Us." At <http://jhcottawa.ca/genpage.asp?sid=6886828&action=contactus>.

Marano, C. 2010. "'Rising Strongly and Rapidly': The Universal Negro Improvement Association in Canada, 1919–1940." *The Canadian Historical Review* 91/2.

McLaren, K. 2008. "'We Had No Desire To Be Set Apart': Forced Segregation of Black Students in Canada West Public Schools and Myths of British Egalitarianism." In Barrington Walker (ed.), *The History of Immigration and Racism in Canada: Essential Readings*. Toronto: Canadian Scholars' Press.

National Post. 2009. "Community Centre's Troubled Tenure Ends." May 9. At <http://www.canada.com/nationalpost/news/toronto/story.html?id=e99d9514-41e6-48af-86bb-fa89a6756bde>.

Rudwick, E.M. 1959. "DuBois Versus Garvey: Race Propagandists at War." *The Journal of Negro Education* 28/5 (Autumn).

Satter, B. 2003. "Marcus Garvey, Father Divine and the Gender Politics of Race Difference and Race Neutrality." In Cornel West and Eddie S. Glaude Jr. (eds.), *African American Religious Thought: An Anthology*. Louisville, KY: Westminster John Knox Press.

Shilliam, R. 2006. "What About Marcus Garvey? Race and the Transformation of Sovereignty Debate." *Review of International Studies* 32.

Toronto Daily Star. 1928. "Negro Leader Sets Sail, Says He Was Muzzled." November 8, Special to the Star.

Universal Negro Improvement Association. 1914. "Objectives of the Universal Negro Improvement Association." *Public Broadcasting Service: American Experience*. At <http://www.pbs.org/wgbh/amex/garvey/filmmore/ps_objectives.html>.

___. 1920. "Declaration of the Rights of the Negro Peoples of the World." *Public Broadcasting Service: American Experience*. At <http://www.pbs.org/wgbh/amex/garvey/filmmore/ps_rights.html>.

Walker, J. 1980. "The Black Loyalists." In *A History of Blacks in Canada*. Hull, Quebec: Minister of State Multiculturalism.

Williams, D.W. 1997. *The Road to Now: A History of Blacks in Montreal*. Montreal: Vehicule Press.

Winks, R.W. 1971. *Blacks in Canada*. Montreal: McGill-Queen's University Press.

21. FROM JAMAICA TO CANADA
Miss Lou and the Poetics of Migration

Andrea Davis

The Honorable Louise Bennett Coverley, or Miss Lou, as she is still best known to Jamaicans, represents more than any other artist, including the iconic Bob Marley, the voice of the Jamaican nation. No artist, social activist or politician had a deeper reach into the heart of the Jamaican folk or was more consistently committed to the project of Jamaican self-identification. With a career beginning in the late 1930s and spanning more than fifty years, she represented before and after independence, the poetic imagination and expressive culture of a people she believed in and loved deeply. The biting social commentary often revealed in her poetry was balanced by an unwavering belief in the resilience and creativity of the Jamaican spirit. When Miss Lou left her island nation in the early 1980s to live first in the United States and then permanently in Canada in 1987, she was more than sixty years old and had already contributed a life's career in the direct service of Jamaican nation building. Like many Jamaicans, she was an unwilling migrant, moved by circumstances (an ailing husband who needed advanced medical care) rather than desire. And like many of these migrants, Canada was a strategic choice, weighed in the balance and found wanting but not intolerable. Until her death on Wednesday, July 26, 2006, at the Scarborough Grace Hospital in Toronto, Canada became the place where she lived, but for Jamaicans at home and scattered across the Caribbean diaspora she continued to represent the spirit of a nation she may have left physically but had never left behind.

The questions this chapter raises circulate around Bennett's location in Canada in the last two decades of her life. How do we explain her enduring cultural and national significance long after she had left Jamaica? And, as a powerful cultural symbol, how did her influence translate across these distinct borders? The answers to these questions lie in part in Bennett's poetry. Miss Lou's poetry and prose monologues had long established the relationship between migration, social unease and cultural loss. While often critical of the bourgeoning Jamaican nation, she was also forceful in the defence of her country against external political and cultural influences. The critique of migration and cultural loss that predominates in her work has to be read, however, in relation to the imperatives of migration that have marked Caribbean living since colonization. Caribbean people, for any number of reasons, do choose to migrate. Miss Lou's own decision to leave Jamaica and her clear location as an unwilling migrant, rather than reducing her national influence, extended it by identifying her through her poetry and lived experiences with the struggles and sacrifices, not only of Jamaicans at home, but also of a growing Jamaican diaspora abroad.

Miss Lou and Life in Canada

When I first met Miss Lou in 1995, she had already been living in Canada for almost ten years. Honor Ford-Smith and I, both graduate students at the time, had decided that we were going to convince her to come to York University for a reading of her poetry. Miss Lou had up to that point been larger than life for me, and the meeting, the "conspiracy" to pull off the poetry reading, all seemed incredibly audacious. I was simultaneously awed by that first meeting in her "home" — an apartment in one of Toronto's suburbs — and saddened by the sense of pathos and loss the meeting evoked. She was an exile, caught in James Clifford's (1997: 250) "entangled tension" of diaspora claims. She and Eric Coverley had exchanged their beautiful estate in the St. Andrew hillside for a cramped urban apartment divided by too many walls and narrow hallways, and neighbours who had no way of knowing the weightiness of her national and cultural symbolism, and who would not have cared. Maybe for this reason, I have always hated Toronto apartments — by-products of the detached anonymity of big-city living. In metropolitan cities, like Toronto, Jamaican immigrants feel both hyper-visible and invisible.

We sat and listened for hours to Miss Lou recreate stories of another "home," another time that all four of us longed for desperately, at least in that moment, but knew there was no return to. She recreated stories of her childhood and adult life: of her father who wanted a son but got the surprising daughter; the market women on the bus who propelled her into writing; her early reception in Jamaica; and her love story. And even there in that small apartment, she recited her poetry—her audience small but rapt. I was pregnant, and as I left the apartment she stopped me, passed her hand over my stomach and blessed the child. She had sealed our connection as displaced Jamaican women: me a young mother-to-be and she the designated mother of the nation.

The college room we reserved was cozy but too small to hold the bodies that lined the walls and spilled into the hallways and corridors to listen to Miss Lou on the winter afternoon she finally arrived on campus. A large section of the audience came from outside the university, and despite the cold it felt as if Jamaica had, indeed, hijacked the university. The university, after all, had no special claim to Miss Lou and had rejected her, in fact, for all of her early career.[1] Jamaican Creole and the untamed laughter of Jamaican immigrants recalling their entangled lives circled and enshrined the college. There was no doubt that Miss Lou belonged to the community — a Jamaican community in Toronto in 1995 that understood and shared the pathos of her exile and came with hands open to receive some gift that could take them through another winter away from the "home" of no return. For this group, the possibilities of diaspora living, like the promise of return, were deferred and bittersweet.

Life for Jamaican immigrants in Canada is framed in large part by precisely these diaspora tensions over social citizenship, belonging and return. Defined in economic terms, Jamaican immigrants who have settled in Canada are generally perceived as primarily escaping poverty and educational disadvantages and as seeking a "better" life in the more developed country. Yet, the rigorous immigration laws and point system that scrupulously select incoming immigrants ensure that the "typical" immigrant of the late twentieth and early twenty-first centuries (when Caribbean migration to the United States and Canada soared) is highly educated and skilled, and he or she often has to endure a reduction in standard of living, despite earning higher wages. While domestic service is a given in Jamaican middle-class households, for example, it is an expensive luxury generally reserved for the wealthiest in Canadian society. Since service jobs, like domestic labor, have historically been reserved for non-White immigrants, Afro- and Indo-Caribbean immigrants have also come to be marked permanently by this history of undervalued working-class labour. As a result, Jamaican immigrants entering societies like Canada find themselves not only economically but also culturally marginalized.

As Augie Fleras (2004: 431) argues, the practice of Canadian diversity is actually a practice of mono-multiculturalism that privileges an Anglo-Canadian identity and culture as the universally accepted norm and allows minoritized cultures expression only within carefully delineated and non-threatening boundaries. Jamaican cultural performances (including language, dress, walk) are often assumed to be too extravagant, too loud, too vulgar and not only fall short of the "ideal," normalized culture but are often perceived as threatening and in need of containment. Since Canadian society tolerates differences only as long as they are contained within private or personal spaces, the tendency of Jamaican cultural expressions and attitudes to seep into the larger society is often seen as problematic and sometimes even dangerous.

Routed to the metropolitan city of Toronto, Miss Lou's migration must be understood within this context of simultaneous gain and loss. Migration, perhaps paradoxically, humanized her. Jamaican immigrants in Canada and elsewhere, "ketching hell a farin," could make better sense of the reasons that had dictated their own movement, could mark their own gains as well as their losses in relationship to her. She continued to bear the weight of Jamaican national identity, rooted by a nationalist rhetoric that established her(s) as its "voice," but she was now more than an icon. Jamaicans across the Caribbean diaspora accepted her routing as a personal sacrifice. She had willingly or unwillingly entered a community of everyday suffering and struggle, accepted a fall in social status and privilege, abandoned her beloved nation in body only but not in spirit.

Jamaicans at home, struggling with their own problems, also understood perhaps better than Miss Lou knew the complexities of the choices she was called to make. When Miss Lou returned to Jamaica in 2003 for the first time since migrating to Canada, adoring Jamaicans lined the streets to greet her and screamed her name as her entourage passed (Mills 2003). While she was surprised and deeply moved by this outpouring of national appreciation (Lowrie 2003), Jamaicans had no misgivings. Old and young, they unabashedly reaffirmed their love of the mother of their young nation as they celebrated the forty-first anniversary of Jamaica's independence.

Establishing Miss Lou's importance as a national and cultural icon in Jamaica while locating her firmly in Canada, paradoxically reminds us, however, that cultural identities are neither fixed nor "pure." In the same way that Canadian society is being called upon to adapt to and be (re)created by the non-White cultures it seeks to absorb, these cultures are also themselves constantly in processes of recreation. As I have argued elsewhere, when "culture" comes to represent any kind of hegemonic nationalist discourse (whether from the centre or the margin) it runs the risk of encouraging oppressive, homogenizing narratives: "For Jamaican identities abroad, where Jamaicanness is in large part a performance of memory based on one's own and/or others' past lived experiences, the need for a fixed, "pure," cultural identity is ... problematic" (Davis 2006: 25). The need to project national and ethnic identities as unalterable and pure leads to an eventual marginalization and fear of any kind of difference.

Bennett's location outside of Jamaica challenges us, therefore, to rethink the role of art as a fixed performance of nation and community. As Ramazani (2009: 50) explains, "Bennett helps us to see that a national poet can also, paradoxically, be a transnational poet — a poet whose work vigorously crosses, and is crossed by, national boundaries." This transnationalism can be traced "through its divided social belongings, cross-national language and allusions, diasporic consciousness, and ambivalent responses to the globe-traversing forces of modernity and decolonization" (50). It is precisely this tension between roots and routes that emerges perhaps unexpectedly in Bennett's poetry and prose. As a younger woman and years before coming to Canada, Bennett had lived briefly in Europe and the United States and travelled widely as a performer. She was always attuned to global politics and had distinct opinions about racial injustice and imperialism. While her poetry was rooted in the Jamaican landscape, it also travelled outward, constantly testing, as it were, the wider position of the world and Jamaica's place within it.

Miss Lou and the Context of Her Poetry

Miss Lou was born on September 7, 1919, in Kingston, Jamaica, the only child for her parents, Cornelius Bennett and Kerene Robinson, and was raised in a single-parent household after her father died when she was seven years old. According to Mervyn Morris in the introduction to *Selected Poems* (1982/2003: iii–iv), her mother's job as a dressmaker exposed Bennett early to a wide range of Jamaican folk influences and language, especially as observed through the eyes and voices of women, and she knew early that she wanted to write. She attended Calabar Elementary School at St. Simon's College and Excelsior High School, and, encouraged by her mother, she pursued her love of poetry and published her first collection, *Dialect Verses*, in 1942. A year later, her poetry began appearing every week in the *Sunday Gleaner*. As Barbara Gloudon (1986: 2), a senior journalist at Radio Jamaica, explains, "Nothing like these poems had been seen before" and Jamaicans were immediately captivated by her ability to recall the spirit of their daily lives in a rhythm and language they understood. Bennett continued her education and fascination with Jamaican folklore, pursued courses in journalism and social work, and in 1945, she won a scholarship to the Royal Academy of Dramatic Art in England. Her studies in England also initiated a successful broadcasting career in London, where she worked for the BBC. After a brief return to Jamaica and then again to England, she lived for three years in New York, where she married Eric Coverley (a promoter of Jamaican theatre) in 1954.[2] A year later, they returned to Jamaica, and she concretized her career in poetry, theatre, radio and television performance and social commentary.

By 1986, just before she migrated to Canada, Bennett had published nine volumes of poetry and stories; recorded several albums, including *Jamaican Folk Songs* (1954) and *Children's Jamaican Songs & Games* (1957); performed in at least twenty-five Jamaican national pantomimes; worked for more than twenty years in radio (*Lou and Ranny Show, Laugh With Louise, Miss Lou's Views* and *Smile Jamaica*); spent twelve successful years in television (*Ring Ding* 1968–1980); and appeared in the film *Club Paradise* (1986). Despite this enormous repertoire of work and her unrivalled popularity among the Jamaican working classes, Bennett's work until at least the late 1970s drew repeated criticism from the Jamaican middle and upper classes, who were uncomfortable with her use of the Jamaican language (Morris 1982/2003: xiii). Her poetry, which was not respected as "real" art, in fact, received no critical attention until Morris's essay, "On Reading Louise Bennett, Seriously" appeared in 1963, a year after Jamaica's independence and twenty years into her publishing career (Cudjoe 1990; Morris 1982/2003).

Bennett's "discovery" in 1963 was not accidental. She provided an emerging group of scholars, poets and writers the context within which to enter debates about the possibilities of independence and also a model from which to craft a distinctly Jamaican and Caribbean poetics, the need for such a poetics made necessary precisely because of the reality of independence. The project of political autonomy in the Caribbean has long been interwoven with the projects of cultural and artistic autonomy. As Rex Nettleford (1990: 32) explains, the work of Caribbean artists has been closely tied to movements for democratic freedom: "Foremost among such artists have been the writers — literate, healthily schizophrenic, insightful, and truly among the first to explain formally the Caribbean to itself, whether in the printed poem, the novel or short story." In referring to Bennett specifically, Nettleford in *Jamaica Labrish* (1966/2005: 2) also concedes that in "the post-independence period when many Jamaicans are asking themselves questions about who and why they are, Miss Bennett has taken on new and important dimensions."

Kamau Brathwaite (1996) extends the relationship between political and artistic autonomy by lamenting the inability of English and the iambic pentameter, the most common metre in English poetry, to reflect the lived experiences and the cultural and geographic landscape of the Caribbean. What is needed, he argues, is "a rhythm that approximates the natural experience, the environmental experience" and "more closely and intimately approaches our own experience" (269). For Brathwaite, the rhythm most capable of carrying the weight of these emotions is one influenced by "the African aspect of our New World/Caribbean heritage." Not surprisingly, Brathwaite, like Morris and Nettleford, identifies Bennett as one of the first to experiment seriously with this form of linguistic creativity and as the literary precursor of the post-independence poet.

Selwyn Cudjoe (1990: 26) perhaps explains Bennett's influence best when he sums up her achievements:

> Bennett's work challenged the privileged status accorded to the poetic tradition of white discourse in Caribbean letters, empowering the voices and expressions of the masses of Caribbean people. Bennett used the power of Jamaican speech to explore the complexity of the Jamaican experience and, in so doing, forced the members of the upper and middle classes to face their own linguistic and class biases. Her use of oral and scribal forms, as she forced the language

to accommodate itself to express the poetic sentiments of the people, was an important breakthrough in Caribbean literature.

The rest of this chapter turns to an examination of these oral and scribal forms, looking specifically at the theme of migration and cultural loss. My desire is to attempt to reveal the ways in which Miss Lou's expression of her nation's poetic sentiments might be balanced between the imperatives of Brathwaite's homebound nation language and the claims of diaspora.

Miss Lou and the Poetics of Migration

I examine seven of what I call Bennett's migration poems, from *Selected Poems*, edited by Mervyn Morris (1982/2003). I begin with her popular poem "Colonization in Reverse," which explores the ironic effects of Jamaican migration to England. The next two poems — "Dry-Foot Bwoy" and "No Lickle Twang" — challenge the notion of shame often associated with the use of the Jamaican language, especially after migration. Since Bennett has been most influential in her use of Jamaican Creole, this discussion is necessary. "Pass fi White," "A Merica" and "Tan a Yuh Yard" are three poems that focus on Jamaican migration to the United States. I conclude with a discussion of Bennett's only truly diasporic poem, "Home Sickness." While none of Bennett's poems engage questions of migration within a specifically Canadian context, the questions she raises in these poems are far reaching and resonate with the experiences of Jamaican immigrants in Canada. Her poetry, I hope, might help those of us who are Jamaican immigrants in Canada re-enter conversations about what it means to contribute to the (re) creation of this nation without abandoning our cultural memories. While I cannot pretend that Bennett's poetry allows us the space to completely explore this desire, it provides a valuable context from which to examine some of the challenges of South-to-North migration and cross-nation coalition.

"Colonization in Reverse" is a tongue-in-cheek examination of the reverse effects of Jamaican migration on English society after World War II. The long and brutal war had left England ravaged and desperately in need of economic revitalization, and skilled and working-class labour from British colonies, like Jamaica, was seen as essential to England's recovery. Estimates of total Caribbean migration to Britain between 1951 and 1961 vary, according to Bonham Richardson (1989: 216), from 230,000 to 280,000. While Caribbean immigrants saw themselves as loyal British subjects, their presence ignited deep racial paranoia, and they were exposed to increasing expressions of racism, especially in the labour market and in housing. Citing the saturation of the labour force, the *Commonwealth Immigrants Act* of 1962 responded to these racial prejudices by successfully cutting off Caribbean migration to Britain (217).

By playing on the meaning of the word "colonization," Bennett's poem draws a parallel between the historic cultural damage of British colonialism on Caribbean peoples and the feared cultural imposition and (re)settlement of Jamaican immigrants in England. The poem rewrites the project of colonization with its assumptions of European conquest and subjugation by bestowing agency and autonomy on the colony itself. The poem, thus, celebrates the Jamaican Anancy-like propensity to triumph over the larger and more powerful adversary. The poem's humour and irony derive, however, from the fact that the speaker understands that the colony's perceived ability to conquer and subdue the "motherlan" is, indeed, born entirely out of the colonizer's misplaced fear of the growing numbers of Jamaican immigrants. By invoking the fear that immigrants take away jobs from other citizens, the poem, indeed, reverses the history of settlement and conquest in specifically Jamaican terms:

> Oonoo se how life is funny,
> Oonoo see de turnabout?
> Jamaica live fi box bread
> Out a English people mout.
>
> For when dem catch a Englan
> An start play dem different role
> Some will settle down to work
> An some will settle fi de dole.
> (Bennett 1982/2003: 107)

The multiple meanings of the word *settle* destabilize the immigrants' motives so that they constantly shift between earnestness and calculated deception. While the poem once again celebrates Jamaican resilience, it also reveals as either potentially naïve or morally suspect those too willing to abandon their island home for the unknown promises of the "mother country." In the end, however, English society will have to decide how to best interpret these shifting social clues because in the short term, at least, the colony has won: "What a devilment a Englan! / Dem face war an brave de worse; / But ah wonderin how dem gwine stan / Colonizin in reverse" (Bennett 1982/2003: 107).

In examining the two poems that directly address the question of language in *Selected Poems* (2003), it is clear that Bennett's critique of Jamaican middle-class aspirations, as part of a linguistic debate, is framed by an awareness of the ways in which migration alters our understanding of ourselves as immigrants or travellers originating in the Global South. "Dry-Foot Bwoy" offers a scathing critique of a young man's abandonment of his island history, once he is exposed to life in England. This abandonment is noted most powerfully in his rejection of the Jamaican language in which he was raised. It is at first unclear whether Mary's son, derogatorily referred to as *dry-foot bwoy* to register his humble origins and false pretensions, is actually living in England or has recently returned home. While the tone of the poem and the images it invokes suggest the feeling of a communal Jamaican yard, the use of the word *come*, instead of the word *go*, implies that the encounter the poem narrates does, in fact, take place outside of the island: "Me tink him *come* a foreign lan / *Come* ketch bad foreign cole!" (Bennett 1982/2003: 1). Read in this way, the poem becomes a commentary on a young Jamaican man's inability to navigate the challenges of English society without abdicating his cultural values. To explain the sharp disjunction between the boy's pretentious behaviour and his humble Jamaican roots, the speaker at first identifies the cultural (dis)ease the boy voices through his body as a kind of physical illness brought on by the harshness of the European environment. The cold he figuratively catches symbolizes the coldness and isolation of British society as well as his growing alienation from his own sustaining community. While the speaker empathizes with the immigrant's struggle within the harshness of the European cultural terrain, she has no sympathy for his easy abandonment of his childhood memories.

In the poem, meaningless English words displace the richness of Jamaican cultural history and erect a barrier of miscommunication between the speaker and the boy. The speaker, then, must re-educate the young man:

> Me seh, 'Yuh understand me, yaw!
> No yuh name Cudjoe Scoop?
> Always visit Nana kitchen an
> Gi laugh fi gungo soup!
>
> 'An now all yuh can seh is "actually"?
> Bwoy, but tap!
> Wha happen to dem sweet Jamaica
> Joke yuh use fi pop?'
> (Bennett 1982/2003: 2)

While being careful to connect the boy's laughter to Nana's (Nanny's) kitchen, the narrator undercuts the weightiness of the historical references with the lines "Gi laugh fi gungo soup" and "Joke yuh use fi pop" (Bennett 1982/2003: 2). In this way, the speaker eloquently joins a long tradition of Jamaican warriorhood to a tradition of cultural resilience.[3] The word *pop* suggests the creativity and vitality of the language but also alludes to its secondary meaning in Jamaican speech, to fool or to trick. Yes, Jamaicans have been through difficult times but have always found a way, like Anancy, to survive. The narrator, thus, again subtly registers a note of empathy with the boy's struggle to find himself in a foreign country but suggests that the clues to his survival lie within the very language and cultural traditions he has abandoned.

The boy's resulting anger and stubbornness, "Him get bex and walk tru de door, / Him head eena de air" (Bennett 1982/2003: 2) indicate an unfortunate willingness to comply with the colonial project of African self-erasure. He fails to realize that his pride is misplaced and that by uncritically walking through the door of British opportunity, he runs the risk of losing more than he gains. The mocking laughter of the community of women that follows him is a final ominous reminder of the consequences of his short-sighted choices.

"No Lickle Twang" shifts the debates about language from a context of British colonialism to one of U.S. cultural imperialism. While again relying on the social and cultural disparities between a mother and her son as its framing device, the poem reverses the central problem by shifting the narrative perspective. By making the mother the poem's speaker and by having her voice her disillusionment over her son's refusal to mimic Euro-American speech and dress, the poem signals cultural loss as a cross-generational problem that may be exacerbated by migration but also functions beyond it.

The poem suggests that the young man who spent six months in the United States and has now returned home, with the money to show for his absence but nothing else, is perhaps a temporary labourer.[4] While the young man's labour abroad seems to have been motivated by a desire to improve his economic situation rather than any desire to romanticize U.S. society, the mother clearly privileges migration as a sign of cultural "improvement." Post-independence Jamaican society has, indeed, increasingly modelled middle-class success, less after English cultural standards and more after the "ideal" of the American Dream. Thus, this mother believes her son's migration, no matter how temporary, should bring with it an enhancement of the family's social privilege. Since the most visible marker of a "real" improvement in class status in Jamaica is facility in British or American English and not just economic success, she demands this facility as the ultimate sign of her son's proven cultural capital.

The mother's demand that the changes in her son's speech and behaviour be distinct and rapid simultaneously alludes to and ignores the potential pain involved in such a process. She fails to recognize her son's self-awareness as a positive trait and sees him instead as trapped in the "ugliness" of Jamaican working-class culture. The contest between the American Dream and Jamaican cultural memory appears most powerfully in the poem's juxtaposition of the words, *Merica* and *Mocho*—one meant to mark the "First

World," progress and advancement and the other meant to mark smallness, "backwardness" and the lingering memory of Africa in Jamaica:

> Suppose me lass me pass go introjooce
> Yuh to a stanger
> As me lamented son what lately
> Come from Merica!
>
> Dem hooda laugh after me, bwoy!
> Me couldn tell dem so!
> Dem hooda seh me lie, yuh wasa
> Spen time back a Mocho!
> (Bennett 1982/2003: 3)

The poem finally ends on a note of dramatic irony when the mother urges her son in one last act of familial redemption to call his father *Poo*, instead of *Pa*. While readers immediately recognize the linguistic slip (*poo* refers to excrement or feces) and know how such a greeting will be received, the mother in her over-zealousness to impress is unaware of her own malapropism. While she uses the word *shame* repeatedly to describe her disappointment in her son's lack of linguistic prowess, in the final analysis the shame is hers since the word she chooses for her husband, rather than a sign of respect and veneration, is one of insult.

The next group of poems — "Pass fi White," "A Merica" and "Tan a Yuh Yard" — offer more explicit critiques of Jamaican immigrants' attempts to integrate into U.S. society. In "Pass fi White," as the title suggests, the problem is one of both cultural and physical erasure. While sensitive to the challenges non-White immigrants have historically faced in negotiating U.S. Jim Crow laws, the poem is, nonetheless, impatient with the strategies they have sometimes employed for survival. The success of the poem revolves around the pun on the word *pass* and the speaker's clever identification of the link between the young woman's inability to pass her exam and her ill-advised attempts at racial camouflage. By reminding us that "Her brain part not so bright" (Bennett 1982/2003: 101), the speaker reaffirms the immediate assessment that this is not a smart decision. The poem's repeated rhyming patterns — *write* and *white*, *bright* and *white*, *right* and *white* — progressively emphasize the link between Whiteness and rightness, and Whiteness as test of citizenship, a test we know the young woman will fail. The tone of anxiety in the poem further heightens when her love relationship is revealed. The undercurrent of anxiety is mirrored in the bodily (dis)comforts she experiences, both literally in the form of heart palpitations and cold sweat and in her metaphoric self-annihilation.

While her mother recognizes the challenges of migration her daughter faces and identifies her attempts to perform the racial "ideal" as one response to the pressures of a racialized society, she dismisses the young woman's choices as ineffectual: "She no haffi tan a foreign / Under dat deh strain an fright / For plenty copper-colour gal / Deh home yah dah play white" (Bennett 1982/2003: 101). Ironically, she recognizes that her daughter's colour combined with an education would afford her far more cultural leverage in Jamaican society.

By inserting the father's perspective, the poem more clearly establishes the reasons for the daughter's social subterfuge, by explicitly naming the United States as racist and critiquing its Jim Crow laws. The father powerfully unmasks the fluidity of racial identities and the shifting social constructions of "race" in a U.S. society that pretends racial rigidity. His attempt to justify her choices as a covert form of cultural resistance is, however, quickly exposed:

> Him dah boas all bout de distric
> How him daughter is fus-class,
> How she smarter dan American
> An over deh dah pass!
>
> Some people tink she pass B.A.,
> Some tink she pass D.R. –
> Wait till dem fine out seh she ongle
> Pass de colour bar.
> (Bennett 1982/2003: 102)

Ultimately, the risks involved in trying to conform to the rules of "race" in U.S. society leave his daughter exposed not only to the damaging effects of racial prejudice but also to social criticism and cultural ostracization within the very community on which her rehabilitation might depend.

In "A Merica" and "Tan a Yuh Yard" Bennett examines the social frenzy around migration to the United States that reached its peak in Jamaica in the late 1970s and 1980s. Two factors combined to encourage this dramatic out-migration. The *Hart-Celler Immigration Reform Act* of 1965 removed explicitly racist criteria from U.S. immigration law by emphasizing skill and family reunification over place of origin, making it easier for immigrants from newly independent countries in the Caribbean to settle in the United States (Kasinitz 1992: 26–27). Increasing political tensions in Jamaica and fear among the Jamaican middle classes over the growing influence of socialism and ties to Cuba's Communist government were also powerful push factors driving Jamaican migration (Kaufman 1985: 122). As Philip Kasinitz (1992: 27) confirms, by the early 1980s approximately 20,000 Jamaican immigrants were arriving annually in the United States. These incoming immigrants, like those coming from elsewhere in the Caribbean, represented a wide variety of class positions: "well-educated members of the urban elite seeking to protect their wealth in volatile economies, children of the middle class searching for broader opportunities, and large numbers of poor people looking for a standard of living above mere subsistence" (27–28).

In "A Merica," Bennett's first linguistic intervention into the construction of the United States as an "ideal" host society occurs in the poem's title. By physically dismantling the word America, she simultaneously reproduces Jamaican speech patterns in which *a* signifies to and interrupts the notion of U.S. cultural and political hegemony. By opening the poem with a proverb, she also establishes the wisdom of the speaker and contrasts historical knowledge with erroneous contemporary belief and practice: "Every seckey got him jeggeh, / Every puppy got him flea, / An yuh no smaddy ef yuh no / Got family oversea!" (Bennett 1982/2003: 109).

The accumulation of voices in the poem emphasizes the sense of frenzied movement and action sustained throughout the poem and reflected in the widespread and growing urgency to migrate. By further invoking the images of a series of natural disasters, the speaker accentuates the poem's sense of out-of-control movement as well as the near-hysterical social response of those seeking to leave: "Me ask meself warra matter, / Me ask meself wha meck: / Is tidal wave or earthquake or / Is storm dem dah expec?" (Bennett 1982/2003: 109). By pointing to the disjuncture between the departing emigrants and the Jamaican landscape, the poem reveals a deep social problem in Jamaican society. Despite the cautionary question — "Ah wonder is what fault dem fine / Wid po li Jamaica / Meck everybody dah lif-up / An go a Merica?" — the poem closes with the speaker's resolve to "falla fashin" and migrate (Bennett 1982/2003: 109–110). The poem, thus, suggests that while many reasons might be offered for migrating, the real reason might be that it is simply in style.

"Tan a Yuh Yard" responds directly to "A Merica" by cautioning Jamaicans to consider their options more carefully and "Lef Merica alone" (Bennett 1982/2003: 110). By once again invoking a Jamaican tradition of resiliency, the speaker suggests that with some amount of creativity Jamaicans can survive without risking the loss of cultural and political autonomy that often results from migration. While the speaker in "A Merica" is caught in the excitement of the perceived promises of migration, the tone in "Tan a Yuh Yard" is far more reflective and self-consciously cautionary. Here Bennett appears to invoke an unapologetic Jamaican nationalism by indicting "First World" racism and revealing the sacrifices often encoded in the notion of American "progress": "Win yuh mine offa foreign lan – / Koo how some a de man-dem / Run back home like foreigner / Dis set bad dog pon dem!"

(Bennett1982/ 2003: 110). By linking images of 1960s civil rights clashes with more contemporary stories of U.S. racism, the poem explicitly reveals the high personal and social costs involved in migration.

In the poem "Home Sickness," the only Bennett poem in which the speaker is an immigrant recording her own experiences, she invokes, as the title suggests, a deep desire for the past. Her homesickness is conjured up in an overwhelming desire for the cultural symbols, the food and landscape of her island home. Yet, in an unexpected turn at the end of the poem, Bennett interrupts any easy resolution of the speaker's romanticized longing for the past by powerfully reminding us of the deep ambivalence of our choices and our divided loyalties. Even as the poem's persona longs for return to a historically suspended home of her past, she realizes that return is impossible because "home" has been reconfigured by the relentless circumstances of migration: "Go back to me Jamaica, / To me fambly! To me wha? / Lawd-amassi, me figat – / All a me fambly over yah!" (Bennett 1982/2003: 108). Her final assertion, "All a me fambly over yah!" registers her awareness of a sense of uncontested responsibility within the new host society. The meanings of home and family are fluid rather than static.

Conclusion

It is impossible to avoid the difficult questions Bennett's poems raise. How does one balance the explicit nationalist critique of a poem like "Tan a Yuh Yard" with Bennett's later personal decisions to migrate first to the United States and then to Canada? Is it enough to mark her as an unwilling migrant, like the speaker in "Home Sickness," forced to depart her beloved nation because of circumstances outside her control? The reality is that Bennett's position is never quite as rigid as one might initially assume. Indeed, even in "Tan a Yuh Yard," her warnings against the desire to migrate are balanced by a genuine awareness of social hardship in Jamaica. Her migration poetry, thus, shifts constantly between empathy and critique, and her nationalism is almost always balanced by a tongue-in-cheek self-mockery.

Among the bodies pressed into the university classroom in 1995 to hear Miss Lou read, the personal stories of migration would have been too many and too complex to recount. What Jamaicans saw in Miss Lou on that cold winter afternoon was the symbol of their cumulative sacrifices and a reminder of their collective resilience. We invoked, out of necessity, her cultural and national significance in order to delineate the contours of a shared community, however fleeting and illusory. Whether in Jamaica or in Canada, we could resist complete self-erasure by holding on for one evening to our island language and laughter; by making them reverberate in that room; by overtaking with our too-loud, too-vulgar and too-colourful bodies the sacred spaces of a re-colonized Canadian university, where not so long ago we would not have studied anything called postcolonial or Caribbean poetry, and even then certainly not Miss Lou. Yes, many of us were Canadian citizens, our family and children "over yah," but our present in that moment joined hands with a shared past to help us (re)create two nations, one here and one a "Yard."

Canadians of Jamaican descent must increasingly grapple with these tensions between *here* and *there*, *roots* and *routes*. In demanding that Canada recognize its social responsibility to all its citizens, we must also increasingly take responsibility for a country that has been home to a Jamaican diaspora now for several generations. Perhaps, what Bennett's poetry best teaches us is that we respond most effectively to Canada's practices of mono-multiculturalism when we insist on joining our cultural memories across the borders of race, class, gender, language and geography we share. It is only then that we can realize the creative power of diaspora living and its ability to recreate, to re-imagine both the local and transnational.

Notes

1. Although Bennett's first published volume of poetry appeared in 1942, she was not included in any anthology of West Indian poetry before 1960. The first critical essay on Bennett's work was Mervyn Morris's 1963 essay, "On Reading Miss Lou, Seriously."
2. Eric Winston Coverley died on August 7, 2002, at the age of ninety-one in Toronto, Canada.
3. Cudjoe was the leader of the Leeward Maroons, and Nanny (suggested by the name Nana) was leader of the Windward Maroons. She was recognized as a Jamaican national hero in 1975.
4. Currently, the most popular seasonal worker program in the United States that hires temporary Jamaican labourers is the H-2A Temporary Agricultural Workers program. These workers, mostly men, are not immigrants and cannot become permanent residents or citizens. They also have little protection under U.S. law (see Cindy Hahamovitvh 2008). Canada has a similar program, known as the Seasonal Agricultural Worker Program (SAWP).

References

Bennett, L. 1993/2003. *Auntie Roachy Seh*. Kingston, Sangster's Book Stores.
___. 1982/2003. *Selected Poems*. (Mervyn Morris, editor.) Kingston: Sangster's Book Stores.
___. 1942. *(Jamaica) Dialect Verses*. Kingston: Herald Ltd.
Brathwaite, E.K. 1996. "English in the Caribbean: Notes on Nation Language and Poetry." In Janet Maybin and Neil Mercer (eds.), *Using English: From Conversation to Canon*. New York: Routledge.
Clifford, J. 1997. *Routes: Travel and Translation in the Late Twentieth Century*. Cambridge: Harvard University Press.
Cudjoe, S. (ed.). 1990. *Caribbean Women Writers: Essays from the First International Conference*. Wellesley: Calaloux Publications.

Davis, A. 2006. "Translating Narratives of Masculinity across Borders: A Jamaican Case Study." *Caribbean Quarterly* 52, 2/3 (June–Sept.).

Fleras, A. 2004. "Racializing Culture/ Culturalizing Race: Multicultural Racism in a Multicultural Canada." In Camille A. Nelson and Charmaine A. Nelson (eds.), *Racism, Eh? A Critical Interdisciplinary Anthology of Race and Racism in Canada*. Concord, ON: Captus Press.

Gloudon, B. 1986. "The Hon. Louise Bennett, O.J.: Fifty Years of Laughter." *Jamaica Journal* 19 (Aug.–Oct.) 2.

Kasinitz, P. 1992. *Caribbean New York: Black Immigrants and the Politics of Race*. Ithaca, NY: Cornell University Press.

Kaufman, M. 1985. *Jamaica under Manley: Dilemmas of Socialism and Democracy*. London: Zed Books.

Lowrie, T. 2003. "Jamaica's Beloved 'Miss Lou' Departs." *Jamaica Observer*, August 21. At <http://www.jamaicaobserver.com/news/47842_Jamaica-s-beloved--Miss-Lou--departs>.

Mills, C. 2003. "Noh Lickle Twang: JA's Cultural Icon Returns." *Jamaica Gleaner*, August. At <http://jamaica-gleaner.com/gleaner/20030806/news/news5.html>.

Morris, M. 1963. "On Reading Louise Bennett, Seriously." *Jamaica Journal* 1/1 (December).

___. 1982/2003. "Introduction." In Louise Bennett, *Selected Poems*. Kingston: Sangster's Book Stores.

Nettleford, R. 1966/2005. "Introduction." In Louise Bennett, *Jamaica Labrish*. Kingston: Sangster's Book Stores.

___. 1990. "Communicating With Ourselves: The Caribbean Artist and Society." *Caribbean Affairs* 3/2.

Ramazani, J. 2009. "Louise Bennett: The National Poet as Transnational?" *Journal of West Indian Literature* 17/2 (April).

Richardson, B.C. 1989. "Caribbean Migrations, 1838–1985." In F.W. Knight and C.A. Palmer (eds.), *The Modern Caribbean*. Chapel Hill: UNC Press.

22. JAMAICAN BY BIRTH ... CANADIAN BY CHOICE

In Conversation with Raymond Chang and Michael Lee-Chin

Royson James

Jamaica's got me hooked.

I don't recall flirting with the bait, chomping on the lure or ingesting the flesh-covered steel that has toyed with me since birth. Yet, now, far from her shores she reels me in — tugging, guiding, letting me run, then jerking me into her embrace. Hook, line and sinker.

Jamaica's got her hooks in me ...

As I write this, I am over the Caribbean Sea. Soon, the MoBay vibe will stir memories set aside, to be dusted off on the drive from Sangster's International Airport, past Doctor's Cave beach and the same question, every time. Why are there so few public beaches in the tourist capital? And the same answer, every time. "Maybe my hometown is really reserved for tourists." No anger accompanies this mental sparring every time I journey home. Maybe it's because home is really not MoBay, but Orange, seven miles into the countryside on the road to Adelphi, where the ram goat is king, the mongoose is a menace, and mother hen emerges from her nest with a dozen chicks and is lucky to deliver three to hen-hood. Or cock-dom.

This time, unlike last Christmas, I'm here to work. What is the story of the Trelawny Maroons and their forced resettlement in Nova Scotia in 1796, only to move again in four years to Sierra Leone? Isn't that a fascinating Jamaican-Canadian story? And are any of their descendants still living in Preston, Nova Scotia, the Canadian town with the largest percentage of Black folks? Then, Why do Jamaicans run so fast? — a pressing question the world ponders on the eve of the 2012 London Olympics. And, What are fifty must-see places in Jamaica? — the kind of question travel sections of newspapers ask when a tourist-heavy island nation celebrates fifty years of independence.

The last time I was in Jamaica to work, I was on a multiple mission as well. That's always the case with this journalist, ever seeking to justify my keep, to prove myself, even though I'm a columnist, holding a newspaper position of trust that allows free rein and wide latitude. It's part of the immigrant's curse, and blessing, I guess. That year, the *Toronto Star* sent me to cover the bar mitzvah of a Canadian kid whose Jamaican-born dad was taking him to Kingston's historic Duke Street synagogue — to connect him to his spiritual and geographic heritage. But to give added value, I tagged on an interview with Michael Lee-Chin, the financial services mogul, billionaire and celebrated Jamaican-Canadian. On another assignment, I doubled up by adding an interview with G. Raymond Chang, another Jamaican-Canadian who made his millions from the financial services sector. Both men are fascinating in what they represent — the highest of Jamaican achievement abroad, in our Canada, based in the Toronto region, as outsiders looking in, but neither constrained nor restrained by their "otherness" — the embodiment of Jamaica's "Out of Many One People" motto and Toronto's "Diversity our Strength" calling card; standard-bearers of the impact, influence and immeasurable worth of Jamaicans in Canada.

When word leaked out in 2011 that a group of Torontonians were busy planning a year of special events to celebrate the fiftieth year of Jamaica's independence, I travelled to Burlington, Ontario, to pick Lee-Chin's brains. I had interviewed him there before, as a lead up to the 2005 opening of the Lee-Chin Crystal at the Royal Ontario Museum (ROM). That's what happens when you donate $30 million to one of the blue-blood institutions rooted in Toronto; they name it after you. And you get to wax poetic about the dichotomous permanence of the nomadic immigrant experience in Canada. I tried then, in 2005, to talk about his wealth and growing fame; he kept talking about the opportunities and challenges of his homeland. Apparently, the hook was fastened in his lips as well.

Months later we met in New Kingston at the National Commercial Bank offices he had acquired in 2002 for a song, and the conversation kept drifting to Jamaica's future and his role in helping to shape it. So now, with the Year of Jubilee approaching, I knew he'd be eager to chat. Somewhat allergic to the media since the *Globe and Mail's* attack dog Jan Wong did a somewhat revealling feature length story on him, thanks to unrestricted access. Lee-Chin met me in his Burlington boardroom. The estate mansion in Flamborough, outside Hamilton, the former preserve of Laidlaw CEO Michael DeGroote and bought in 1996 for $1.5 million, was out of bounds. We would not be counting the number of car garages to see if there were eight as reported; neither verify if there are indeed two two-bedroom cottages, a swimming pool, tennis court and trout pond on the eleven-hectare property ringed by century-old trees. Overlooking the helicopter pad — launch site of one of Lee-Chin's toys, which include a private jet and a stable of fancy cars — this titan of business assumed the job of newspaper editor, leaned forward in the firm leather chair and pitched potential stories that are uniquely Jamaican or which highlight historical Jamaican-Canadian links.

"Did you know that Jamaica is the most profitable operation for the Bank of Nova Scotia?" Lee-Chin asks, a mischievous smile curling up to meet his salesman's eyes.

"That 25 percent of Scotia Bank's international profits are from Jamaica?" he asks, toying with the overmatched reporter.

Jab. "Scotia Bank in Jamaica, 1877."

Jab. "Eight per cent of the bank's profits in 2001, were earned in Jamaica."

Jab. "Jamaica had electricity before New York."

Jab, jab. "Running water before New York. And the second country in the west with a railway."

Then, the knockout. "Did you know the Bank of Nova Scotia was in Jamaica before it was in Toronto?" — to finance the rum and codfish trade out of Halifax.

And to make sure the sparring partner stays down: "In 1976, the Jamaican currency was stronger than the Canadian dollar. One U.S. dollar cost you just $1.09 Jamaican." Now it's about 85 to 1.

Despite Jamaica's appeal, Canada rocks as a close second. It's cold when Jamaica is hot; reserved and understated where Jamaica is bumptious and expressive. Canada picks her battles as Jamaica goes about her business unmindful of exploding grenades. One is polite to a fault; the other exuberant to the point of excess. One creeps up on you; a marching band precedes the other. With its broad shoulders spread across a vast land, Canada, second only to America in the role of Atlas to the world, lifts up the planet's displaced towards sunlight; Jamaica punches above its weight, a tiny cultural colossus whose reach positively exceeds its grasp. Opposites attract, yes, but why so easily?

I'm not sure what it is that first awakened me to Canada's charms, watching as I must have been, from island repose. Maybe it was those ads about Expo 67, featuring the glistening geodesic dome. Or was it the photographs of a multicultural populace, branding a country open to citizens sporting turbans, kilts, parkas and dashikis? There is room there for me, I may have thought, before finding it exactly so. Canada may indeed be too vast for true intimacy, but there is much to embrace.

I landed at Pearson International the night a man first landed on the moon. July 20, 1969. I was joining my parents — mom a domestic in Forest Hill; dad an orderly at Sunnybrook Hospital. I was supposed to improve the family's status, if not its fortunes. A year later, Port Antonio-born Lee-Chin arrived as a civil engineering student at McMaster University. He had very little money, Jamaican or Canadian currency. Chang had emigrated from Kingston in 1967, leaving behind a thriving family business. Family assets strained to cover eleven siblings, so Chang chose a Canadian education over a more expensive U.S. version and graduated in 1970 from the University of Toronto with a degree in solid state physics-electrical engineering; he later gained a chartered accountant designate.

Chang dabbled in a custom furniture business in the Jane-Finch area and finally jumped into the money fund game with some partners. Lee-Chin, meanwhile, worked as a bouncer to get through university. And when he was still short of tuition, he got a scholarship from the Jamaican government to finish his studies. By twenty-six he had become a financial adviser, and six years later, at age thirty-two, he borrowed $500,000 to purchase Mackenzie Financial stocks. That same year, 1983, Chang and partners bought into a tiny investment fund firm. It was managing just $5 million in assets and, in Chang's words, "was in a horrific administrative mess, but we recognized the potential and brought in the right people," including partner Bill Holland. Twenty years later it had morphed into CI Financial and manages upward of $80 billion in 190 funds. Meanwhile, Lee-Chin's stock value in Mackenzie Financial would appreciate seven-fold in four years. With the profits he purchased a small Kitchener investment firm, AIC Ltd., and watched its controlling assets balloon from $8 million in 1990 to $8 billion in 1998; it would later spike at $14 billion before falling back with at least five straight years of redemptions outstripping investments. By the time Chang had ceased active work in his firm he had a value of some $300 million. Lee Chin's personal worth is measured in multiples of that, once topping $2.5 billion in 2005.

Two Jamaican boys, just out of short pants, both with Hakka Chinese roots, Lee-Chin with the added African flavour, had travelled to Canada to study, picked up a few tricks along the way and were beating the Canucks at their money game. CI Financial is the second-largest publicly traded fund company in Canada and Chang has three million of its shares. AIC Ltd., one of Canada's largest privately run mutual fund operations, was sold to Manulife in 2007 and in exchange, Lee-Chin is a significant shareholder in Manulife. Jamaica, renowned for its coffee, bauxite and beaches; famous for its cultural influences in music and hairstyle and an accent that invites imitation; infamous for its dons in the Kingston garrisons and drug trade gangsters in Toronto's social housing complexes, was now hearing its name in corporate boardrooms, government offices, social clubs and in the highest circles of the land. And the sentences were ending with phrases like "role models," "success," "philanthropy," not "immigrants" or "criminals" or "deportation."

Once Lee-Chin started appearing on the *Forbes Magazine* list of world's wealthiest men, his cover was blown. Soon, the everyday media would be talking about him, and with that, the emergence of a public persona. Instead of operating on Bay St., Lee-Chin ran his operations ninety minutes away, where, he says, he could listen to his own voice without being contaminated by the chatter of those around him. But money talks — especially when you spend it as flamboyantly as the wealthy Jamaican with the Chinese-induced olive skin. Chang, though, slipped under the radar, by intent and by nature. Where Lee-Chin is well over six feet tall, outgoing and obviously athletic, Chang is six feet, of modest built and has no interest in being anything but retiring and understated. Self-effacing, he tells many interviewers that people tell him he is cheap and that he throws money around like manhole covers. Not so. Still, when Chang bought his mansion on the Bridle Path, Toronto's toniest neighbourhood, for $4.75 million in 2005, few noticed, except the friends who attend his annual summer soiree, where one can bump into David Suzuki or former Jamaican prime minister Edward Seaga and media types from the contact list of Chang's well-connected wife, Donette Chin-Loy. It's on such occasions one gets a glimpse of the opulence and comfort that wealth affords Chang — living in a post-modernist glass house with indoor swimming pool resting atop a two-acre ravine lot tamed with lovely gardens, a gazebo and tennis court. But new recognition and fame were just around the corner. Both men were soon to discover that nothing brings adoration and accolades and honour like giving your money away.

Chang and Lee-Chin are proof of the Biblical injunction less affluent mortals sometime forget. The more you give, the more you receive. Lee-Chin gave $5 million to his alma mater, McMaster University, in 2001. The next year he bought 75 percent of one of Jamaica's most popular but poorly performing banks, National Commercial Bank (NCB), for a song. Naturally, the bank's profits skyrocketed to US$130 million, from US$6 million. It is now Jamaica's largest, with 2,400 employees and forty-five branches. The next year he gave $30 million to the Royal Ontario Museum, the gift that would catapult him into public prominence. McMaster conferred on him an honorary Doctor of Law degree in 2003. The next year Lee-Chin donated $10 million to the University of Toronto to establish a school of management — and he received the International Humanitarian Award in New York. In 2005, his holding company, Portland Inc., created Columbus Communications — a Barbadian company that has controlling interests in telecommunications providers in the Caribbean. Think Flow Jamaica, Flow Trinidad, Cable Bahamas, Fibralink Jamaica and a range of digital telephone, highspeed internet and cable television services in twenty-one Caribbean and Latin American companies. Then he jumped into the tourism sector, purchasing the high-end Blue Lagoon, Reggae Beach and Trident Villa and Spas in Jamaica. And seeing that people do get sick, Lee-Chin bought a private hospital in Kingston in 2006. Once engaged in the medical business, he donated $4 million to Northern Caribbean University (NCU) in Mandeville to build a world-class nursing school, named for his mother, Hyacinth Chen, and accommodating eight hundred nursing students.

When Ray Chang was named Outstanding Philanthropist of 2010 by the Toronto chapter of the Association of Fundraising Professionals, he was reclaiming the award Lee-Chin won in 2005. In the last few years alone, Chang has donated some $20 million we know of, mostly in areas of education and health, his passion. He gave $5 million to Ryerson University for continuing education, and that school bears his name. He followed that with $7 million to fund research at the Centre for Addiction and Mental Health. The Toronto General and Western Hospital Foundation has a teaching chair for internal medicine named after his parents, Gladstone and Maisie. He also established a fellowship to train University of the West Indies (UWI) doctors at the hospital, an achievement the philanthropist beams about. And he supports the Dr. Herbert Ho Ping Kong Centre for excellence in education and practice of general medicine at the hospital. Then, he's good for about a million dollars to the ROM and UWI. Still, much of the money Chang has donated over the years has flowed anonymously.

After donating $1 million, he turned down a request by an academic institution for naming rights on a chair in medicine, and it wasn't the first time. He won a car on his annual deep-sea fishing trip in Panama and gave it to charity. He also sits on numerous boards and gives his directorship money to charity. He gave away so much money in 2010 he wasn't able to deduct it all, he told Tony Wong of the *Toronto Star*.

"It's not about the recognition. I really am not doing anything different than my grandfather, or father, who always gave back," says Chang. "They just did things and they didn't expect anything back. It wasn't something to talk about."

Universities and agencies and corporate bodies and associations in Canada and Jamaica are tripping over themselves to honour the men. Their business interests span Canada and the Caribbean. They sit on corporate and institutional boards in both countries. Chang has honorary degrees from Ryerson University and the University of the West Indies (UWI); Lee-Chin has honorary Doctor of Laws degrees from McMaster, University of Toronto, NCU, Sir Wilfred Laurier, UWI and York University. Both are university chancellors — Chang at Ryerson; Lee-Chin at Wilfred Laurier. They have been vested with the Order of Jamaica, the country's fourth highest. And they function with ease and effectiveness and equal honour and approval in Canada and in Jamaica.

I didn't apply for Canadian citizenship until some eighteen years after landing at Pearson. I wanted to feel Canadian, without divesting emotionally in Jamaica. The year before I became Canadian, I had returned to Orange for the first time since leaving. I cried and cried as I saw the little kids walk up at my church to recite the Bible verses, like I had in the very spot. I stopped and stared at the bougainvillea and hibiscus, enthralled. Common everyday objects of beauty during my childhood were now, surprisingly, treasures to store and cherish. I knew then that this land of wood and water was mine forever, no matter where I would roam. In Paris, I had seen the image of Bob Marley, on a mural listing the greatest figures of the twentieth century. Marcus Garvey had stood the test of time. In Ghana, I would stand on the shore off Cape Coast and feel the pull of the ancestors, the will to survive the African Maafa of slavery. Yes, the proud, indomitable Jamaican spirit bred into me could never be dulled by adopting Canadian citizenship. I felt Jamaica in my bones. The country had its hooks in me.

And, so, I grew to love Canada, as I do Jamaica; the way a man grows to love his wife, as himself.

Ray Chang puts it his way. "I am Jamaican by birth, Chinese by heritage and Canadian by choice. Each has played a significant part in my life." It is a beautiful thing that Canada allows. It is the genius of our adopted country, the very essence of a duality, a multi-dimension that conservatives would destroy.

Lee-Chin says that in Canada, "I came to a country and developed a business that I probably couldn't have done anywhere else. I love this country. It's been very good to me. Canadians are gentle and decent. This is a great country; every country in the world can aspire to be like us. And what is fantastic is how Toronto, over the years, has evolved to absorb the melting pot."

He made the stupendous $30 million donation to the ROM as a statement of the permanence of Jamaicans in Canada and as an "inspiration to every single immigrant, to every single person, every Canadian that whatever you put your mind to achieving, you can achieve it in this country." It was also, he says, to give everyone pause before they used the stereotype to judge Jamaicans. "We need to recalibrate people's views of themselves, particularly immigrants, and particularly Jamaicans. When your son goes to the ROM, he will see a name that relates to him and he will say, 'Holy, mackerel. I have a connection to this institution. I have a connection to this country'."

This increased love for Canada takes nothing away from the affection for Jamaica. It's the liberating fact of Canada.

Chang admits he feels most comfortable as a Jamaican. His first brush with discrimination was in Canada. And when he travelled to Hong Kong, cognizant of his Hakka-tinged accent and speech that was not part of the dominant group, he concluded, "No matter where I live, I'm going to be a minority. I will stick out in appearance, accent, heritage. I'm different. But I will use that difference to my advantage. I'm not going to let it hold me back. I won't hesitate to step out of the box or enter into any box. It's not a limitation. What I've found is, those who are going to accept you, fine. I'm not going to force anything on anyone. I am who I am. If you don't like it, tough. My parents taught me, 'Nobody is better than you. You are not better than anybody'."

When Chang's uncle died in the mid-1950s, the number of kids in his immediate family doubled to ten. By age thirteen he was working the family business, selling fruit cakes and Easter buns, and mixing with the salesmen in a way, he says, Chinese don't normally do. That, plus his education at Jesuit-influenced St. George's College high school in Jamaica, prepared him for the future. "It gave me a running start." He'd learned early that education is the great equalizer, that it is portable and to be obtained at all cost. And when Jamaica tilted politically to the left, and it appeared that the "good standard of living that two generations of my family had built up could disappear," the lesson was reinforced.

Lee-Chin loves to tell the story of how he grew up dirt poor. His mother, Hyacinth Chen, who now owns real estate interests and one of the largest supermarket chains in Jamaica, a millionaire in her own right, doesn't like hearing it. The son hasn't stopped telling it. It's what drives him. It's the link to the past, his African roots, a Jamaica of another time, a legacy that grips the island economy and threatens its future, one he's determined to influence and shape.

"I spent my formative first eighteen years in Jamaica and I'm an amalgam of all the opportunities presented in Canada. I'm Jamaican in attitude, accent, behaviour and mannerisms," he says. "The son of an orphan whose teenage mom worked three jobs as a clerk, and it's possible in one generation that I could buy the National Commercial Bank? This country nurtured me to believe I could be anything I wanted." One takes that for granted until one considers the prospects of another child, born the same year, 1951, but in another country torn by war, limited by a cast structure, or in which there are no examples of success among people of his kind — factors that "truncates one's confidence," he says. His mixed heritage, which prevented total acceptance from Chinese or black Jamaicans, seemed not to have had any impact, he says.

His parents had high expectations. And he grew up in an era open to opportunities in a country where, "250 years earlier, I would have been a slave. So, I'm blessed. I have to work hard. I wouldn't be where I am today if Jamaica hadn't made me confident. I would be ungrateful if I didn't hold Jamaica in highest esteem." Now, the task of his life is to inject some struggles and challenges into the lives of his five children. That's needed, he says, when you get driven home from the maternity ward in a Rolls Royce.

His other struggle is to help Jamaica pull itself up economically. To that end Lee-Chin has invested hundreds of millions in his native land, promises to keep his bank's profits in the country, donates 1 percent of its credit-card purchases to scholarships and school supplies, and is treated as a hero on his frequent visits. He finds motivation in the story of his African ancestors, and his improbable existence considering the death rate of slaves on the way to Jamaica and on its plantations. The idea that he has thrived and earned a fortune is overwhelming at times. "I can't let them down," he says.

Jamaica suffers from an erosion of wealth, unable to optimize its intellectual and financial capital. Its people leave, taking the brain power. And investors run away with the money they make, taking job-creation potential and creating a vicious cycle. Was there an iceberg that hit Jamaica, Lee-Chin asks, then answers:

> No, it's been continuous. Historically, from colonial days we've had people coming here, making it here and shipping out the profits. That's happened and continues right up to day. We are denuding ourselves, not reinvesting. This year, $1 billion US will be shipped out of Jamaica. That's wealth destruction. The solution is to reverse both the denuding of intellectual capital and the denuding of financial capital. It's a long-term solution. So, what we are doing here? We want to build a business starting with NCB, with a reputation that is so strong that it will provide an entrepreneurial, professional outlet for the brightest people. They don't need now to go to the United States or Canada; and we will stop the exporting of our best.

The vision is to make NCB the most successful bank in the world, Lee-Chin says. "And why not? ING and Amro are the fifth and sixth largest banks in the world and are from a small country of thirteen million. If they can do it, why can't we? All it takes is a little brains, will and ambition, and we have lots of that. The mission is to instill confidence to keep the brightest people here."

Chang, on a smaller scale, is helping pepper farmers in St. Ann to pull themselves up by the bootstraps. He's invested in the renowned Walkers Wood spice business. "When I talk to farmers and ask what's holding them back, they tell me it's land, money and secure markets," Chang says. So, he approached a bauxite company with its large acreage sitting idle and negotiated land leases. Then he sent out the message to the farmers, promising startup funds, training and a guaranteed price for all the peppers they produced. I visited one such farm with Chang in 2005. On two and a half acres, a farmer like Micey Coombs could net $10,000 Canadian a year — double the average wage. He has also invested in Corrpak, a packaging manufacturer, employing nearly 200 people in Greenich Farm, one of Jamaica's major inner city communities.

Lee-Chin and Chang are just two men, albeit rich ones, challenging a huge country with massive economic problems, even as it dominates the world on the Olympic track and influences global music and fashion. And, adding to their difficulty is a massive public relations headache, brought on by what

Lee-Chin says is about a hundred dons and gunmen who have hijacked the country's image and defined it in public consciousness as a place of violence and mayhem. The reputation, like capital, has gone abroad.

"It hurts me. I want the perceptions of us to be more reflective of who we are, of our contributions. We have a reputation we have to clean up. Someone gets shot and you say, 'Please, God, let it not be a Jamaican.' You cringe. Every upstanding Jamaican feels the same way. We are embarrassed by it."

I took my son, Darnell, on separate interviews with the two moguls, the type of titan he dreams of becoming. The boy sees his mom and his dad as typical misguided immigrants — working, working, working and not reaching heights attained by people who let their money do the work. He's driven to make family fortunes, not just improve the family status. So he wants the key to striking it rich.

"A good life is not measured by the wealth you accumulate. It's evaluated by the contribution you make to society," Chang tells him. Lee-Chin backs up Darnell's co-mentor, saying:

> This is for you, Darnell, if you're going to be a full-fledged human being. I had to be a disciple of something. Initially, I didn't know what that something was going to be, but I saw people who were fulfilled, who made the right choices through thick and thin, were the ones who had a purpose in life and dedicated their life to a cause. So I thought I want to find a cause that I can dedicate my life to. So it was having a purpose that gave me confidence, that gave me focus, that gave me discipline, that allowed me to persevere, that gave me courage.

And so, in Canada and in Jamaica, exhibiting the Jamaican pride, competitive spirit, can-do attitude and indomitable will, Raymond Chang and Michael Lee-Chin have changed the conversation about Jamaicans. Still, at another stirringly positive UWI Toronto benefit gala — Chang is the patron of the annual event — at the Four Seasons Hotel in March, the media is not there to record the exhilaration of a room full of doctors, lawyers, professors, engineers and scholars from Jamaica and the rest of the Caribbean, raising money to send Haitian and Jamaican students to UWI. The room is bursting with potential, a little-seen, unknown display of a community's reach, influence, power and impact. Lee-Chin states the obvious: "Their contributions are not the headlines, so they are unsung. Our reputation has been ambushed. A few bad men have hijacked our reputation."

So, what about that reality? One of the tougher tasks of my job as a newspaper columnist is the vicious and vile emails that pile into the inbox on the matter of Jamaicans and crime. Everyone's an expert. Many lay claim to a Jamaican friend or a Jamaican lover or spouse who has the answer to the miasma of crime and gunmen and the slaying of our boys on Toronto's streets. Frequently, the tirade begins with the declaration that it is Jamaicans, not Bajans or Trinidadians or the studious continental Africans who are the troublemakers. And the evidence, piled up online, in blogs, in the newspapers and police files and court cases, paint a discouraging profile. The evidence is an effective silencer. Dare to complain about police harassment or racial profiling or heavy-handed policing, and citizens cite crime statistics as justification. "Control your kids. Father your children. Either teach your boys to keep their thing in their pants or your girls to close their legs or don't bother us," is the attitude. And one more thing, "Go back to your hell-hole of a country." That offered solution is not a majority view, but the issue is a majority concern.

While the majority of Jamaicans lead extraordinary lives of tremendous contribution, often woven into the fabric of Toronto society, a few drops of blood contaminate the pool and attract the sharks. Most destructively, the blood also sends the productive majority scurrying for cover — leaving the arena unpopulated, except by the bad men. It's the great issue for Jamaicans over the next fifty years in Canada, especially in its largest city.

Those who watched the creeping violence of rude boys morph into gangstas, then ruthless posses and indiscriminate killers that rule Kingston's garrisons, fear Toronto is in the first stage of a march towards this madness. And, with typical aggressiveness and flare, Jamaicans are the visible foot soldiers in the trade.

What to do? What's the problem? How to solve it? Who do you enlist to reverse the death march? Education, the great equalizer Ray Chang talks about, is absent from the lives of these young men. They are at the end of a familiar cycle that often begins with a baby mother and an absent father, limited supervision, childrearing by the street fathers and the inevitable slide into crime. To stop the flow of blood, one must stop its conception. And who can conceive of an abortive regimen that's moral, legal, ethical and practical. In essence, the impact of identifiable Jamaican gunmen shooting one another in broad daylight might be diluted by identifiable Jamaicans helping, teaching, healing, serving, interacting with the city in broad daylight. Incapable as we are of stemming the virus that infects some of our youth, considering the dysfunction of their lives and station, Jamaicans in Canada may want to focus on a campaign of Jamaican goodness to counteract the debilitating effect of Jamaican badness. The former outnumber the latter 1000 to 1. It may be time to showcase it.

Go to the UWI fundraising gala — a stellar event delivered with precision and verve — and your head swells with pride. Where are these people all the time? Do they exist in some subterranean city, muted, invisible, managing hospital emergency rooms, running police divisions, leading school boards, conducting life-changing research, sitting in court in judgment of law-breakers, managing the crown attorneys, designing buildings, strategizing political campaigns? The operative words are "muted" and "invisible." It's as if the majority of our people have chosen to flee rather than fight, to hide their deeds under a bushel, lest they be associated with the evil. That must end, or the heroic efforts of high-achievers like Lee-Chin and Chang will be dismissed as a statistical anomaly to be expected when you have some 300,000 people in one place.

In Jamaica in March 2012 to explore why Jamaicans run so fast, I ran straight to the hovel of a home of the mother of the "suitcase murder." The exclusive interview ran on Sunday, April 1. I'm writing now on Tuesday, April 3. I have not heard from a lawyer willing to tackle the case, neither a social worker nor an ex-copper. There is no battery of community services workers and professionals ready to jump to the woman's aid. Were it not for Councillor Michael Thompson, the lone Black councillor at Toronto city hall, trying heroically to set up a bank account to accept donations, Opal Austin would lack someone in her corner.

Austin sent her two children to live with their father and stepmother in Toronto in 1990. They were aged ten and thirteen. The ten-year-old boy, Dwayne, plunged from a twenty-second-storey balcony in 1992, and police ruled it a suicide. By 1994, Melonie, then seventeen, was murdered, and her starved and fractured body tossed in a suitcase and set ablaze in Vaughan. Police saw the burning suitcase, recovered the body but were unable to identify it because the foot and finger prints were burned off. The girl was not reported missing. Nobody here missed her. Apparently, she was not enrolled in school. The father told her mother in Jamaica that Melonie had run away to the U.S. And nobody knew — until a police tip eighteen years later revealed her identity and led to the arrest of the caregivers. How could that happen, in Canada?

A visible, engaged, vibrant, empowered community of Jamaicans would have sprung into action. Immediately. A top criminal lawyer would have jumped on the case and started advocating for the suicide case to be re-opened. Social policy wonks would have drafted necessary changes to immigration and child welfare protocols, to make sure such kids are tracked. Average Jamaican-Canadians would voice their outrage and concern and condemnation. But if the past is any indication, good Jamaicans will have vacated the public square. Afraid of another bad publicity moment about a bad Jamaican apple, they overturn an entire bushel basket of potential goodness that could salvage a bad situation.

One of the legacy projects of Toronto's Jamaica50 celebrations will be publication of a book, "When Ackee Meets Codfish." It profiles some two hundred Jamaican Canadians of influence and achievement, many of them in Toronto. If only they could unshackle and unmask themselves and assume their destiny.

In one of our interviews, I asked Lee-Chin if anyone had ever approached him to bankroll or be lead donor in the creation of a space, a centre, for Caribbean and Black people in Toronto. That would speak to permanence, address the need to look after Jamaica's young before they are tossed to the wolves. That would signal a certain maturity, the creation of community capacity and the coming out of the closet, so to speak, of the Caribbean community, led by its largest group, the Jamaicans. Talk about a made-in-Toronto legacy for Jamaica's Year of Jubilee.

Lee-Chin joked that he is already too busy and doesn't need another cause. But he didn't close the option. It's just that nobody, with the gravitas of a Hilary Weston, who solicited the $30 million ROM donation, has asked. On the most crucial issue of our time, our silence is killing us, even as the achievements of two of Jamaica's finest speak volumes.

For a people spawned on the edge of the sea, fifty years is long enough to find one's voice, if not one's legs.

PART SEVEN – EDUCATING CANADIANS

23. ENHANCING EDUCATION

Jamaican and other Caribbean Teachers in Alberta

Etty Shaw-Cameron

In his book *The Courage to Teach*, Sam Intrator (2002: xxxvii) writes: "Teachers believe that teaching is more than a job and more than merely doing routine work — that teaching is a vocation to which they were summoned because they have something worthy and important to contribute to the world." Because Caribbean teachers subscribed to this belief, we were motivated enough to leave the warmth of the tropics, sacrifice our accustomed ways of life and take up teaching in Alberta schools. Currently, Alberta's population is comprised of a large number of people from the Caribbean region — people who were prepared not only to leave the warmth of their islands but also the white sand beaches, a supportive system of family, friends and community and a more relaxed pace of life to live in Alberta's intemperate and often harsh climate.

This chapter[1] documents the contributions of Caribbean teachers — a majority of them Jamaicans — who worked in Alberta schools. It is appropriate that the stories of these teachers be included in this anthology as a way of honouring fifty years of autonomy for the island nations of Jamaica and Trinidad and Tobago, both of which achieved independence in 1962. The teachers came to Alberta in the 1960s; some of them entered the profession by way of career changes, and many came on the direct invitation from school jurisdictions. These qualified professionals were highly sought after at a time when Alberta education's system was experiencing a severe shortage of teachers. We contributed to the development of education and consequently to the enhancement of Alberta communities.

Several conditions precipitated the need for Caribbean teachers in Alberta schools. It was the aftermath of World War II — a war in which many of Alberta's trained teachers participated as a way of fulfilling their patriotic duties. During the war, the education of the province's children suffered — the schools became run down, support services were almost non-existent, and trained teachers were hard to find. The few teachers who did not go to the war preferred to work in city schools or larger centres, where work-ing conditions were somewhat better. Some schools in remote areas of the province were almost deserted; others closed because there was not enough trained personnel to meet the needs of school jurisdictions. And the situa-tion was even worse on First Nations reserves. The government responded by putting grade eleven students in the classrooms as teachers (they found it hard to cope with the conditions),[2] and to avoid potential disaster some schools were converted to correspondence centres.

Some Caribbean teachers worked at the correspondence centres, mark-ing papers and teaching students from a distance in subjects like science, social studies, mathematics and English. They provided students the opportunity to do school work at their own pace until such time as trained teachers were more in abundance and became available to staff schools.

Few rural teachers had help in dealing with the difficulties of language and cultural differences as there were no instruments in place to address these issues. Normal school training did not prepare teachers to teach non-English speaking students or to communicate with their parents. When Jamaican teacher Clair Burgher found out that not all the students in her class could communicate in English, she quickly devised ways and means to remedy this problem. Success came over time, and eventually all students started understanding and enjoying the lessons and participating fully in classroom activities. There was no philosophy in place to cover the special needs of children with disabilities, to meet the needs of the slow learners or extra bright students, or even students with special skills. Conscientious Caribbean teachers did what they could, though they had few resources to work with. Their teacher college training background became their greatest source of reference.

Irrespective of the conditions, teachers were expected to set sterling moral standards for their students. We were constantly watched by the com-munity to the point where one teacher felt that she lived and worked under a microscope. In small communities, there were regular personal contacts as everyone went to the same church, post office, general store and curling and skating rinks. Outside of the classroom, there was not much else. It was not uncommon for teachers to share the personal opportunities they were engaged in for growth and development with their students and their parents. Such things as professional development days, furthering their studies at universi-ties or colleges and conducting workshops all demonstrated to students that education is lifelong learning. Teachers modelled that good organizational planning, complemented with the wise use of time, were important strategies to the achievement of a person's desired goals at any age.

Teacher turnover was always a problem for rural schools. Teachers changed schools frequently, opting for better pay, better working conditions or better scenery. However, when Caribbean teachers came on the scene, they guaranteed school jurisdictions years in the classroom. With this type of stability in place, school jurisdictions were able to focus their attention on fine tuning such things as philosophical needs, the provision of much needed classroom materials, support services for teachers and upgrading of infrastructures to make schools and the teaching profession more appealing, all of which would attract prospective teachers and perhaps reclaim other teachers who had embarked on different careers.

Caribbean teachers were well liked by parents, students and administrators in the communities where they worked. We exuded a vivacious and bubbly personality, a panacea for coping with difficulties. We were kind and caring and possessed excellent classroom management skills. Clear boundaries were established for expected behaviours, and consistency was maintained. Students had a say in simple rules for the smooth running of the classroom, and they exhibited pride in the ownership of their creations, which were displayed on the walls inside the classroom. A walk into a Caribbean teacher's classroom was like a visit to an art gallery. In addition, Caribbean teachers brightened the classroom with our keen sense of humour and our upbeat personalities. We spoke with confidence and sincerity, and we were firm and consistent in our expectations; these qualities helped the students to develop good rapport with us. As teachers, we had excellent organizational skills and were able to accept and overcome challenging situations.

In-depth evaluations revealed that Caribbean teachers were respected and held in high esteem by First Nations people as well as those in the mainstream. We easily measured up to and surpassed the criteria used for evaluating our performance in the schools. Some teachers, like Vernal Smith and Walter Subadan (both Jamaicans), left the classroom to work with government and private agencies after a time. Vernal Smith was appointed by the Alberta Solicitor General Department to coordinate and supervise provincial inmate education. In fulfilling this mandate, Smith established and directed a vocational program at St. Paul Correctional Centre. Walter Subadan became project manager in the Federal Lands and Statutory Requirements Section for the Department of Indian Affairs and Northern Development. Guyanese teacher Sybil Sargeant-Simmons was lauded by her principal as one who "had good leadership potential in the areas of curriculum development and general school administration. Her broad background and varied experiences make her an asset in any position for which her competencies qualify her." These teachers substantiate the belief that teachers are generic to all professions — a teacher can easily cross from one field into another.

Concerning classroom discipline of students, Caribbean teachers were neither permissive nor punitive. We maintained a kind but firm attitude while successfully guiding our students to achieve their ambitions without being stifled. As skills were learnt, the students developed a keen sense of responsibility, which ultimately led them to accept new challenges with confidence and courage. We accentuated the positive; we found something good in every child and used it to promote the child's self-esteem. The results were compensatory as the students in turn performed to the best of their ability and achieved phenomenal results.

The successes experienced by Caribbean teachers stemmed from our love of children and teaching. Many of us spent hours trying to find new ways to bring a lesson alive in the classroom so the children would be motivated to learn. One very successful contribution that the author made to students' learning was the introduction of special projects, which engaged students and their parents in extra-curricular activities that had to be carried out at home. These practical and fun projects created the climate for parents and children to work together, to communicate and to solve problems in creative ways. Designed as extensions to learning, these special projects gave students the opportunity to practise problem-solving skills independent of the teacher's direct guidance. The author also left the legacy of Carnival Days, which the school and community celebrate as their annual year-end activity.

In caring for students, teachers found remarkable ways to transcend unfavourable conditions in the schools and communities. Principal Steve Ramsankar, from the islands of Trinidad and Tobago, is one teacher who overcame adverse conditions at his inner-city school in Edmonton. There he initiated a nutrition program to help alleviate the problem of hunger, which was prevalent among the students and their parents in the community. As time progressed, the school opened a clothing bank, which provided the students choices of clean clothes and warm outfits in winter. Principal Steve used his own money to buy unbudgeted classroom materials that students needed in order to take the next steps because he believed that "when the basic needs of students and community are met, a climate for good learning is created." And when the climate for good learning was created, Steve and his students travelled internationally to his island home of Trinidad and Tobago — quite an adventure for inner-city students. This memorable experience helped students develop a greater sense of appreciation for living in a multicultural society like Canada. There is always that passion among Caribbean teachers to help children learn, grow and stretch even if it means making personal sacrifices.

One success led to another, and before long Steve phased in aspects of a program that later became the model for "safe and caring schools" throughout the province of Alberta. Within the school he incorporated the Police Liaison Program for safety, opened up a child-care centre and introduced English as a second language (ESL) for students and their parents. Regularly scheduled activities like Cub Scouts, Brownies and Girl Guides were allowed to operate within school hours so students could benefit from attending within a safe and caring environment. Steve worked with the Department of Education to promote safe and caring schools throughout the province.

It is a sad reflection on our world today that it appears that everyone is talking but no one is listening — hence, little or nothing gets done. Parker J. Palmer, in the *Courage to Teach* (Intrator 2002: xix), states: "Listening is what the human self most yearns for: to be received, to be heard, to be known, and in the process to be honored… deep listening is what gives rise to the impulse toward personal and social change." Indeed, the federal government of Canada must have listened to Enoch Henry, the assistant principal who recommended that a school be built on the Louis Bull Reserve. As the assistant principal's concerns were honoured, the students of this reserve had the opportunity of receiving their schooling close to home. The school is often the centre of a community, the place where people congregate for communal activities. This was a tangible and lasting legacy that Enoch got for the Louis Bull Reserve. This Mico University-trained Jamaican teacher showed that teachers are community leaders and builders whose vision is all encompassing.

Charles Green, a Jamaican-born teacher, took a literary approach to voicing his concerns about the education of First Nations children. Charles experienced the difficulties of working in the education system on the reserve. He saw first hand the plight of Native education and was motivated to write an article, "Coming of Age: Native Education in the 21st Century." This document has been used as a resource material in some senior classes for Native Studies at Simon Fraser University. Charles worked for many years among the First Nations population, reaching the rank of superintendent and was frequently consulted on the subject of Native education.

In my opinion, teachers are among the most versatile people in the world. The skills they utilize in the classroom often spill over in the communities as added benefits to others. Teachers are like Boy Scouts and Girl Guides, who practise the motto "be prepared." Jeannette Austin-Odina is an example of versatility and preparedness in that she affords herself multiple career choices to the extent her employers are drawn to her. You could say she is "Jill of all trades and master of all" in the fields of guidance counsellor, social work, French language instructor, founder of the Council for Canadians of African and Caribbean Heritage (CCACH) and co-founder and promoter of the annual Afro-Quiz competition in Edmonton. The sky's the limit for this teacher who hails from the twin islands of Trinidad and Tobago.

When the Alberta government decided to comply with Canada's bilingual policy, appropriate classroom materials in French were not readily available at all grade levels. To prevent the teaching of French being restricted to rote learning at the level she taught, Valerie McIntosh, a teacher from Grenada, voluntarily wrote a basal reader called *Periscope*. Not only did the students in her French immersion class benefit from using this book, other districts, including Edmonton Public, found the book useful in their system. This book is among the suggested resource materials for the French program in Alberta at the elementary level.

The presence of numerous ethnic groups in Alberta led to the government overhauling the social studies curriculum to provide content with greater forms of ethnic identity. Jamaican couple Hal and Hazel Rogers and their children became the resource engine for the Kanata Kit at the lower elementary level. After the materials were developed, the couple was among those who piloted and gave their input to what became the new social studies curriculum for the lower elementary grades throughout the province. Inroads were gradually made into the ways the Department of Education developed and delivered school curricula, partly because of the presence of Caribbean teachers. Our children did not fit the mainstream curricula, and we voiced our dissatisfaction with the status quo, thus initiating change in an aspect of cultural identity.

Caribbean teachers who taught in Alberta schools have been recognized in public and private arenas ranging from *Time Magazine's* International Man of the Year, municipal, provincial and federal governments, clubs, volunteer organizations, colleagues, parents, students, administrators, First Nations band leaders and community members. They have been gifted with personal memorabilia and honoured at retirement functions. Many have been recommended for special awards, some given scholarships and others, special citations. There is a large photograph in honour of teacher Hal Rogers at the entrance to Willow Park Elementary School in Leduc. Each year, a member of the Rogers family attends a ceremony at the school to present the Hal Rogers' Citizenship Award to a grade six student who has demonstrated exceptional qualities of citizenship.

School jurisdictions throughout Alberta have benefitted considerably from the superb health enjoyed by Caribbean teachers. Despite the change in climate, Caribbean teachers attended school regularly, hardly taking time off work. By not using substitute teachers, school jurisdictions accumulated excess funds. In appreciation, some boards remunerated teachers who had unused sick leave. Places like the Yukon and Northland School Divisions offered incentives in the forms of isolation bonuses and a one-way ticket from Edmonton or Vancouver to teachers who were appointed to teach in these regions.

Caribbean teachers were highly sought after because we were articulate in the English language and could communicate easily with the students. We were well trained in classroom management and maintained discipline while we adhered to the philosophy of education for every child who was capable of learning. We used our spare time to find and devise creative ways to motivate student learning, and the results were compensatory. At the end of a school year, requests came in from parents to have their children placed in a Caribbean teacher's class if there was more than one class at a particular grade level. In order to maintain a balance in numbers, principals had to do much juggling in compiling class lists.

Caribbean teachers helped define the education system in Alberta and contributed to the multicultural mosaic of the province and of Canada. Our presence in Alberta during the crisis years helped to restore professionalism to teaching; as well we helped to stabilize, energize and maintain the education system, which today ranks high in Canada.

Not only did the people of the host province benefit from having Caribbean teachers among them, life was made easier for the governments of the islands. Previously unknown in this part of the world, the Caribbean islands have been gaining visibility. Ultimately, the islands benefitted from this exposure as tourists started going to these places. In later years, educational exchanges fostered relationships among universities. Where there was once a teacher shortage, Alberta now experiences a workforce shortage, and a new wave of people from the Caribbean are coming to the province to assist the operation of businesses and farms.

Before honorary consuls came to Alberta, Caribbean teachers acted as unassigned ambassadors for their region. Some have sponsored West Indian days at the University of Alberta, appeared on CBC radio to talk about the Caribbean, educated people in its culture and competed in the sports of cricket and netball, which were foreign to Albertans. Above all, we have shown people how to "party" in Caribbean style. This garnered a following of many who felt the urge to learn rhythmic movements. Caribbean teachers are found at the forefront of clubs, organizations, associations, boards and other leadership positions. We have been role models and community leaders who are highly sought after because of our strong organizational and interpersonal skills. We have been dedicated volunteers who have given unsparingly of our time to community endeavours, hoping to leave the school and communities better places for those who follow.

Notes

1. This chapter is a condensed version of a self-published book: *Roll Call: Caribbean Teachers in Alberta Schools* by this author, Etty Shaw-Cameron, who was trained at Shortwood Teacher College in Jamaica. The book was written in an effort to validate the presence of Caribbean teachers who have lived and worked in the province of Alberta since the 1960s. In the process, these teachers have made invaluable contributions to the education of Alberta's children and to the many communities where they lived and worked.

2. These untrained student teachers were placed in schools that were far from their homes and were devoid of basic educational materials or support personnel.

References

Caribbean Times. 1989. "Stephen Ramsankar Receives Honorary Doctor of Law Degree." 93.325/4. June.

Cochrane, Jean. 2001. *The One Room School in Canada.* Calgary: Fifth House.

Dreikurs, Rudolf, Pearl Cassel and Eva Dreikurs. 2004. *Discipline Without Tears.* Toronto: John Wiley & Sons.

Intrator, Sam. 2002. *The Courage to Teach.* San Francisco, CA: Jossey-Boss.

McKenzie, Robert J. 2002. *Setting Limits in the Classroom.* NY: Three Rivers Press.

McLachlan, Elizabeth. 1999. *With Unshakeable Persistence.* Edmonton: NeWest Press.

___. 2001. *With Unfailing Dedication.* Edmonton: NeWest Press.

Provincial Archives of Alberta. 1983. "The Communicant.Ramsankar — A Man for all Countries." 93.325/6.November.

Shaw-Cameron, Etty. 2009. *Roll Call: Caribbean Teachers in Alberta Schools.* Edmonton, AB: Etty Shaw-Cameron.

Stamp, Robert M. 2004. *Becoming a Teacher in 20th Century Calgary.* Calgary: Detselig Enterprises.

24. MAKING A DIFFERENCE

Reflections of a Results-Oriented Jamaican Canadian Educator

Avis Glaze

As a young girl growing up in rural Jamaica, my first career choice was to become a lawyer. I spent countless nights watching Perry Mason on television in an effort to learn his techniques. And then one day I met a very special teacher, and my future direction was firm. I instantly switched from law to teaching and set my sights on a career in education. In choosing this profession, I knew that I could fulfil my desire to make a difference in the lives of others. My strong sense of social justice and of the importance of education sharpened my resolve to pursue a career in an area that makes it possible to have a positive influence on the lives of young people.

A good education has always been important to me. Education liberates the human mind and the human spirit and can instill an insatiable appetite for learning. It can ignite within students a strong motivation to achieve. It can also promote, among other things, a high regard for democratic principles and human rights. Education and democracy are inextricably linked. And democracy is strongest where education is strongest.

As a young teacher, I became convinced that a society must value educational equity. We must ensure that all of our students graduate from our schools with the skills, knowledge, attitudes, dispositions and sensibilities necessary to become productive and self-sustaining citizens. The costs are too great otherwise — in terms of the disengagement of our youth, poor levels of health and high levels of crime. Our quest for educational equity must therefore be relentless.

In my early years as teacher, I also recognized that literacy is the master key to future life chances. It is a foundation for learning and a primary means of social and economic empowerment. Statistics Canada, for example, tells us that a mere one percentage gain in average literacy and numeracy skill levels in Canada would add a permanent increase of $18.4 billion per year to the country's GDP (gross domestic product). We do know that investment in human capital leads to economic growth. And we also know that low levels of literacy skills contribute to unemployment.

While I have held many positions in education, including that of being Ontario's first Chief Student Achievement Officer and founding CEO of the Literacy and Numeracy Secretariat, I still consider myself first and foremost, a teacher. I chose a profession that is intensely noble, moral in its intent, multifaceted in its scope and boundless in its possibilities to make things happen for all students from all backgrounds, including those in our African-Canadian community. It is a profession that allows us, each day, to nurture their potential so that they can fulfill their role in contributing to the future of Canada — a future we *all* want to create as proud immigrants to this country who take very seriously what the notion of responsible citizenship means.

I believe strongly in the importance of building a robust education system that ensures excellence and equity for all students. That is certainly the best hope for a country to ensure a promising future for all. That is also why I embraced every opportunity to influence education policy both within Canada and beyond and have worked with fellow educators around the world to support teachers and educational leaders in their quest to provide *every* student with the best possible education.

Throughout my career, I have been responsible for many innovations in Canadian and international education policy. In this article, I will describe those policies that, I feel, have had the greatest impact on the education of African-Canadian students and on all students in Canada and other jurisdictions.

Ontario's Royal Commission on Learning

The system of education in Ontario is recognized as one of the best in the world. There are many pockets of excellence, along with some areas which need improvement. It has, however, become imperative that the education system, as a major change agent in our society, consistently evaluates its role and effectiveness in responding to its increasingly diverse population and to the rapidly changing needs of the individuals we are expected to serve.

In 1993, I was asked by the Ontario government to be a commissioner on its Royal Commission on Learning. This initiative was created in response to continuing concerns about the quality, efficiency and responsiveness of the system of education in Ontario. The Commission was charged with the responsibility of bringing all partners in the education system together in a process of public consultation and of taking the public's concerns and translating them into a concrete plan of action for the future of elementary and secondary school education in Ontario. The Commission's mandate posed several questions under the following themes: the purpose and direction of our school system; the program in our schools; accountability in education; the organization of our system; and the issue of governance.

Public consultation was extensive, including eighteen months of public hearings in twenty-seven cities throughout the province. In an effort to reach those who might not respond to these more formal processes, the Commission also visited such places as shopping malls, community centres, newly arrived immigrant groups and specific cultural organizations, detention centres and homes for pregnant teens.

As a result of this very extensive consultation with the widest possible cross-section of Ontarians, the Commissioners of the Royal Commission on Learning concluded that Ontario did have a good education system with some excellent schools and many committed educators. They also stated, however, that there were many aspects of the system which required dramatic improvement if the system was to enhance the opportunities and life chances of students in general and those from racial minorities and homes with low incomes in particular.

After examining some 5,000 briefs, my fellow commissioners and I concluded that the conventional tools of school reform were just not enough to transform Ontario's massive education system in the many ways we considered necessary. Thus, we redefined the primary and shared responsibilities of schools with a clear focus on schools as centres of teaching and learning. We advanced a two-tiered system of recommendations and identified four engines or levers of change. These included a new kind of school-community alliance in which parents, community organizations, social agencies, businesses and unions, religious, cultural and athletic groups all played a part (the African saying, "It takes a village to raise a child," is reflected in our thinking). In this regard, the commissioners recommended that every school establish a school-community council, comprised of staff, students, parents and community representatives, to create links between the school and the community and to provide advice on key issues. Our conclusion was that schools cannot do it alone. They need assistance with the shared aspects of education so that they can focus their attention on the academic achievement of students.

We also highlighted the importance of early childhood education and the professionalization of teachers. Early learning has a tremendous impact on future success in school, as those children who experience high quality early programs not only gain significantly in coping skills but also develop positive attitudes to learning. At the same time, the commissioners recognized fully that no real reform could take place without the participation of teachers. Professionals learn throughout their lives; they are expected to engage in ongoing professional development to ensure continuous improvement. We recommended that professional development be mandatory for all educators and that an Ontario College of Teachers be established as an independent body to determine professional standards and be responsible for certifying teachers.

In the end, we made 167 recommendations in a variety of areas, all addressing the many challenges facing education in Ontario. If implemented, Ontarians would be in a better position to meet the educational challenges of the twenty-first century with confidence. The Commission (1995) was especially impressed with the "astonishing diversity that characterizes the people of Ontario." Indeed, a wide range of religious, linguistic, racial and ethno-cultural groups seized on the opportunity to air their concerns about the education of their children. It was clear to the Commission "that schools must welcome students of every background, faith, language, culture, or colour. On this there can be no compromise or qualification." In particular, representatives of the various racial and ethno-cultural groups and organizations submitted briefs, often including irrefutable empirical data such as abnormally high drop-out rates and the low number of students going into university, demonstrating "forcefully and convincingly that the educational system was failing their community." This was particularly true for the Black, Hispanic/Latin, Portuguese, Francophone and First Nations communities.

Many concerns were expressed by parents and community leaders of African descent. Their primary focus was on how Black children are casualties of negative differential treatment, stereotyping, bias in testing and evaluation, streaming, a mono-cultural curriculum, unfair and unusual discipline, racism and, most damaging of all, the self-fulfilling prophecy of low expectations. Many of the concerns, some of which were shared by other ethno-cultural groups and organizations, were voiced with a sense of urgency and the notion that there was a crisis in the African-Canadian community in terms of the education of their students.

In short, the briefs suggested that many Black students felt alienated from and marginalized within the education system. As a result, two of our key recommendations were: 1) in jurisdictions with large numbers of Black students, school boards, academic authorities, faculties of education and representatives of the Black community collaborate to establish demonstration schools and innovative programs based on best practices in bringing about academic success for black students; and 2) whenever there are indications of collective underachievement in any particular group of students, school boards ensure that teachers and principals have the necessary strategies and human and financial resources to help these students.

As I never tire of repeating, the African-Canadian community has *always* placed a high value on education. This was demonstrated by the range and quality of briefs submitted to the Commission and in the discussions during the consultative process and visits to schools. Those who are more recently from the Caribbean, Africa and other parts of the African diaspora know that, like women in Canadian society, they must work very hard to achieve their goals. But, in their homelands, role models of academic and professional excellence were in abundance.

Yet somehow, even for those Black students who are descendants of earlier settlers in Ontario, academic excellence is perceived to be the exception rather than the role. The myth that Black people do not value education, that they cannot, in general, achieve academic excellence and that parents are not interested in their children's education must be dislodged. Black parents, educators and organizations have not stood idly by waiting for someone else to address their concerns about their children's education. They have cooperated with school boards and the Ministry of Education in the cause of their children's academic achievement.

Indeed, it was the persistent lobbying of the Black Educators' Working Group and the Anti-Racist and Multicultural Education Network of Ontario (AMENO) which resulted in the establishment of the position of Assistant Deputy Minister of Anti-Racism and Equity. These two organizations, as well as others, worked very closely with the Ministry to help define policy.

The Literacy and Numeracy Secretariat

In 2003, I was chosen to be Ontario's first Chief Student Achievement Officer and CEO of the newly formed Literacy and Numeracy Secretariat. We moved quickly to forge consensus around the philosophy, modus operandi, resources, strategies and tools that would be needed to ensure success for all students.

In Ontario, excellence and equity go hand in hand. We recognize that educators can enhance the life chances of students within our diverse population and prepare our young people to participate fully in the global economy. With our belief that factors such as poverty should not truncate the possibilities of students, we have used focused intervention strategies to ensure that all children learn regardless of personal factors. The aim is to build an even more robust society by strengthening the education of students in general and students from diverse backgrounds in particular.

One of the most important foundations of success in school and beyond is literacy. Recognizing this, Premier Dalton McGuinty created the Secretariat with a mandate to drive change and create a new way of working with the school districts to bring about improvement in student achievement. It was the responsibility of the Secretariat to provide strategic leadership in building strong linkages and alliances with system partners to support learning.

Early on, the Secretariat recognized that a "one size fits all" approach would not work. A range of strategies were implemented to recognize the diverse needs of district boards and schools across the province. For change to happen and be sustained, it was critical to have ownership at all levels.

Top-down approaches have not proven to be effective in the long term. Instead, the Secretariat worked alongside districts and schools to provide a range of supports and build capacity for them to take ownership of their own improvement efforts.

The Secretariat implemented a number of strategies that have had a positive influence on student achievement. The result was improved capacity for administrators, board and school staff to effectively plan for improvement and to change practice when necessary. Many of the following strategies focused on students who were not performing well in the system:

- providing targeted intervention to the lowest achieving schools and those that have been static in their improvement efforts;
- creating a network of schools that had demonstrated continuous improvement in order to facilitate the sharing of successful practice;
- funding tutoring programs to ensure that struggling students received additional support;
- creating a data analysis tool, Statistical Neighbours, that helps boards and schools use data to improve student achievement; and
- providing special funding to support students from designated groups in urban settings.

Having built a solid foundation, the government's literacy and numeracy strategy has been achieving steady results. The Secretariat is now moving forward with greater precision and intentionality to sharpen the focus on student achievement. What is most significant is that this is being done with the support of teachers, principals, superintendents and all those who have a vested interest in the improvement of the system. There is, undoubtedly, a high level of enthusiasm and commitment within the field. This is by no means accidental. It is the result of a carefully crafted strategy that is humane, that brings out the best in people and that uses all that we know about what motivates people towards inspired performance and to sustain improvement over time.

The Promise of Diversity

In 2008, I was asked by the Ontario Minister of Education to co-chair the Ministry's steering committee for the creation of an equity strategy and implementation plan. Our report, *Realizing the Promise of Diversity: Ontario's Equity and Inclusive Education Strategy*, focused on the most effective ways to eliminate the systemic barriers that impede student achievement and student success in this province. We highlighted the need to move from tolerance to acceptance in embracing diversity, while providing each child with the resources and encouragement to achieve the maximum of their ability. Our aim was, and remains, to help Ontario become one of the most inclusive places in the world.

The strategy reflected the government's commitment to raising the bar for student achievement while reducing the achievement gaps for students who traditionally have not done well in schools. The document highlighted the fact that recent immigrants, children from low-income families, Aboriginal students, boys and students with special education needs were (and continue to be) just some of the groups that may be at risk of lower achievement. We called for all partners in education to work at identifying and removing barriers to success and ensuring that all students are engaged, included and respected and that they see themselves reflected in their learning environment.

Our report emphasized that Canadians have, over the years, embraced multiculturalism, human rights and diversity as fundamental values. We are known worldwide as one of the most tolerant of societies. At the same time, we have had our share of troubling incidents of prejudice and racism exemplified in terms of religious intolerance, homophobia and discrimination. This awareness calls for constant vigilance and, more importantly, ensuring that our students in schools today develop a strong commitment to eradicating all forms of prejudice.

Acknowledging that good work had been done and that Ontario educators possessed a strong commitment to equity, the document asked school boards and schools to work collectively on further actions to realize our vision of an equitable and inclusive education system. Clear actions were laid out for the Ministry of Education, school boards and schools to take over a four-year period, in order to make Ontario a global leader in building and sustaining an equitable and inclusive education system. These actions included the following:

- the Ministry issuing a policy/program memorandum (PPM) to provide direction to boards on the development, implementation and monitoring of equity and inclusive education policies;
- school boards reviewing existing equity and inclusive education policies and/or developing or extending such policies; and
- schools developing school improvement plans aligned with Ontario's equity and inclusive education strategy.

As a co-chair of the committee that developed this document, I am very proud of our province, teachers and school leaders for making this commitment to such important aspects of education. Our teachers' unions and principals' councils have also developed innovative equity programs and have, over the years, promoted the cause of equity.

As an immigrant to Canada and as someone who builds capacity internationally, I speak with pride about a country that works hard at integrating its immigrant populations. We have been praised by Organization for Economic Co-operation and Development (OECD), based on our Programme for International Student Assessment (PISA) results, as one of the few places in the world that is both raising the bar and closing the achievement gaps. This augurs well for the future prosperity of our country.

Character Development: Education at Its Best

Increasingly, governments are recognizing that a holistic approach to education includes some form of character development. A common theme that runs throughout these programs is respect for self and others. This idea ties in with my own firm beliefs that we must recommit ourselves to the higher mission of schooling: to transmit from one generation to the next the habits of mind and heart necessary for good citizenship to thrive. Admittedly, many parents do teach what we call "character" in their homes. In fact, they are the first character educators. But the fact remains that character development is also a responsibility of educators, who are charged with nurturing *all* aspects of learning.

Character education, of course, is not a new curriculum; it is a way of life. It is the way we treat others and hold ourselves accountable by ensuring that our actions are compatible with our stated values and beliefs. In implementing the strategies that embed the character attributes into the fabric of the school, all members of the school community seize the "teachable moments" to reinforce the attributes which are determined in cooperation with a wide cross-section of community members.

We all want our schools to foster positive attributes — to be the embodiment of caring and civility. We want them to be models of effective human relationships, where students continue to learn what it means to be humane, empathetic and respectful. A systematic character development program nurtures the universal attributes that transcend racial, religious, socio-economic, cultural and other lines of division in our communities. It is a whole-school effort to create a community that promotes the highest ideals of student deportment and citizenship.

It is easy to bemoan the turbulence of our times, invoke the challenges that beset us or join the critics who assert that our young people have no moral voice guiding their actions. I do not adopt this approach because it is reactive. Our motivation as educators must be based on our fundamental beliefs about what constitutes excellence in education and what we believe will contribute to the future well-being of individuals and our society as a whole. Character education is about taking care of the common good and the universal values that we can all agree upon — those that bind us together as one human family and that take us to a new level of consciousness about who we are, what we believe in, how we wish to live our lives and how we choose to relate to others.

In the nineties, I spearheaded initiatives to implement character education in two Ontario district school boards, first in York Region (outside Toronto) and later in Kawartha Pine Ridge (in Peterborough, Ontario). Then in 2008, I helped the Ontario government launch a province-wide character development initiative. It's important to note that we did not see character development as a panacea; rather, we believed in its possibility to create positive school cultures. We also recognized that it would take all the institutions in our community working together for character education to be successful.

In Ontario, we first implemented character education district-wide in the York Region District School Board. We convened three education forums for a wide cross-section of the community: parents, community leaders and educators. They were asked to reflect on the culture they wished to foster in the region's schools. The forums created a space for a conversation about the role of schools in preparing citizens for the future and enabled us to forge consensus on the attributes we wanted our students to embody as members of their schools and community, and as future citizens.

We convinced our community participants that by focusing on our youth during these very challenging times, we were helping to create the future we all wished to have. In particular, we also emphasized that we would be nurturing characteristics identified by the business community as integral to a strong work ethic and success in the workplace.

At the end of the three sessions, the participants decided on ten attributes that they wanted us to develop in our schools. These were respect, responsibility, honesty, integrity, empathy, fairness, initiative, perseverance, courage and optimism. (Interestingly, when we conducted a similar exercise in the Kawartha Pine Ridge District School Board, members of that community chose the same ten attributes.)

In York Region, I approached the mayor of Markham and asked him to work with the school district to engage our community in an ongoing, systematic and focused character education effort. We engaged a wide cross-section of the community, including parents and educators as well as members of our business and faith communities, government officials, the police and labour and social representatives — all individuals who were interested in making our community safe, inclusive and inviting.

Through our collective efforts, York Region became the first jurisdiction in Canada to develop a character initiative to serve as an example of how community development could be led by the education sector. The Kawartha Pine Ridge District School Board, meanwhile, established a "Character in the Workplace" initiative in a systematic and intentional manner. We brought school district employees together and asked them to consider participating in a program similar to those we were developing in the district's schools and the wider community. I selected a school board secretary and a member of the business department to lead this strategy. The initiative introduced staff members to the common purpose of character development and assisted them in modelling and demonstrating the highest standards of character in dealing with their colleagues and with the public. The board also began to celebrate a character attribute each month and encouraged everyone working for the board to put these tenets into daily practice.

In Ontario, through mandatory courses in civics and history as well as optional courses in law and world issues, our public education system has introduced students to the ideals of a democratic society and fostered pro-social concepts of citizenship among our younger generation. We also require mandatory community service for students prior to graduation to encourage a sense of community involvement and responsibility — an initiative that resulted from the recommendations of the Royal Commission on Learning.

It is important that, in a world dominated by popular culture in which very confusing messages reach our young people every day, we reinforce the need for an active and involved citizenry. We need to teach these important elements of democracy in a manner that engages young minds and redirects their enthusiasm towards causes outside of themselves and that contribute to the common good.

If I were to sum up my own education philosophy in a few words, it would be this: let us realize the immense potential of our young people and their passions, interests and willingness to take on responsibilities that we, as adults, do not always provide for them. Let us work with them to sustain and create a world where citizenship and all its privileges, rights and responsibilities are extended to all.

Many of our schools, I feel, represent the world in miniature. They mirror our larger society, which has become increasingly diverse. Futurists like Gary Marx tell us that minorities will become majorities. The opportunity presented to educators will be to ensure that diversity is welcomed, explored and celebrated and its ramifications are managed effectively. Schools in general, but secondary schools in particular, need to address the issues that cause marginalization and a lack of connectedness among students. It is necessary for secondary school teachers to work at reinvigorating the ethic of care. At a time when the need for affiliation and a sense of connectedness is so high, secondary teachers must continue to be mentors to students from diverse backgrounds so that they can feel that someone cares. Many children from diverse backgrounds or children who live in poverty look at their teachers and say to themselves, "I don't care how much you know until I know how much you care!" A strong commitment to demonstrating the ethic of care is essential in diverse settings.

Teachers, as well as the community as a whole, have a key role to play in moving our students beyond minimalistic notions of tolerance, for example, to the level of empathy, especially for those who are different. And as someone who has been a guidance counsellor in my not-so-distant past, I can assure you that empathy can be taught!

In conclusion, the key purposes of education, to my mind, can be placed on a continuum. At the one end is the instrumental notion that the purpose of education is to prepare individuals for the workforce. At the other end are loftier aims. Plato, for example, said that the primary purpose of education is to create a more just and harmonious society. In my view, if we want a society in which citizens care about one another — in which qualities such as honesty, integrity, fairness, courage and optimism are pervasive and violence of any kind is discouraged — we have no choice but to nurture these qualities in our homes, in our schools and in our communities.

As we concluded in our recent book, *Breaking Barriers: Excellence and Equity for All*:

> The time is now for all educators to intensify our efforts to realize the promise of diversity and the possibilities it holds for the achievement of excellence and equity. We are called upon to sharpen our resolve, strengthen our commitment, and break the barriers that stand in the way of success for all students. (Glaze, Mattingley and Levin 2012: 193)

References

Glaze, Avis, Ruth Mattingley and Ben Levin. 2012. *Breaking Barriers: Excellence and Equity for All*. Toronto: Pearson Canada.

Royal Commission on Learning. 1995. "For the Love of Learning: Report of the Royal Commission on Learning." Toronto: Queens Printer.

25. WHERE SURF MEETS SHORE
Reflections from the Edge
Mary Lou Soutar-Hynes

Incorporating both prose and poetry, this chapter touches on two pivotal and defining aspects of my life in Canada: education and writing — poetry, in particular. It sheds light on my life's trajectory in these two areas since my arrival in Canada and on the ways in which my Caribbean perspective and my lived experiences revealed themselves and influenced that trajectory. The first part, The Path of Education, is mainly prose, while the second, Poetry: A Parallel Path, interweaves poetry and prose.

The Path of Education

[Excerpt from "writing / a life"]

"...no road
caminante —   *se hace*   one creates it
al andar   as one walks"
(Soutar-Hynes 2006: 9)[1]

It was the summer of 1969 when I arrived in Canada as a landed immigrant, chest X-ray in hand. Two weeks earlier I had left the convent, having been dispensed by the Vatican from my vows as a Sister of Mercy — vows of "poverty, chastity, obedience, and the service of the poor, sick and ignorant."[2] Leaving the island of my birth, my large supportive family and the religious community where I had lived, worked and prayed for the previous twelve years was a radical step.

I might not have left Jamaica at all if the religious community had accepted my offer to continue working, but as a secular, at the Mandeville high school where I had been teaching English, Spanish and Religion. For three of those years, I had also been administrator of the boarding school, which accommodated almost a hundred girls and young women from Latin

America, other parts of Jamaica and the surrounding islands. My teaching years as a religious ensured that education would be both an enduring passion and a professional path.

After my decision to leave the island was confirmed, Canada, a Commonwealth country, beckoned, and Toronto became my city of choice — an English-speaking urban centre where, for the first time in my adult life, I was not singled out by either religious habit or family connections. The city has proven to be a place where I could create a space for myself and make a contribution.

For the first six years in Canada, my work in educational publishing allowed me to travel the country as a teacher-consultant. I visited school boards and districts, community colleges and adult and manpower retraining centres, and ran professional development sessions to assist in the integration of reading materials and equipment into their programs. It was an invaluable opportunity to explore my new country from coast to coast to coast, to appreciate its beauty and regional diversity and to make connections with educators at all levels. These connections ultimately facilitated my return to teaching.

The publishing industry also provided the first opportunity to build on my Caribbean roots. In the early 1970s, I was invited to contribute a chapter on the Caribbean for the grade six social studies textbook *The World of People: The Western Hemisphere,* part of a series being developed for use in elementary schools across the country. It was the first time I had been challenged to approach the Caribbean region as a whole, to think beyond the confines and limitations of one island. I took responsibility for the chapter very seriously, determined to include information, maps and photos from original sources and to get informed, authoritative Caribbean feedback on the work, which was to be published by McGraw-Hill Ryerson.

The publishing project became a significant source of identity affirmation. It reinforced the value and power of the Caribbean cultural capital that I could offer to my adopted country, particularly in the field of education, to which I returned in 1975. This included my experiences in a multiracial society, familiarity with Jamaican standard and vernacular languages, deep knowledge of the education system and personal experience with the dislocation of being an immigrant.

Complementing my growing interest in pursuing graduate studies in reading and language, the chapter project sowed the seeds of the work I would do thereafter, often in collaboration with like-minded professionals in the large urban school boards and educational institutions of the day in Metropolitan Toronto. This work included professional development workshops with teachers and administrators and the development of policies to work toward the successful assessment, placement and program planning for immigrant students — in my case particularly, for those from the English-speaking Caribbean. During those years, I built enduring networks, professional affiliations and friendships with colleagues, who became sources of support and encouragement through later challenging and tumultuous times.

The mid-1970s, however, marked the early days of "immigrant education," the development of professional qualifications courses in English as a second language/English as a second dialect (as they were known then) and reading specialist courses in which I was involved. In 1976, my article "West Indian Realities in the Intermediate Grades: The Emerging Role of the ESD Teacher" was published in the special issue of TESL TALK on "The Immigrant Student in Secondary School."

In 1977, an important catalyst was Walter Pitman's report on the state of racism in the city of Toronto. Entitled *Now Is Not Too Late*, the report was submitted to the former Council of Metropolitan Toronto by the Task Force on Human Relations. That same year, the Task Force also received a report by fellow Jamaican, Dr. Inez Elliston, entitled *Racial Attitudes and Racial Violence in the School and School Community: A Survey of the Opinion of Personnel*." The information served as a wake-up call for school boards in the city and across the province.

Through the Reading Centre in our board, I was instrumental in developing a system-wide response to the issues raised in the Pitman report. Billed as "A Creative Response to the Pitman Report," the session was facilitated by an interdisciplinary team supported by the Reading Centre and Program Department where I worked as a teacher-consultant; in addition, the director of education ensured that participants in the first session included senior officials and trustees of the board.

Innovative for its time, the session invited participants to consider the changing population in the board's schools and the impact of pre-conceived biases on the decisions being made for the placement of — and programs offered to — new-Canadian students. Also addressed was the need to provide training to ensure that teachers, counsellors and administrators could make informed decisions that would be in the best interests of these students. Despite the progress made in the intervening years, many of these challenges remain and continue to draw on the expertise, collaboration and innovative solutions of educators, researchers and scholars.

I, however, found those years both energizing and hopeful. They reinforced my belief in the efficacy of collaborative endeavours, an approach I continued to favour, whenever possible, in my work — in schools and the school board, in Jamaica with education colleagues, in the Ontario Ministry of Education and in the literary world of poetry.

One example of such endeavours highlights a key focus for my work: In the late 1970s and early 1980s in both my master's and doctoral course work at OISE, my interests included composing-process theory and the teaching of writing. These interests led to the development and implementation of a sabbatical leave project — the multi-year, six-day Teachers' Writing Workshop Series for educators from kindergarten to senior years of secondary studies. Offered throughout the school year, the workshops brought together teachers from across levels, grades and disciplines, shared current theory, encouraged and supported the notion of "the teacher as writer" and reflective practitioner and initiated collaborative, inter-school, cross-grade writing projects.

The series later became a model for the four-year summer Residential Writing Workshop Series organized with the Jamaican Ministry of Education and the island's National Association of Teachers of English (NATE). The idea for the project was generated by a chance meeting with an education officer from Jamaica at an international conference of teachers of English in Ottawa, at which we were both presenting workshops. Once back in our respective jurisdictions, we initiated support for the concept, and the collaborative project was born.

My work in the teaching of writing also led to an invitation from Harcourt Brace Jovanovich to develop a writing textbook for senior English courses in the Canadian market. *The Writer Within: Dialogue and Discovery*, co-written with colleague and friend Trina Wood, was published in 1989.

Poetry: A Parallel Path

Poetry chose me many years ago. During my teaching, consulting and co-ordinating years, I shared my poetry and poetic practice with students and teachers in writing courses and at such workshops as the Writing Workshop Series. Wherever possible during these years, I also invited Caribbean poets into my courses — Bruce St. John of Barbados, Mervyn Morris of Jamaica and Ahdri Zena Mandiela of Toronto.

Apart from occasionally submitting a poem or two to a literary journal, a small number of which were accepted, it was only in my fiftieth year that I began to move my work into the public domain. I joined a women's writing workshop facilitated by the poet Libby Scheier and began the serious work of engaging and developing my poetic voice. My portfolio of poetry, fine-tuned through these workshops, enabled my acceptance eight years later into the six-week Writing Studio Program at the Banff Centre for the Arts. There, the opportunity to consult with leading poets over a sustained period of time was incredibly affirming and deepened my commitment to the craft.

Writing, although a solitary occupation, has deep roots. As poets and writers, we draw on influences and antecedents — the work of both those who went before and those contemporary writers whose words sustain and inspire. My poem "for writers whose work i have loved" acknowledges those influences and antecedents.

for writers whose work i have loved

your words are sweet
like my grandmother's blackie mangoes
stewed succulent
with slivers   of the skins of limes
green and tart

they fill my mouth
and roll around my tongue
      warm and golden
           flesh   heavy with summer

i suck them dry
and one by one   plant them in my mind
      seeds stripped   bone white
          fibres flat   and smooth

patient
anticipating harvest   as seeds
give birth   bearing fruit
in their own good season
(2001: 41)

Not surprisingly, island, sea and Caribbean images and issues would permeate my work. A latecomer to the literary world, I could mine years of memory and the complexities and dilemmas of a long-lived life. This process of exploration began with *The Fires of Naming* (2001), my first collection of poetry, continued with the second, *Travelling Light* (2006) and is evident still in my third collection, currently being considered for publication. It is also evident in poetry that appears in anthologies, essays and other writings. I write elsewhere that, in terms of poetics, the

> form and structure, the shape of the poem as it emerges on the page, and its articulation are as important to me as the content, the impulse, the image that give rise to the piece. My early work emerged unencumbered by traditional forms of syntax — all lower case, a semantic breathing punctuated by caesuras, line breaks and long dashes, often claiming the full span of the page.... Three collections later, some poems are going radical, insisting on a comma here or a period there, sometimes reclaiming capitals and fixating on left-justified lines.... I continue [however] to be faithful to the form, the shape that each new piece assumes. As a painterly poet ..., I see the page as my canvas, and I paint in words. (Forthcoming)

Once my first collection was published, I started to reach out to the literary community, becoming a member of the League of Canadian Poets and the Writers' Union of Canada. The Arts and Culture Jamaica organization and its president, Paula DeRonde, were instrumental in arranging my first introduction as a poet to the Jamaican community in Toronto. I was invited to read at an Independence Day celebration at the Consulate. It was a moving experience. To that point, my profile in the community derived primarily from my work in education and related causes.

My only Caribbean literary contact had been the writer and poet Rachel Manley. I knew her only through her work and approached her at the launch of *Slipstream: A Daughter Remembers* (2000), her moving memoir about her relationship with her father, Michael Manley. She agreed to read the manuscript of my first collection and wrote an eloquent blurb. Slowly, over the years, opportunities to participate in Caribbean-initiated literary activities and publications began to come my way: reading at the first Caribbean-Canadian Literary Expo (CCLE), sponsored by the CARICOM Consular Corps in 2003; being one of six poets featured in the anthology *Calling Cards: New Poetry by Caribbean/Canadian Women*, published in 2005 by Sandberry Press; invitations to read at Caribbean bookstores such as A Different Booklist; and invitations to submit to anthologies celebrating Jamaica's fiftieth year of independence.

Surfacing Issues: Family, Migration, Race

Toronto had become for me a site of creative encounter. Despite the all-engrossing commitment required for my work in education, I was drawn to explore through poetry a multiplicity of issues that clamoured for a voice — among them, the implications of family, race, class and migration.

Both my parents were from well-known families.

> My maternal grandfather ... along with a business partner, established what was to become one of Jamaica's successful corporate ventures. Steeped in Roman Catholicism, the family was deeply involved with the church.... With a Jamaican-born father and a mother from the Dominican Republic, theirs was a bilingual family — Spanish was my mother's second "mother tongue"....
>
> My father's family had Scottish roots on the Soutar side and names such as Vendryes (French) and Levy (Jewish) on his maternal side, although both his parents were Jamaican-born.... My great-grandfather Soutar, who had emigrated to Jamaica from Scotland in the 1850s, was eulogized in articles and editorials in the newspapers of the day ... "respected by all who knew him, he was honest in his convictions on trade, politics and the development of a sound healthy spirit of co-operation in our midst ... he never sought the

limelight of publicity ... or the applause of those who knew what he was doing to benefit the land of his adoption." (2011)

School and family were the focus of my formative years, and, by growing up Jamaican, I was implicated in issues of race and class. My years of schooling with the Sisters of Mercy and the opportunity to be part of a community of students and educators from all walks of life, races and religions had reinforced a strong sense of social justice and an idealistic desire to serve the country. "Out of many, one people," Jamaica's motto, seemed a real possibility. Although other factors were also in play, my decision to enter the convent in September of the year I sat my Cambridge Higher Schools Exams was prompted in great part by a desire to fulfill those ideals and to transcend the boundaries of race and class.

The convent, like all institutions, is itself a reflection of the society in which it exists, with all its accompanying complexities, strengths and weaknesses. Although I learned much during those young adult years that has held me in good stead, I chose, after much soul-searching, to move on from both the convent and Jamaica. Migration, however, will never erase the indelible birthmark of one's country of origin. One continues to be drawn toward it and to be implicated in its trajectories. This experience is not without dilemmas or conflict, as the poem "Implicated" suggests.

Implicated

> *"what magic words for the getaway"*
> — Olive Senior

Wash your hands before the multitudes,
    declare innocence.

Stay clear of
pharisees and popular demand,
lest   wrongful prisoners be freed.

Like Pilate's wife,
    pay heed   to dreams.

If there are *magic words*, they've yet
    to be invoked.
Perhaps   you've toyed with a few —

diaspora

                redemption

      exile

(2010)

In the poem "Anatomy / of green," which began with memories of swimming in the river that flowed through my great-grandfather Soutar's property at Temple Hall, issues of colour and degrees of pigmentation soon insinuated themselves into the lines — familiar preoccupations in a mixed-race society with its complex implications and roots.

Anatomy
    of green

I never really knew the   moss-green river,
its uneven washes,   subtle bracing.

Rarely touched the sucking ooze   of sand-
fogged bays,   palettes seaweed-streaked.

        Needed to see clearly
    what to step on
or over —
        To sense the underlying
layers,   how pigment
can be diluted —

        Waking each morning
to trace the edges
light to dark.

      Wet
           in the wash.
(2010)

Island Themes: When Hyphens Open

Although much of my poetry gives voice to the joys, dilemmas and complexities inherent in a long-lived life, I am constantly drawn back to island themes. They surface in unexpected ways, creating and mining the space-time continuum, the cracks through which can surge childhood memories, familiar images and reflections on life and time. Such was the case with the poem "Of fragments / and heartwood," which began in the Galleria Italia of the Art Gallery of Ontario, in Toronto.

**Of fragments
and heartwood**

after "Cedro di Versailles, by Guisseppe Penone

I

They say the roots of certain trees grow up, not down,   while some grow knees,
                    interrupt the story —

                                        plum, baobab, and casuarina,
            Bombay, tamarind and frangipani

                        Anchors and deviations

                            Vendors with their baskets and wares
gathered each day around the baobab —
girls tumbling from classrooms,   eager to spend their round bronze pennies,
and tiny silver coins,
                on grater cakes,
                        gizzadas and Bustamante's backbone

                            Mrs. Dalhouse,   with her large glass jar
of tamarind balls   (twelve for sixpence)
astute librarian,   year after year,   ignoring rules and limits   for the girl
                    who lived on a diet of books

                Some roots are permanent   and sweet

II

Today,   the air's like August in St. Andrew,   still and heavy,   waiting for thunder —
            sharp, thick downpour flooding roads,   newly minted potholes
                    forcing traffic through and round —
                        each car   intent on seizing   its sliver
                            of advantage

                        Faced with obstacles,   roots thicken,   grow up
and over —
            sense gravity,   which way is down,
                        perception at the tip

III

                              Each life a galleria,   of sorts,
self and world,   under constant
      observation —
           stone, resin, leather and wood

The boulder beneath the bougainvillea   where she stood as a child on July
afternoons carefully noting licence plates,   the provenance of cars
                    inching up Lady Musgrave Road —
the leisurely meander   of a herd of cows,   back from grazing King's House
grounds,
         home of the British Governor

            Some roots   are opportunistic,
    others may need to be trimmed —

IV

      Childhood certainties,   all sunlight and fierce truths —

Cable Hut,   its wild, black-pebbled beach,   steep,   slack drop to the sea,
           open mouth of waves
and summers,   painting logos for her father's booth at the Denbigh Fair

     Pot a tree, and roots will circle, tie themselves
        in knots

Time   a forest,   wood-breathing ribs,   polished smooth —
     sapling,   mother to the tree

          heartwood —
   limestone,   mountains,
     coral-sea

(2011)[3]

There is no statute of limitations for poetry — no site, timeframe, context or location that precludes inspiration. The poem "off and on" had its beginnings late one cold and rainy night as I listened to the radio on my drive home from work. As often happens, I scrambled to find paper and pen to capture images before they disappeared — in this case, a conflux of memories of Mandeville nights and an experience in Madrid, merging with Toronto blackouts and Bob Marley.

off and on

I

it's a rain-slick asphalt   black like *mandeville*-night
tail lights luminous   liquid-red

shifting gears   i play the lanes   fly-fisher
reeling out the flow

a radio talk show host   discusses reggae-coups
the post-marley revolution

the lights are out   between eglinton and lawrence
avenue road   a masque of darkness

II

i first heard the rhythms of bob marley   on the streets
of spain   "no woman nuh cry"   pulsing through mcdonalds

there's no forgetting   fire-light and trench-town
mingling   in madrid

another day held together   tight
against the bone   paper-

thin   susceptible
to fluctuation   and to flames

III.

north of lawrence   power is restored
the rain subsides

the payne's-grey night sky   freshly laundered
above trees   and undulating roads

edging the city   a platinum
moon   stippled silver

abundant   poised
no ambiguity there   no tears
(2001: 72–73)

Conclusion

As my forty-second year in Canada draws to a close, education in all its facets remains a passion, even as I continue to seek out and engage new areas of interest — the field of poetic inquiry and ekphrastic (poetry/art) collaborations with artists. Moving sometimes into prose as well as poetry, I continue "writing my life," reflecting on facets as disparate as spirituality, sexuality and the incessant, challenging, yet life-affirming waves — family, race, class, migration — that surface upon the shores of one Jamaican-Canadian, born and raised in a multiracial colonial Caribbean.

I also follow with interest the evolution of the religious life and the religious community of women I left so long ago. As the following excerpt from the poem "measure / of wings: a triptych" in *Travelling Light* might suggest, the former nun in the poem (a thinly disguised self) seems to have negotiated some sort of truce with life.

[Excerpt from "measure / of wings: a triptych"]

panel 1

released   from the constraints
of convents
she negotiates the abyss
between microns   and light years
following   a new
obedience

frames
clause by clause   her tacit
constitution
ordinary rhythms   ordering
her days

terse texts   penned
in the sanctuary of trains
speeding
towards light   a liturgy
in-transit
(2006: 17)

Notes

1. Excerpt from the poem "writing a life" that incorporates a variation on the line by Spanish poet Antonio Machado: *Caminante, no hay camino, se hace camino al andar.* Translation: *Traveller, there is no path; one creates the path as one walks* (2006: 9).
2. The vows required of all Sisters of Mercy during the years I was a religious.
3. This poem was inspired by Guiseppe Penone's tree-sculpture, *Cedro di Versailles,* installed in the Galleria Italia of the Art Gallery of Ontario. Grater cakes, gizzadas and Bustamante's backbone are Jamaican coconut candies. Bustamante's backbone is named after Sir Alexander Bustamante, one of Jamaica's national heroes and the island's first prime minister. It is said to represent his firmness of character.

References

Elliston, I. 1977. "Racial Attitudes and Racial Violence in the School and School Community: A Survey of the Opinion of Personnel." Report submitted to the Metro Task Force on Human Relations. Toronto, ON

Manley, R. 2000. *Slipstream: A Daughter Remembers.* Toronto, ON: Knopf Canada.

Pitman, W. 1977. "Now Is Not Too Late." Report to the Council of Metropolitan Toronto by the Task Force on Human Relations.

Soutar-Hynes, M.L. 1976. "The Caribbean." In Benjamin Vass, Series Editor, Susan Kiil (eds.), *The World of People: The Western Hemisphere.* Toronto, ON: McGraw-Hill Ryerson.

____. 1976. "West Indian Realities in the Intermediate Grades: The Emerging Role of the ESD Teacher." TESL TALK, *Quarterly for Teachers of English as a Second Language* 7, 4.

____. 2001. *The Fires of Naming.* Toronto, ON: Seraphim Editions.

____. 2006. *Travelling Light.* Toronto, ON: Seraphim Editions.

____. 2010. Manuscript for *Dark Water Songs.* Toronto, ON: Author.

____. 2011. "of fragments / and heartwood." Unpublished poem. Toronto, ON: Author.

____. (forthcoming). "Points of Articulation: A Letting Go and a Reaching Towards, A Poet's Journey." In Suzanne Thomas, Ardra Cole, and Sheila Stewart (eds.), *The Art of Poetic Inquiry.* Toronto, ON: Backalong Books.

Soutar-Hynes, M.L., and Wood, T. 1989. *The Writer Within: Dialogue and Discovery.* Toronto, ON: Harcourt Brace Jovanovich.

PART EIGHT –
ECONOMIC AND SOCIAL RELATIONS

26. MYTHS AND REALITIES

The Challenge of Social Transformation through Canada/Jamaica Diasporic Exchange

Beverley Mullings, Kay-Ann Williams and Alexander Lovell

The Jamaican government, international development and financial institutions, scholars and Jamaicans resident abroad all agree that the Jamaican diaspora offers the island its best hope for future growth and development (Franklyn 2010; Government of Jamaica 2009; Meeks 2007; Patterson 2007; USAID 2003). This near universal agreement comes largely from the recognition of the significant economic contribution that Jamaicans abroad have steadfastly made throughout the long period of crisis the country has struggled to emerge from since the 1980s. The diaspora, they argue, has consistently risen to the challenge that diminishing government spending, weak exports and declining inward investments have posed since the first International Monetary Fund/World Bank austerity programs were introduced. Jamaicans abroad have remained remarkably consistent in their efforts to support the economic well-being of families and whole communities over the last thirty years. And many have continued to send money and goods back home even during periods of economic crisis when their own personal economic fortunes have declined.

Remittances have been an economic lifeline for Jamaica, a salvo as it were, to the injuries that high levels of debt, sluggish gross domestic product (GDP) growth, weak foreign exchange earnings and high levels of crime have exacted on the Jamaican economy and society. Rising from US$96 million in 1980 to US$236 million a dozen years later, diasporic remittance rose at a meteoric rate during the 1990s and into the twenty-first century (from US$522 in 1994 to $1,058 million in 2001 to an all time record of $2,181 million in 2008). Even in the face of the current economic downturn in Europe and North America, remittances have remained relatively robust, accounting for 13.4 percent of Jamaica's GDP in 2009, a figure twelve times more than the value of overseas development assistance (World Bank 2012).

It is this faithful flow of remittances from Jamaicans abroad since the 1980s that partially explains why so many have come to believe that the Jamaican diaspora offers the island its best chance for economic and social transformation. And as the government's 2009 national development plan —*Vision 2030 Jamaica* — indicates, the developmental possibilities that diasporic engagement promises go beyond the US$100–160 that members of the Jamaican Canadian diaspora are estimated to send to family members and communities back home. The document states:

> The Diaspora can play a strategic role in our economic development in a number of ways, including: as a source of investment and entrepreneurship for business ventures; by providing lobbying support for Jamaica in international fora; as a source of academic and technical expertise; as a market for tourism and our exports of goods and services; and as a network for advancement of Jamaicans in international businesses and other endeavours. (Government of Jamaica 2009: 142)

In the opening address of the first Jamaican Diaspora Conference in 2004, former Prime Minister P.J. Patterson stated: "The already existing levels and intensity of diaspora engagement are indeed encouraging. But I am convinced that we can build on the currently prevailing patterns to move to even greater and more exciting possibilities."

In this chapter, we take a critical look at the enhanced role envisaged for members of the diaspora in Jamaica's future development trajectory because we believe that the current rush to celebrate the developmental power of diaspora overlooks important realities regarding the capacity and/or willingness of Jamaican communities abroad to participate in the island's development strategies. In particular, we focus on the extent to which members of the Jamaican Canadian diaspora are committed to taking on these developmental roles.

We write this chapter as members of the Jamaican diaspora, but we are cognizant of the fact that our attachments to the island are as complex, circuitous and contradictory as the concept of diaspora itself. Like many, our attachments to "the rock" are linked to our ancestral ties (we all have at least one relative who was born on the island), but our connections are complicated by our places of birth (Canada, the United Kingdom and Jamaica), our emotional and social ties and the degrees to which we share nationalist sentiments that animate us to forge solidarities with others who are oriented towards the preservation and enhancement of levels of prosperity on the island. We recognize that although we maintain differing degrees of attachment to the identities "Jamaican," "Canadian" and "Jamaican Canadian," there is a certain durability in the ties that bind together the heterogeneities that differentiate us. We therefore hope that in much the same way that our identities as Jamaicans, Canadians and Jamaican Canadians represent "names we give to the different ways we are positioned by, and position ourselves within, narratives of the past" (Hall 1994: 225), this chapter will draw attention to the diverse locations from which members of the diaspora identify with Jamaica and consequently the diverse expectations with regard to development that different members embrace.

Like many, we believe that the Jamaican diaspora has the capacity to play a significant role in building a Jamaica that is more equitable and socially just, one that offers all Jamaicans the opportunity to live a fulfilled life where capabilities and choices are maximized. But we argue that the orientation of the emerging diaspora strategy focuses too narrowly on generating flows of capital from diasporic locations to Jamaica, with insufficient regard for the economic, social and political challenges that affect the ability of diaspora members to meet these expectations. The consequence of prioritizing efforts to generate capital inflows over building other forms of diasporic engagement has been the creation of a diaspora strategy based on fairly broad assumptions about the characteristics, expectations and desires of the diaspora as a whole, with very little concrete evidence to support them. We believe that there are at least two key assumptions that currently shape and direct the nature and orientation of Jamaica's evolving diaspora option. The first is that members of the Jamaican diaspora can generate the levels of investment and skills transfers needed to generate significant levels of economic growth in Jamaica; the second is that members of the Jamaican diaspora share a common vision of development that is compatible not only with the views of the Jamaican state but also with the views of Jamaicans in Jamaica. We seek to offer a more nuanced understanding of the possibilities the diaspora offers to the ongoing challenge of building a socially, economically and environmentally sustainable Jamaica in the twenty-first century.

The Jamaica Canadian Diaspora

Jamaican Canadians represent the smallest of the three main Jamaican diasporic communities abroad. Of the estimated one million Jamaican-born persons estimated to be living outside Jamaica, approximately 134,320 live in Canada (Todoroki, Vaccan and Noor 2009). Adding the second and third generations to this number renders the Jamaican Canadian diaspora significantly larger. The 2006 Census records estimates this combined figure at 231,110 persons, of whom 160, 205 (69 percent) live in the Toronto Metropolitan Area and a further 11,130 (5 percent) in greater Montréal (Citizenship and Immigration Canada 2012). Prior to 1967, very few Jamaicans migrated to Canada, largely because Canada's immigration policy gave explicit preference to White European and American migrants. The so-called "White

Canadian" immigration policy ended in 1967, when the points-based immigration system was adopted. Based on individual skills and experience, this system opened the door to large-scale Jamaican immigration. The large and dramatic rise in Jamaican migration to Canada can also be attributed to changes unfolding in Britain's immigration policy that made it more difficult for Jamaicans to enter that country.

The effect of the opening up of Canadian immigration to non-Whites can be seen in the rapid increase in the number of Jamaican emigrants. In 1966, for example, only 1,407 Jamaicans emigrated to Canada, but by 1967 the number of migrants had increased by two and a half times to 3,459 (Ministry of Manpower and Immigration 1967), after which, Jamaican immigration settled into a relatively predictable annual inflow of approximately 3,600 persons per year. This trend, however, changed significantly in 1974, when the number of Jamaicans migrating to Canada surged to 11,286. This movement was without doubt a reflection of the growing economic insecurities that emerged with the oil price-induced debt crisis. Thereafter, patterns of Jamaican migration to Canada closely mirrored the unfolding economic crisis in Jamaica, spiking to over 5,000 persons in 1987, and again in 1992 and 1993 following periods of sharp economic decline in the island's economic fortunes, but otherwise maintaining a consistent and gentle declining trend. Since 1993, when 5,989 Jamaicans migrated to Canada, the number of persons migrating to Canada has remained in a state of relatively steady decline, falling in 2006 to the lowest level recorded since the adoption of the points-based system (Citizenship and Immigration Canada 2012).

The Jamaican Canadian community is smaller than the Jamaican American and the Jamaican British communities; however, figures suggest that the Canadian community is generally more highly skilled thanks in large measure to Canada's emphasis on skill as a criterion for the selection of unsponsored applicants.[1] A comparison of the categories through which Jamaicans migrated to the United States and Canada in 2010 gives some indication of the relative differences in levels of skill and entrepreneurialism that might exist between these two diasporic populations. While approximately a quarter of immigrants to Canada gained permanent residency as economic class[2] migrants, only 3 percent of Jamaicans immigrating to the United States did so through similar employment-based immigration channels (Citizenship and Immigration Canada 2012; Office of Immigration Services 2011).

The Rise of Jamaica's Diaspora Option

Jamaicans across the diaspora have always maintained close ties with family and friends on the island, with numerous studies documenting the role that diasporic community organizations have historically played in securing and defending the rights and freedoms of Jamaicans at home and abroad (Davis 2008; Hill 2011; Austin 2007). In Canada, for example, from as early as the 1920s, members of the Jamaican diaspora had a significant influence on questions of national development in Jamaica. Groups such as the Montréal and Toronto chapters of the United Negro Improvement Association (UNIA), for example, had strong ties with Jamaicans on the island, recognizing that the networks they forged helped to advance the interests of Jamaicans both in Canada and on the island (Hill 2011). David Austin documents the important role played by people of African and Caribbean descent in Montréal in the creation of a politically conscious and mobilized Black community in the 1960s (Austin 2007). In addition to these earlier, well-known efforts, a number of smaller community organizations' philanthropic and community building efforts have been foundational to the everyday survival of families and communities at home and abroad. Many of these organizations have been instrumental to the survival of local communities in Jamaica. Their fundraising efforts have given hospitals, schools and households equipment and resources that the Jamaican government has not been able to provide. Recognition of the importance of these contributions to the continuity of everyday life encouraged the Jamaican government in the 1990s to seek new ways of developing closer and more formal institutional ties between Jamaicans on the island and those in the diaspora.

Modelled on policies to engage their diaspora in countries like India and Israel, the Jamaican government initiated a series of dialogues with selected diaspora representatives throughout the 1990s with a view to developing a more systematic and coordinated approach to forging relationships with Jamaicans abroad. The Jamaican government's orientation towards what some describe as the "diaspora option" did not emerge in a vacuum. Indeed, the orientation in state policy and practice towards the Jamaican diaspora throughout the 1990s reflected the findings of the 1992 West Indian Commission, which concluded at the end of its consultations with West Indians in Britain, Canada and the United States: "Here we have voices and talents and interests and resources which we must find organized ways, and devise systematic preferential arrangements, to involve in work and lives back home" (1993: 26). The report recognized the challenges posed by an increasingly globalized, integrated and competitive world economy. The fear that the region risked becoming "a backwater, separated from the main current of human advance into the twenty-first century"[3] was a crucial driving force behind the West Indian Commission investigation and is reflected in its introduction:

> We face a new time of threat to those achievements; new social concerns that we could be falling back; new economic problems like shortages of foreign exchange which had not been a part of past

experience. And with all our gains for democracy over the years there are deep concerns about the quality of governance now – indeed of disaffection with the entire political process. And on top of it all we face the menace of the drug problem. (xxvi)

The report's acknowledgement of the importance that West Indians abroad attached to assisting efforts to improve quality of life in the region and its belief that there was much to be gained from engaging this extra-territorial wing of the West Indian nation was reinforced by the growing reliance throughout the 1990s on economic remittances, which by the end of the twentieth century had outstripped the value of overseas foreign aid and foreign direct investment to the region.

Jamaica's efforts to engage its diaspora in the 1990s corresponded with the unprecedented rise in the number of returning residents. Between 1998 and 2008 the number of Jamaicans taking up permanent residency on the island increased by 14,738 (see Planning Institute of Jamaica 2009 and earlier years). Returning residents represented a relatively new and economically significant population because of the developmental contribution they made in terms of increased flows of capital but also revitalization of both rural and urban economies. In 1993 the government responded to the rising numbers of returning residents by establishing the Charter for Long-term Returning Residents, which included the creation of the Returning Residents Facilitation Unit to harmonize and standardize the information and procedures needed to permanently return to reside on the island. The conversion in 1998 of this early facilitation unit to a department dedicated to diaspora affairs — the Jamaican Overseas Department — and later, in 2002, the appointment of a minister with specific responsibility for advancing diaspora affairs highlighted the growing importance the Jamaican government placed on the creation of stronger developmental ties with not only its returnee population but the broader Jamaican diaspora as a whole (see Franklyn 2010).

Deepening Diaspora Ties: The Institutionalization of the Diaspora Option

Efforts to institutionalize a strategy for engaging the Jamaican diaspora expanded significantly at the start of the twenty-first century as the issues that had emerged from a series of dialogues initiated in 1999 with key members of the diaspora had begun to take root. By 2004 the first of a series of institutionalizing strategies had been initiated. The diaspora conference, attended in 2004 by 400 Jamaicans from Canada, the U.S., the U.K. and the island itself, was a tremendously exciting and optimistic event that attracted approximately 700 participants by 2008. Members of the diaspora from its far flung parts not only had the opportunity to express their concerns and commitments directly to members of the Jamaican government but were invited to "sit at the table" as partners in charting the island's future development path. The subsequent establishment of the Diaspora Advisory Board, comprising diaspora representatives resident in Canada, the U.K. and the U.S.; the Diaspora Foundation; and trade councils and lobby groups; as well as the proclamation of Jamaican Diaspora Day and the initiation of efforts to create a diaspora bond all speak to the dedication and commitment that the diaspora and the Jamaican government share to the island's future well-being and development.[4] While most hail these efforts to "harness" and "tap" the potential of the diaspora, as essential to Jamaica's ability to turn around its economy, few question the broader political context within which Jamaica's diaspora option has emerged and its embeddedness within a set of policies that privilege economic production over social reproduction and depoliticize the processes, through which market freedom increasingly trumps all other freedoms.

Many of the strategies that have been actively pursued within Jamaica's diaspora option have been oriented towards encouraging investments in Jamaica, opening up opportunities for the Jamaican private sector to gain access to markets abroad and more recently generating new sources of capital that the Jamaican government could use to finance education and health as well as to pay down the national debt. There are efforts to launch a diaspora bond by August 2012, with celebrations marking the island's fiftieth anniversary of independence beginning to indicate the growing importance of the faithfulness of diaspora capital to the financing of future social investments. Diaspora bonds are debt instruments that allow the issuer to gain access to fixed-term funding at discounted interest rates. The benefits of a diaspora bond to the Jamaican government lie in the potential improvement to the country's credit rating that the existence of a faithful source of funding from the diaspora indicates. Benefits also accrue from the differences between the rates of interest the government would have to pay in order to borrow money at market rates and the lower rates of interest that could be obtained on loans derived from the diaspora. The government estimates that the Jamaican diaspora saves approximately US$5billion a year, an amount equivalent to 40 percent of the island's GDP (Thame 2012). For diaspora members, the benefits lie not only in the satisfaction that bond holders are likely to derive from directly contributing to socially needed projects but also from the belief that diaspora members might gain some influence over policy decisions in the future. On the question of risk, the distribution of costs is stacked more unevenly towards the diaspora, for as World Bank advocates of diaspora bonds for development point out in the worst-case scenario, the issuing country may be unable to make debt service payments in hard currency — governments are likely to be able to pay interest and principal in local currency (Ketkar and Ratha 2011).

Whether Jamaica's diaspora option can generate the flows of skill and investment that countries like Israel and India are purported to have successfully achieved remains an illusive question that very few scholars or policymakers have seriously explored. Instead, most continue to make assumptions about the capacity of the diaspora to re-invigorate the Jamaican economy with very little recourse to the economic, employment and social realities of the diaspora itself. In the following sections, focusing largely on the Jamaican diaspora in Canada, we explore some of the assumptions that inform the foci and orientation of the current diaspora option, with a view to inviting more critical reflection on the limits and orientation of this current approach.

Assumption One: Members of the Jamaican diaspora can generate the skills transfers, business networks and levels of investment needed to boost economic growth in Jamaica.

Much of the economic promise of diasporic engagement is predicated upon two main beliefs. The first is that there is a highly skilled, entrepreneurial and networked Jamaican diaspora out there that is able to generate the business opportunities and networks that Jamaica needs. The second is that the emotional and patriotic ties that members of Jamaican diaspora have with the island are sufficiently strong to motivate them to take on levels of risk that other investors would be unwilling to assume. In relation to the first, scholars examining the economic success of India note the important role that its diaspora plays in creating linkages between investors in their home and host countries (Saxenian 2006; Kuznetsov 2006). Pandey et al. (2006) attribute the Indian diaspora's success in building global production networks to their strong presence in the technology industry in the United States and their crucial role in the creation of India's IT outsourcing industry. The ability of diaspora members to act as "bridges," as Kuznetsov describes them, that link private sector interests in the countries where they reside to countries with which they hold ancestral ties, is a powerful incentive for states to develop closer ties. Given the fact that Jamaica has the second highest percentage of its tertiary educated population living outside of the island's territorial borders in the world,[5] it is not surprising that many regard the diaspora as an untapped resource with the potential to not only boost the island's stock of human capital but also to help generate new market opportunities for the Jamaican private sector. The ability of the Jamaican diaspora to generate such market opportunities is a fairly grey area because we know very little about the labour market experiences of skilled Jamaicans abroad and importantly, the influence they exert within overseas labour markets.

In Canada, the fact that a large proportion of new immigrants are arriving through the economic class channels would seem to suggest that the Jamaican Canadian diaspora is increasingly well placed to help Jamaica to tap into overseas business and entrepreneurial networks. But it is important to note that gaining access to Canada through the skilled worker class is no guarantee of gaining access to professional and business opportunities. As Todoroki, Vaccan and Noor (2009) note, since 2002, immigrants under the economic class category have not come with the security of assured employment because direct sponsorship by an employer is no longer a requirement for migration to Canada. This migration opportunity therefore is a double-edged sword because there is no guarantee that Jamaicans will find work commensurate with their level of skill and education. There is mounting evidence that new immigrants face barriers in Canada's labour markets as a result of the discounting of their credentials. Some scholars argue further that this experience is racialized and that there are systemic barriers in place that maintain the under-representation of visible minorities in highly skilled capacities in the Canadian labour force (Teelucksing and Galabuzi 2005).

Data from the 2006 census suggest that the skills that facilitate Jamaican migration to Canada do not necessarily help them to access commensurate positions in the Canadian labour market. Whereas the number of Jamaican's over fifteen years of age with tertiary degrees or higher (30 percent) matched that of the Canadian population as a whole, Jamaicans were less likely than other Canadians to hold managerial positions (9 percent for all Canadians versus 6% for Jamaicans). While Jamaicans were more likely than Canadians as a whole to be concentrated in business, finance and administrative occupations (21% for all Jamaicans vs. 18% for Canadians), data generated from a smaller sample of the census (twenty-five to fifty-four years of age) indicate that as many of 25 percent of persons of Jamaican descent in Canada are concentrated in administrative, clerical and technician positions compared with approximately 20% of Canadians as a whole (Statistics Canada Online Database). In addition, overall, Jamaicans in Canada are more likely to be unemployed and more likely to earn lower incomes than other Canadians. Thus, the assumption that significant numbers of the Jamaican Canadian diasporic community will act as bridges that link network investors in Jamaica with those in their home countries deserves further scrutiny.

In relation to the second underlying premise, that the emotional and patriotic ties held by the Jamaican diaspora will be sufficient to motivate them to take on levels of risk that other investors would be unwilling to assume, similar critical questions need to be posed. Is the hope pinned on the ability of diaspora to generate new flows of investment capital through the diaspora bonds a realistic one? What assumptions about the nature of the Jamaican diaspora would have to hold true for the diaspora as investor model to be successful?

Current efforts to issue a diaspora bond in time for the fiftieth jubilee are predicated on a belief that there will be sufficient nationalist fervour to overcome the fact that diaspora bonds carry higher levels of risk and lower rates of return for investing members. It is possible that members of the diaspora would be willing to take on these conditions in order to help finance specific and identifiable national investments. As Ngozi Okonjo-Iweala and Dilip Ratha (2011) argue in the journal *Foreign Policy*: "Diaspora bonds can tap into the same kind of emotion migrants feel when cheering on their national team in a football match, a long way from their homeland. Patriotism could in effect become the effective tool for helping a developing country fulfill its development dreams."

But far more important to the success of a diaspora bond issue is the question of trust. Israel, and to a lesser extent India, are often cited as evidence of countries that issued bonds successfully, and both are viewed as models that the Jamaican government or private sector should follow. Suhas Ketkar and Dilip Ratha argue that since 1951 Israel has annually issued a diaspora bond that has raised over US$26billion. This investment capital has been used to finance projects in transportation, energy, telecommunications and other essential areas. Ratha, who currently serves as a consultant to the Jamaican government, believes that if multiple maturities and denomination amounts that were as low as US$100 were offered, the diaspora would positively respond to a bond at a 4 percent interest rate (Inter Press Service 2012). However, few acknowledge that significant differences exist between the economic power of the Israeli and Jamaican economies, the political contexts that give rise to the forms of patriotism expressed by each diaspora and, importantly, the levels of trust and reciprocity that exists between the governments and the diaspora in each country.

The extradition of Christopher "Dudus" Coke to the United States in 2010 and the Manatt-Dudus Commission of Inquiry that followed have both brought issues of patronage and corruption to the fore. What advocacy group Jamaicans for Justice describe as the "growing level of cynicism" and "pervasive sense of lack of accountability and trust in governance structures in the country" among Jamaicans may ultimately challenge the assumption that patriotism can conquer all (Gleaner/Power 106 News). It may, in fact, be more instructive to examine the low take up of the diaspora bond issued by Ethiopia in 2009 in order to establish the role that accountable, democratic and trustworthy governance structures play in the success of diaspora options as a whole.

Assumption Two: Members of the Jamaican diaspora share a common vision of development that is consistent with not only the views of the Jamaican state but also with the views of Jamaicans in Jamaica.

The growing despair over the divisive nature of Jamaica's Westminster parliamentary system of government and the endemic nature of political patronage and its contribution to the levels of violence found in the poorest urban communities, as well as the growing levels of corruption across state, private sector and civil society institutions, have led a growing number of scholars to advocate for a different vision of development. Brian Meeks (2007), for example, argues for a vision that is founded on new modalities of democracy, new forms of popular participation and new social arrangements that not only include the vast majority of the Jamaican people but critically, also the diaspora. While we agree with the broadly defined ideals that Meeks eschews, there is much variation in the Jamaican diaspora — in its composition and, crucially, in the variety of alternative and conflicting visions that its members embrace. Like the term the "Jamaican people," the Jamaican diaspora is often imagined as a single community that shares a common vision of development. But, as Mullings (2012) has outlined elsewhere, if not problematized, the term "diaspora" can be reduced to an invocation that is used to justify a host of interventions that may be neither democratic nor just.

To truly embrace the Jamaican diaspora as partners in governing, there would need to be a concerted effort on the part of the Jamaican state to encourage, recognize and incorporate the truly diverse viewpoints and priorities of the diaspora. This is not yet being done. While a number of voluntary and philanthropic organizations have been incorporated into the network that the government officially recognizes as the "Jamaican Diaspora," there are many others that have not. And while we recognize that it would be virtually impossible to have every Jamaican organization abroad participate in the current diaspora meetings, greater effort must be made to create an institutional framework capable of incorporating the visions, opinions and voices of a wider range of groups – including those with visions of development that radically differ from that of the Jamaican government.

There is evidence that even among groups with seats and voices at the table, there are limits to the level of governance that diaspora groups are afforded. Efforts by members of the present diaspora network to secure a senatorial seat in Parliament, for example, have been stymied by section 40 (2) of the Jamaican Constitution, which bars persons who have not been ordinarily residents in Jamaica for the preceding twelve months, or who have pledged allegiance or obedience to a foreign power from sitting in the houses of Parliament. While the government and opposition have been generally favourable to amending this requirement in the Constitution, other, ostensibly more difficult, obstacles to greater inclusion in the governance process remain. As the threat to boycott the 2011 diaspora conference indicates, the balance of power between the Jamaican state and the diaspora is presently one that has the potential to limit the role of the diaspora to simply that of an agent of the state.

Concerns over the Jamaican government's handling of the 2011 diaspora conference and, in particular, its attempt to control the content and format of the meeting, as well as to hand pick preferred members of the advisory board, led the then future leader representative on the Diaspora Advisory Board for the U.S., David Mullings, to issue a public statement detailing the reasons why a boycott was imminent. In this statement he claimed that, indeed, it had been the failure to engage diaspora conference members as partners the year before that had provoked the boycott and eventual postponement (see Mullings 2011). Many believe that the current Jamaica diaspora movement (as some members describe this loose government supported network) does not represent the views of either Jamaicans at home or in the diaspora. This belief has persisted from the very start of efforts to institutionalize the diaspora option. Williams (2012) found that these concerns also exist among skilled Jamaican immigrants in the Greater Toronto Area (GTA), many of whom have chosen to support organizations that directly focus on local philanthropic projects, such as the establishment of basic schools or specific childhood education facilities.

The 2006 Canadian census indicates that 28 percent of the Jamaican Canadian diaspora are from a second generation and an additional 6 percent from a third. If Jamaica is to sustain its relationship with its diaspora it will also need to develop an inclusive and genuinely consultative relationship with this growing population, who undoubtedly will hold visions of development that are significantly different from those of Jamaicans of the first generation and possibly from Jamaicans in Jamaica. If these extra-territorial citizens are to be mobilized, they too must be given the space to potentially shape social, economic and political relations of the island.

Conclusion

The 1992 West Indian Commission (1993: 27) emphasized the importance of avoiding a mercenary approach to the diaspora, advocating instead: "We must treat these men and women of the diaspora as West Indians all, far from home but close at heart." And it is clear from Jamaica's earliest efforts to develop a diaspora option that balancing strategies to mobilize capital with those aimed at creating an open and inclusive framework for governance was of the utmost importance. We therefore see the Jamaican government's desire to develop a strong institutionalized relationship with the diaspora as a positive initiative that has the capacity to go a long way towards boosting levels of inward investment and ultimately reducing debt. But we believe that much more needs to be known about the Jamaican diaspora – the factors that affect their capacity to generate wealth and, importantly, the factors that motivate the forms of participation in Jamaica's economy and society that they seek. The Jamaican diaspora is not the same as the Jewish or Indian diaspora and so the successes recorded by these countries in their efforts to "harness" forms of capital in their diaspora need to be tempered by the realities that racism, labour market exclusion, brain abuse[6] and lack of political representation exert upon this community. Recognition of the challenges facing members of the Jamaican diaspora particularly within labour markets and within politics and civil society is essential because it will lay the groundwork for alternative approaches to the mobilization of diasporic economic and human capital, perhaps approaches that require the Jamaican government to offer some creative incentives and support.[7]

We believe that Jamaicans in the diaspora continue to be stalwart patriots who are willing to contribute to the health of the nation, but there are limits to the degree to which diasporic obligation to "those left behind" can, and should, be "tapped." Patriotism and obligation, however, are sentiments that operate at different scales. While Jamaicans are likely to continue to remit money to family, close friends and community out of a sense of obligation, there is no guarantee that patriotism can always be channelled into financial support for the government. Without trust in political institutions or a sense of having some influence in the governing practices of the state, patriotism can quickly turn to disaffection and the withdrawal of support. This is a possible danger when governments seek to pick and choose groups within the diaspora that it would prefer to "do business with."

The importance of maintaining an open dialogue aimed at creating solutions to the challenges facing the island is evident in the Delano Franklyn's documentation and communication of the conversations and resolutions that emerged in the early years. In the intervening years since the first diaspora conference, more attention has been placed on developing policies and institutional frameworks to orient diaspora capital towards national development objectives than has been given to establishing and institutionalizing the governing role that the Jamaican diaspora could play. In the rigorous search for practical solutions to the real and pressing foreign exchange crisis that the West Indian Commission so poignantly identified,[8] broader questions about the nature of the political structures needed to foster greater democratic participatory deliberation across the island have tended to be drowned out. In the spirit of the West Indian Commission, P.J. Patterson envisaged a political role for the diaspora – as a special interest lobbying group that could influence their host country governments. He did not, however, place emphasis on the need for the diaspora to play a similar role within Jamaica.

Yet as the debates that are beginning to emerge from consultative groups within the diaspora clearly show, the relationship between political and economic inclusion is mutually constitutive and intertwined. Without a commitment to building stronger institutional frameworks for including the voices, experiences and differences of not only the wider Jamaican diaspora but also Jamaicans from all walks of life and political persuasions in broader conversations about the nature of social transformation, the diaspora option as presently constituted will be challenged to sustain itself beyond a second generation.

Notes

1. Of course this does not mean that entrants through other categories are necessarily less skilled.
2. Persons who immigrate to Canada under the economic class category include skilled workers, investors, entrepreneurs, self–employed persons and recently, live-in caregivers. Successful applicants within the skilled worker class must demonstrate their possession of essential and transferable skills that contribute to success and adaptability in the Canadian labour market.
3. This quote is reported in the 1992 West Indian Commission (1993) as a statement made by the then prime minister of Trinidad and Tobago, A.N.R Robinson, in a paper entitled "The West Indies Beyond 1992," which was delivered at the historic CARICOM Grenada Summit in July 1989, which gave rise to the Grand Anse Declaration that established the CARICOM Single Market And Economy (CSME) and gave birth to the West Indian Commission.
4. Delano Franklyn, a key and dedicated architect in the institutionalization of the diaspora option, has painstakingly documented the processes involved in his essay "The Jamaican Diaspora: Building an Operational Framework."
5. Cohen and Soto (2001) estimated that over 82 percent of Jamaicans live outside of its territorial borders.
6. Bauder (2003) defines brain abuse as the exclusion of skilled immigrants from the upper segments of the Canadian labour markets because of the non-recognition of the foreign credentials and the devaluation of their foreign-acquired skills.
7. Strategies to engage diasporic economic and human capital in China and in Mexico typically include some level of state financial assistance. Mexico's tres por uno programme for example, provides matching funds for local projects that diaspora members identify and pool money to support (Orozco 2005). In China, the state similarly provides incentives to University professors and students to form collaborative transnational networks (Zweig and Fung 2004).
8. A more comprehensive critique of the importance of the neoliberal market solutions in current diaspora options is provided in Mullings 2012.

References

Austin, David. 2007. "All Roads Led to Montréal: Black Power, the Caribbean, and the Black Radical Tradition in Canada." *The Journal of African American History* 92.

Bauder, Harald. 2003. "Brain Abuse, or the Devaluation of Immigrant Labour in Canada." *Antipode* 35.

Boyce Davies, Carole. 2008. *Left of Karl Marx: The Political Life of Black Communist Claudia Jones*. Durham, NC: Duke University Press.

Citizenship and Immigration Canada. 2012. "Provided Data Tables on Permanent Residents to Canada by Country of Birth." Ottawa: Citizenship and Immigration Canada

Cohen, D., and M. Soto. 2001. "Growth and Human Capital: Good Data, Good Results." OECD Development Centre, Working Paper 179." Paris: OECD.

Franklyn, Delano. 2004. "Overview: Jamaica and the Jamaican Diaspora." *Jamaica Diaspora Conference 2004: 'Unleashing the Potential.'* Kingston, Jamaica June 15–16.

Gleaner/Power 106 News. "Jamaicans for Justice Disappointed with Manatt-Dudus Report." *The Gleaner*. At <http://go-jamaica.com/news/read_article.php?id=29523>.

Government of Jamaica. 2009. "Vision 2030 Jamaica National Development Plan." Kingston: Government of Jamaica.

Hall, Stuart. 1994. "Cultural Identity and Diaspora." In J. Rutherford (ed.), *Identity: Community, Culture, Difference*. London: Lawrence & Wishart.

Hill, Robert A. 2011. *The Marcus Garvey and Universal Negro Improvement Association Papers: The Caribbean Diaspora 1910–1920*. Durham, NC: Duke University Press.

Inter Press Service. "Harnessing Diaspora Funds for Development Financing Thalif Deen Interviews Dilip Ratha of the World Bank." At <http://Ipsnews.net/news.asp?idnews=105421>.

Ketkar, Suhas L., and Dilip Ratha. 2011. "Diaspora Bonds: Tapping the Diaspora during Difficult Times." In S. Plaza and D. Ratha (eds.), *Diaspora for Development in Africa*. Washington DC: World Bank.

Kuznetsov, Yevgeny. 2006. *Diaspora Networks and the International Migration of Skills: How Countries Can Draw on Their Talent Abroad*. Washington DC: World Bank.

Meeks, Brian. 2007. *Envisioning Caribbean Futures*. Kingston, JA: University of the West Indies Press.

Ministry of Manpower and Immigration. 1967. *Immigration Statistics 1967*. Ottawa: Canada Immigration Division.

Mullings, Beverley. 2012. "Governmentality, Diaspora Assemblages and the Ongoing Challenge of 'Development'." *Antipode* 44.

Mullings, David. 2011. "Setting the Record Straight about the Jamaican Diaspora 'Convention' and the Boycott Threat." At <http://www.jamaicans.com/articles/primecomments/setting-the-record-straight-aboutthe-jamaican-dia.shtml>.

Office of Immigration Services. 2011. *2010 Yearbook of Immigration Statistics*. Washington, DC.

Okonjo–Iweala, Ngozi, and Dilip Ratha. 2011. "A Bond for the Homeland." *Foreign Policy*. At <http://www.foreignpolicy.com/articles/2011/05/24/a_bond_for_the_homeland?page=0,2>.

Orozco, Manuel. 2005. "Hometown Associations and Development: Ownership, Correspondence, Sustainability and Replicability." In B. J. Merz (ed.), *New Patterns for Mexico: Observations on Remittances, Philanthropic Giving, and Equitable Development*. Cambridge, MA: Global Equity Initiative, Harvard University. At <http://www.ssrc.org/workspace/images/crm/new_publication_3/{6a12f169-3f55-de11-afac001cc477ec70}.pdf>.

Pandey, Abhishek, Alok Aggarwal, Richard Devane, and Yevgeny Kuznetsov. 2006.

"The Indian Diaspora: A Unique Case?" In Y. Kuznetsov (ed.), *Diaspora Networks and the International Migration of Skills: How Countries Can Draw on Their Talent Abroad.* Washington DC: World Bank.

Patterson, P.J. 2004. "Address by Most Hon. P.J. Patterson, ON, PC, QC, MP, Prime Minister at Jamaica Diaspora Conference on Wednesday, June 16, 2004." At <http://www.jis.gov.jm/special_sections/DiasporaConference/PMAddress. html>.

___. 2007. "The Importance of the Caribbean Diaspora to Economic Development." In "Lecture by the Most Hon. P.J. Patterson, former Prime Minister of Jamaica given at the Schomburg Center for Research in Black Culture, NY, November 3, 2007 on the occasion of the 4th Annual CIN Caribbean Lecture."

Planning Institute of Jamaica. 2009. *Economic and Social Survey of Jamaica 2008.* Kingston.

Saxenian, Annalee. 2006. *The New Argonauts: Regional Advantage in a Global Economy.* Cambridge, MA: Harvard University Press.

Statistics Canada online database. "2006 Census Data Products: Special Interest Profiles" At <http://www12.statcan.gc.ca/census-recensement/2006/dp-pd/ prof/sip/Rp-eng.cfm?LANG=E&APATH=3&DETAIL=1&DIM=0&FL=A& FREE=0&GC=0&GID=0&GK=0&GRP=1&PID=97614&PRID=0&PTYP E=97154&S=0&SHOWALL=0&SUB=0&Temporal=2006&THEME=80&V ID=0&VNAMEE=&VNAMEF= >.

Teelucksingh, Cheryl, and Grace-Edward Galabuzi. 2005. "Working Precariously: The Impact of Race and Immigrant Status on Employment Opportunities and Outcomes in Canada." *Directions: Canadian Race Relations Foundation* 2, 1.

Thame, Camilo. 2012. "Jamaica Diaspora Bond Possible for Jubilee." *The Jamaica Observe,* March 09. Kingston. At <http://www.jamaicaobserver.com/business/ Jamaica-diaspora-bond-possible-for-Jubilee_10997570>.

Todoroki, Emiko, Matteo Vaccan, and Wameek Noor. 2009. *The Canada-Caribbean Remittance Corridor: Fostering Formal Remittances to Haiti and Jamaica through Effective Regulation* Washington, DC: World Bank.

USAID. 2003. "Leveraging the Jamaican Diaspora for Development." Washington, DC: USAID Office of Development Credit.

West Indian Commission with Sir Shridath Ramphal. 1993. *Time for Action.* Kingston: University of the West Indies Press.

Williams, Kay-Ann. 2012. "Immigrant Civic Engagement via Organized Social Networks: A Case of Jamaican Immigrants in the Greater Toronto Area." Paper presented at the Association of American Geographers conference. New York City. February.

World Bank. 2012, "World Bank Online Database." At <http://www.worldbank. org/data/onlinedatabases/onlinedatabases.html>.

Zweig, David, and Chung Siu Fung. 2004. "Redefining the Brain Drain: China's 'Diaspora Option'." *Center on China's Transnational Relations Working Paper No. 1.* Hong Kong: The Hong Kong University of Science and Technology.

27. THE CHANGING JAMAICAN ECONOMY
From Independence to Now
Gervan Fearon

Over the past fifty years, the economic developments of Jamaica have been filled with moments of opportunities and challenges. There is a natural interest in understanding these developments as well as forecasting what the future may entail. This curiosity is represented by two key questions: first, what have been the key economic developments and drivers over the past fifty years and, second, what are the implications of these developments to Jamaicans in Canada as well as those at "home"? To address these questions, I look at the economic development of Jamaica over the last five decades, including the challenges and choices of decision-makers and those likely to emerge in the future. I begin by presenting a profile of Jamaicans in Canada.

Jamaicans in Canada

The Jamaican population in Canada currently stands at about 250,000, representing nearly 10 percent of the 2.7 million individuals residing in Jamaica itself. Statistics Canada's analysis of the Jamaican community in Canada suggests that Jamaicans make up the fourth largest non-European ethnic group in the country, with the Chinese, East Indian and Filipino communities being larger. It is interesting to note that Jamaicans generally report their ethnic background to simply be Jamaican, emphasizing the Jamaican motto: "Out of many, one people."[1] In 2001, Statistics Canada census data indicated that there were 210,000[2] Jamaicans residing in Canada — the majority of them (181,000[3]) in the province of Ontario, mostly in the city of Toronto (150,000[4]) (Lindsay 2001). The 2001 numbers permit comparisons even though the population has grown since then. For instance, in 2001, 21 percent of Jamaicans were college graduates, compared to 15 percent of the general adult population within Canada. Additionally, Jamaicans are known for their strong work ethic, with 68 percent employed, compared with 62 percent for the general population. Jamaicans in Canada tend to have a strong sense of belonging to both countries. This can also be linked to the demographic profile of the community. Statistic Canada data further revealed that 34 percent of the community arrived in Canada between 1971 and 1980; 24 percent in the 1980s; and another 26 percent between 1991 and 2001 (Lindsay 2001). Hence, only 16 percent of the population entered Canada before 1971.

The affection of Jamaican Canadians for their homeland is reflected in the level of remittances they make to Jamaica. In 2010, remittances from Canada to Jamaica reached US$193.8 million, nearly 10 percent of the US$1906.2 million in total remittances to Jamaica in the same year (Bank of Jamaica 2011). These figures mean that Jamaicans in Canada are remitting an average of $774 per person to Jamaica. The United States at US$1,110 million and United Kingdom at US$332 million both rank higher than Canada as sources of remittances. Bank of Jamaica data show that remittances from all sources, including Cayman Islands and other places, represent nearly 15 percent of overall economic activity in Jamaica (i.e., as measured by gross domestic product). This level of transfers is approximately equal to the economic size of the Jamaican tourism industry. Remittances received by individual Jamaicans averaged around US$700 per year over the past five years. Since per capita annual income in Jamaica is less than US$10,000, remittances represent a significant source of income to the Jamaican economy and, correspondingly, constitute an important component of overall economic activity.

In 2001, 24 percent of the Jamaican population in Canada was between the ages of forty-five and sixty-five. These data suggest that by 2021 this population will be over sixty-five, with potentially important implications for remittances to Jamaica. Therefore, the relationship between the Jamaicans in Canada and the nation of Jamaica will evolve in the coming years, with the next fifty years likely to be very different than the past fifty.

In addition to Jamaican immigrants, a second group of Jamaicans in Canada are seasonal agricultural workers.[5] The Canadian Seasonal Agricultural Workers Program (SAWP) was first established in 1966 between Canada and Jamaica, and it sent 264 Jamaican workers to Canada (mostly Ontario). The program was modified to include workers from Barbados and Trinidad and Tobago in 1967, Mexico in 1974 and additional Caribbean islands in 1976. By 2010, the program had expanded to involve nearly 6,400 seasonal agricultural workers. Individual farm workers are generally paid just over the minimum wage. For example, in 2003, workers earned approximately $7.45 per hour, while the minimum wage in Ontario was $8.00 per hour (Ross 2006). Those workers who have been at the same agricultural enterprise for more than a single year often earn an end-of-season bonus.

Canada and the Caribbean have also established the Caribbean Compulsory Savings Scheme, which involves 20 to 25 percent of a worker's earnings being remitted to the government of the country of origin, which can only be collected after the individual has returned. Some 5 to 8 percent of these "savings" is retained by the government to cover administration and processing costs (Ross 2006; Hercog and Siegel 2011). Extrapolating from Ross's (2006) analysis, a farm worker who earned approximately $8,000 for working a period of five months (at forty hours per week and $10 per hour) would pay a remittance of about $2,000 under the Caribbean Compulsory Savings Scheme and about another $2,000 in personal remittance. These numbers would represent as much as J$960 million or CAN$12 million in remittances to Jamaica from these workers. Jamaican farm workers therefore contribute a potential 6 percent of the remittances to Jamaica.

The scale of bi-lateral trade between Canada and Jamaica reached $521 million in 2008, with Jamaica exporting goods worth $327 million to Canada. These exports from Jamaica included inorganic chemicals, beverages, vegetables, preserved food, fruits and nuts and knit apparel, according to the Government of Canada data. The export of these products to Canada reflects the demand for a "taste of home" by Jamaicans in Canada.

The population of Jamaica increased from under 1.5 million in 1950 to about 2.6 million in 2010. The labour force in Jamaica is about 1.1 million. Overall economic activity reached US$6.5 billion in 1980, increasing steadily to US$24 billion in 2008, and is projected to reach over US$25 billion in 2012. In comparison to Canada, Jamaica's per capita income has grown at a slower rate over the years. In 1970, Jamaica's per capita annual income stood at $750, compared with US$4,000 for Canada.[6] By 2010, the level was US$5,300 for Jamaica and US$46,000 for Canada. This gap in the standard of living has widened between Canada and Jamaica over the years, with Canadians in 1970 earning about 5.3 times as much as the average Jamaican, increasing to 8.7 times as much by 2010. Jamaicans in Canada might ask: what have been the key economic developments and drivers of the Jamaican economy over the past fifty years that have helped to shape these trends? In what follows, I look briefly at the developments over the decades since independence.

Toward the Development of a Viable Economy

The foundation of the Jamaican economy of the 1960s was established in the 1940s and 1950s. The discovery of bauxite in the 1940s transformed the economy as bauxite production moved from less than 1 percent of overall economic activity in 1950 to nearly 10 percent by 1960 and over 15 percent by 1970. Similarly, tourism changed from being an experience of the few to an activity of the many, resulting in tourism becoming an important component of the economy during this period. The mining and tourism industries became an increasing source of employment and foreign currency earnings for the nation. Nonetheless, the Jamaica agriculture sector remained a primary employer during the period, with the production of well-established products, including banana, sugar, coffee (e.g., Blue Mountain Coffee) and tobacco. Tobacco production had already started to decline in prominence by the 1960s, pointing towards some of the challenges that Jamaica would soon face in the competitiveness of its agricultural products. Changes in the agricultural sector and population growth induced movement from the rural to the urban centres of Jamaica, as well as migration to Canada and other countries.

Jamaica had been blessed with a productive land mass both in terms of its agricultural potential and its natural resource capacity (e.g., bauxite and minerals). Its people were industrious and would indeed form an important part of the labour force for many countries in the 1960s, including Britain, the United States and Canada. However, the attraction and formation of capital (i.e., investment in plant and equipment) were challenges facing the Jamaican economy that can be traced back to the plantation economy of the 1800s, with the rise of competition from sugar beet production in France and Germany in the 1870s. Consequently, it is not surprising to see the establishment of favourable tax legislation during the period of 1947 to 1949, which aided the formation of the textile and cement industries. Additionally, tariffs were reduced in the early 1950s to support the importation of inputs needed to promote a manufacturing sector. The Jamaica Industrial Development Corporation, established in 1952, aimed to promote foreign investment and industry in the country. These actions supported economic growth of the period into the 1960s. The 1960s saw the rise of national independence across the Caribbean as well as in other regions of the world as nations began to chart their own socio-political and economic futures. Conversely, colonial powers focused more on domestic concerns following War World II. The industrial rebuilding and growth of the 1950s and early 1960s triggered greater global competition for capital investment. Jamaica's independence in 1962 also meant that British and others investors evaluated whether to keep their capital investment in Jamaica or repatriate it. It is therefore not surprising that in the early 1960s, tax holidays, accelerated depreciation and tax concessions were implemented in Jamaica. These actions supported the capital formation and foreign investment needed to foster the textile, bauxite, cement and tourist (e.g., construction of hotels) industries. Investment share of overall economic activity peaked at 35 percent in the late 1960s, corresponding to the growth in the bauxite industry and the supportive investment climate established in Jamaica. On the other hand, the tax holiday and concession regime resulted in insufficient government revenues to fulfill the demands for education and health care in this newly independent country (examples of infrastructure investment included the New Deal Education Programme, the growth of the University of the West Indies and the highway from Kingston to Spanish Town).

Jamaica's monetary policy had been anchored to the British pound through a number of steps, including the establishment of the Bank of Jamaica in 1836, the printing of the British pound by the Bank in 1837, the *Currency Notes Law* of 1939 and the printing of the first Jamaican notes in pound currency in 1962. In 1969, Jamaica switched from the pound to the dollar.[7] At the time of independence, the currency was fundamentally the British pound. When the Jamaican dollar was introduced, monetary policy acted in support of a pegged exchange rate relative to the United States currency, which would have been important to foreign investors who were being attracted by the conciliatory taxation regime. By 1965, the rising competitiveness of the United States and the rise of new economies (e.g., Japan — every Jamaican can remember having a transistor radio) was affecting the Jamaican manufacturing sector's prosperity, and import restrictions were established to purportedly protect Jamaican industry. In 1968, the British pound was devalued against the United States dollar, which helped the competitiveness of Jamaican exports and, correspondingly, increased the cost of imports. Nonetheless, the introduction of the Jamaican dollar in 1969 did not see any deviation in the currency value against the U.S. dollar even though the trade positions of Britain and Jamaica relative to the U.S. were significantly different.[8]

Jamaica entered the 1970s having had economic growth at around 5 percent during the 1960s, which was driven by the vibrant bauxite and tourism sectors. Jamaica was also becoming more involved in regional socio-political and economic development. For instance, Jamaica would play a significant role in the formation of the Caribbean Community (CARICOM) following the formation of the 1968 Caribbean Free Trade Association (CARIFTA). In 1972, Jamaica initiated and became a founding member of the International Bauxite Association (IBA), which included Australia, Guinea, Guyana, Surinam and Yugoslavia. The IBA aimed to achieve greater control of the production and price of bauxite. Through its *Bauxite Production Levy Act* of 1974 Jamaica pushed for a rise in the bauxite levy to support the growing demand for public investment in education, health and infrastructure. The bauxite industry wanted to see the government tax concessions of the 1950s and 1960s continued. This placed the industry in direct conflict with the interests of the government, as demonstrated by the legal case *Kaiser Bauxite Company vs Jamaica*. In 1973, the actions of the Organization of the Petroleum Exporting Countries (OPEC) triggered a significant rise in oil prices, causing the costs of producing bauxite and alumina in Jamaica to sharply rise. These forces corresponded to a drop in bauxite production, motivating the government to increase its ownership of bauxite production.

In 1974, inflation and currency upheaval springing from the oil crisis were met with foreign exchange restrictions in Jamaica that permitted only commercial banks to engage in currency exchange; this was to address the leakage of foreign currency out of the country. The government therefore was standing against the outward flow of capital. Concurrently, the government acted as a substitute for capital formation and investment in the economy by expanding public sector ownership of enterprises and thus a rise in public sector employment. Specifically, the government moved to take a financial position in the banking sector (e.g., Barclays Bank in Jamaica was purchased), in public utilities (cable and wireless and thereafter the television station became publicly owned) and in mining and other enterprises (e.g., hotels).

In the 1980s, Jamaica's economy continued to be challenged by external economic forces. The United States' economy was undergoing the fallout from the savings and loans crisis between 1982 and 1989. This had a negative impact on Jamaica's tourism sector, which had grown to be a substantial component of the economy. The bauxite industry faced greater competition from production capacity in Guinea, Australia and Vietnam. Consequently, in 1985 bauxite production dropped to 50 percent of 1980 levels, and since bauxite represented over 70 percent of foreign earnings capacity, this decline severely affected the country's foreign currency earnings. It is estimated that Jamaica lost approximately $2.4 billion in U.S. foreign currency earnings and government revenues lost $800 million over the ten-year period ending in 1985 (*Daily Gleaner* 2008).

Between 1974 and 1984, foreign exchange restrictions stipulated that only commercial banks could engage in currency exchange. The country was therefore focused on controlling capital and currency outflow, which is fundamentally different from fostering capital formation and attracting investment. Additionally, the government moved to maintain its control of import-substitution and currency management through the establishment of high import tariffs, as well as through import purchasing controlled by the Jamaica Commodity Trading Corporation (originally established in 1977). The government also established Jamaica Nutrition Holding Ltd., Jamaica Building Material Ltd. and other mechanisms that reflected a growing role for the public sector in the economy.

The Jamaican exports and tourism sectors were fundamental to employment and foreign currency earnings for the nation. Adjustment of the exchange rate would have been the usual mechanism to change the terms of trade between countries. Yet, the government maintained a tight currency trading range through a pegged foreign exchange rate regime against the U.S. currency. The maintenance of this policy was certainly costly to the Jamaican economy since the government used foreign currency earnings to defend the Jamaican dollar, kept interest rates artificially high and restricted currency movement. High interest rates were maintained through high cash and liquid assets, with reserve ratios being imposed on Jamaican commercial banks and financial services companies (Guilde et al. 1997).

These high reserves rates meant that banks held a high level of government bonds/securities, thereby supporting the domestic population and financing a large share of the national debt, which would eventually crowd out private investment and consumer expenditures. Still, the foreign exchange rate storm would eventually become too strong for the government to withstand. By 1989, the Jamaican economy was moving towards market liberalization due to internal (export competitiveness) and external (IMF) pressures. A government currency auction was established in 1984, replacing the earlier strict currency control mechanism. The auction was abundant in 1989, and the exchange controls were fully removed by 1991. Not surprisingly, by 1991, the currency moved quickly to its market equilibrium, sliding against the U.S. dollar. On the other hand, the government dependency on debt financing meant that interest rates would be further increased and the crowding out of private investment continued, slowing economic growth despite flexible exchange rates. The economic implication involved unemployment rising to the 30 percent range.

By the 1990s, government revenues tended to hover at around 29 percent of GDP. Tax reform that had been initiated in the 1980s continued, with a move towards greater reliance on expenditure tax as opposed to income tax. Expenditure taxation was efficient and had a greater scope for collecting government revenues, given that nearly 40 percent of economic activity takes place in the informal economy.[9] Furthermore, changes in labour regulations and taxation were implemented with an aim of improving the conditions for a growth in employment. Taxation reform is important since government provision for services, such as education, health care and infrastructure, cannot be achieved without an effective tax revenue collection mechanism. In fact, government policies such as high cash and liquid assets reserve ratio for the financial services sector and import levies were directly related to the need for government revenues in the face of an ineffective tax collection system. Unfortunately, these alternative approaches to government revenue generation tend to distort economic activity and cause a drag on economic growth and development.

Government expenditures averaged about 30 percent or more of GDP, and social services expenditures averaged around 10 percent of GDP. Between 1980 and 1998, the Jamaican government committed over 50 percent of its social service expenditures to education and about 25 percent to health care. During these years, the annualized government expenditures exceeded the 29 percent mark eleven times and resulted in mounting government deficits. Jamaica's debt levels during the 1990s approached 90 percent of GDP, which was largely attributable to its purchase of and support of production capacity in the sugar industry, as opposed to social service expenditures. In fact, debt repayment costs became a significantly large component of government expenditures, which limited government's capacity to fund social services and infrastructure investment (King and Richards 2008).

Public borrowing tended to crowd out private sector investment in the physical capital needed to support the productivity and competitiveness of firms in the economy. On the other hand, debt repayment costs tended to crowd out human capital investment and limit the capacity of the nation to expand the funding of public education initiatives. In the 1990s, for instance, nearly 20 percent of the expenditures on education went to tertiary education; however, only about 5 percent of the population had access to tertiary educational opportunities. Individuals in the richest quintile represented 46 percent of the students attending tertiary education, while this figure was less than 4 percent for individuals in the poorest quintile.

Jamaica's economic growth lagged that of other countries in the Caribbean over the period of 1980 to 1996, with the region's growth reaching an average of 3.0 percent, while Jamaica's only achieved 1.4 percent. Still, the 1990s saw a reshaping of the economy that would bring down unemployment from nearly 30 percent in 1980 to nearly 15 percent by the end of the 1990s.

The Jamaican economy began the 2000s with promises and opportunities, and the low bauxite prices of 2000–02 would soon transition to higher prices between 2002 and 2005. Hurricanes Ivan in 2004 and Dennis and Emily in 2005 would foretell a coming economic storm. Jamaica had adopted what appeared to be a countercyclical fiscal policy, such that government expenditures tended to increase during poor economic times to curtain economic downturns. On the surface, this seems to be an appropriate role of the government. However, in the decade beginning in 2000, the capacity of government to support this policy would be challenged.

Along with the strengthening of world bauxite prices, Jamaica's bauxite production reached 14.9 million tonnes (higher than the output 1974). Additionally, alumina made up 67 percent of these exports, compared to 47 percent in 1974. Correspondingly, Jamaica began to seriously talk about improving its processing capacity through greater natural gas imports, investment and usage. The limited budgetary capacity of government meant that this would have to be driven by foreign investment and/or public-private partnership. China was seen as a national partner given the forecasted strong growth in its bauxite demand. Bauxite generates nearly 60 percent of Jamaica's foreign currency, and, on the other hand, the primary use of the country's foreign currency is for oil imports.

The International Monetary Fund reported that the national debt for Jamaica had reached 144 percent of GDP for the fiscal year 2003–04. The composition of this debt involved a large portion held by domestic interests, resulting in the internationally held Jamaican debt being only 77 percent of GDP (Blavy 2006).[10] By 2006–07, government deficits reached J$34,476 million, with interest expenditures (J$97,817 million) nearly twice as high as program spending (J$49,120). Based on Bank of Jamaica Statistical Digest[11] data, wages and salary reached J$78,660 million in the same period; revenues had increased to J$211,625 million, driven by tax revenues of J$188,300; in comparison the tax revenue in 1992–03 was only J$19,050 million.

Jamaica was subject to the global economic downturn, which resulted in a drop in overall economic activity by nearly 1 percent in 2008 and 3 percent in 2009. Nonetheless, the downturn in Jamaica was more modest than in some of the other Caribbean islands (Barbados and Trinidad and Tobago), according to the analysis of Bangwayo-Skeete, Rahim and Zikhali (2011). The economic pressure had already started in 2007 with falling bauxite prices, and the government conducted expansionary fiscal policy (i.e., increased spending) aimed at cushioning the effects on the national economy. By 2009, public debt at US$13.4 billion had reached 135 percent of GDP, with 55 percent held internally (primarily domestic banks, insurance companies and pension funds) and 45 percent externally (primarily by private external bond holders, Inter-American Bank, Caribbean Development Bank and World Bank). This debt had accumulated primarily over the period of 1996 to 2003 (Hurley 2010). The high cost of debt serving was also driven by the high interest rates within the Jamaican economy over an extended period. These realities precipitated the need for debt rescheduling, which was facilitated by a debt swap in 2010, which resulted in an estimated US$525 million in interest savings, or 3.5 percent of GDP for the period 2010 to 2011 (Hurley, Pham and Stewart 2010).

Jamaica has made tremendous progress over the past twenty years to reduce unemployment and the cost of capital in the country, in the process weathering debt and capital storms. Jamaica has experienced a chronic period of total factor productivity (e.g., labour and capital productivity) being relatively low. Investment in research and development is estimated at 0.016 percent of GDP for CARICOM countries, well below the 2–3 percent spent by many developed countries or, put another way, lower than the rate of population growth in the region.

The future holds a new and emerging challenge regarding the performance in the knowledge economy, of which the Internet is often considered to be a prime factor. This view suggests that simply making Internet service available means participation in the knowledge economy. In the 1960s, education and infrastructure were viewed at the two catalysts to economic growth, and Jamaica's economic policy has tended to focus on today's problems that emerged from yesterday's decisions. The scope of the nation's vision will be defined by the knowledge of its people. Hence, tomorrow, it will be knowledge and its application that will define the future of the nation. The fundamental economic problems facing Jamaica do not have a political face; rather, it is about the management and allocation of economic drivers: land, labour, capital and knowledge. Social and political conflicts have proven to be costly to the economy. The ability of Jamaica to establish a governance mechanism that permits problem-solving and conflict resolution without resorting to strong-arm politics and that supports employment opportunity without appeal to the informal economy (as well as criminal activity) will help define the socio-economic climate for the attraction and application of knowledge from Jamaicans inside and outside of the physical boundary of the nation.

Conclusions

The Jamaican economy entered the 1960s and independence with a sense of optimism and enthusiasm. However, there were economic clouds gathering that dated as far back as the development of the sugar beet industry in France and Germany in the 1870s, foretelling a need for productivity gains if the industry was to be competitive in the future. The rise of the U.S. sugar industry and imposition of import restrictions furthered the need for productivity gains. The outflow of capital from the sugar industry reflected these pressures, so the Jamaican government's expenditures to support the industry required action to support productivity gains, not only keeping facilities open.

In the 1940s, the discovery of bauxite in Jamaica led to a new economic driver (ore and mineral acquisition) that spared development and capital investment inflows during the 1950s and 1960s. By the 1970s and 1980s, bauxite production in Guinea, Australia and, eventually, Vietnam and other countries changed the competitive position of Jamaica. The challenges facing the sugar industry over more than a hundred years, starting in the 1870s, was now playing itself out in the bauxite industry less than fifty years after its establishment.

The oil crisis period — 1973 to 1977 — were defining years for the Jamaican economy. The government attempted to insulate the country from imported inflation, through higher oil prices and by controlling imports through the formation of a number of import-export trading companies. The adherence to a pegged exchange rate relative to the U.S. dollar would further cost the government precious foreign currency and infer high interest rates, including restrictive capital markets and foreign currency exchange. Additionally, the Jamaican government became further induced into a policy of import substitution as well as using public ownership as a mechanism for maintaining economic activity in the sector. In Canada, the United States and England, governments also struggled with their role in counter-balancing the impact of the oil crisis and dealing with stagflation (i.e., high unemployment and high consumer goods prices). For instance, wage and price controls were established in Canada in 1975 and remained until 1979.

The Jamaican government made significant financial expenditures to support industry, including the sugar, bauxite, cement, airline, tourism and banking sectors. These efforts were often done through debt financing supported by a monetary policy requiring bank and financial services sector deposit and liquid asset reserves and, in turn, holdings of government securities. This policy contributed to the crowding out of private sector investment and consumer expenditures because of the high cost of capital (i.e., high interest rates) and distorted financial intermediation. High debt servicing costs in turn weakened the government's capacity to effectively respond to the growing demands for education, health care and infrastructure investment. Correspondingly, Jamaican exchange rates were held artificially high for an extended period of time up to the 1990s, thus adversely affecting the export competitiveness of the economy.

Jamaica has struggled to find a reasonable balance between private and public sector involvement in the economy. Correspondingly, the debate has had numerous instances of "strong-arm politics" and violence due to an inadequate problem and dispute resolution mechanism. The economic losses from this violence correspond to the loss of life, increased health costs, drops in remittances and direct foreign investment avoidance. Yet, the social consensus to focus on fundamental drivers of economic growth (e.g., labour productivity, capital formation and knowledge acquisition and its application) remains elusive. On the other hand, the experiences of both the United States and China as well as Brazil and Chile suggest that getting the fundamental economic drivers, education and infrastructure investment supported by an effective government revenue collection framework can lead to productivity and prosperity improvements within a wide range of balance between public and private sector involvement in the economy.

A review of the literature pertaining to the Jamaican economy suggests that a consensus is being formed. Recent tax reforms, for instance, point to a growing understanding that governments must have revenue to support investment in education, health care and infrastructure. There is also a growing consensus that government debt is choking off the vitality of the Jamaican economy and that there is a need to focus on the fundamental drivers of economic growth.

Between 1950 and 1960, Jamaica witnessed a significant out-migration to Britain, the United States and Canada, which inadvertently reduced the pressures on the Jamaica government to meet the growing demands of the population. These individuals left the country at an age when family and personal ties had been fundamentally established and a sense of obligation and belonging adequately forged, which is reflected in their remittances back home. By the 1970s, these remittances were becoming a significant portion of the economy and represented a form of capital flow into the country supporting land purchase and house construction as well as providing an informal safety net to a considerable portion of the society.

In addition to their remittances, Jamaicans in Canada contribute to the Jamaican economy through tourist activities, purchase of export products and investment within the country. Yet, the Jamaican diaspora's greatest contribution is maybe not its remittances but rather the application of its skill, knowledge, management, governance principles and goodwill (i.e., human capital) in support of the nation. This may even be true of Jamaicans in the U.S. and the U.K. Jamaica's ability to engage this capacity will be important in defining its future. However, the demographic profile of Jamaicans in Canada suggests that they will be second, third or even fourth generation, and their ties will likely be more with their new home than with Jamaica unless the engagement is meaningful.

Jamaicans in Canada need a formal mechanism for contributing and engaging human capital in Jamaican society. For instance, this engagement might take the form of serving on the boards of Jamaican private and public sector corporations, agencies and commissions; conducting joint research activities with university colleagues; and investing in joint ventures in Jamaican mutual funds or companies that are cross-listed including those on the Toronto Stock Exchange. The current debt situation of the Jamaican government might potentially result in a focus on the financial capacity of Jamaicans in Canada to support debt financing through bond purchases or even indirect taxation on remittances. These actions may yield short-term benefits for the Jamaican government, but today we need possibilities and opportunities to define the path for the future, a path that will certainly be determined by human capital and Jamaica's ability to engage in the knowledge economy. The knowledge economy is much more than access to the Internet — it is the ability to use research and development to solve technological, engineering, product development and socio-economic challenges for the betterment of members of the society. Ironically, it was Sir Arthur Lewis's work that first formally articulated the concept of human capital, and it may yet be these ideas that save Jamaica.[11]

In 1962, at the time of independence, most of us could not have imagined the year 2012 would be here and we would be reflecting on the economic developments that have shaped the nation. In 2062, the story of the first hundred years of Jamaica will be written. A consensus on the vision of Jamaica and the actions needed to get there are crucial. This requires an understanding that the drivers of economic development are labour productivity, capital formation and knowledge acquisition and its application. We can point to the role of the government and the private sector in fostering these drivers of economic development. On the other hand, we can, as individuals, make choices that support the enhancement of each of these economic drivers by our decisions about education, investment and problem solving. Hence, together government, the private sector and individual Jamaicans will chart the next fifty years of Jamaica's history. Along the journey, Jamaicans in Canada will be making a contribution. Indeed, a portrait of the Jamaican economy includes us all.

Notes

1. Jamaicans reporting Jamaican roots as ethnicity was 65 percent in the 2001 Canadian Census, meaning 35 percent reported multiple ethnic roots as compared to the general population in Canada reporting multiple ethnic roots at 40 percent.
2. <http://www12.statcan.ca/english/census01/products/highlight/ETO/Table1.cfm?T=501&Lang=E&GV=1&GID=0>.
3. <http://www12.statcan.ca/english/census01/products/highlight/ETO/Table1.cfm?T=501&Lang=E&GV=1&GID=35&S=1&O=D>.
4. <http://www12.statcan.ca/english/census01/products/highlight/ETO/Table1.cfm?T=501&Lang=E&GV=2&GID=535&S=1&O=D>.
5. This group is not counted as part of the Statistics Canada census numbers of Jamaicans permanently in Canada.
6. Per capita income is measure here in terms of GDP per capita in current U.S. dollars on a purchasing power parity basis so GDP (PPP) per capita.
7. A history of Jamaican currency is provided by the *Jamaica Gleaner* (2003). Additionally, a history of the currency can be attained through the Bank of Jamaica.
8. Exchange rates are generally considered to be mechanisms for adjusting the relative price of traded goods and services to reflect the relative competitiveness or purchasing power between trading nations. For instance, the devaluation of a currency supports the relative competitiveness of exports while making imports more expensive. It should be noted though that devaluation does not by itself make an economy more productive (e.g., output per capita or per labour hour input when evaluated in real prices or real GDP). Gross domestic product is the value of all goods and services produced in an economy adjusting for exports less imports. Real GDP purges the evaluation from price changes over time so can be considered to be a measure of the amount of overall economy activity in terms of quantity as opposed to nominal value (e.g., quantity multiplied by current prices).
9. It is worth noting that expenditure taxation can be regressive (i.e., not equitable), meaning the poor pay a greater portion of their income in taxes than higher income earners. Hence, there is an issue of taxation policy efficiency versus equity, which remains a challenge for economists and policymakers.
10. The relationship in the portion of a country's public debt held by domestic as opposed to international interests has provided Jamaica with a scope of national debt management that would have otherwise been crippling to the country's economy (e.g., Greece started to hit the debt wall prior to reaching a debt to GDP ratio of 140 percent).
11. <http://www.boj.org.jm/publications/publications_show.php?publication_id=1>.

12. Human capital involves the skills, knowledge, management and values (e.g., governance framework and ethics) applied by individuals to close the gap between desired and existing situations or outcomes through constructive problem solving and/or conflict resolution.

References

Bangwayo-Skeete, P.F., A.H. Rahim, and P. Zikhali. 2011. "Does Education Engender Cultural Values That Matter tor Economic Growth?" *Journal of Socio-Economics* 40, 2.

Bank of Jamaica 2011. *The Balance of Payments Remittance Report.* Kingston, Jamaica: External Sector Statistics Unit, Economic Information & Publications Department, Research and Economic Programming Division.

Blavy, R. 2006. "Public Debt and Productivity: The Difficult Quest for Growth in Jamaica." International Monetary Fund (IMF) — African Department, October, IMF Working Paper No. 06/235. At <http://papers.ssrn.com/sol3/papers.cfm?abstract_id=944073###>.

Guilde, Anne-Marie, Jean Claude Nascimento and Lorena M. Zamalloa. 1997. "Liquid Asset Ratios and Financial Sector Reform." Working paper of the International Monetary Fund, Monetary and Exchange Affairs Department.

Hercog, M., and M. Siegel. 2011. "Promoting Return and Circular Migration of the Highly Skilled." UNU-MERIT working paper. At <http://www.merit.unu.edu/publications/wppdf/2011/wp2011-015.pdf>.

Hurley, Gail, Minh H. Pham, and Machel Stewart. 2010. "Discussion Paper — Jamaica's Debt Exchange: A Case Study for Heavily Indebted Middle-Income Countries." United Nations Development Programme, Bureau for Development Policy, New York.

Jamaica Gleaner. 2003. "Money — The Roots of Jamaican Currency." March 10.

____. 2008. "Financial Crisis and the Jamaican Economy." October 19. At <http://jamaica-gleaner.com/gleaner/20081019/focus/focus1.html>.

King, Damien, and Latoya Richards. 2008. "Jamaica's Debt: Exploring Causes and Strategies." Caribbean Policy Research Institute Policy, Caribbean Policy Research Institute, Kingston, Jamaica, Paper #W0801.

Lindsay, Colin. 2001. *Profiles of Ethnic Communities in Canada: The Jamaican Community in Canada, Social and Aboriginal Statistics Division.* Statistics Canada, Catalogue no. 89-621-XIE-No. 12, Ottawa, Ontario.

Ross, L. 2006. *Migrant Workers in Canada: A Review of the Canadian Seasonal Agricultural Workers Program.* Ontario: The North-South Institute.

Statistical Digest. *Bank of Jamaica.* Various issues. At <http://www.boj.org.jm/publications/publications_show.php?publication_id=1>.

Statistics Canada. 2001. *Selected Ethnic Origins, for Canada, Provinces and Territories —* 20% Sample Data, Ontario. At <http://www12.statcan.ca/english/census01/products/highlight/ETO/Table1.cfm?T=501&Lang=E&GV=1&GID=35&S=1&O=D>.

____. 2001. *Selected Ethnic Origins, for Census Metropolitan Areas and Census Agglomerations —* 20% Sample Data, Toronto. At <http://www12.statcan.ca/english/census01/products/highlight/ETO/Table1.cfm?T=501&Lang=E&GV=2&GID=535&S=1&O=D>.

28. WORKING TO BETTER THE LIVES OF JAMAICA'S CHILDREN

Armand P. La Barge

Some of you may know that I am fifty percent Newfoundlander and I spent a great deal of my childhood summer vacations in the tiny central Newfoundland community of Botwood. If you have ever visited the rock before, you know that Newfoundlanders like Jamaicans go out of their way to make visitors feel at home. To become an honorary Newfoundlander, all one has to do is drink a shot of Jamaican Rum, known on the island as Screech, kiss a codfish on the mouth and answer the question, "Is ye an honorary Newfoundlander?" with the phrase "Indeed I is me ol' cock, and long may your big jib draw."

I am told by my good friend Dr. Sylvanus Thompson that becoming an honorary Jamaican citizen is a little more difficult. He told me to become an honorary Jamaican you have to be able to run 100 metres in 9.58 seconds like Trewlany's Usain Bolt; bowl a cricket ball as fast as Kingston's Michael Holding; punch as hard as Port Antonio's Trevor Berbick; create a worldwide movement to feed and house the poor and disabled like Kingston's Father Richard Ho Lung; lead a rebellion against an oppressive regime like Morant Bay's Paul Bogle and Montego Bay's Samuel Sharpe; emancipate and unify the minds of an entire race of people like St. Ann's Marcus Garvey; draft a constitution and lead a nation to independence like Hanover's Sir Alexander Bustamante and Manchester's Norman Manley; become the chancellor of a university like Kingston's Ray Chang; create a billion dollar financial empire like Port Antonio's Michael Lee Chin; become a member of Parliament and provincial minister like Clarendon's Margaret Best; lead an international bank like Kingston's Dr. Mary Anne Chambers; become the president of the Ontario Conference of Seven Day Adventists like Stoney Hill's Reverend Dr. Mansfield Edwards; found a radio station and black business professional association like Negril — the King of Cool's Denham Jolly; and sing and perform like Johnny Osbourne, Millie Small, Lee "Scratch" Perry, Peter Tosh, Bunny Wailer, Big Youth, Jimmy Cliff, Dennis Brown, Desmond

Dekker, Shaggy, Grace Jones, Shabba Ranks, Super Cat, Sean Paul, I Wayne, Manchester's Byron Lee and the Dragonaires, St. Ann's Bob Marley and the Wailers, and Kingston and the world's Louise Bennett-Coverley, or Miss Lou. On reflection, kissing the cod and drinking a shot of Jamaican Rum or Newfoundland Screech doesn't sound all the bad now.

I have said it before and I will say it again there are now over seven billion people in this world, and it never ceases to amaze me how much of an impact the population of the tiny island nation of Jamaica and its diaspora have had on this globe. Here in Canada we only have to look at individuals such as Audrey Campbell, Bromley Armstrong, Pat Howell, Dr. Mavis Burke, Dr. Alvin Curling, Dr. Herbert Carnegie, Dr. Lincoln Alexander, Dr. Vince and Fay Conville, Dr. Sylvanus Thompson, Dr. Pamela Appelt, Deputy Chief Peter Sloly and Dudley Laws, to name but a few, to appreciate how Canadians of Jamaican heritage have helped make Canada one of the greatest countries in the world.

Dr. Thomas Lickona is a developmental psychologist and professor of education at New York's State University. He directs the Center for the Fourth and Fifth Rs — Respect and Responsibility — and I am a firm believer in his saying that "a child is the only known substance from which a responsible adult can be made." That's why PACE Canada and organizations like the Missionaries of the Poor, Future Aces, the Markham African Caribbean Association and the Jamaican Canadian Association are so important. The dedicated people in these organizations are working hard to provide children the tools they need to not just survive but to succeed in this very competitive world, and I would urge everyone to support them in any way you can.

As you have heard, I have had the pleasure of travelling to Jamaica each year for the past several years along with a number of my former colleagues from York Regional Police. There we work in Father Richard Ho Lung's missions on Hanover, Tower and Highholborn Streets in downtown Kingston and at the Beatitudes Home on Mount Taber at Iron River, Constant Spring near Stony Hill. Father Richard Ho Lung is the Superior General of a world-wide religious congregation that he founded in 1981 known as the Missionaries of the Poor.

Somewhere along Davis Ahlowalia's journey through life, he became interested in policing, and he left the priesthood and became a member of York Regional Police.[1] Davis nonetheless continued to visit and work in the missions in Kingston and in India, and one day he appeared at the Chief's office at HQ and asked if we could do anything to help support Father Ho Lung and the important work he was doing in Jamaica. Davis had only been on a year at that time and I could not help but admire his courage, his conviction and his overwhelming desire to help those in need. We decided then and there to adopt Father Ho Lung's Stony Hill mission in Jamaica, and we decided to send a team of officers there to work alongside Davis and the brothers. Sadly, we never got the opportunity to go there together. At the age of twenty-eight years, Davis was killed in an off-duty motor vehicle collision just north of Woodbridge (north of Toronto). Our work in Father Ho Lung's missions in Kingston and Stony Hill and our work with PACE Canada is our way of keeping Constable Davis Ahlowalia's legacy of helping others alive, but it is also our way of saying thanks to the people of Jamaica for helping make their adopted homeland of Canada one of the greatest countries in the world.

When my wife Denise and I first learned about the work that PACE Canada was doing to advance childhood education in Jamaica from Lorna King and Dr. Mary Anne and Chris Chambers, we jumped at the opportunity to get involved. We jumped at the opportunity to get involved because both of us know from the work of the late Dr. Fraser Mustard how important it is to better the lives of children by focusing on early childhood education and development. That's what Basic Schools do in Jamaica and that's what Basic Schools that are supported by PACE Canada do very well.

When Tony Browne, Errol Lee, Don Yirenkyi, Pat Brown and Ricky Veerappan and I were helping rebuild homes in some of the most impoverished and crime ridden areas of Trench Town after Hurricane Katrina, we used to watch the little boys smartly dressed in their khaki uniforms and little girls in their blue skirts and white blouses make their way to and from school. We often commented on the fact that you couldn't tell from watching these kids whether they were from Trench Town or Beverly Hills. You couldn't tell whether they lived in a ten foot by ten foot house south of Torrington Bridge on Maiden Lane in what the Jamaica Constabulary call an Unplanned Urban Development or in a three thousand square foot home on Montclair Drive, Kingston 6, or in Mona Heights or Barbican. That's because, as Horace Mann once said, "Education is, beyond all other devices of human origin, the great equalizer of the conditions of men and women. It is the balance wheel of the social machinery" (Mann, 1868: 669).

Education allows an individual to put their full potential to maximum use because it gives us greater insight into the world around us. Education provides us with a perspective of looking at life, and the right education helps us develops opinions and points of view on everything. Education enables us to convert information to knowledge, and it enables us to learn from the experiences of Rosa Parks and Martin Luther King, Terry Fox and Rick Hansen, Dr. Herbert H. Carnegie and Dr. Avis Glaze, Barrack Obama and His Honour Lincoln Alexander, to name but a few. Someone far wiser than me once said, "You can't make this world safe for democracy until you make it safe for diversity."[2] Education can shatter stereotypes and wrongly held myths, and it helps us develop opinions and points of view on poverty and the dispossessed, on crime and civil rights, on the environment and on domestic violence and on such inhumane aspects of world history as racism, discrimination and slavery. Education teaches us the right behaviour, and most importantly — education teaches us how to lead our lives.

Tony Browne and I and about eight other members of York Regional Police had the opportunity after working in Father Ho Lung's mission for a week to visit our adopted school — the Brooks Level Basic School in Stony Hill — last year. We took full advantage of the opportunity to spend some time with Principal Patricia Sayers, her seven dedicated teachers and the sixty-nine boys and sixty-one girls who make up the student population. It was inspiring to see these boys and girls ranging in age from three to six years smartly dressed in their school uniforms learning how to read and write and count. The teachers and the students were ecstatic to receive the colouring and children's books, the crayons, pencils and rulers that we brought with us. We were ecstatic to see that the money we had contributed through PACE Canada was used to paint the school, to purchase tape recorders, DVD players and charts for the classrooms and to fund lunch and graduation programs and table top activities and aids for the students.

Thirty-five days from now we will be celebrating Christmas. As you know Christmas means much more than sitting down to a meal of ackee with salted fish, baked ham, curry goat, rice and gungo peas, mouth-watering stewed ox tail and a glass of sorrel. Christmas in Jamaica and Canada is a time of great giving and great love. The sons and daughters of Jamaica and the Caribbean have given a lot to this country and to this world, and I am confident that the grandsons and granddaughters of Jamaica will continue to do their part to make this world a safer, a more inclusive and a more caring and place in which to live by supporting the groundbreaking work of organizations like PACE Canada.

What better way to end my remarks then with the moving words of Hugh Sherlock's "Jamaica — Land We Love": "May the Eternal Father bless our two lands, may he guide us with his mighty hand, and may he keep us free from evil powers and be our light through countless hours."[3] Thank You.

Notes

This chapter is a portion of a speech given at the annual PACE Canada Adopt-a-School Brunch, held at the Jamaican Canadian Centre in Toronto on November 20, 2011. It was the day that the United Nations and the Canadian government have recognized as the International Day of the Child and recognition that all children and youth have inherent rights, which can be defined as those basic things that are necessary to live and grow with dignity as human beings. Children have rights to a supportive family, to the protection from all forms of harm and to the provision of adequate food, clothes, housing and education.

1.   Davis Ahlowalia was raised in York Region (north of Toronto) and as a young

man entered the seminary in Toronto to become a priest. He studied with some of Father Ho Lung's Missionaries of the Poor and became fascinated in with the work that they were doing in Jamaica and around the world. Davis visited the missions in Kingston and India several times and worked alongside the brothers feeding the poor, tending to the sick and orphans, and comforting the dying.

2. Speech by His Highness the Aga Khan IV (2006) to the School of International and Public Affairs, Columbia University.

3. Adaption of the opening lines of the Jamaican National Anthem.

References

Mann, H. 1868. "Twelfth Annual Report to the Massachusetts State Board of Education." In M. Mann (ed.), *Life and Works of Horace Mann* (Vol. 3). Boston: Walker, Fuller and Co.

Aga Khan IV. 2006. "Speech by His Highness the Aga Khan to the School of International and Public Affairs, Columbia University." At <http://www.amaana.org/agakhan/speechcolumbia506.htm>.

Jamaican National Anthem. 1962. *Jamaica: Land We Love.*

29. PROJECT GROUNDINGS

Canadian and JamaicanYouth [Re]Define Violence

Andrea Davis

Reflection One: Chantel Dunn

Early Tuesday morning, February 7, 2006, Chantel Dunn, a second-year York University student majoring in business and society, died from gun-shot wounds she received the night before while driving in the Jane and Sheppard area, close to the university campus. The nineteen year old, nicknamed Angel by her family, had just picked up her boyfriend from a basketball game when gun shots engulfed their vehicle. The car she was driving crashed into a nearby home. Her boyfriend, who was also shot, managed to escape the vehicle and tried to flee the scene. He survived and is believed by police to have been the intended target in the shooting. He has never cooperated with the police, and the case remains unsolved.

When I first heard that a York University student had been shot, my body went into a state of physical shock that lasted several minutes, because nobody told me, but I knew she was Black. I was not at home. I received the news second-hand and I called my friends, "What is her name?" Nobody knew; it took about a day to find her name and to realize that she was not actually one of my students. But it did not matter, because she could have been. Chantel was an honour roll, bilingual student with hopes of becoming a lawyer. She came from a close, nurturing extended suburban family. Her life, her dreams were tied up with those of every Jamaican immigrant family in Canada, most of them moving to this country in search of a "better" life for their children. Yet, the country mourned for Jane Creba but did not mourn for Chantel Dunn. Her death affected me deeply. She was of Jamaican descent; I needed to own her. She was first-generation Canadian; this country had a right to protect her. She was a York University student; I have a responsibility to remember her.

> *The pickney dem a dry*
> *The youths dem a cry*
> *The pickney dem a dry*
> *Like the clothes pon de line*[1]

Canada and Jamaica and Shared Narratives of Violence

Canada and Jamaica have been linked historically through shared political ties to Britain and through ongoing political and economic initiatives. The transformation of Canadian immigration laws in the 1960s further encouraged an increasing number of Jamaican immigrants to choose Canada over the United States or England as a preferred country of settlement. More recently, however, the countries have also been linked in reports of violence, as violence has become a global concern. In 2005, Jamaica and Canada experienced a marked increase in violent deaths particularly in the urban centres of Kingston and Toronto. Amnesty International (2009) reported Jamaica's murder rate as the highest in the world in 2005 when it peaked at 1,674 (a rate of 60 per100,000). Alternately, in Toronto, the media dubbed 2005, "The Year of the Gun," because of the sharp increase in gun-related homicides in the city most of them involving young Black males, which almost doubled over the previous year and culminated in the Boxing Day shooting of Jane Creba, a White Canadian girl. What was most shocking about Jane Creba's death was the fact that it shifted the terrain of violence beyond the boundaries of ethnic minority enclaves in Toronto and positioned it in the sacred heart of the multicultural city. For the first time, Torontonians realized they could no longer simply register uneasiness with near daily occurrences of violence or dismiss them as problems relegated to visible-minority, low-income communities.

More recently, on May 3, 2010, police arrested seventy-eight people in Ontario, about a dozen of whom were alleged members of Jamaica's Shower Posse. According to media reports, the Shower Posse had wide networks extending from Toronto to Windsor and Sault Ste. Marie and back to the Caribbean (Freeze 2010). In the same month, efforts in Jamaica to execute a US extradition order against the Shower Posse's leader, Christopher (Dudus) Coke, resulted in the deaths of more than seventy Jamaicans and reports of widespread human rights abuses by Jamaican security forces.

What is striking about the patterns of violence proliferating in cities like Kingston and Toronto is that a disproportionate number of violent crimes involve youth. The Inter-American Commission of Human Rights (2008) confirmed that between 2003 and 2008, 398 children were killed violently in Jamaica and another 441 were injured by guns. In addition, many of the people reportedly killed by police were adolescent youth. In 2000, twenty to twenty-five year-old males were also identified as the principal offenders in all types of major crimes in Jamaica and accounted for 37 percent of all murders in that year (World Bank 2003). Between 1995 and 2005, 45 percent of homicide victims in Toronto were Black, representing a 300 percent increase from the previous decade (Janhevich,

Bania and Hastings 2009). Of the seventy-nine murder victims in Toronto in 2005, more than forty were young Black men, and at least three were young Black women.

While Jamaica has had a national youth policy in place since 1974, Canada has yet to carry out an in-depth review of the situation of its youth or develop a youth policy framework (Franke 2010; McMurtry and Curling 2008). As Franke (2010) rightly argues, based on the context and changing realities of Canadian youth today, the time is right to assess all the emerging challenges facing this important segment of the population. Alternately, while Jamaica's youth policy has sought to decrease anti-social behaviour and develop strategies for youth participation, decision-making and social and economic development, studies about Jamaican youth continue to see them as merely reacting to the situations in which they find themselves rather than as critical agents who can bring about social change (World Bank 2003). Many youth programs exist, but little is known about their effectiveness.

Reflection Two: Shauna-Kaye Shaw

On Sunday, July 31, 2011, I held hands with Woodside residents in a small rural village in St. Mary, Jamaica, chanting "The Pickney Dem a Dry" with Jamaica Youth Theatre, thinking of Chantel Dunn, and weeping uncontrollably for Shauna-Kaye Shaw, another young woman I had never met. Six months earlier, villagers discovered her body close to the Woodside Community Centre in which we stood. The seventeen year-old youth leader had been missing from home from the day before, and concerned villagers had organized a search. When they found her, she had been sexually assaulted, stabbed and her throat slashed. Residents suspect she was murdered by a young man who had recently moved into the village and whose advances she may have spurned. Two men were arrested and charged and are awaiting trial. Her death was shocking for the close-knit community that had never experienced violence in this way. Violence might happen elsewhere, far away, but not in this "mossy covert, dim and cool" (Brodber 1980: 9).

The feelings of grief and the sense of recognition on that July afternoon were too painfully familiar. Another shining light of her family and community was gone too early, without any formal leave-taking. As I wept for these two women to whom I was now linked, I understood something of the enormity of my responsibility as a scholar involved in community-based research. As a Black woman of Jamaican descent, I am framed by the communities I work in and study—Canada and Jamaica—both places delineate the borders of my experiences. Here I was in Woodside, trying to do something called community research, holding the memory of a Toronto girl and weeping for another. What did these two young women have in common? How were their lives linked by violence and pain and loss across two national boundaries I claimed? As members charged us to "Live up! Live up!" I wondered how the research I do could live up to the weight of such recognitions.

Live up! Live up!
We all bleed red!
Live up! Live up!
We all bleed red!

Project Groundings

The research project that took me from Toronto to Woodside, St. Mary, is a Social Science and Humanities Research Council of Canada funded partnership titled Project Groundings.[2] The project employs a holistic approach to youth development to explore new approaches to youth violence. By defining violence in its broadest terms, it seeks to increase public awareness of the causes and effects of violence among Canadian and Jamaican youth. Rather than assuming that Black youth are naturally predisposed to risk, the initiative examines how systemic and social violence (such as racism and poverty), as well as physical and gendered violence, mediate in the lives of some youth and disrupt their desires to function as engaged citizens by promoting feelings of social isolation and cultural estrangement. Since violent crimes in Canada continue to be linked in the popular Canadian imagination with performances of Jamaican masculinity, the study also explores how a greater appreciation of Jamaican society and culture (both rural and urban) might help Black Canadian youth develop an understanding of self that can challenge the stereotypes evident in Canadian society and produce the critical discourse needed to (re)insert themselves as active agents in their communities. By helping youth rearticulate their social identities through arts-based programs, history and literature, the project seeks to change the behaviour and action of those youth most affected by violence.

The partnership brings together researchers from five Canadian universities as well as the University of the West Indies (Mona). It also includes three community partners: JYT in Kingston, the Woodside Development Action Group in St. Mary, and Nia Centre for the Arts in Toronto. JYT and Woodside provide the research team with models of successful youth engagement in urban and rural Jamaica, which we hope to replicate and expand in Toronto, allowing for a critical assessment of a range of shared approaches to youth development.

The research partnership launched in summer 2011 with two youth forums: one in Kingston on July 28 and the other in Woodside on July 31. A third youth forum took place in Toronto on January 21, 2012. Canadian and Jamaican youth travelled to meet each other in their respective countries to participate in all three events[3] and together confronted issues related to systemic and physical violence and initiated conversations about how they might interrupt these complex patterns of violence.

The most important revelation of the conversations among the three groups of youth has been their consistent prioritization of systemic violence (poverty in Jamaica and racism in Canada) over physical and gendered violence. While youth do not ignore the latter, they see these expressions of violence as linked and as byproducts of social alienation, poverty and racism. In the rest of this chapter, I provide a summary and critical analysis of the youth forum findings. Since these forums were meant to prioritize the voices and opinions of youth, I structure the summaries so that the voices of Jamaican and Canadian youth frame the academic debates and analysis.

Poverty as Systemic Violence and Effects on Education, Employment and Socialization

> *Male youth at Kingston forum*: Well, for one, right now my main priority, it was crime and violence, but right now it's just poverty, really. I am trying to stay out of poverty. Being a student, I am unemployed. Travelling from August Town to Rock Fort on a daily basis is $320 on bus fares only. That does not include a bag juice, you see what I'm saying? I'm not working. Where, where should I work? I'm doing a course in general construction. They don't have any work in that field that I can do part time.

> *Male youth at Kingston forum*: Once you are coming out of a poor home, you're not expected to become nutten good. Yuh know, the stigma, let me talk about the stigma. You have four schools downtown on North Street and the only ghetto school down there is Trinity. KC is not a ghetto school; George's is not a ghetto school; Alpha is not a ghetto school because those are traditional high schools, and all of those schools encircle Trinity, but Trinity is the ghetto school. So the way that you're stigmatized also is a very big problem for us as young people and you function accordingly. Now you're living in Cherry Gardens, which is uptown, they're not going to come and put a police post at your community. As a matter of fact, if you're going to do that you have to write a letter stating that you're going to do it. Nobody asked Tivoli Gardens if they want a police post put down there or the one at Denham Town. So these things, they treat you according to the geographical area which you are in.

In both the Kingston and St. Mary youth forums, youth identified poverty as the most debilitating violence they experienced. In the Kingston youth forum, youth particularly lamented the lack of access to education and training, which was precipitated by poverty. The inability to secure bus fares and lunch money or to buy uniforms means that many youth cannot participate in educational training as often or consistently as they desire. Extra classes are expensive and sometimes exclusive, and students are being ejected from exam rooms because of unpaid tuition. Youth also acknowledged that lack of education means greater unemployment, trapping them in cycles of poverty and underachievement. They believed the education system should place more emphasis on "ordinary" skills and professions, and they wanted schools to focus more on diverse arts, including spoken word, dance and visual arts.

Youth also linked poverty to the ways they had been socialized and positioned in Jamaican society. They identified this largely in relation to geographic location and social class and community groupings (country versus town, uptown versus downtown). Since class lines are easily identifiable through neighbourhoods, youth who live in poor communities suffer from deeply entrenched stereotypes and negative stigmatization, which makes it difficult for them to secure employment and improve their social status. Youth felt stigmatized if they wore certain clothes or attended particular schools. They were also discriminated against based on political affiliations identifiable through community location.

Rural Jamaican youth identified similar difficulties as their urban counterparts, prioritizing their challenges in the same order, that is, poverty as their most immediate experience of systemic violence. Speaking from a rural context, youth also identified a lack of facilities and resources as a major concern and expressed feelings of alienation resulting from few recreational and developmental opportunities. Where they could find resources and facilities, transportation fees, poor roads and other obstacles to travel were major deterrents to social and civic participation and personal advancement. While they recognized the necessity of agricultural pursuits, a lack of crop diversification and financial compensation was increasingly forcing them to abandon agriculture and entrenching them even more deeply in poverty.

> *Male youth at Woodside forum*: For the most effective [strategies] we put hustling and for the non-effective farming, 'cause meanwhile you get tired a dat yuh move inna something else. But dem nah get the good money when dem just move inna farming. The money nuh really a come in same time, so as a youth now we jus a jump outta dat and jump inna de quickest way fi mek money.

> *Female youth at Woodside forum*: There was a youth group here and since January, the death of Shauna-Kaye, there hasn't been much things going on in this community. So you find people being unemployed without any kind of activities to do, yuh know? And, if you don't keep your mind active, you're going to find something else to do with it.

The Kingston and Woodside youth's identification of the damaging social and personal effects of poverty on Jamaican youth is supported by a number of studies. According to UNICEF (2004), people living in poverty face enduring obstacles that prevent them from experiencing their most fundamental human rights. In addition, poverty reduces the economic, physical and psychological resources available to families (Ashiabi 2000). Smith and Ashiabi (2007: 840–41), who look specifically at the effects of poverty on Jamaican children and youth, link expressions of physical violence directly to poverty and confirm that Jamaican children are disproportionately poor: "In Jamaica, children under 18 years account for 39% of the Jamaican population but 50% of people who live in poverty; one in every four Jamaican children is poor with the highest percentage (28.4%) living in rural areas." Their study further corroborates that 31 percent of Jamaican youth aged fifteen to twenty-four are unemployed (841) and that school attendance among poor Jamaican youth is problematic (845). Again, according to the Inter-American Commission on Human Rights (2008), violence unduly affects the poorest sectors of the Jamaican population, especially women and children who are often forced to make incredibly difficult choices to survive.

Physical and Sexual Violence

> *Female Youth at Kingston forum*: There are young girls who are prostituting themselves for money and they're doing it in front of their parents. So, what we have are little girls on the corner. There is no money in the home; they need to eat. Mommy realizing that she either have a boyfriend or she is doing this decides to leave her alone, to not pay any school fee, to not take care of her anymore because you have a man now. So, Mommy say, "Yow! You have a man! Gwaan now, me nah wan nutten fi do wid yuh cause you have man now! Gwan go do weh you a do!" So Mommy is passing her between the legs of a forty year-old man and just looking at her and just walking up the road. And I don't know if Mommy doesn't realize that she is also guilty and committing a crime. But Mommy has given up. So the child needs to eat [and] the child cannot get a job outside of selling her body because this is what she knows.

Closely linked to questions of poverty and unemployment for Jamaican youth were questions of physical and sexual violence. Youth insisted, for example, that poverty contributed directly to child labour and sex work. They described incidents of children being taken out of school by parents to work in family businesses or the sex trade and to perform transactional sex. Many of these children, in attempting to escape abuse at home become abused on the streets where they are also unprotected. In some communities there is also a culture of sexual abuse where dons[4] have control over women. Youth were careful, however, to also identify the sexual agency of girls who enter sex work despite their parents' objections or choose to have relationships with older men to escape poverty and advance their educational and long-term goals. Still, youth problematized this agency by criticizing parents' abdication of their parental responsibilities. Most importantly, youth felt unprotected by the Child Care Protection Act, which they insisted does not adequately enforce the law.

Amnesty International (2006) supports the expressions of concern about explicit violence against youth and women voiced in the Jamaican forums. Expressions of social unease about violence have also been proliferating in the Jamaican media as Jamaicans struggle to find answers to these pressing problems (Sinclair and Barrett 2012; Gloudon 2011; Reid 2011). While Sinclair and Barrett (2012) reveal significant increases in incidences of rape between 2010 and 2011, Gloudon (2011) blames the increasingly grotesque nature of violence on gangs, which use extreme violence as a way of intimi-dating their rivals and controlling poor communities.

Importantly, increases in violent crimes in Jamaica have also been blamed on the failure of North American societies to socialize and integrate youth into full social participation. Bernard Headley (2006), in his discussion of deportees, focuses on the public perception in Jamaica that the country's soaring crime rate can be linked directly to the growing numbers of former emigrants being forcibly returned "home" from the United States, Britain and Canada. When Canadian residents who have spent all of their forma-tive years in Canada are deported to Jamaica, they rarely have families or communities to reintegrate them into Jamaican society and have no sense of national or civic loyalty, encouraging ongoing and more deeply entrenched participation in criminal activities. Thus, violence in Canada and Jamaica is neither discrete nor unrelated.

Racism and Social Disengagement in Canada

> *Male youth at Toronto forum*: My biggest challenge in Toronto is racism. I have an Italian name. When they see my name, they're expect-ing someone else when I apply for jobs. I used to drive a very nice vehicle, and I would be automatically pulled over [by the police]. So stereotypes are my biggest issue.

> *Female youth at Toronto forum*: People are homogenized in a black group. Toronto people don't take time to learn about each other. They have Taste of the Danforth and Caribana to distract us. They talk about

Jamaica as a race. They have stereotypes and expectations of you and they're negative. They don't give people a chance.

At the youth forum in Toronto in January 2012, youth addressed the conviction that Canada is failing its youth and that this failure is experienced directly as both systemic and physical violence. Youth identified racism as their greatest concern and felt they were negatively stereotyped based on their age, "race" and perceived social class as mostly first- or second-generation immigrants. When speaking about violence in relation to sexual, gender and physical aggression, youth linked this violence consistently to racism and attributed this violence to specific social and racial markers: male, Black, young, priority neighbourhoods. By linking race and class, youth identified ongoing physical violence as largely affecting "inner-city," racialized communities. They identified young Black men as the most exposed to the effects of both physical and systemic violence and critiqued, in particular, the ways in which male youth are stereotyped and targeted by the police. In further discussing the ways stereotypes are constructed and deployed, Toronto youth explicitly critiqued Canada's tendency to homogenize blackness as a problematic performance of Jamaicanness.

Education Practices and Systemic Violence

> *Female youth at Toronto forum*: Kids are not learning about their history. If you don't know yourself then how will you move forward. If they change the syllabus to represent diverse histories then people can better understand themselves and move forward.

> *Male youth at Toronto forum:* I think teachers should really know how to deal with students. I don't know like teaching students something; like knowing how students learn. Like you're teaching them business and they're not engaged and you say "that's how they are." But if that's the case, you're not a [good] teacher.

At the forefront of youth's discussions in Toronto were also expressions of deep dissatisfaction with Canadian education practices. Youth articulated systemic violence most often in terms of the racism they encountered in the education system. In this regard, youth made no distinctions in the challenges faced at the elementary, secondary or postsecondary levels. The general consensus was that there is a lack of explicit policy guidelines on the part of administrators, and apathy and incompetence on the part of educators. In a 2006 Student Census conducted by Yau and O'Reilly, seventy-two percent of grades 7–8 students agreed that learning about their culture or racial background would make learning more interesting for them. Students also believed they would do better in school if they could learn about their history in the classroom. In line with these findings, youth at the Toronto forum demanded changes in school curricula to express the cultural history of Black people. They saw this as essential to addressing youth's disengagement in Canadian society.

At the heart of both Jamaican and Canadian youth, then, is this deep desire to advance their life chances through education and to participate as full and engaged citizens in their societies. Still, there is the overwhelming belief that their societies for different reasons withhold these possibilities. Most Jamaican parents who choose to migrate to Canada or the United States are motivated precisely by the desire of better education opportunities for their children. Yet, Jamaican immigrant students entering the Canadian educational system are negatively labeled by the fact of their migration and are expected to have difficulty integrating into Canadian society. Many of these students are streamed, without adequate assessment, into special ed programs. African Canadian children who have difficulties with their teachers are also labeled as 'behavioural' or learning disabled and placed in specialized classes, which effectively bars them from more advanced levels of study (Codjoe 2001).

> *Male youth at Toronto forum*: I believe that school is not for everybody. I got kicked out of school in grade nine and I realized my skills and I put myself to work and have been successful. We need to realize that there are alternatives for other people. I have nothing against the idea of learning to advance oneself [but] I believe everything that I have to learn comes from within, understanding my lineage, my history, etc.

> *Female youth at Toronto forum*: There is discussion of school not being for everyone. I find that bothersome because there needs to be a reality check. We need to be real about how people can be successful in Canadian society. You can't even explore some of these other options without a high school option. Maybe we need to talk about including students in programs in the K-12 education process.

Students' disengagement results precisely from experiences of negative social and racial stereotyping in the classroom. Since racialized students are not exposed to curricula that reflect the complexities and contestations of Canadian history and are offered instead an education that reproduces Euro-Canadian privilege and power, they feel excluded from access to empowering and creative education opportunities. James and Brathwaite (1996: 30) go further to demand that the deliberate exclusion of Black experiences from Canadian classrooms be recognized as a specific kind of violence:

These "acts of violence" must be eliminated from the education system. The schools with our input must provide resources that will truly educate black students as well as others to survive in the complex global community of which we are all a part. The changes that are sought in curriculum cannot wait for another generation.

Perhaps not unsurprisingly, data from the 2006 Toronto District School Board reveals that the dropout rate for Black youth is high and highest among English-speaking youth of Caribbean descent at forty percent. Most of these dropouts were young men born in Canada to Caribbean parents—the very children considered likely to inherit their parents' dreams. At the Toronto forum, some youth reflected this sense of deep disaffection from the Canadian education process while others although critical of the system, were willing to find ways to work within it.

Youth Empowering Themselves and Other Youth

Male Youth at Kingston forum: We need to within ourselves think that okay I am going to make the change. The change begins with me. No matter what society say I am going to make a difference in society. And if we can't do that, we are going to continue down the path, okay, my father was a robber. My father was a gunman. I'm going to follow in that line because that's as I see it. And I'm not seeing anyone to say, yow, I'm going to take a stand. And I think that we as young people need to start doing that, taking the stand, taking the responsibility for everything that we do because we have the choice to do or not to do.

Male Youth at Toronto forum: People have to learn how to define themselves and not pay attention to what people think. People stereotype Black men as violent and if people continue to define them that way then they will behave this way unless they resist this consciously and say they will define themselves differently.

Youth's insistence on surviving against all odds was echoed in all three forums. They consistently demonstrated attitudes of resiliency and were willing to take responsibility for and ownership of their futures. Youth insisted they were important contributors to their societies and encouraged each other to take initiative. In particular, they felt they needed to rethink definitions of success and be more creative in their career and life choices. All three sets of youth also confirmed their belief in the importance of the arts in personal healing and social and civic engagement. Overall, youth agreed that the arts play a positive role in their development and that they could achieve positive changes in thought and cultural socialization through arts-based programs.

Conclusion

In all three youth forums, youth recognized that childhood and youth are heterogeneous and socially negotiated categories and that there are significant disparities in the experiences of children and youth from varying racial, class and geographic locations. These youth, thus, delineated in powerful ways the specific problems they faced, in all instances prioritizing the systemic violence of poverty and racism above physical violence.

For the youth participating in the Jamaican forums, the challenge was how to retain their potential to function as viable and engaged citizens despite the overwhelming odds that appeared stacked against them. By naming poverty as the most ingrained and enduring violence they experience, youth called upon each other, their government, educators and parents to recognize both their vulnerability and enormous potential. While youth were movingly honest, they were also incredibly hopeful and passionately desired the opportunity to shape their futures in the most positive ways, identifying education, integration into the workforce, and economic stability as primary goals.

Youth in Toronto, like youth in Jamaica, insisted on identifying physical violence only in relation to larger, more pervasive systemic violence. In this case, they identified racism, particularly as it is expressed at all levels of the education system as the greatest challenge they face. While Jamaican youth identified an unwilling disengagement from school because of a lack of resources, Black Canadian youth in resource-rich schools confirmed that they often willfully disengage. This disengagement results from being constantly marginalized and estranged from processes of learning in which they are stereotyped and culturally erased. While some Canadian youth felt entirely alienated from the education process, others continued to demand ongoing changes in school curriculum to express the diverse cultural histories of Black people and their contributions to Canadian society.

Reflection Three: Chantel Dunn and Shauna-Kaye Shaw

As I look back at the first year of this project, the daunting sense of responsibility has not waned, but I am more persistently optimistic that the work we do as researchers in and around our communities has enormous value. When I first started this project, I had no idea where it would take me. I had already faced Chantel Dunn, but I did not anticipate Shauna-Kaye Shaw. As a research team, we chose Woodside because it was so safe, so protected from the violence that stalks Kingston. Woodside was to be a model of community development where Black Canadian youth, long lamenting the absence of Black history in their classrooms, could learn about the interrelated histories of people of African descent, could reenact narratives of Emancipation and be reunited into an African diasporic com-munity. Woodside will still be all of these things, but on that fateful July afternoon as we held each other and cried, we recognized more powerfully than any of us could have imagined how much we need each other—Jamaica and Canada reaching out of necessity across two worlds divided by race, class, gender and geography but linked by our pain and our relentless desire for healing. I offer this chapter in humble memory of Chantel Dunn and Shauna-Kaye Shaw, the two women I carry with me now.

Live up! Live up!
We all bleed red!
Live up! Live up!
We all bleed red!

Notes

1. *The Pickney Dem a Dry* is a performance piece that resulted from a collaborative arts project between Jamaica Youth Theatre and a youth group in Denmark, in which youth created a theatre piece around photographs of graffiti in Kingston, Jamaica. In the performance, participants write the names of young people who have died violently, hang them on a clothes line and speak a sentence about who they were. The performance importantly acknowledges a shared humanity among youth. It also challenges us to take responsibility, to "Live up! Live up!"
2. The formal title of the project is "Youth and Community Development in Canada and Jamaica: A Transnational Approach to Youth Violence."
3. Rural and urban youth, as well as Toronto youth participated in both Jamaican forums. Jamaican youth also participated in the Toronto forum.
4. "Dons" are leaders of community gangs in Jamaica. Since dons control com-munities, they often have sexual access to adolescent girls within their territory with impunity. See Amnesty International 2006.

References

Amnesty International. 2006. "Sexual Violence Against Women and Girls in Jamaica: 'Just a Little Sex.'" 22 June. At <http://www.unhcr.org/refworld/docid/44c5f2a24.html>.
___. 2009. "Jamaica: Public Security Crisis—Facts and Figures and Case Studies." At <http://www.amnesty.org/en/for-media/press-releases/jamaica-public-security-crisis-facts-amp-figures-and-case-studies-200907>.
Ashiabi, G.S. 2000. "Some Correlates of Childhood Poverty in Ghana." *Journal of Children and Poverty* 6.
Brodber, Erna. 1980. *Jane and Louisa Will Soon Come Home.* London: New Beacon Books.
Codjoe, H.M. 2001. "Fighting a 'Public Enemy' of Black Academic Achievement — The Persistence of Racism and the Schooling Experiences of Black Students in Canada." *Race, Ethnicity and Education* 4/4 (December).
Franke, S. 2010. "Current Realities and Emerging Issues Facing Youth in Canada: Analytical Framework for Public Policy Research, Development and Evaluation." Policy Research Initiative, Government of Canada.

Freeze, C. 2010. "Police Connect Jamaican Shower Posse to Toronto Gangs." *Globe and Mail,* 4 May.

Gloudon, B. 2011. "Beheading the Spirit of Our History." *Jamaica Observer,* July 29. At <http://www.jamaicaobserver.com/columns/Beheading-the-spirit-of-our-history_9328752>.

Headley, B. 2006. "Giving Critical Context to the Deportee Phenomenon." *Social Justice* 33/1.

Inter-American Commission on Human Rights. 2008. "IACHR Issues Preliminary Observations on Visit to Jamaica." Press release 59/08. At <http://www.cidh.org/comunicados/english/2008/59.08eng.htm>.

James, C.E., and K. Brathwaite. 1996. "The Education of African Canadians: Issues, Contexts, and Expectations." In K. Brathaite and C.E. James (eds.), *Educating African Canadians.* Toronto: James Lorimer.

Janhevich, D., M. Bania, and R. Hastings. 2009. "Rethinking Newcomer and Minority Offending and Victimization: Beyond Hate Crimes." Institute for the Prevention of Crime/Department of Criminology, University of Ottawa.

McMurtry, R., and A. Curling (co-chairs). 2008. "The Review of the Roots of Youth Violence." Toronto: Service Ontario Publications. At <www.rootsofyouthviolence.on.ca>.

Reid, T. 2011. "MURDEROUS! More than 1,500 Children and Teenagers Killed Since 2001." *Sunday Gleaner,* July 17. At <http://jamaica-gleaner.com/gleaner/20110717/lead/lead1.htmlgleaner.com/gleaner/20110717/lead/lead1.html>.

Sinclair, G., and L. Barrett. 2012. "Rape on the Rise." *Jamaica Gleaner,* January 19. At <http://jamaica-gleaner.com/gleaner/20120119/lead/lead1.html>.

Smith, D.E., and G.S. Ashiabi. 2007. "Poverty and Child Outcomes: A Focus on Jamaican Youth." *Adolescence* 42/168 (Winter).

UNICEF. 2004. *The State of the World's Children 2005.* New York: UNICEF.

World Bank. 2003. *Caribbean Youth Development Issues and Policy Directions.* Washington, DC: World Bank.

Yau, M., and J. O'Reilly. 2007. *2006 Student Census, Grades 7–12 System Overview.* Toronto: Toronto District School Board.

Postscript

My very first meeting with Professor Carl James, co-editor of this work, at McMaster University in 2011 at the handover of the archives of the Honourable Louise Bennett-Coverley, oM, OJ, MBE to that venerable institution was an auspicious occasion. Not only were we honoured to be among the many who attended that event to pay tribute to our dear Miss Lou, featured in one of the essays in this publication, Carl and I were to discover that we were at one in having a vision for capturing the presence, role and contribution of Jamaicans in Canada, in a manner that had the benefit of the rigour of intellectual scrutiny and the credibility that comes with that process. My proposal to Professor James of having an academic work of this nature resonated with him, clearly in line with ideas he had previously contemplated.

It is to the credit of Professors Carl James and Andrea Davis that they have been able to produce a work of the breadth and depth of this important contribution to our knowledge and appreciation of the Jamaican, and by extension the Caribbean, diaspora, on the country of Canada. We owe them and all who contributed chapters, distinguished personalities in their own right, a debt of gratitude. From the stories of the arrival of Jamaicans to the shores of Canada, the sifting out to ensure "that only suitable persons are sent" — a feature of Canadian immigration policies, much like those of many other countries — to meeting the challenges head-on of their new homeland and creating productive lives out of the opportunities presented, weaving desirable features of their former home into their present realities, the Jamaicans in Canada today perhaps best epitomize the most positive outcomes of immigration.

It was from the outset and even now remains my hope that this body of essays, coming as it does from the pen of a broad spectrum of our people in terms of their personal and professional abilities and experiences, would lend itself to serious contemplation by policymakers as much as by students, academics and members of the public more generally. The extent to which decision-makers at all levels are able to grasp the depth of the transition which Jamaicans have made, the commitment they have developed towards their new homeland while maintaining a practical and admirable sense of loyalty to their country of birth or heritage would help to facilitate their broader appreciation of the value of multiculturalism, a policy to which successive Canadian governments have been wedded.

It is also my belief that one of the best investments that this work could ever make is to deepen the understanding and pride that our young people have in their history and those who created and preserved it for them. No one will challenge the adage that a people who forget their history are doomed to repeat it. It is sometimes felt that the struggles of the past are too often denigrated and diminished by those who have inherited a more bountiful present. We do not wish for later generations to be paying for debts which we incurred, but neither do we wish for them to ignore that their more secure future in many ways is determined by the legacies they have inherited.

At another level, we are fully conscious of the increased attention being given by governments to the value and role of the diaspora in national development. The Jamaican Government has made no secret of its own intentions in that regard and has sought to accelerate action to structure the process of engagement. All of this gives new meaning to the cause for integrating diaspora issues in foreign policy and foreign relations.

As we celebrate in 2012 the fiftieth anniversary of the independence of Jamaica and simultaneously commemorate the fiftieth anniversary of the formal establishment of diplomatic relations between Jamaica and Canada, I am pleased to be associated in a modest way with the genesis of the conceptualization of this work and even more gratified by its completion and the high quality of its content. The Jamaican presence in Canada predates Canada's confederation and Jamaican's own independence. The relations between the two countries have been long, deep and wide and have been beneficial on both sides. Yet nowhere is this more evident than in the Jamaican people who have made Canada their home and that of their off-springs and who, having benefitted from the opportunities which they were privileged to receive, have given back in equal measure, in almost every field of endeavour.

May this work be a lasting tribute to our people and all that they have accomplished for themselves, for Jamaica and for Canada. We owe a debt of gratitude to the International Development Research Centre (IDRC) for its ready response to request for their financial support to this effort.

Sheila Sealy Monteith
High Commissioner for Jamaica to Canada

Acknowledgements

We owe a tremendous debt to all the contributors — scholars, artists, other professionals and community workers — who have willingly participated in this project. We appreciate and are encouraged by your enthusiasm, support and belief in this endeavour and your contribution to the conversation about Jamaica and Jamaicans that this book begins. Like us, you saw this as an opportunity, not only to highlight the accomplishments of Jamaican Canadians and their contributions to Canadian society and the world, but also to paint a portrait of a small but impactful island and its people in this the fiftieth year of Jamaica's independence. Our individual and collective contributions mark the importance of the ongoing social, cultural and political relationships between Canada and Jamaica, which we believe will continue to strengthen in the next fifty years.

Our sincerest gratitude goes to Her Excellency Sheila Sealy Monteith, High Commissioner for Jamaica to Canada, for her support and encouragement from the conception of this project to its completion. She gave generously of her time and energy and supported us in securing funding from International Development Research Centre. To the staff at IDRC, we say thank you.

We also acknowledge Selom Nyaho-Chapman, Desmond Miller and Kai James for their valuable research assistance and work on the manuscript; Marshall Beck at the Centre for Research on Latin American and the Caribbean; and Louise Gormley and Tara Fernandes from the York Centre for Education and Community for their commendable assistance with this project. Our sincere appreciation goes to Trevor Massey and Pamela Appelt of the Jamaica 50th Anniversary Committee for their encouragement and support of this project, and their recognition of its contribution to the Jamaica 50th celebration.

A very special thank you goes to Brenda Conroy for her superb copyediting and helpful suggestions, which strengthened the manuscript. And, to the cover designer, John van der Woude, thanks for your excellent representation of the link between Jamaica and Canada. We are also grateful to the staff of Fernwood — Errol Sharpe and Beverley Rach — for their interest, support and cooperation in making this project come to fruition.

Finally, we acknowledge and name our family and friends for their patience, support and ongoing encouragement. Carl thanks his family — Kai, Milderine, Dorne and Sammy — as well as his friends, Everton and Joan Grant-Cummings and Alexander Francis. Andrea thanks her son, Kamau, and mother, Magetta, and her extended family and friends, especially Michele Johnson and Michael McKee.

Contributors

Dwight Barrett holds degrees in psychology and nursing from York University. His professional interest is in critical care and nurse practitioner studies. A first generation Canadian, he has a strong interest in helping Jamaican nurses learn about their history.

Sharon Morgan Beckford is an assistant professor in the Department of English at Rochester Institute of Technology, where she teaches literatures and cultures of the Black diaspora. Her research interests include Black diaspora as well as cultural and feminist studies, and Caribbean, Canadian and postcolonial literatures. Born in Falmouth, Trelawny, Jamaica, Beckford grew up in Kingston, where she attended Wolmer's High School for Girls. Upon graduating, she attended the University of the West Indies, Mona Campus, migrating shortly thereafter to Canada. Her publications include *Naturally Woman: The Search for Self in Black Canadian Women's Literature.*

Kevan Anthony Cameron, also known as Scruffmouth, is a poet, performer and advocate for indigenous peoples of African descent at home in Canada and elsewhere in the diaspora. Born in Edmonton, Alberta, to Jamaican parents, Kevan is a graduate of Simon Fraser University, where he played varsity soccer and received his bachelor's degree in general studies with a focus on liberal arts, philosophy and history. He is creative director of Black Dot Roots and Culture Collective, where he engages in educational, creative and community program activities.

Mark V. Campbell is a postdoctoral fellow at the University of Guelph, where he is currently pursuing work in improvisation, community and social practice (ICASP). He holds a PhD in sociology and equity studies, specializing in cultural studies, and is currently involved in a project that examines the relationships between turntablism, improvisation and consumption in late capitalism. A Canadian of Jamaican ancestry, Dr. Campbell's research interests also include Afrodiasporic theory and culture, Canadian hip hop cultures, Afrosonic innovations and community development for youth.

Mary Anne Chambers is a retired bank executive and former Ontario cabinet minister whose extensive volunteer activities have included senior positions on boards of institutions in the education and health care sectors. Chambers is president of PACE Canada and chair of the Advisory Committee of the York Centre for Education and Community, York University. She has received numerous awards including a Medal of Appreciation from the Prime Minister of Jamaica, a Golden Jubilee Medal from Queen Elizabeth II and a Doctorate of Laws, *honoris causa*, from the University of Toronto. Access to opportunity, especially for children and youth, has long been a primary focus of her contributions to corporate social responsibility, public policy and philanthropic causes.

Maxine C. Clarke is a clinical neonatologist currently teaching medical education at both the undergraduate and postgraduate levels at Queen's University and has been on staff at the Kingston General Hospital since 1993. She received her medical degree from the University of the West Indies in 1975, a postgraduate degree in paediatrics from the University of British Columbia and a neonatology fellowship at the University of Toronto and UBC. Dr. Clarke has worked at hospitals in Bathurst, New Brunswick, and at the Hospital for Sick Children in Toronto. She is currently developing a diversity curriculum for undergraduate medical students.

Andrea Davis is an associate professor in the Department of Humanities at York University and interim director of the Centre for Research on Latin America and the Caribbean (CERLAC). She came to Canada on a Canadian Commonwealth Scholarship to pursue graduate studies after completing a first degree at the University of the West Indies, Mona Campus. She has published widely on Black women's fiction and gender and sexuality and is currently the lead investigator on a project on Jamaican and Canadian youth, funded by the Social Sciences and Humanities Research Council of Canada (SSHRC).

Cecille DePass is an associate professor in education and associate director of the Cultural Diversity Institute at the University of Calgary. She was recently chair of the Education Sector of the Canadian Commission, UNESCO, and former president of the Comparative and International Education Society of Canada. DePass was a visiting lecturer at Liaoning University, Dalian, China, in summer 2000. Well-known for her work with professional and community associations, her Jamaican/ Caribbean heritage is evident in her sensitivity to social justice issues in both her teaching and publications.

Gervan Fearon is dean of the G. Raymond Chang School of Continuing Education at Ryerson University, where he holds cross-appointments as an associate profes-sor in the Departments of Economics and Global Management Studies. He has supported partnerships with the University of the West Indies and the University of Technology in Jamaica. Born in Birmingham, England, to Jamaican parents, Fearon lived in May Pen, Jamaica, between 1964 and 1968, and moved to Toronto in 1968 with his parents and three siblings.

Avis Glaze is a well-known international leader in education. She has worked at all levels of education in Ontario, as well as in urban and rural Catholic and public schools. As Ontario's first Chief Student Achievement Officer and CEO of the Literacy and Numeracy Secretariat, she played a pivotal role in helping to improve education in the province. Presently, she is president of Edu-quest International Inc., which offers a wide range of educational services across the globe.

Most Honourable Sir Kenneth O. Hall, ON, GCMG, OJ, Governor-General of Jamaica 2006–2009 (the fifth person to hold this position) is currently an Honorary Distinguished Fellow of the Mona School of Business at the University of the West Indies. He is renowned for his contribution to advancement of the regional integration process during his tenure at the CARICOM Secretariat 1975–1977 and 1994–1996, and as Governor-General established the Governor-General's Youth Award for Excellence Programme. A former professor, Sir Hall holds a PhD in history from Queen's Universityand was pro-vice chancellor/principal of the University of the West Indies, Mona Campus. He has published widely in the fields of history and international relations.

Annette Henry is a professor and head of the Department of Language and Literacy Education at the University of British Columbia. Her scholarship examines Black students, Black women teachers' practices, language and curriculum in the socio-cultural contexts of schooling. Henry has taught in education institutions at various levels and settings in Canada, the United States, Haiti and Jamaica. She owes her love of Jamaica, its language, culture and people to her parents who met in England, where she was born and raised until the age of nine. Their family of five migrated to Canada in 1965.

Carl E. James teaches in the Faculty of Education and in the Graduate Program in Sociology at York University, Toronto. He is currently director of the York Centre for Education and Community. James has researched and written extensively about the educational, occupational, cultural and athletic experiences and achievements of Black youth in Toronto. Building on his ongoing work with Caribbean youth, he is co-investigator on a Jamaica/Canada youth and community development project funded by SSHRC.

Royson James is the municipal affairs columnist for the *Toronto Star*, Canada's largest daily newspaper. A journalist for more than thirty years — starting in 1979 with *Contrast*, a Black community newspaper, and with the *Star* in 1981 — he received his journalistic training at Andrews University and was named an honoured alumnus of the university in 2004. Other recognitions include a Canadian Achievement award from *Pride Magazine* and the Bob Marley Award. A native of Jamaica, James immigrated to Canada in 1969. He is married with four children.

Jamil Jivani is a juris doctoral candidate at Yale Law School. Born and raised in the Greater Toronto Area, he is a graduate of York University, where he studied non-profit management and international development. Jivani has worked as an entrepreneur, teacher, project manager and fundraiser for organizations in Canada, Kenya and the United States. He continues to lead youth development programs in Toronto and Nairobi. Jivani is a 2012 summer associate at Wachtell Lipton Rosen & Katz and has served as president of the Yale Black Law Students Association.

Michele A. Johnson previously taught in the Department of History at the University of the West Indies, Mona Campus. She is an associate professor in the Department of History, York University where she teaches a variety of courses on Blacks in the Americas. Her research interests focus on the cultural history of Jamaica, gender relations, race/racialization and labour, domestic slavery and service in Jamaica/the Caribbean and Canada, as well as migration and African diaspora/s.

Naila Keleta-Mae is an artist-scholar and a assistant professor in the Department of Drama and Speech Communication at the University of Waterloo. Keleta-Mae's practice and research engage with performance and feminist and critical race theories and methodologies. As a performance poet, recording artist and playwright, her work has been commissioned by the *Toronto Star*, played on CBC radio, produced by Black Theatre Workshop and published by Playwrights Canada Press. Keleta-Mae, who is of Jamaican descent, has received awards from the International Federation for Theatre Research and York University and has been published in *Canadian Theatre Review*.

Tamari Kitossa is an associate professor of sociology at Brock University. Jamaican born, Kitossa migrated to Toronto with his parents and three siblings in 1973. He lives in southern Ontario with his partner, who is Macedonian, and their two children. His research interests include the social construction of Blackness in Western culture, repressive tolerance toward interracial couples, racial profiling and criminalization of African Canadians, and race and colonialism in criminology.

Armand La Barge is the former chief of York Regional Police, where he worked since 1973. Now retired, he has been recognized with numerous awards for his community service and work with young people locally and internationally. He is the founder and past chair of the Adopt a Mission Jamaica Committee, and each year he travels to Jamaica with other officers to work with children supported by the Mission. La Barge is currently completing his doctorate in multiculturalism studies at Charles Sturt University.

Alexander Lovell is a doctoratal candidate in geography at Queen's University. His research examines the development of the Caribbean "ethnic food" industry in Canada, focusing on Jamaica's diaspora-based development strategy. Born in Canada, Lovell is a second-generation member of the Jamaican diaspora whose heritage can be traced to Dumfries, St. James.

Rachel Manley is a Jamaican Canadian author/poet widely recognized for her non-fiction trilogy *Drumblair: Memories of a Jamaican Childhood*, *Slipstream: A Daughter Remembers* and *Horses in Her Hair*. The first memoir won the Canadian Governor General's Award for non-fiction, and together all three present an intimate, yet historical, view of Jamaica. A member of one of Jamaica's most influential families, Manley was born in Cornwall, England, to Jacqueline Kamelard-Gill and former Jamaican prime minister, Michael Manley.

Desmond Miller is a master of education candidate at York University, where he is pursuing research on the intersections of race, education, sport and recreation in the lives of student athletes. A third-generation Canadian who grew up in Toronto, Miller played varsity basketball in high school and at the University of Toronto, he captained his track and field team, garnered Ontario University Athletics All-Star honours and went on to hold the university record in pentathlon. His community-based activities include Drum Artz Canada and the Canadian Sport Film Festival.

Sheila I. Sealy Monteith has been the High Commissioner for Jamaica to Canada since February 2010. She has been in service to Jamaica's Ministry of Foreign Affairs and Foreign Trade for more than twenty-five years, including six years in the Permanent Mission of Jamaica to the United Nations in New York. Fluent in Spanish, Her Excellency Sealy Monteith has served as ambassador to the United Mexican States and the Republics of Costa Rica, El Salvador, Guatemala, Honduras, Nicaragua and Panama and high commissioner to Belize. Mme. Sealy Monteith holds a master's of science in international relations and maintains an interest in international development issues.

Beverley Mullings is an associate professor of geography (cross-appointed to gender studies) at Queen's University. Her research engages broad questions of social transformation, the political economy of globalization and the politics of gender, race and class in the Caribbean and its diaspora. Mullings was born in the United Kingdom, but many of her formative years in the 1970s/80s were spent in Kingston, Jamaica. She has lived for the past twenty years between the United States and Canada. She is currently an editor of the journal *Gender, Place and Culture*.

Robert Pitter is a professor in the School of Recreation Management and Kinesiology at Acadia University, where he teaches about sport, physical culture and media. His research and publications, which have examined topics pertaining to sport and society in the areas of sport policy, racial issues, pain and injury, have appeared in a number of academic journals. He is also co-editor of *Sporting Dystopias: The Making and Meaning of Urban Sport Cultures*.

Joan Samuels-Dennis is an assistant professor in the School of Nursing at York University, having completed her doctorate in nursing in 2009. She was born in Westmoreland, Jamaica, and migrated to Canada in 1983 at age ten. Samuels-Dennis's research interests focus on the long-term effects of violence on the mental health of men and women. Her background as a first-generation Canadian Jamaican nurse and her interest in critically appraising how we record people's history inform her research.

Olive Senior is the prizewinning author of over a dozen books of poetry, fiction and non-fiction, including *The Encyclopedia of Jamaican Heritage*. Her work has been translated into several languages, published in numerous literary journals and anthologies and widely used in schools and universities. She is a winner of the Commonwealth Writers Prize, the Norman Washington Manley Foundation Award for Excellence (preservation of cultural heritage — Jamaica) and the Gold Musgrave Medal of the Institute of Jamaica.

Etty Shaw-Cameron is one of the many teachers who have worked in the education system in the province of Alberta for over thirty years. She was trained at Shortwood Teachers College in Kingston, Jamaica, where she excelled in methodology and was a college athlete. Now retired, she lives with her husband, Locksley. Her son, Orville, performs occasionally at Stage West — a dinner theatre in Edmonton. Kevan, her second son, is a writer and promoter of spoken word.

Mary Lou Soutar-Hynes is a Jamaican Canadian poet/educator and former nun with an interest in poetic inquiry. A 2009 Hawthornden Fellow, her work has appeared in journals such as *Poetry Wales*, *Quills* and *Canadian Woman Studies*, and anthologies including *Calling Cards: New Poetry from Caribbean/Canadian Women*. Her poetry collections include *Travelling Light*, long-listed for the 2007 ReLit Poetry Award, *The Fires of Naming* and *Dark Water Songs*.

Leanne Taylor is a assistant professor in the Faculty of Education at Brock University. Her research explores the social construction of multiracial identities, the use of digital media in social justice education, transnational and immigrant student aspirations and marginalized students' access to and experiences in post-secondary education. Born in Canada to a Jamaican father from Montego Bay and a Canadian mother of Scottish and Irish descent, Leanne grew up with her brother in small-town Eastern Ontario and made yearly trips to visit family and friends in Jamaica.

Lisa Tomlinson holds a master's degree in education and is completing her doctoral studies in humanities at York University. A scholar of Jamaican origin residing in Toronto, Tomlinson's research and teaching focus is in the area of literary and cultural studies of the Caribbean and African diaspora. Her recent publications include "The Black Diapora North of the Border: Women, Music and Caribbean Culture in Canada," in *Transnational Caribbeanities: Women and Music*, edited by Ifeona Fulani.

Barrington Walker is an associate professor of history, Queen's University. The first Black tenured faculty member in the Department of History at Queen's University, he specializes in the history of Black Canadians and of race and immigration in Canada. He is the author of *Race on Trial: Black Defendants in Ontario's Criminal Courts, 1858–1958*. Walker is a first-generation Canadian of Jamaican ancestry. His father's family hails from Montego Bay and his mother's family from Saint Mary. They met and married in Canada.

Ewart Walters is a writer, consultant, triple gold-medalist journalism recipient, dramatist, former diplomat, public servant, community activist and sportsman who has lived in Ottawa for over forty years. He has received national honours from his homeland, Jamaica, for his work among visible minorities in Canada. His self-published autobiography, *To Follow Right – A Journalist's Journey*, was published in 2011.

Kay-Ann Williams is a doctoral candidate in geography at Queen's University. Her research explores the relationship between Jamaican immigrant labour market experiences and levels of civic engagement in Canada. Williams was born in Jamaica and lived there for thirty years before migrating to Canada. She also resided for a brief period in Sweden, where she completed a master's of science degree.

Melanie York graduated with a bachelor of science in nursing degree from York University. A second-generation Jamaican Canadian with cultural and familial roots in St. Thomas and St. Anne, Jamaica, York aims to pursue effective clinical practices in nursing and contribute to historical studies that will strengthen the voice of Jamaican health-care practitioners in Canada.

Jamaica 50 Celebration

Jamaica 50 Celebration Inc. recognizes *Jamaica in the Canadian Experience* as an important contribution to the celebration of Jamaica's 50th anniversary of independence. By showcasing Jamaicans and the contributions we have made to Canada, this anthology represents a commemorative legacy of the successes of Jamaican communities in Canada and the possibilities that Canada has afforded them.

Jamaica 50 Celebration Inc. is a not-for-profit organization, established under the patronage of the Jamaican High Commissioner, Her Excellency Sheila Sealy Monteith, and the Jamaican Consul General to Toronto, Seth George Ramocan. The organization is made up of a group of dedicated volunteers who aim through charitable and other social and cultural initiatives and events to highlight the positive impact and influence that Jamaicans have had on Canada, showcase the best of our people, arts and culture, place a spotlight on Jamaicans' accomplishments and encourage youth of Jamaican heritage to become better informed.

The most important legacy that can result from this year of independence celebration is to encourage and enable future Jamaican Canadian leaders and their continued advancement in the Canadian mosaic. *Jamaica in the Canadian Experience* is an important part of the Jamaica 50 mission — a book whose remunerations will help to support our future generation of leaders, providing youth with resources, mentorship and the tools necessary to continue the successes of the independence won by their forebears for another fifty years and beyond.

Jamaica 50 heartily endorses this book, seeing it as an initiative that provides the evidence of why we must all "Jump for Jamaica."

Pamela Appelt and Joe Halstead
Co-chairs
Jamaica 50 Celebration Inc.